MONTE CARLO OR BUST

Also by Joseph Buchdahl

Fixed Odds Sports Betting
How to find a Black Cat in a Coal Cellar
Squares & Sharps, Suckers & Sharks

JOSEPH BUCHDAHL

MONTE CARLO or BUST

SIMPLE SIMULATIONS *for* ASPIRING SPORTS BETTORS

HIGH STAKES

First published in 2021
by High Stakes Publishing,
an imprint of Oldcastle Books Ltd,
Harpenden, UK

highstakespublishing.co.uk

Editor: Steven Mair

A CIP catalogue record for this book is available from the British
Library.

ISBN
978-0-85730-485-8 (print)
978-0-85730-486-5 (Ebook)

2 4 6 8 10 9 7 5 3 1

Printed and bound in Great Britain by Severn, Gloucester

CONTENTS

Chapter	Page
The Story of the Monte Carlo Simulation	7
A Little Probability & Statistics	13
How to Build a Monte Carlo Simulation	46
Prediction Models	54
Winning	99
Losing	160
Staking	196
Tipping	272
Odds & Sods	301
A Game of Luck or Skill	323
A Cautionary Tale	348

THE STORY OF THE MONTE CARLO SIMULATION

The name 'Monte Carlo' (literally Charles' Mountain, after Prince Charles III of Monaco) has been synonymous with gambling ever since the opening of its Casino de Monte-Carlo in 1863. It lends its name to the Monte Carlo fallacy, otherwise known as the gambler's fallacy or the fallacy of the maturity of chances, the erroneous belief that if a particular event has occurred more frequently than normal during the past it is less likely to happen in the future, and *vice versa*. On the fateful night of 18 August 1913, the roulette ball kept landing on black spin after spin. The longer the sequence continued, the more people started to take notice and place bets on red, believing that such an unlikely sequence could not possibly continue if reds and blacks occur about half of the time each, discounting the influence of the green zero. After the 26th consecutive black, with a probability of less than 1 in 136 million, a lot of roulette players had lost a lot of money. It did not stop there; having seen a long sequence of blacks end on the 27th spin, some players now believed it would be followed by another long sequence of reds to redress the balance.

Belief in the Monte Carlo fallacy stems from a mistaken interpretation of the law of large numbers, more commonly and wrongly understood as the law of averages, where the individual believes that, following an unlikely sequence of events, things **must** even out to ensure that observations match expectations. Independent events like coin tosses or roulette wheel spins, however, do not have memories. There is nothing compelling them to return towards an expected average, just a mathematical tendency for this to happen as the sample of observations becomes larger and larger.

Monte Carlo is also famous for its car rally, first raced in 1911 and immortalised in the 1969 film *Monte Carlo or Bust!* Whilst this book has nothing to do with car racing, it has afforded me the opportunity to come up with a snappy book title; all the more fortunate since the film was originally intended to be called *Rome or Bust!* So why Monte Carlo? In addition to the fallacy, the municipality's connection to gambling also lends itself to a computerised method of repeated random sampling to obtain numerical results when more formal mathematical approaches prove too difficult. It is a technique used to understand the impact of uncertainty in prediction and forecasting. It helps us define the most likely or expected outcome, for example a result of a tennis match given some quantified superiority of one player over another, or the most likely betting returns from a series of wagers given some information about the predictive abilities of the bettor. In addition to the most likely outcome, we can also use it to estimate the range of possibilities that surround it, which is very often more informative than simply knowing what is most probable. Since chance and random outcomes are central to the modelling technique, much as they are to games like roulette and dice played at the Monte Carlo Casino, it was perhaps an obvious choice of names. Indeed, its 1946 origin story is all about cards, as we shall see.

While there is some debate about the nature of the first application of the Monte Carlo method, with some suggesting its use may date back as far as the times of the ancient Babylonians, it is generally accepted that the first modern Monte Carlo experiments were carried out during the latter part of the 18th century. One notable example was the Comte de Buffon's needle problem: what is the probability that a needle thrown randomly on to a horizontal plane ruled with parallel straight lines will intersect one of them, assuming the length of the needle is less than the distance separating the lines. The problem was named after George-Louis Leclerc, a French polymath, also known as the Comte de Buffon, who first proposed the thought experiment. Amongst his other scientific exploits was his estimation of the age of the Earth at about 75,000 years, at a time when the 18th century consensus was that, following the Old Testament, it could not be older than about 6,000 years. Whilst his needle problem can be solved precisely with integral geometry, a simpler way to estimate a solution is to throw a sample of needles on to the surface and count how many of them intersect a line. By repeating this many times and calculating an average, one can arrive at an ever more refined estimation of the probability.

Perhaps the most beautiful Monte Carlo experiment involves the estimation of the number pi, the ratio of a circle's circumference to its diameter, denoted by the Greek letter π. First draw a circle so that it fits perfectly inside a square, as shown below. If the circle's radius, that is the distance from its centre to its edge (or half its diameter) is r, then the square must have edges of length 2r. The area of a square is, unsurprisingly, the square of the length of its edge, that is the edge length multiplied by itself: 2r x 2r = 4 x r-squared, written as 4r^2. The area of a circle is π x r-squared, or πr^2. This means that the ratio of the area of the circle to the area of the square must be πr^2 divided by 4r^2 which is π/4 (since r^2 divided by r^2 = 1). Let's throw some rice grains on to the picture and count the number of grains in the circle and the number of grains in the square. Divide the total number of grains in the circle by the total number of grains in the square. Finally multiply your answer by 4 and you will have an estimate of π.

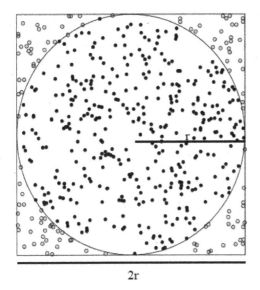

Adapted from Johansen, Adam M. (2010) Monte Carlo methods. In: Baker, Eva L. and Peterson, Penelope L. and McGraw, Barry, (eds.) *International Encyclopedia of Education* (3rd Edition). Burlington: Elsevier Science, pp. 296-303.

2r

A single run of this experiment might not provide a reliable answer. Perhaps the grains happened to clump more in the middle than at the edges, just because of luck. To increase the accuracy of the estimate, one would repeat this many times. The greater the number of runs, iterations or samples, the more we can be sure that we eliminate the influence of luck in the way the rice grains land, provided there is no underlying bias in the way we are throwing them.

This repeated random sampling is the basis of the Monte Carlo method. It was not until the middle part of the 20th century, however, that the Monte Carlo method gained its name and popularity as a technique for solving deterministic problems probabilistically. Stanisław Marcin Ulam, a Polish-American scientist who had worked on the Manhattan Project into the development of nuclear weapons towards the end of the Second World War was, in January 1946, recovering from surgery following a bout of encephalitis, when his mind wandered on to the topic of calculating the chances of winning a game of Canfield Solitaire. Named after noted gambler Richard Canfield, owner of the Canfield Casino in Saratoga Springs, New York, at the end of the 19th century, the game is notoriously hard to win, with only about 1 in 30 attempts successful. Ulam recounted his inspiration as follows:

'After spending a lot of time trying to estimate them by pure combinatorial calculations, I wondered whether a more practical method than "abstract thinking" might not be to lay it out say one hundred times and simply observe and count the number of successful plays.'

By writing a bit of code to replicate the rules of play, Ulam was suggesting a computer could be used to replicate the evolution of many games far more quickly than playing a series of hands oneself. Having done so it would then be a simple matter of counting how many of the played hands ended with a successful completion to estimate the probability of it happening. Obviously, the more repetitions in the simulation, the more reliable the estimate will be. The Manhattan Project had been a motivating force behind the development of computers. Ulam realised that the availability of such computing power made such a statistical method easily achievable. Computers such as ENIAC, or Electronic Numerical Integrator and Computer to give it its full title, were being designed with military purposes in mind. The simulations that were run on such computers were thus regarded as secret government work, and hence needed a code name. 'Monte Carlo' was chosen as a nod to the Monte Carlo Casino, where Ulam's uncle, borrowing money from relatives, would gamble. It would seem to represent a very appropriate choice.

The Monte Carlo method is now used in many fields of investigation where uncertainty of outcome plays a significant role, including finance, weather forecasting (where it is known as ensemble forecasting), engineering and the development of artificial intelligence to name but a few. It has even been used in baseball to prove that the sacrifice bunt, where a batter aims to advance his fellow team players to other bases, often at his own expense, is an ineffective strategy. We can use it in betting too. In this book, I will look at how simple Monte Carlo simulations can be used to assist the bettor in a number of domains: forecasting outcomes, expectations about winning and losing, the role of money management, the influence of luck, and the assessment of touts and tipsters amongst other things. I will do this with the aid of arguably Microsoft's best consumer product, Excel, the ubiquitous spreadsheet tool first released in 1985, which organises data in columns and rows that can be manipulated through formulas to perform mathematical functions on the data. Whilst there are other more powerful data analysis and programming packages like SPSS, SAS and R available, they may require a more comprehensive mathematical and programming background to use comfortably. Excel, however, is easier to learn and has a proven longevity, having been made available via Microsoft's suite of

Office software. It's probable that most of you reading this will have either used it at one time or are familiar with its basic functionality on a more regular basis. And it's great for organising the sorts of data – bets, odds, stakes, profits, losses etc. – that you will be handling if you have any aspirations of becoming a more serious bettor. Throughout, I have assumed that readers will have a basic working knowledge of Excel's functionality. If you don't, it doesn't take much to self-teach; that, after all, is how I acquired it, and what you don't know already can easily be Googled.

In writing this book, I've attempted to do something that thus far, I possibly haven't been particularly good at, but which a friend of mine challenged me to try: to explain betting to those who know nothing about probability. This is like trying to explain skiing to someone who's never seen snow. I don't think that's practically possible, so instead, I'm going to try to explain the world of probability from the bottom up, in the easiest possible terms, introducing new concepts gradually without, hopefully, losing too many readers along the way. Explaining betting without explaining probability is pointless, because betting odds, after all, are just another way of representing probability. Any sensible and serious discussion about betting, therefore, must always begin with understanding the mathematics of likelihood: statistics.

The poet John Lydgate once famously said, "You can please some of the people all of the time, you can please all of the people some of the time, but you can't please all of the people all of the time". I fear with this project this is where I will end up. There will be some who will chastise me for encouraging anyone, via the subtitle of this book, to aspire to be a bettor. To those I say this: yes, betting has its dangers, and unfortunately for a few this will come to impact their lives, and the lives of those close to them, in unpleasant ways. But for most, it can be fun, provided it is not indulged excessively and beyond one's means, and for some, if they are prepared to put in a little effort, it can be rewarding too, even if not necessarily profitable. But a word of caution here, and again, I can hear the criticism ringing in my ears. Betting to win, that is to make a consistent and sustained profit over the long term, is exclusively the domain of the "one percenters". It takes hard work to make it pay. There are reasons for this, which I intend to address within. I apologise if you find this message discouraging, but I'd rather be a realist than an idealist when it comes to telling the story about betting.

Then there will be those with a suitable mathematical training who may consider most of what follows largely superfluous and obvious. For those I hope at least they might find something new and of value inside. Finally, there will be those who either can't remember how to multiply together two fractions or have little inclination to want to learn; they will probably lose the will by the second page of the next chapter. For you, unless betting is simply a recreational pastime (and that's perfectly acceptable, by the way), I would suggest not to bet ever again. Otherwise, I hope that you will make the effort to learn new things. The reason I've chosen to tell this betting story via the Monte Carlo simulation is that perhaps it, more than any other tool, allows me to find a balance between these mathematical backgrounds. It's sophisticated enough to provide a meaningful interpretation to some of the ideas that bettors deal with, yet simple and intuitive enough to easily understand what it tells you without having to know any of the mathematics that powers it. Despite this, however, you will always be better prepared to take on the bookmaker if you know a little maths. Thus, I will begin, first, with a little primer on probability. By the end of the next chapter, hopefully the mathematical novices amongst you will be more comfortable with statistics, the concept of expectation and a probability distribution.

A LITTLE PROBABILITY & STATISTICS

A few things are certain. We might include in that subset the sun rising tomorrow, or that it will not rain at the South Pole, although even those events technically have a finite but infinitesimally small chance of being false. But many things we experience in everyday life are uncertain; will it snow on Christmas Day, will I pick a King when drawing a card from a deck, will Liverpool win the Premier League again? We humans like to quantify the likelihood of uncertain things happening. It gives us a sense of being in control, even if, ultimately, we often prove to be wrong about the numbers. The likelihood or chance of something happening has, since its development in the 18th century, been described by the mathematics of probability.

Probability

On probability, Wikipedia has this to say:

> *Probability is the branch of mathematics concerning numerical descriptions of how likely an event is to occur, or how likely it is that a proposition is true. The probability of an event is a number between 0 and 1, where, roughly speaking, 0 indicates impossibility of the event and 1 indicates certainty. The higher the probability of an event, the more likely it is that the event will occur. A simple example is the tossing of a fair (unbiased) coin. Since the coin is fair, the two outcomes ('heads' and 'tails') are both equally probable; the probability of 'heads' equals the probability of 'tails'; and since no other outcomes are possible, the probability of either 'heads' or 'tails' is ½ (which could also be written as 0.5 or 50%).*

It is as useful and simple a description as is reasonably possible. While in everyday life probabilities are typically described with percentages (for example a 75% chance of rain), mathematicians conventionally prefer to use decimal notation (in this case 0.75). Sometimes you might also hear probability expressed as a 1-in-x chance, where x is some positive number. For example, the chance of rolling a 6 on a fair dice is 1-in-6, since there are 6 equally likely possibilities. Essentially this is just like a fraction. Naturally, it follows that the sum of the probabilities for all possible outcomes is 1 (or 100%). It also follows that if the probability of an event A occurring is p(A), then the probability of A not occurring is 1 – p(A). In my rain example above, the probability of no rain is 1 – p(rain) = 1 – 0.75 = 0.25 (or 25%). Mathematicians call this the complementary rule.

Complementary Rule:

$$p(not\ A) = 1 - p(A)$$

For bettors who simply bet on one single thing at a time, for example the winning team in a football match or the correct score, this is pretty much the only probability rule they need to know. Unsurprisingly, such bets are known as singles. The hard part, of course, is figuring out how to calculate, or forecast, those probabilities. Others, however, may prefer betting on more than one thing at the same time, for example the outcome of two matches together. Provided they are independent of each other, with the outcome of one match not influencing the outcome of the other, then the probability of both occurring is described by the multiplication rule.

Multiplication Rule for independent events:

$$p(A\ and\ B) = p(A)\ x\ p(B)$$

For example, what is the probability of throwing a 3 on one fair die and a 6 on second die? With the dice being independent, we multiply the probabilities for both outcomes. p(3) = 1/6 and p(6) = 1/6. Hence p(3 and 6) = 1/6 x 1/6 = 1/36. (For those who don't remember how to multiply fractions, you can always use a calculator.) For additional events, you simply continue to multiply the probabilities, provided all events are independent. Such bets are known as doubles, trebles, 4-folds, 5-folds etc., depending on how many events go into them, or simply just accumulators or 'accas' for short. American bettors know them as parlays. There is a slightly more complicated version of the multiplication rule for non-independent events but generally speaking, bettors need not worry about this. Where the probability of B is dependent (or conditional) on the outcome of A, this will give rise to what is called a related contingency bet, for example Liverpool to win and Liverpool to win 2-0. Such bets are not permitted anyway.

The final probability rule that will prove useful for bettors to know is the addition rule. Where two events, A and B, are mutually exclusive, that is to say they cannot occur at the same time, the addition rule states that the probability of either A or B occurring is given by p(A) + p(B).

Addition Rule for mutually exclusive events:

$$p(A \text{ or } B) = p(A) + p(B)$$

Obvious examples include coin tosses and die rolls. You cannot get both heads and tails on one toss of a coin, or a 6 and a 3 on one roll of a die. Here, then, the probability of rolling a 6 or a 3 is given by $p(3) + p(6) = 1/6 + 1/6 = 2/6 = 1/3$. (Again, if you can't remember how to add fractions, just use a calculator.) In sports betting we might want to back more than one possible result. There are three possible outcomes to a 90-minute football match: home, draw or away. Perhaps we might want to cover both the home win and the draw, meaning we would win our bet if either home **or** draw wins. Since home win and draw are mutually exclusive – they can't both happen at the same time – we then have p(home or draw) = p(home) + p(draw).

For events that are not mutually exclusive, for example drawing a queen or a spade from a deck of cards, the rule changes subtly. Here, one of the possible cards satisfies both conditions. Now we must use the following rule:

Addition Rule for non-mutually exclusive events:

$$p(A \text{ or } B) = p(A) + p(B) - p(A \text{ and } B)$$

Suppose Federer is playing Nadal and Djokovic is playing Thiem. Federer has a win probability of 60% or 0.6 whilst Djokovic has a win probability of 70% or 0.7. We'd like to bet on either of them winning. What is the probability that either Federer or Djokovic (or both) will win? Using the addition rule for non-mutually exclusive events we have p(Federer or Djokovic) = p(Federer) + p(Djokovic) − p(Federer and Djokovic) = 0.7 + 0.6 − (0.7 x 0.6) = 0.88 or 88%. It may not be intuitively obvious how the addition rule for non-mutually exclusive events is derived but for those motivated to try, it can be done using a simple probability tree and the first three aforementioned probability rules. Fortunately, such non-mutually exclusive bets are not very typical. Perhaps betting to win either half in a football match is the only obvious example that springs to mind.

Odds

So much for probability; but don't bookmakers quote things in odds? Yes, they do, but odds are just another way to describe the likelihood of something to happen; that is to say, the probability. Bettors in the UK are familiar with expressions like 2 to 1 against (written as 2-1, 2:1 or 2/1). These don't mean quite the same thing as a 1-in-x chance, and hence don't exactly correspond to the probability fractions, even though this odds notation is known as fractional. Here, 2 to 1 against means that 2 out of every 3 times we expect our forecast outcome not to happen, whilst 1 out of every 3 we expect it to occur. Consequently, odds of 2 to 1 against imply a probability of 1/3. Conversely 2 to 1 on (written as 1-2, 1:2 or 1/2) would imply that 2 out of 3 times our predicted forecast will happen and fail to happen 1 in 3 times.

Although UK odds tells you precisely how much profit you will make for a specified stake – in this bet £1 in the hope of making a £2 profit – I find UK odds notation confusing and less disposed for doing probability calculations. Suppose we want to make a double bet where each part is 2 to 1 against. What are the odds? It's not at all obvious. Intuitively we might think it is 4/1 since 2 x 2 = 4. But that would be incorrect. Consider each probability and then use the multiplication rule. The probability of each part of the bet is 1/3, so making a double means the probability of both parts occurring is 1/3 x 1/3 = 1/9. How do I then turn this fraction back into odds? Usually at this point I give up and turn to a better way of expressing odds: the European decimal notation.

Whilst UK odds notation tells you your profit for a winning bet, European notation tells you your total return, including your stake. Furthermore, to keep things as simple as possible your stake is always assumed to be a standardised 1 unit (of £, $, € or whatever your preferred currency). A winning bet of 2 to 1 against would then give you a return of 3 for a 1-unit stake, 2 for the profit and 1 for the original stake you get back. This would be written as 3 (or 3.00). Perhaps it is already becoming obvious why this notation is more useful. The odds of 3 are the reciprocal, or inverse, of the probability, 1/3. To find the decimal odds from the probability, or for that matter the probability from the odds, just calculate the inverse. What about our double bet? Simply multiply the odds together, since each part is the reciprocal of its probability; hence the multiplication rule applies directly in a way that it cannot be used for UK fractional notation. 3 x 3 = 9; thus, the odds for the double bet are 9 (or 9.00) and the probability is 1/9.

Returning, just briefly, to the fractional notation, we can now say that if the total return is 9 from a 1-unit stake, that must mean the profit for a winning bet would be 8, and the odds written in UK fractional format 8 to 1 against. I challenge anyone to argue that they can intuitively calculate 2:1 x 2:1 = 8:1 in their heads, and furthermore tell me that this is useful. The UK might be, in many ways, the cultural home of sports betting, but I would argue that its contribution to the world of odds notation is best forgotten, at least for those motivated by a more quantitative approach to betting analysis. Of course, I have no doubt that many bettors who will have grown up with them will completely disagree. You're welcome to do so, but fractional odds have no place in the calculations and simulations that will follow in the rest of this book. Without wishing to cause further offence, I would say the same about other odds notation, including American, Hong Kong, Indonesian and Malay. None of them translates as easily into probabilities, and hence for my purposes are effectively useless in comparison to decimal odds. Probability, after all, is what betting is all about. For those interested, there are many online sources that will tell you how these other odds notations work, with odds calculators for how to convert between them.

If the sum of the probabilities for all possible outcomes of an event is 100% (or 1), then why do the probabilities implied by bookmakers' odds come to more than 100%? Let's look at an example. The final of the French Open in 2020 was played between Nadal and Djokovic. The bookmaker bet365 quoted decimal odds of 1.72 and 2.1, respectively. This implies that bet365 believed Nadal had a 1/1.72 or 58.1% (or 0.581) chance of victory, whilst for Djokovic it was 1/2.1 or 47.6% (or 0.476). Summing the two makes 105.7% (or 1.057). That makes no sense; you can't have the probabilities for all possible outcomes sum to more than certainty, right? The answer to the original question is to be found by remembering that bookmakers are not charities designed to give you a fair chance of winning. They are businesses which exist to make money themselves for the effort they go to offer people bets in the first place. Instead of charging you an entry or subscription fee, they charge you by shortening the odds. The amount they do this by can be seen by the size of the excess beyond 100%. In this case the excess is 5.7% (or 0.057). This is called the bookmaker's margin. In reality, bet365 probably believed that Nadal had a 56% chance of winning, Djokovic 44%. Had they quoted fair odds without their margin included, we would have seen 1/0.56 or 1.79 and 1/0.44 or 2.27.

The bookmaker's margin provides a measure, albeit indirectly, of how much profit they are aiming to make. Sometimes you might hear the term 'overround'. The overround is simply the sum of the probabilities, or the margin plus 100%, in this case 105.7%. Confusingly, you might also have come across the term 'vig', short for 'vigorish'. Its usage is more common in America. The vig is analogous to the margin but not precisely synonymous. It is a direct measure of the bookmaker's expected percentage profit on the total stakes taken on an event. The vig and margin are related in the following way:

1) Payout = 1 / Overround. Payout is the percentage returned to the bettors by the bookmaker. Here, it is 1 / 1.057 = 0.946 (or 94.6%)
2) Vig = 1 − Payout. Here, it is 1 − 0.946 = 0.054 (or 5.4%)

Thus, the margin and vig are what are called bijective reciprocals.

$$vig = \frac{margin}{1 + margin}$$

$$margin = \frac{vig}{1 - vig}$$

And since the margin = overround − 1, putting this into the first expression above and then simplifying, we also have:

$$vig = \frac{overround - 1}{overround} = \frac{margin}{overround}$$

If bookmakers' odds are unfair, how can you make a profit? Well, firstly you can get lucky. Betting is largely a game of chance where you win some and you lose some. The problem is that if you kept betting and betting many times like this, in the end all the good and bad luck would cancel out and you'd end up losing an amount that would be dictated by the bookmaker's margin, or more precisely the vig. Betting, unlike roulette, however, can also be a game of skill, although it's a rather difficult game to become good at. This possibility arises because the true probability of an event in sports cannot be known perfectly, unlike in roulette where simple mathematics allow one to calculate the odds exactly. Given this, the possibility always exists that the bookmaker has made a mistake. The skilled bettor's job is to learn how to find those mistakes. Sometimes they are large enough that even after the bookmaker has applied their margin, the odds will still be longer than the true odds (whatever they may be). Suppose in this example Nadal really had a 60% chance of winning, and he really would win 60 out of every 100 matches played against Djokovic indefinitely in exactly the same circumstances, more than the number bet365 believes. OK, so we still don't know which ones he wins and which ones he loses – luck will dictate in the short term how well we will do – but we do now know that 60 times out of every 100 we will make a profit of £0.72 for a £1 stake, whilst the other 40 times we'll lose £1. A quick summing up of the net profits and losses reveals that, overall, we should make a net profit of £3.20 for every £100 staked. This sum is known as our expected profit. It's not guaranteed because good and bad luck can influence it just as they do for a coin toss, but the mathematics of the probabilities tell us that this is what profit we should expect to make on average after good and bad luck have cancelled out. We will return to the concept of expectation again a little later. For now, there is an important take-home message: the accuracy of our expected profit calculation depends entirely upon our accuracy in 'knowing' the 'true' chances of Nadal beating Djokovic. (I use inverted commas to remind you that, in reality, knowing the true probability perfectly is impossible; I will review why a little later.) If we're wrong, then what we expect to happen may be far removed from what actually ends up happening, on average. Furthermore, the problem of good and bad luck in the short term (in fact even over quite long terms, as I'll show later in the book) will often have us deceived.

Some statistics

To many non-mathematicians, 'statistics' can be a dirty word used in conversations to argue that your opponents can basically say anything they like because the 'statistics' prove their case. Perhaps there is a kernel of truth to that, but for the most part statistics should simply be seen as a way of organising, analysing, describing, and interpreting data to help answer questions that you may be asking about uncertain events. For example, when attempting to forecast the likelihood that a team or player you want to bet on has of winning, you might want to know how many times they have won in the last 4, 6 or 10 games. Perhaps you might also want to know how many goals a football team has scored in the last 10 games. If the total is 30, then that tells us the average is 3 goals per game, since 30 divided by 10 is 3. You might also want to see how those goals have been scored in the past 10 games. It's highly unlikely that the team scored 3 goals in every game. Perhaps they won their most recent 4 games 6-0 and then scored only once in each of the 6 games before that. There are statistics that can give us useful information about how those goals have been distributed. Perhaps most significantly of all, statistics can help us unpick the competing influences of luck and skill that are so deeply intertwined in betting.

Broadly speaking, there are two types of statistics that will concerns us here: descriptive statistics, which summarise the nature of the data, like the average or by how much it varies; and inferential statistics, which attempt to infer or draw conclusions from data that are subject to random variation. Random is just another word for chance or luck, implying no cause, or at least hidden causes that we are unable to ascertain. For Henri Poincaré, the famous 19th French mathematician, luck was simply a measure of our own ignorance.

> 'Every phenomenon, however trifling it be, has a cause, and a mind infinitely powerful, and infinitely well-informed concerning the laws of nature could have foreseen it from the beginning of the ages. If a being with such a mind existed, we could play no game of chance with him; we should always lose.'

So much of what happens in sport is luck. Think of a tennis player with a 70% first serve percentage. 70% of the time they will make a first serve. But what determines whether their next serve will be successful or a fault? There are so many factors – hidden variables as Poincaré might call them – which will dictate the outcome, operating in a sequential line of cause and effect. The speed and trajectory of the ball toss will depend on the state of the player's arm muscle fibres, the positioning of the opponent, the movement of the air and so on. The way the racket connects with the ball, and ultimately the speed and direction it is sent, will depend on the movement of the serving arm, the server's eyes and perhaps even the movement on the opposite side of the court of the opponent. All these influences will, in turn, depend on the nerve impulses operating in the server's brain, that send signals to the nerves of the muscles engaged in the serving action. Tiny differences in the starting conditions of any of these can, in some instances, magnify through the cascade of events that takes place during the serve, to the point where we might see a completely different outcome. Colloquially, this process has come to be known as the butterfly effect, from the idea that the simple air perturbation arising from the flapping of a butterfly's wings could, two weeks hence, result in a hurricane thousands of miles away. In chaos theory, the butterfly effect describes the sensitive dependence on initial conditions in which a small difference in one state of a system can result in large differences in a later state. If we could know precisely all these tiny initial differences in the server's action, the motivations behind them, and how their influence cascades through the system over time, we'd know for every serve whether it would be successful or not. But we can't possibly know this much, as much as Poincaré's hypothesised infinitely powerful and infinitely well-informed mind. All we can know is that over a large number of previous first serves, the player has historically been successful 70% of the time, from which we infer that they have a 70% chance of being successful with their next serve. It is the imprecision of knowledge about causes that creates uncertainty, and it is the uncertainty which means we must use the language of probabilities, not guarantees or certainties, to describe outcomes in sports, and hence outcomes in betting too.

Never mind a single tennis serve; imagine the number of hidden variables operating in a 90-minute football game with 22 players on a 100m by 65m football pitch making 1,000 passes of the ball that could potentially influence the outcome. The number and nature of these competing but hidden variables is so immense that it is simpler to give them all a name: random. The word is often understood to mean uncaused. In the context we are talking here, that is not quite correct; certainly, Poincaré would say so. Rather the word is best used to describe a process that is sufficiently complex, such that the outcome is completely unpredictable given the information we have. For our purpose that will suffice, although it is worth noting in passing that at the scale of the subatomic (quantum mechanical) world, the meaning of 'random' can indeed imply 'causeless'. Since big things like players' brains are made up of little things like atoms and quarks, philosophically speaking, at least, we might be forced into redefining what 'random' actually means. But this is neither the time nor the place for a philosophical debate about causality. For another book, maybe.

If sporting outcomes are heavily influenced by random variables, that must mean the bets we strike on them are heavily influenced by them too. Statistics provides us with the tools to reveal what influence they have and gives the bettor some means of separating luck from forecasting skill, if indeed they have any. The job for the bettor is to try to uncover as many hidden variables as they can to make a better estimate of the 'true' probability of an outcome than the bookmaker. The task is fraught with danger. We might, for example, forget to pay attention to a highly significant variable. Suppose our tennis player's opponent is a top 10 player. Against top 10 players they have a first serve success percentage of 60%, because they try harder to serve faster and with more precision against a better player. If we happen to overlook this variable – the quality of whom they are playing – we are likely to draw less reliable conclusions than our bookmaker, and that can cost us financially.

We can, in addition, draw incorrect inferences from correlations between variables. Correlation, a mutual relationship or connection between two (or more) things, doesn't always imply one of them caused the other; when it doesn't, it is known as a spurious correlation. Some spurious correlations are obvious, and funny, for example the number of Americans who drowned by falling into a pool correlates very well with the number of films Nicolas Cage appeared in between 1999 and 2009. Only a fool, however, would believe Nicolas Cage's level of creative output had an influence on pool drownings. Others, however, are trickier to spot, particularly when the patterns which emerge from correlations make it easier to infer a causal relationship. Between 2012 and 2017, teams that played away in the English League 2, the fourth tier of English professional football, won so often that, even after taking into account the bookmaker's margin, you could have made a good profit just betting on all of them. But does that mean something had changed in League 2 that caused teams playing away to win more often than the bookmaker believed, and which, furthermore, the bookmaker hadn't noticed? Almost certainly not. This profitable run, from the point of view of the bettor, was almost certainly nothing more than pure luck. In the end, if there is no causation, good luck should eventually run out, as it did in this case.

Let's looks at some descriptive statistics. Recall the 10-game goal-scoring record, where our team has scored 30 goals. Dividing 30 goals by 10 games gives a figure of 3 goals per game. In common parlance, this would be known as the average. Statisticians, however, use different types of averages, or more technically called central tendencies, which mean slightly different things, just as the Inuit have different words for 'snow' and Hawaiians have different words for 'wave'. These different averages can prove more, or less, useful depending on the context and the data that you have. Our 3-goal-per-game average here would be known to a statistician as the 'mean', or more specifically the 'arithmetic mean'. An arithmetic mean is calculated by adding several quantities together and dividing the sum by the number of quantities. Provided there are 30 goals scored over 10 games, you will always calculate the same arithmetic mean regardless of which games those goals were scored. Even if the teams scored 30 goals in 1 game and no goals in the other 9, the arithmetic mean is still 3. There are three other means: the weighted mean, the geometric mean and the harmonic mean, but it would be rare for a bettor to ever need these, so I won't waste time now describing them. Feel free to look them up. I'll introduce one or two of them later as and when I need to. Where the word 'mean' is used on its own, it's safe to say that it is the arithmetic mean that is implied. It is certainly the most commonly used. Recall from a little earlier the expected profit of £3.20 for every £100 bet. 'Expected' is just another way of saying 'mean'. We didn't know which order we would win and lose bets on Nadal but our expectation was that, on average, we would make £3.20 for every £100 bet, or £0.032 for every £1 wager, if all our wagers were £1. 'Expected' and 'mean' essentially mean the same thing, pardon the pun.

Sometimes, however, the arithmetic mean is not a particularly useful way of describing the average. Suppose in the 10 games, our team scored the following goals: 3, 0, 1, 0, 11, 8, 0, 0, 6, 1. An unlikely set of goal tallies, granted, but it will help to describe two additional averages. Here, you will notice that as many as 6 of the goal counts are below the arithmetic mean and only 3 of them above it. For such a skewed set of data, the arithmetic mean is then not as useful at describing the central tendency. Instead, we might observe that the most common number of goals scored is 0 – it happens in 4 out of the 10 games. This would be called the 'mode', the most frequent value in a set of data. It describes what our team does most often. Another type of average is known as the 'median'. It describes the middle number in a given set of data when it is ordered sequentially. Re-ordering the goals scored we have: 0, 0, 0, 0, 1, 1, 3, 6, 8, 11. The middle number in the sequence is 1, so the median of the data is 1. Like the mode, the median is typically a better measure of the central tendency of some data when that data is skewed or asymmetric. In the chapter on staking, we will see that the median can be a much better measure of profit expectation than the mean where the amount you bet is measured in percentages rather than fixed units.

The central tendency of a set of data is just one way to describe it. Another is knowing how it varies, or how it is spread. The most basic way is by means of the 'range'. The range is simply the difference between the highest and lowest values, in this case 11. It's descriptively informative but not very powerful. A measure of variability far more widely utilised by statisticians is something called the standard deviation. The standard deviation, written as 's' or with the lowercase Greek letter σ (sigma), is the average amount of variability in your data. It tells you, **on average**, how far each score lies from the arithmetic mean, which is often denoted by the Greek letter μ (mu). The larger the standard deviation, the more variable or spread out the data is. It's with the introduction of the standard deviation that most non-mathematicians start to lose the will, and that's hardly surprising when you see the formula,

$$\sigma = \sqrt{\frac{\sum(x_i - \mu)^2}{n}}$$

Nevertheless, it is an incredibly important descriptive statistic to know for bettors who are serious about trying to win and profit beyond the simple entertainment that betting may offer, so I will persevere in explaining how it is calculated. You only have to bother reading this once. Thereafter, calculators or Excel can do all the work for you. The important point is that you understand the concept behind it, rather than the mathematics involved. The arithmetic isn't that hard anyway. You only really need to know what a squared number and a square root are.

Let's go back to our ten goal tallies. There are 6 steps to finding the standard deviation in these data, all of which are contained in the formula above. Going through them is a much easier way than trying to interpret it if you lack a mathematical background.

1) Calculate arithmetic mean. We already know this is 3. This is your value of μ in the formula.
2) Subtract the mean from each of the ten goal tallies to calculate each difference, or deviation, from the mean. In the formula, each goal tally is described by the letter x. The subscript 'i' merely describes how many x's there are, in this case 10 of them. x_i means the ith value of x.
3) Square all the deviations. A square of a number is a number multiplied by itself. 5-squared, written 5^2, is 25, 10^2 is 100. $(\frac{1}{2})^2$ is $\frac{1}{4}$.
4) Add all the squared deviations together. The shorthand used in the formula is the character $\sum$. This simply means 'the sum of' and is a

quicker way of writing the formula than to have to write $(x - \mu)^2$ 10 times in a long line.

5) Divide this number by the total number of data points, n, in this case 10, since there are 10 goal tallies.

6) Calculate the square-root of this number. A square root is just the reverse of squaring. For example, the square root of 36, written as $\sqrt{36}$, is 6.

It is easier to show these steps in a table.

Goals	Deviation from mean	Squared deviation
3	0	0
0	-3	9
1	-2	4
0	-3	9
11	8	64
8	5	25
0	-3	9
0	-3	9
6	3	9
1	-2	2
Sum = 30	Sum = 0	Sum = 140

You may remember that squaring a negative number makes a positive number, since any two negative numbers multiplied make a positive one. That is the point of squaring since the sum of the deviations from the mean will always come to zero, so would be a useless statistic to measure the variability of a set of data. Our goals data has a sum of squared deviations of 140, hence an average squared deviation of 14, and finally a standard deviation, σ, of the square root of 14, written $\sqrt{14}$, which equals 3.74. This means that, on average, a goal tally deviates from the mean by 3.74 goals.

Sometimes there is a slight difference to step 5, depending on what type of data you have. If the data being analysed represent a population on its own, we divide by the number of data points, in this case 10. More usually, however, the data will represent a sample taken from a larger population. For example, the population might be all 38 goal tallies for a team scored in a Premiership season, from which we select a sample of 10. At other times, we may not know the population but assume that our data represents a sample from it; we then draw inferences from its descriptive statistics and extrapolate those to the population. In such cases, the number we use to divide the sum of the squared deviations by is $n - 1$. In this case it would be 9, and we use the symbol 's' instead of 'σ', which is used for population standard deviation. Why we divide by $n - 1$ and not n for samples is rather complex and beyond the scope of this book. All that you need to observe is that as the sample size, n, of data points increases, the closer s approaches σ, since $n - 1$ as a proportion of n tends increasingly towards 1.

Sometimes you may also see the word 'variance' used. Descriptively, it is a qualitative measure of how much your data vary or are spread. Mathematically it is the average of the squared deviations from the mean. In other words, it is just the square of the standard deviation. The more spread out the data, the larger the variance is in relation to the mean. In later chapters you will see how these descriptive statistics are used to describe the data that you will be handling as part of your betting, from building forecast models to analysing profits and losses.

Distributions

The standard deviation and variance of a set of data tell you how that data is spread. However, it is also useful to know how the data is distributed, and most significantly how often each value occurs. Typically, the data in a distribution will be ordered from smallest to largest, and by means of a chart or histogram, allows you to easily see both the values and the frequency with which they appear. A distribution can help you calculate the probability of any one particular observation in some data, or the likelihood that an observation will have a value which is less than or greater than a point of interest.

Let's plot a simple frequency distribution of the 30-goals data, showing the number of times a particular number of goals were scored over the 10 games. From the distribution below, what is the probability that our team scores 0 goals? If this sample of goals is representative of our team's goal scoring output over a much larger number of games (the population), we could say that they have a 4-in-10, or 40%, chance of failing to score. To calculate this, simply divide the number of times they failed to score, 4, by the total number of observations, 10. What is the probability our team scores more than 3? Again, we simply divide the number of times in this sample where that has happened, 3, by the total, 10, giving 30%.

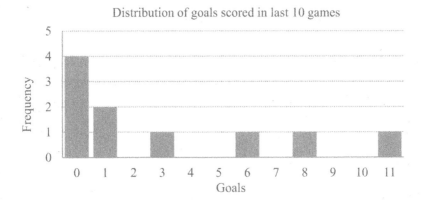

Distribution of goals scored in last 10 games

Of course, in our example, the sample is so small that we probably didn't need to bother drawing the distribution to make these calculations. When data sets are much larger, however, and particularly when they may be closely represented by well-known data distributions that have predefined mathematical functions that describe them, they can be particularly useful. Let's look at some of them.

A uniform distribution is a probability distribution in which all outcomes are equally likely. The drawing of a suit from a card deck will conform to a uniform distribution because the likelihood of drawing a heart, a club, a diamond or a spade is equally likely, 25%. So, too, for drawing any of the 13 numbers. On a frequency histogram, every bar would have the same height. In practice if you were to draw cards, you might see deviations from those expected probabilities. These deviations from expectation are just down to chance but if you kept drawing cards for an infinite length of time, the heights of the bars would be the same. I drew a card (with replacement after drawing) from a deck 10,000 times – well, actually I simulated it on a computer – and here were the results.

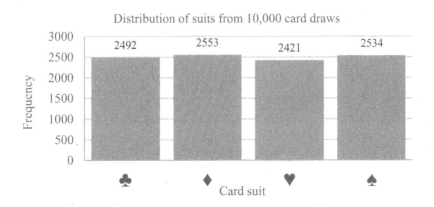

Distribution of suits from 10,000 card draws

Mathematically, this uniform distribution would be described by the expression p(suit) = 1 / number of suits. Since there are 4 suits, the probability, p, of drawing any suit is ¼ or 25%. Such an expression is called a function, which describes the distribution of a random variable. In this example, the random variable is the suit of the card. A fair coin toss also has a uniform distribution because the probability of getting either heads or tails in a coin toss is the same, 50%. Its function would be p(heads or tails) = ½. More usually, the distribution of a random variable that has only two possible outcomes is known as a Bernoulli distribution, after the 17th century Swiss mathematician Jacob Bernoulli. Unlike the uniform distribution the two outcome probabilities need not be equal. For a fair coin toss, obviously they would be. Where they are not, p is the probability of one outcome (for example a win) and q is the probability of the other outcome (for example a loss). Following the complimentary rule, q = 1 – p.

Look again at the distribution of goal tallies in the histogram earlier. Clearly, that is not a uniform distribution. There are more occasions when fewer (or no) goals are scored than when many are scored. In fact, if we look at goal scoring by football teams in general, this remains the case for large numbers of games. The frequency distribution below shows how often a particular number of goals were scored by Premier League home teams during the 2017/18 to 2019/20 seasons, a total of 1,140 separate goal tallies with a total of 1,754 goals scored.

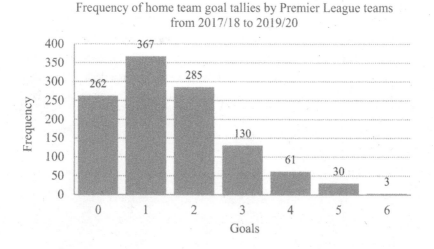

Frequency of home team goal tallies by Premier League teams from 2017/18 to 2019/20

I've shown the frequencies for 0 to 6 goals. There were only two occasions in the three seasons when the home team scored more. We see a similar distribution for away teams, although because of home advantage, there are proportionally more low-score tallies. Again, for clarity, I've omitted the single occasion when there were more than 6 goals scored (Leicester's 9-goal thrashing of Southampton).

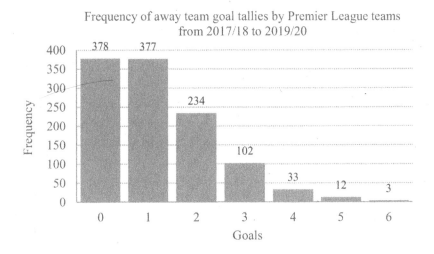

Frequency of away team goal tallies by Premier League teams from 2017/18 to 2019/20

Rather than showing the absolute frequencies or counts of different goal tallies, we can instead display them as percentages of the total. For example, 3 home goals were scored on 130 occasions, or 11.40% of all the goal tallies (130/1,140).

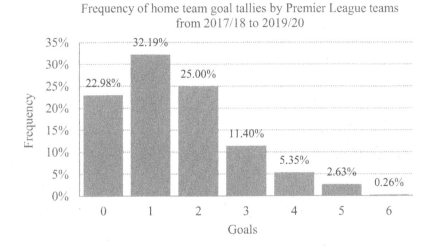

Frequency of home team goal tallies by Premier League teams from 2017/18 to 2019/20

These distributions have low arithmetic means, 1.54 goals for home teams and 1.20 goals for away teams. Consequently, they are highly asymmetric, or skewed, where most of the data are pushed towards the left-hand side and there is a longer tail with higher values to the right. This asymmetry also ensures that the median is even smaller than the mean, since a few much larger tallies will introduce an arithmetic bias when calculating the mean. In this case the halfway point in both home and away distributions (at the 570th data point) is 1 goal.

The distribution of goals in football conforms quite closely to something called the Poisson distribution, named after the French mathematician Siméon Denis Poisson, who developed the mathematical function that underlies it. Like the uniform distribution, the Poisson distribution counts the number of things, in this case the number of times a particular tally of goals was scored. Such distributions are called discrete since we are counting discrete events. For the uninitiated, the Poisson distribution function, unlike the uniform distribution function, is algebraically more complex, so I won't frighten you with it. You can always look up Wikipedia if you'd like to see what it looks like. For our purposes here it's worth noting one significant aspect of the Poisson distribution: the arithmetic mean is equal to the variance, or the square of the standard deviation. Poisson distributions with a low mean and variance, as above, will tend to exhibit a high degree of asymmetry. Those with a higher mean and variance will be more symmetrical. For my Premier League goals, the variance is actually a little higher than the mean for both home and away distributions, 1.69 and 1.41 goals respectively, but these are not terrible matches and Poisson is not a bad approximation for the distribution of goal tallies in football. I've calculated the precise home goals frequencies that would be predicted if the data perfectly fitted a Poisson distribution, and plotted these as a comparison to the original data.

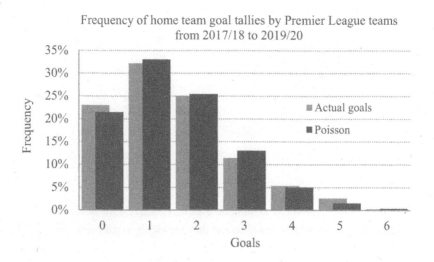

Frequency of home team goal tallies by Premier League teams from 2017/18 to 2019/20

Similarly, for away goals.

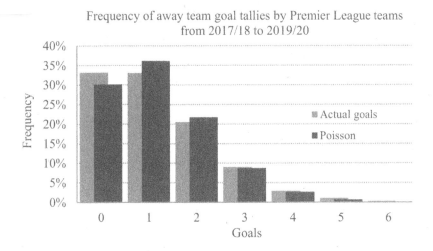

Frequency of away team goal tallies by Premier League teams
from 2017/18 to 2019/20

In the next chapter I will explain how you can perform this calculation in Excel.

A coin toss may exhibit a Bernoulli distribution, but what if we wanted to count the number of heads, or tails, in samples of independent Bernoulli trials? For example, suppose we grouped our coin tosses into batches, or samples, of 10; how often would we see 5 heads / 5 tails, 4 heads / 6 tails, 3 heads / 7 tails and so on? Let's do a little arithmetic to find out. We know that the chance of throwing heads or tails is 50%, or 0.5 in decimal notation. What is the chance of throwing two consecutive heads, or tails, in two independent coin tosses? Using the multiplication rule for independent events, we can calculate this as 0.5 x 0.5 = 0.25. What about 10 consecutive heads, or tails? Same rules apply, so 0.5 multiplied by itself 10 times is 0.0009765625 or 1 in 1,024. Now, what about 9 heads and 1 tail? The probability of throwing a tail is the same as for throwing a head, so wouldn't the answer be the same, that is 1 in 1,024? Indeed, yes, but there is a subtle difference. This time, there are more ways of combining 9 heads and 1 tail. You could land the tail on the first toss, or the last toss, or any of the intervening 8 tosses. Overall, there are 10 possible ways of ordering 9 heads and 1 tail. Since each combination is equally likely (1 in 1,024), the probability of landing 9 heads and 1 tail in a series of 10 independent coin tosses is 10 in 1,024 or 1 in 102.4. For all heads or all tails there is obviously only one way to order it. For combinations of heads and tails there are more ways, and the more mixed the combination, the more ways to do it. A good scientific calculator will calculate the numbers for you, or you can Google 'combinations calculator' (or 'nCr calculator') for an online version. Excel will perform this task too, using the function COMBIN(n,r), where n is the total number of items (in this case, the total number of coin tosses) and r is the number of items in the combination (in this case, the number of heads, or indeed tails). For 8 heads and 2 tails (or 2 heads and 8 tails) there are 45 ways; for 7 and 3 there are 120 ways; 6 and 4, 210 ways. Perhaps it may come as no surprise that the 5 heads and 5 tails is the combination with the most ways to achieve it. In fact, there are 252, meaning the probability of seeing 5 heads and 5 tails is 252 in 1,024 = 0.246 or 24.6%. The full distribution is shown below, and it is called the binomial distribution.

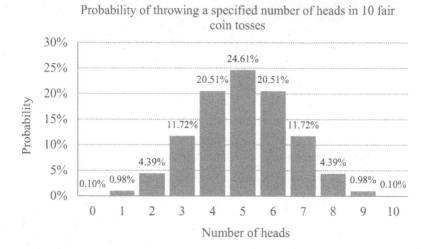

Probability of throwing a specified number of heads in 10 fair coin tosses

The binomial distribution deals with the counting of binary (or Bernoulli) yes or no propositions, including success or failure, true or false and win or lose, in a series of n independent Bernoulli trials, where n is a positive integer number. When there is only one trial (n = 1), the binomial distribution is the same as the Bernoulli distribution. Since the arithmetic mean of a Bernoulli distribution is p, the arithmetic mean of a binomial distribution is np, provided all Bernoulli trials are independent of each other and have the same binary probability p. Here we have 10 trials. Since the probability of heads on each trial is 0.5, the mean is 5. Notice that whilst intuitively we might have expected 5 heads and 5 tails to come up about half of the time, in fact we see it less than a quarter of the time. Nevertheless, it is still the most likely or expected of the 11 possible outcomes. The mean is thus equivalent to the expected outcome. Using the generic formula for the standard deviation of a set of data I showed you earlier, it can be proved that the standard deviation for a Bernoulli distribution $= \sqrt{pq}$, and hence the standard deviation for a binomial distribution $= \sqrt{npq}$. Recall that q is the complementary probability to p and equals $1 - p$. In our coin toss example above, the standard deviation $= \sqrt{10 \times 0.5 \times 0.5} = \sqrt{2.5} = 1.58$. Note, also, that p does not necessarily have to be 0.5 in a binomial distribution. Where it is, meaning q will also be 0.5, the distribution will be symmetric. Where p and q differ, the distribution will display some asymmetry. Suppose our coin is biased 70-30 in favour of tails. Now p(heads) = 0.3, so the mean is $10 \times 0.3 = 3$, and the standard deviation is 1.45. The distribution for this case is shown below.

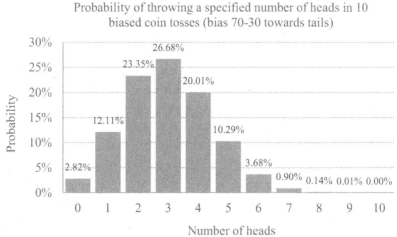

Probability of throwing a specified number of heads in 10 biased coin tosses (bias 70-30 towards tails)

One final observation worth remembering about the binomial distribution is that, whilst in general there is no single formula to find the median for a binomial distribution, if our value for np is an integer or whole number, then the mean, median and mode will all equal np. This means that, in our first example, the mean, median and mode will all equal 5, and 3 in the second asymmetric example. So many betting propositions are fundamentally binary in nature, with just two possible outcomes: win or lose. Consequently, understanding these simple rules behind the binomial distribution can prove immensely useful for bettors analysing their prediction strategies, staking plans and betting histories.

The Poisson and binomial distributions are examples of what are called discrete distributions. Discrete data is information that can only take certain values. They don't have to be whole numbers (integers), but they should be fixed values. Counts of things are an obvious example of discrete data. Goals, baskets, profits and losses are all discrete. The uniform distribution of card suit draws was made from discrete data. However, a uniform distribution can also contain continuous data. Continuous data is information that can take any value, for example height, weight, temperature and length. They are best shown on a line graph to emphasise the infinitesimal differences between data points. For data to be continuous, we should always be able to find another data value between two existing data points. Whilst in practice, the finite resolution of measuring tools used to make such observations will typically render the data discrete, it is nonetheless conventional to consider such fine-resolution data as continuous. Bets have discrete stakes sizes, but when there are hundreds or thousands of them, with many alternative outcome histories, it can sometimes be preferable to regard profit and loss data as continuous. Excel can generate a random number between 0 and 1. Any is theoretically possible with an infinite number of decimal points. Since every random number has the same likelihood as any other of being selected, these data would make a continuous uniform distribution. Excel's processing power constrains how many decimal places the random numbers will have meaning the data are really discrete, but to all intents and purposes it makes sense to regard them as continuous.

Perhaps the most famous of all continuous distributions is the normal or Gaussian distribution, named after its inventor Carl Friedrich Gauss, a 19th century German mathematician and scientist. High school students may remember it as the bell-shaped curve. Suppose instead of 10-coin toss samples, we use 1,000. What would the distribution look like?

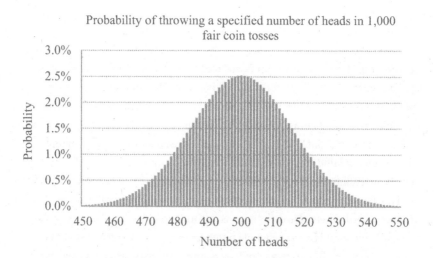

Probability of throwing a specified number of heads in 1,000 fair coin tosses

I've only shown the data points for the middle 100, that is 450 heads and 550 tails to 550 heads and 450 tails. The others are too improbable to bother including. Note that the data is still discrete but the step changes between data points are now much smaller. Consequently, we can start to see the shape of a bell-curve that looks a lot like the continuous normal distribution. Below, I've redrawn the histogram as a line graph.

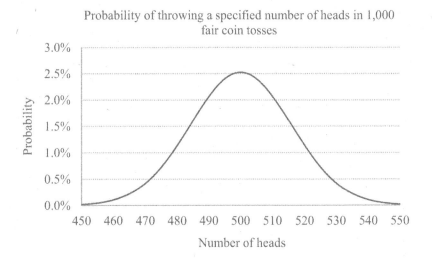

As the number of coin tosses in each sample increases, the discrete binomial distribution is ever more closely approximated by the continuous normal distribution. In the limit when the sample size reaches infinity, the two distributions will be equivalent. In fact, the normal curve still provides a fairly reliable approximation for the binomial when np and nq are greater than 5. For samples of 1,000 coin tosses, np and nq are 1,000 x 0.5 = 500. Certainly, when n is large, working out a problem, either mathematically or computationally, can be easier using the normal distribution than using a binomial. With the binomial you must count all the possible ways of arranging the heads and tails. For 1,000 coin tosses that would be a very laborious task. With the normal distribution, we only need to know the mean and standard deviation, and given it is a good approximation of the binomial we can simply use the square root of npq to calculate the latter. Additionally, when the probability is not the same for each trial, using the binomial becomes impossible. In betting, for example, it's exceptionally rare for all bets to have the same odds. Here, again, the normal distribution, as we will see, provides an excellent approximation.

Conventionally, the mean for a normal distribution is denoted by μ; it is also equal to the median and the mode since the distribution is perfectly symmetric about the mean. The standard deviation is written as σ. The area under the normal curve represents probability and the total area under the curve equals 1. As for a discrete distribution, the height of the curve at any point provides a relative measure of the likelihood of the observation being investigated, whilst an area to the left or right of any vertical line drawn from a particular point on the curve down to the horizontal axis provides a direct measure of the likelihood that an observation will have a value less than or greater than the point of interest.

The normal distribution exhibits what is known as the empirical rule. The empirical rule states that 68.2% of the data falls within plus or minus one standard deviation of the mean, 95.5% within two standard deviations, and 99.7% within three standard deviations. Let's use this rule to see how well the normal distribution approximates the binomial for my samples of 1,000 coin tosses. Using the square root of npq as the standard deviation of a binomial, we have $\sqrt{(1000 \times 0.5 \times 0.5)}$ = 15.8. Thus, assuming a good approximation, we should expect 68.2% of samples to have between 484.2 and 515.8 heads, with the mean being 500. Obviously, the actual number of heads is discrete so I can only count those between 485 and 515. This comes to 67.3%. Within 2 standard deviations the figure is 95.4%, and within 3 standard deviations, 99.7%. If my samples contained 10,000 coin tosses, the approximation would be even more reliable.

The normal distribution is the most important probability distribution in statistics because it fits many natural phenomena, for example heights, blood pressure and IQ scores. This may be because the processes which underscore normal distributions are random in nature. Obviously, different normal distributions will have different means and standard deviations. To help standardise them, statisticians often refer to something called the 'standard normal distribution'. This is simply a normal distribution with μ = 0 and σ = 1. If x is a normally distributed random variable (like IQ scores) with a mean μ and standard deviation σ, then z is the standardised form of x such that:

$$z = \frac{x - \mu}{\sigma}$$

For example, the average IQ of a person is about 100, with standard deviation about 15. If person x had an IQ of 115, z would be (115 − 100) / 15 = 1. It is sometimes also called the standard score or z-score and is a measure of the number of standard deviations a particular data point lies away from the mean.

To gain admittance to Mensa, the high IQ society, you need an IQ of at least 132, which would be equivalent to a z-score of +2.13. I've drawn a standardised normal distribution below. Following the empirical rule, 68.2% of area under the standard normal curve falls within a z-score of plus or minus 1, 95.5% within a z-score of plus or minus 2, and 99.7% within a z-score of plus or minus 3.

The standard normal distribution

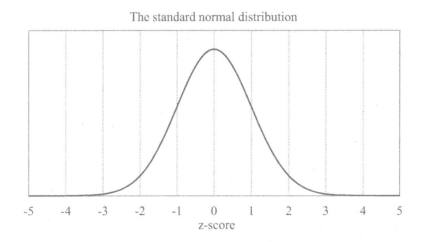

z-score

Random events in sports will give rise to random distributions of profits and losses from the bets that are struck on them. Before I have you hurling the book out of the window in disgust, this is not to argue that everything in sports betting is random. Rather, you should think of betting as the toss of a coin, where the coin may, or may not, be biased. Whether it is depends on any skill. No matter what the bias of the coin (your skill as a bettor who can beat the bookmaker's odds), there will still be a variance of outcomes around the expected mean that will be influenced by the random (hidden) variables that we are unable to decipher. It is for this reason that even skilled profitable bettors must understand the laws of randomness and learn how to tell apart the influence of luck and the influence of their skill, if any does exist. The normal distribution plays a key role in this task as we shall discover.

Statistical testing

Suppose I tossed a coin 1,000 times and saw heads on only 50 occasions, I'd be pretty certain that there was something wrong with the coin. To see just 1 head in every 20 coin tosses would surely imply that the coin was not fair, right? What about 460 heads? Now I'm not so sure. We can use the normal distribution to deduce the likelihood of this happening. This is the basis of a lot of statistical testing. The aim of any statistical test is to determine whether there is enough evidence to confirm or reject a hypothesis about the process we are studying, where that process is influenced by random variables. Traditionally there are two mutually exclusive hypotheses: the null hypothesis and the alternative hypothesis. The hypotheses are conjectures about a statistical model of the population, which are based on a sample taken from the population. In our case the sample is 1,000 tosses of a coin. The null hypothesis is the statement or proposition that is being tested and is typically a default position that there is no difference between the sample observation and what we would expect to observe from the population. Here our expectation is that I am tossing a fair coin, which if tossed an infinite number of times (the population) would land heads 50% of the time. The alternative hypothesis is the proposition being tested against the null hypothesis. In this case it would be that the coin is not fair. The point of the statistical testing is to reject one of the hypotheses. Since they are mutually exclusive, one must be true and the other false.

Using the normal distribution, we can calculate the probability of fewer than 460 heads in 1,000 tosses of a coin. Diagrammatically, this is simply the proportion of the area under the curve to the left of 460 heads in the graph above. You can see that this is quite a small area in proportion to the total area under the curve, which represents all possibilities and a total probability of 1 (or 100%). Mathematically the answer is about 0.006 (or 0.6%) of the total area. (Later in the book I will show you how to perform this calculation easily in Excel.) This tells us that the probability of seeing fewer than 460 heads in 1,000 coin tosses, assuming that the coin was fair – that is, the null hypothesis is true – is 0.6%. Is that small enough to reject or confirm either hypothesis? More simply, does such a low probability tell us that the coin is biased?

The final step in the test involves a rather subjective judgement. Traditionally, statisticians have set arbitrary thresholds below which they reject the null hypothesis in favour of the alternative one. The highest or weakest threshold is 5%. A stronger one is 1%. When physicists are looking for new subatomic particles, they will use a threshold below 0.0001%. Let's use the 1% threshold. What does our result mean? Since the chance of seeing 460 heads or fewer, assuming the coin was fair, is lower than the threshold we have set, we therefore reject the null hypothesis in favour of the alternative one and conclude that the coin is not fair. However, we should always remember that such a conclusion is based on a subjective judgement, the point at which we decided to reject the null hypothesis. There actually isn't much sound scientific basis for these thresholds. Arguably the weakest one of 5%, used by many scientists in their hypothesis testing, is very unsound. Consider what it means. 5% of the time, we can expect to see such a deviation from expectation just by chance. At a fundamental level, this type of statistical testing doesn't prove anything at all; it just informs us about the likelihood of seeing an unusual number of heads given a fair coin. The judgement of whether the coin is, or is not, fair is then left to us.

It's always worth remembering that in random systems, given enough random sampling, pretty much everything is possible. Here, if we collected enough 1,000-coin toss samples, eventually one of them would have no heads, even with a fair coin, but it would take an inordinately long time to happen, indeed, so long that it will be practically impossible to occur before the heat death of the universe, expected in roughly a googol number of years (that's 1 followed by 100 zeros). Remember the 26 consecutive blacks at the Monte Carlo casino roulette table? With a probability of 18/37 (assuming a single zero wheel) for a single black, we'd expect a sequence of 26 about once in every 136 million wheel spins. Yet it happened, and that's because there's an awful lot of wheel spinning around the world, not because the wheel was biased towards black. Indeed, the longest recorded streak of one colour in roulette in American casino history happened in 1943 when red won 32 consecutive times. With a double zero wheel the probability was about 1 in 24 billion. But given the number of casinos and roulette tables worldwide that have been spinning day after day, year after year for over a century since that famous night in Monte Carlo, I've calculated that it's quite probable an even longer sequence will have been witnessed somewhere else.

A little bit more on Expectation

Throughout this chapter you've seen me use the words 'expected' and 'expectation' quite a bit. To recall, 'expected' is really just another word for the 'arithmetic mean'. It is a weighted average of possible values of a random variable over a large number of events. Sometimes it goes by the name 'expected value'. In fact, the origins of the concept date back to the 17th century and underpin the birth of modern probability theory. In 1654 the French mathematician Blaise Pascal was asked by his friend and writer Chevalier de Méré to consider the problem of points. The problem of points concerned a game of chance, called balla, where two players had the same likelihood of winning a round. Each player contributed equally to a prize pot and agreed in advance that the first player to have won a certain number of rounds would collect the entire prize. Chevalier de Méré asked Pascal to consider how a game's winnings should be divided between two equally skilled players if, for some reason, the game was ended prematurely. Pascal decided to correspond with his friend and colleague Pierre de Fermat (famous for Fermat's Last Theorem) on the matter. The work that they produced together helped define a new field of mathematics: probability theory. In doing so they introduced the concept of mathematical expectation or expected value, understood by every sports bettor with more than a passing interest in numbers.

The expected value is calculated by multiplying each of the possible outcomes by the probability that each outcome will occur, and then summing all those products. For discrete distributions like the binomial, that just involves basic arithmetic. For continuous distributions like the normal, that involves more complex integration, a process invented by Sir Isaac Newton, but the principle is the same. I've illustrated the process in the table below for 10 tosses of a coin.

Heads	Probability	Heads x Probability
0	0.000976563	0
1	0.009765625	0.009765625
2	0.043945313	0.087890625
3	0.1171875	0.3515625
4	0.205078125	0.8203125
5	0.24609375	1.23046875
6	0.205078125	1.23046875
7	0.1171875	0.8203125
8	0.043945313	0.3515625
9	0.009765625	0.087890625
10	0.000976563	0.009765625
Sum	1	5

What is the expected number of heads in 10 coin tosses? You may remember from our earlier discussion of the binomial distribution that the answer is 5. However, this time I've calculated the expected value by multiplying each possibility by its corresponding probability. The first column shows the number of heads, whilst the second shows the binomial probability of seeing them for each possibility. Finally, the third column calculates the product of the two. Summing the 10 product values in the third column gives the answer 5. This is the expected value and is the same as the arithmetic mean. Consider a fair die. The chance of rolling any number from 1 to 6 is 1/6. Multiply each number by its probability and sum; the expected value is 3.5.

The concept of expectation has crept its way into sports, most recently football, with the notion of expected goals or xG. Expected goals is used as a performance metric to evaluate football team and player performance. It is used to represent the probability of a scoring opportunity that may result in a goal. For example, based on historical data of high quality shots from a similar distance from the goal with similar player positions at the time the shots were taken, it may be observed that 4 out of every 10 actually result in a goal being scored. Consequently, a shot of comparable nature in a game would be graded with a 40% probability of success. Since success means 1 and failure means 0, the expected goals value for this shot would be $(0 \times 0.6) + (1 \times 0.4) = 0.4$. A game may witness a number of goal scoring opportunities, each with its xG value. Summing them gives the xG for the game, or more usually the xG for each team in a game. In theory, xG provides a truer representation of the quality of play of teams in a game, and the superiority of one team over another, than the actual goals do. Goals are scored with a fair degree of luck and using an actual score line to predict what a team might do in their next game might be less reliable than using their xG. For example, a team might have scored 14 goals in their last 5 games and conceded only 6, but its 'for' and 'away' xG totals might be 8.11 and 8.29. Looking at only the goals data you might conclude an easy win is likely in their next game. In contrast, looking at the xG data, you would arrive at a completely different conclusion. These numbers might be equivalent to tossing a fair coin 20 times and getting 14 heads. If we knew the coin to be fair, we wouldn't then assume the next coin toss had a 14/20 (or 70%) chance of being heads; likewise, for goals and expected goals. xG strips out a lot of the randomness in goal scoring. Reading FC in the English Championship were very much in a similar position regarding their goals and xG performance in the first 8 games of the 2020/21 season, having won 7 and drawn the other, a goal difference of +12 and a 6-point lead at the top of the league. However, their xG difference – just 0.03 after the 8 games as calculated by Infogol.net – told a completely different story. They had simply been lucky to score so many goals (15 compared to an xG of 6.21) and win so many games. Subsequently, they lost the next 4 and dropped to 6th place. They had, to coin a phrase familiar with statisticians, regressed (reverted) towards the mean (expectation).

Unsurprisingly, there is a strong correlation (relationship) between a good xG model and the actual goals scored. If there wasn't, it wouldn't be a reliable way of estimating the expected number of goals. Below is a graph of the correlation between expected goal difference (home team minus away team), as modelled by Understat.com, and actual goal difference for the 380 games played in the 2019/20 Premier League season. Each data point represents one game.

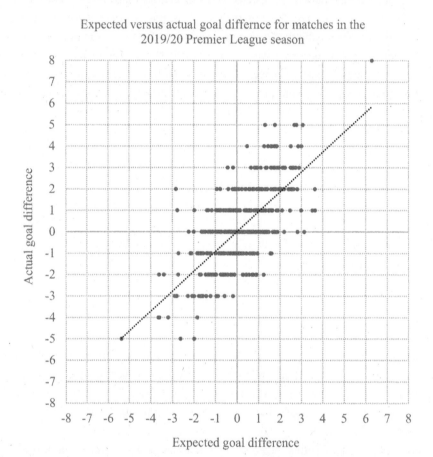

Expected versus actual goal differnce for matches in the 2019/20 Premier League season

You can certainly see a lot of random variability; for example, games that finished with a draw (actual goal difference = 0) had expected goal differences ranging from as low as -2.23 to as high as +3.13. However, you can also see that, on average, games with an expected goal difference of -2, -1, 0, 1, and 2 finish with an actual goal difference, respectively, of close to -2, -1, 0, 1 and 2, highlighted by the dotted trend line. This tells us that, despite the random variability – what statisticians call noise – xG is, on average, a good measure – or signal – of the actual goals scored. The way the individual data are spread about the average trend line provides a measure of the strength of the signal-to-noise ratio. The closer the points cluster about the average trend, the stronger the signal relative to the noise.

Bettors have come to understand 'expected value' as a measure of the size of advantage they hold over the bookmaker, and thus how much they can expect to win or profit. Rather confusingly, the word 'value' has a second meaning here in addition to simply 'figure' or 'number', representing the importance or (financial) worth of something, in this case their advantage. Recall the example I used earlier, where we expected Nadal to have a 60% chance of beating Djovokic. With the bookmaker offering odds of 1.72, we calculated an expected profit of £0.032 for a £1 stake. More generally, the formula for calculating expected value in betting is relatively straightforward – simply multiply your probability of winning by the amount you could win per bet and subtract the probability of losing multiplied by the amount lost per bet. For this example, that would be (0.6 x £0.72) – (0.4 x £1) = £0.032. In fact, there is an even easier method: simply divide bookmaker's decimal odds by the 'true' decimal odds and subtract 1. Of course, to perform this calculation we need to know what the 'true' odds are. As we know, those pesky random (hidden) variables effectively mean we can never know what they are perfectly, we can only have a kind of pseudo-truth as estimated by our prediction model, hence my use of the inverted commas. But if our prediction model, on average, is accurate, then it will give a pretty reliable idea of those 'true' odds. Recall, the 'true' decimal odds are simply the inverse (or reciprocal) of the 'true' outcome probability. Here, if that is 0.6, then the 'true' odds are 1/0.6 = 1.6667. Thus, with the bookmaker's odds at 1.72, the expected value is (1.72/1.6667) – 1 = 0.032 (or 3.2%). Since the odds are just the reciprocal of the probability, we could have alternatively divided the fair probability by the bookmaker's implied probability, giving (0.6/0.5814) – 1 = 0.032. The expected value is equivalent to the expected profit for a 1-unit stake. If we don't bother to subtract the stake, then we have the expected return, which here is 1.032 or 103.2%. Dividing the bookmaker's odds by the 'true' odds is an incredibly fast and useful way of determining expected value. Anything more than 1 implies that over the long term, if we are correct, we should expect to make money; anything less than 1 and we should expect to lose money. If, instead, the bookmaker is correct, then our expected return will simply be equivalent to the bookmaker's projected payout, which you will remember is 1 divided by the overround. Obviously, bets either win or lose, and here that would mean either a profit of £0.72 or a loss of £1. But over hundreds or thousands of the exact same bets, the random noise of the hidden variables cancels out and we are left with our signal, our expected value.

A quick word on accumulators. Since the expected value is simply a ratio of two probabilities, that implies that we can use the multiplication rule to calculate the expected value of doubles, trebles, 4-folds and so on. We just multiply the expected values for all parts of the accumulator, or more strictly the expected returns. Suppose we have two singles, and for both the bookmaker has mistakenly priced them at 2.10 when their 'true' prices should be 2.00. The expected return for each single would be 2.10/2.00 = 1.05. Multiplying, the expected return for the double is 1.05 x 1.05 = 1.1025. Now, for a £1 stake we have an expected profit of £0.1025. A treble and 4-fold would have expected returns of 1.158 and 1.216, respectively. The rate at which expected return grows as the size of the accumulator increases is exponential. It's like we've turned water into wine.

As always in betting there are caveats, in this case two. Firstly, whilst increasing the size of the accumulator might increase your expected return, you're also less likely to win the bet. You have a 50% chance of winning a single bet with 'true' odds. That falls to just 6.25% for a 4-fold where each part has 'true' odds of 2.00. Using the multiplication rule, 0.5 x 0.5 x 0.5 x 0.5 (or 0.5 to the power 4, written as 0.5^4) = 0.0625. All gambling is a trade-off between risk and reward; if you want more reward, you must take more risk to acquire it. Secondly, if you're wrong about the 'true' odds, the compounding of expected return will conspire against you, quickly. Now, you've turned wine into water. If the 'true' odds are, in fact, 2.2, the expected return for a single is 2.1/2.2 = 0.955. For a 4-fold, that would fall to 0.955^4 = 0.830. Accumulators can indeed be a great way to compound your advantage, but only if you have one. Bookmakers know that most bettors don't, which is why they encourage their customers to bet accumulators; it increases their profit margins. If you use them, do so wisely. Don't try to run before you can walk; focus on finding the value in singles first.

The concept of expected value forms the bedrock of any bettor's attempt at longer term success in the world of betting. Indeed, it provides the only meaningful route towards it. Some bettors subscribe to the 'pick winners' philosophy of betting; it's a complete red herring. Anyone can pick winners, but if you're not picking more than the bookmakers believe you should be picking, you will fail to return a profit in the long run. Something with an 85% win probability will be a more likely 'winner' than something with a 15% win probability, but if the bookmaker is pricing them as 95% and 5% respectively, it's the latter that you should be betting on. You'll always be more likely to win the former but see how your bank balance might be looking after betting a 1,000 of them. I can categorically tell you that it will be in the red.

I think those who believe in 'picking winners' subconsciously accept this logic; they just fail to appreciate the probabilistic nature of outcomes, possibly because it involves some mathematics. There's a similar argument against the usefulness of xG, and probably for much the same reasons. However, through understanding the principles of expected value and with a basic grounding in statistics, in particular an awareness of the common distributions that can be used to describe a plethora of sports and betting data, the aspiring bettor should have at their disposal some wonderful tools with which to attempt to gain an advantage. Nevertheless, there are many occasions where real data do not yield themselves easily to simple mathematical functions that define common probability distributions. In such cases, we must look for help elsewhere. Following Stanisław Ulam, in his quest to solve the probabilities of success for a game of solitaire, we will now turn to the tool that he helped to develop for just such a purpose – the Monte Carlo simulation.

HOW TO BUILD A MONTE CARLO SIMULATION

If we wanted to design a prediction model to forecast who would win a penalty shootout, assuming both teams to be equally matched at scoring penalties, we wouldn't need to be particularly sophisticated about it. Given that the chances of either team winning are 50-50, the outcome can be forecast using a discrete uniform distribution, which we met in the last chapter. In common parlance that's equivalent to a coin toss. Suppose, additionally, we wanted to know how likely it was that one of the teams would win 7 such penalty shootouts in 10, we would turn to the binomial distribution, or perhaps the normal distribution if considering a much larger number of shootouts. But what would we use if we wanted to predict the expected number of penalties that each team was likely to score, or the expected total number of penalties taken, or the probability that the penalty shootout would reach sudden death, where it hasn't been settled after each team has taken 5 penalties? Now, the problem is a little more complex. Let's consider why.

The rules of a penalty shootout are fairly simple, but the way these can impact on the evolution of a penalty shootout means that attempting to mathematically calculate the outcomes can become complex. Each team can take up to 5 penalties before the possibility of sudden death. Effectively this means that the initial stage is a 'best-of-10 competition'. Thus, it can be settled before reaching a total of 10 penalties. For example, team A could score their first 3. If team B misses their first 3, the shootout would end, since there is no possible way for team B to catch up once 10 penalties have been taken. The shootout would have been settled with only 6 penalties taken. Alternatively, team B could miss their first 2 and score their third. Team A could then score their fourth, and the shootout ends, because team B won't be able to match team A's total of 4. This time, the shootout finishes with only 7 penalties taken. Further scenarios are possible if team B, which always shoots second, is leading. Some will involve an even number of penalties taken by the time the contest is settled, others an odd number. Given the possibility of either team scoring or missing up to 5 penalties, there are potentially a lot of routes for the penalty shoutout to take. Yes, if I know the probability of team A and team B scoring a penalty, I can use the multiplication rule to calculate the probability for one particular route through the penalty shootout. But my head starts to hurt when I try to visualise all of the routes together as a distribution and hurts even more when I wonder whether a mathematical function could be found that would calculate the probabilities of any particular outcome for me, much like I suppose it did for Stanisław Ulam when he pondered the problem of solitaire. Furthermore, I haven't even considered what happens if the teams are still tied after a total of 10 penalties have been taken. Beyond this point, if team A misses and team B scores, team B wins; if team A scores and team B misses, team A wins; if both score or miss, they continue. This means that beyond 10 penalties there must be an even number of penalties taken in total, although the total number taken could potentially be infinite. Again, my mathematics isn't good enough to consider this problem formally, so I built a Monte Carlo simulation in Excel to consider the problem.

Modelling a Penalty Shootout

The Monte Carlo method relies on a large number of simulated random samples, sometimes called iterations, to obtain numerical outputs which approximate a solution to a problem when other mathematical approaches would prove to be too complex. They are particularly useful for those who may be less familiar with formal mathematical and statistical methods, as they require little mathematical knowledge. Whilst there are different approaches suited for different tasks, the method broadly follows a particular series of steps. Firstly, define the domain of your problem and what it is you want to solve. In my case the domain is the evolution of a penalty shootout and the possible chain of events that lead to its conclusion. The problem I would like to solve, for example, might be to find the probability that a penalty shootout will reach sudden death, assuming all players taking a penalty have a 72.5% (or 0.725) probability of scoring. Whilst typically about 75% of penalties are scored in open play, an analysis of historical penalty shootouts reveals this drops a little, presumably due to the increased pressures given the circumstances in which they take place, players taking penalties who are not typically required to take them, and the inability to score via a follow up after a save.

Secondly, simulate the virtual outcome of each penalty taken using a random input from a known probability distribution. Since I have already defined penalty success (72.5%) or failure (27.5%) probabilistically, intuitively I know that I should use the uniform distribution to generate a random number between 0 (0%)

and 1 (100%). You will recall, from the previous chapter, that within a uniform probability distribution, all possible values are equally likely. Generating 0.124 (12.4%) will be equally likely as generating 0.845 (84.5%). Generating a number above 0.2 will be four times as likely as generating one below. Hence, a number below 0.725 is 0.725/0.275 more likely than one above it, which is precisely the likelihood superiority we want. In terms of penalty success, if the number is less than 0.725, then the penalty is scored; if the number is equal to or greater than 0.725, then the penalty is not scored. This computation is then repeated for each penalty as the shootout evolves. With each new penalty taken, count the cumulative penalties scored for both teams until one of them either wins or loses following a success or failure according to the defined rules of the shootout, and the shootout concludes. Make a note of the outcome with respect to your initial problem, in this case whether the penalty shootout reached sudden death or was concluded before it.

Thirdly, repeat the virtual simulation of a penalty shootout in this manner a large number of times, potentially thousands, tens of thousands, hundreds of thousands or even more, depending on the constraints of your processing power, and record the outputs of each iteration. The more iterations you perform, the more reliable your conclusions will be. Finally, aggregate your results with respect to your identified problem. Here I will count the number of iterations which reached sudden death and calculate this as a percentage of the total. This, finally, gives me an estimate for the probability of a penalty shootout going to sudden death, given my defined initial parameter – a 72.5% probability that all players will score a penalty.

How is such a Monte Carlo simulation performed in Excel? Here I will assume that the reader has a basic knowledge of Microsoft's Excel functions. For those who are new to Excel or who have forgotten how to use it, I would recommend spending a little time reviewing the basics, and in particular, how to use Excel's formulae and functions, and how to populate columns and rows with repeated data. Excel's RAND() function is used to define a random number between 0 and 1. The additional parentheses are just Excel syntax. When you refresh your spreadsheet (traditionally via the F9 key, but if that is assigned by your keyboard for some other purpose, I find the delete key works just as well), you will see that the output changes to a new random number. We can combine this function with another, the IF function to generate a rule: =IF(RAND())<0.725,1,0. This rule determines the outcome of the virtual penalty. If the random number is less than 0.725, then the penalty is scored and counts as a goal. If the random number is greater than or equal to 0.725, then the penalty is not scored and counts as no goal. We can easily populate a data column with the same function. Each cell in the column performs exactly the same task, and because each RAND() function will calculate a different random number, in this way we can simulate a sequence of virtual penalties. How many penalties should we simulate? In theory, a penalty shootout could continue forever; even in practice it could go on for a considerable length of time, but the longer it is, the less likely it happens. When I set up my simulation, I guessed that 100 consecutive penalties by each team would be more than enough to account for 100,000 Monte Carlo iterations. The record for the longest penalty shootout came in 2005 when the Namibian Cup had to be settled by a record-breaking 48 spot-kicks. In the event I was right; the longest sequence in my 100,000 iterations was 64, or 32 by each team. Of course, if I'd used a larger Monte Carlo simulation, it might have been a different story.

The next step is to count the cumulative penalty totals by each team (using Excel's SUM function or simply by addition) and apply a set of rules matching those of a real penalty shootout that will cease the counting and record the final score when one team wins or the other loses. In addition to the final score, I might also want to record the total number of penalties taken in each virtual shootout, as well as which team wins (for example 1 for a win, 0 for a loss). My spreadsheet might look something like this.

H	I	J	K	L
Team A	Team B	Penalties	A Wins?	B Wins?
5	4	10	1	0

Pressing the F9 (or other) refresh key will repopulate your spreadsheet with a whole new set of random numbers and create an entirely new penalty shootout evolution with new outputs. Here was the output from my next iteration.

H	I	J	K	L
Team A	Team B	Penalties	A Wins?	B Wins?
6	7	14	0	1

We could manually make a note of the output data every time we run an iteration, but if we want to repeat this process hundreds or thousands of times, that will prove to be laborious and time consuming. I wanted 100,000 Monte

Carlo iterations. If each one takes even 10 seconds to refresh and record the data, I would be doing this all day and night for the best part of a fortnight. Thankfully, Excel offers us a quick and easy method to run many iterations in one go, by using its Data Table function. You will find this in Data > What If Analysis > Data Table via the Excel ribbon at the top of your spreadsheet page. There are three easy steps to this process. Firstly, highlight the cells containing your output data and a number of empty cells below them using your mouse, which you wish to populate with your outputs for new iterations, in addition to an extra single column to the left. I've shown an example for populating a total of 9 new rows of data for a total of 10 including your original output formulae in the top row.

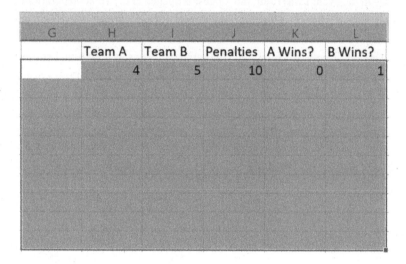

G	H	I	J	K	L
	Team A	Team B	Penalties	A Wins?	B Wins?
	4	5	10	0	1

Next, call up the Data Table in Excel. You will see a box like the one below. In the Column input cell, simply type or mouse-click a single cell reference. It can be any cell, provided it's not one of your highlighted cells from the previous step.

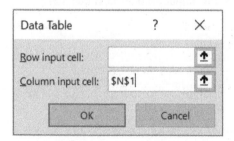

Finally, click OK and watch Excel run its magic. The highlighted cells beneath your first one will be populated with new outputs for each of the 10 iterations, as shown below.

G	H	I	J	K	L
	Team A	Team B	Penalties	A Wins?	B Wins?
	9	8	22	1	0
	5	6	12	0	1
	3	4	10	0	1
	6	7	14	0	1
	4	5	10	0	1
	4	1	7	1	0
	4	5	10	0	1
	5	4	12	1	0
	2	4	8	0	1
	4	5	10	0	1

If you press your refresh key again, the full data table will repopulate with new outputs. Beware, however, if you have a large data table with many iterations (100,000 is quite a large number), this process can take some time to complete (it took around a minute to complete on my PC). Furthermore, if you don't disable the automatic refreshing of Excel formulae calculation (use File > Options > Formulas > Manual), you may inadvertently run the whole simulation again. To preserve the data, simply copy and paste the values to a new workbook. You are then free to run the simulation again, changing the input parameter of one or both probabilities that players in either team have of scoring a penalty.

So how many penalty shootouts in my Monte Carlo simulation went to sudden death? Using the Excel function COUNTIF(J:J,">10"), I can easily count the number, since the shootout enters sudden death if it hasn't been settled after the first 10 penalties. The answer was 27,963. Thus, we can conclude that the estimated probability of a penalty shootout going to sudden death is 27.963%. With a fair bit of head-scratching I did finally manage to calculate the probability from first principles. There are 6 possible scores that result in sudden death after 10 penalties: 0-0. 1-1, 2-2, 3-3, 4-4 and 5-5. There are in fact 1, 25, 100, 100, 25 and 1 respective ways of achieving these scores. Multiplying these by their respective probabilities (using the multiplication rule where success has a probability of 0.725 and failure a probability of 0.275), the exact probability of sudden death is 27.987%. My Monte Carlo simulation yielded an incredibly close match to the true probability.

My simulation also gave me estimates for the mean (Excel function AVERAGE) number of penalties taken (10.62), the mean number of penalties scored (7.70), and the mean number of penalties scored by team A (3.96) and team B (3.74). I could never have calculated these expectations from mathematical first principles. You might be wondering why team A, on average, scores more than team B, despite being equally rated. This is simply a reflection of the fact that team A shoots first. Thus, prior to the shootout reaching sudden death, team A has a chance of claiming victory after it has taken one more penalty than team B, which has no opportunity to catch up. The reverse will never be possible, since team B will never have taken more penalties than team A.

My simulation also confirmed that the teams were evenly matched. Team A won 50,005 shootouts, just 10 more than team B. Over 100,000 shootouts that's incredibly close to the expectation of 50% each. What happens if team B is weaker? I ran a series of new simulations, where team B's penalty success percentage was decreased incrementally by 1% at a time, from 72.5% down to 67.5%, whilst team A remained at 72.5%. The following table reveals how this impacted their chances of success.

Team B penalty shot success percentage	Team A shootout win probability	Team B shootout win probability
72.5%	50.01%	49.99%
71.5%	51.49%	48.51%
70.5%	53.27%	46.73%
69.5%	54.87%	45.13%
68.5%	56.70%	43.30%
67.5%	58.11%	41.89%

The outputs of a Monte Carlo simulation can also easily be plotted as a distribution. For example, the chart below shows the frequency distribution of all 200,000 team scores at the time the shootout is concluded. For clarity, only frequencies up to 12 goals are shown; frequencies for higher tallies, the highest being 26, were too small to be worthwhile including. These frequencies can be equated with goal tally probabilities. For example, my Monte Carlo simulation estimates the probability that a team will score 7 goals is 2.9%. If any bookmaker decided to offer a market on how many goals a team would score in a penalty shootout, this sort of information could prove valuable.

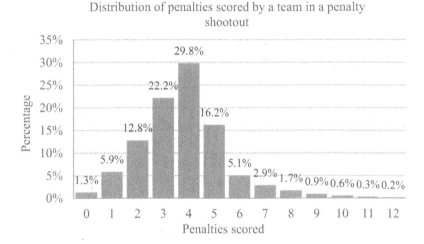

Distribution of penalties scored by a team in a penalty shootout

It should go without saying that the outputs of any model are only as reliable as the inputs that go into it. For my penalty shootout model, there were two key assumptions. 1) Every player has the same scoring probability; 2) the probability of success for one penalty success is independent from all other penalties. There are clear and obvious reasons why these assumptions may be invalid. With regards the first assumption, it's not rocket science to recognise that some players will be better at scoring penalties than others, and some goalkeepers better at saving penalties than others. With regards the second, the psychological pressures on subsequent penalty takers after previous successes or failures must surely call into question the independence of penalties. Footballs, like dice or roulette wheels, may not have memories, but football players certainly do. When developing a model to predict the outcome of sporting events that we can bet on, the importance of remaining alert and sensitive to the possibility of flawed assumptions that might invalidate your model outputs cannot be stressed enough. It is to the use of the Monte Carlo simulation in more traditional sports betting markets that I will now turn my attention.

PREDICTION MODELS

On 13 March 2020, the 2019/20 Premier League was suspended because of the COVID-19 pandemic. The last match had been played 4 days earlier. There followed what became more than a 3-month hiatus until the UK Government allowed the resumption of elite level football. The remaining 92 games were played between 17 June and 26 July. The intervening period would have offered a suitable time to build a model to predict the final outcome, including Champions League places (Liverpool were so far ahead by the time of the league suspension that they had effectively already won it) and relegation to the Championship. Model outputs could then have been compared to bookmakers' odds, with the view of exploiting any potential errors. Let's take a look at how we might have built this model.

Modelling the outcome of the Premier League

The standard approach to predicting the outcome of a football match is to model, in probabilistic terms, the number of goals each team will score. For example, we might predict that team A has a 30% chance of scoring 1 goal, whilst team B has a 40% chance of not scoring at all. Assuming these to be independent, then using the multiplication rule we can say that the probability of team A beating team B 1-0 will be 0.4 x 0.3 = 0.12 (or 12%). If we repeat this exercise for all scores, we can then calculate the probability of a home win, a draw and an away win. For practical reasons, we will probably restrict the number of possible goals a team might score to 6 or fewer; anything more happens so rarely that it's not worth the bother of including them. Using the addition rule for mutually exclusive outcomes, the probability of a draw will be the sum of the probabilities for 0-0, 1-1, 2-2, 3-3, 4-4, 5-5 and 6-6. We can do similar for the home and away win probabilities. Finally, you may recall that to convert to fair decimal betting odds (before a margin has been applied), we simply invert the decimal probabilities.

But how do we calculate the probability of a team scoring a certain number of goals? One well documented approach, first published by Mark Dixon and Stuart Coles (of Lancaster University) in the journal of *Applied Statistics* in 1997

(Volume 46, Issue 2), develops the concept of attack and defence strength, by comparing individual teams goal scoring and conceding to the league averages (means) over a specified number of previous games. These are then used to estimate the expected number of goals each team will score in a game. Finally, the Poisson distribution is used to calculate the probabilities of individual goal tallies, where the expected number of goals is the distribution's mean. Recall that 'expected' and 'mean' are effectively the same thing. One area of debate is how many games one should include, over which the averages should be determined. Too many, and the data may not be relevant for a team's current strength, while too few may allow outliers to bias the data. For my model, I will use the games played in the 2019/20 Premier League season up to the point of suspension. Furthermore, I will use the xG metric instead of actual goals to further reduce the influence of luck in goal scoring over that time, which will hopefully make it more reliable. Let's pick the first game after the resumption of the League – Aston Villa v Sheffield United on 17 June 2020 – as an example to illustrate the process.

To calculate attack strength, the first step is to calculate the Premier League mean xG per game. Since home teams, on average, perform better than away teams, we should consider them separately for this purpose. Indeed, pretty much all football prediction modelling does so. Prior to the League suspension, there were 288 games played and 455.94 xG, as calculated by Understat.com, attributed to home teams. Hence the mean Premier League home team xG scored during this period was 455.94/288 = 1.583 xG. Similarly, for away teams, with a total of 384.97 xG, the mean scored was 1.337 xG. The next step is to calculate the mean xG for both Aston Villa and Sheffield United. In their 13 home games prior to suspension, Aston Villa amassed 17.96 xG. Consequently, their mean home xG was 1.382. Sheffield United amassed 13.33 xG in their 13 away games, implying their mean away xG was 1.025. Finally, to calculate team's attack strength, divide the home/away team's mean xG scored by the Premier League's mean home/away xG scored. For Aston Villa this is 1.382/1.583 = 0.873. For Sheffield United it is 1.025/1.337 = 0.767. The larger the attack strength number, the stronger the attack.

The defence strength is calculated in exactly the same way, using xG conceded instead of xG scored. Unsurprisingly, the Premier League mean xG conceded is just the reverse of the mean xG scored for home and away teams respectively, since goals scored by the away team are goals conceded by the home team, and vice versa. Thus, home teams conceded a mean of 1.337 xG prior to 13 March 2020, with the away teams conceding a mean of 1.583 xG.

With Aston Villa conceding 27.04 xG in 13 home games (mean = 2.08 xG) and Sheffield United conceding 18.83 xG in 13 away games (mean = 1.448 xG), the defence strengths for the two teams are 1.556 and 0.915 respectively. This time, the smaller the defence strength number, the stronger the defence.

Finally, we are in a position to calculate the expected number of goals Aston Villa and Sheffield United will score in their match. For Aston Villa, this is done by multiplying Aston Villa's home attack strength (0.873) by Sheffield United's away defence strength (0.915) and the mean number of home xG scored in the Premier League (1.583). The answer is 1.264 xG. For Sheffield United, we multiply their away attack strength (0.767) by Aston Villa's home defence strength (1.556) and the mean number of away xG scored in the Premier League (1.337). The answer is 1.596 xG. Thus, if our model is correct, and if this game could be played an infinite number of times to eliminate the influence of the random variables, we would expect Aston Villa to score an average of 1.264 goals and Sheffield United to score an average of 1.596 goals. On that basis, it looks like the away team would be favourites to win. The bookmakers certainly thought so, pricing Sheffield United at 2.32 on average (the top bookmaker offered 2.43), whilst making Aston Villa 3.28 (with a best price of 3.50). For the record, the draw was priced at 3.29 (best 3.44).

The Dixon-Coles model gives us the expected goals in a football match. It further assumes that the scoring of goals is independent, that is to say one goal does not **cause** another to be scored, and that they are Poisson distributed. We can then use these assumptions to calculate the probability of any goal tally for either team. I introduced the Poisson distribution to you earlier in my primer on statistics and showed how the distribution of home and away goals conforms quite closely to the Poisson distribution. How did I calculate those Poisson goal tallies in my comparison chart? Knowing that the mean of a Poisson distribution is equal to the variance, it is quite straightforward to calculate the probabilities for any goal tally. Well, it is for a trained statistician. Fortunately, we don't need to worry about learning the mathematics. Excel will do the job for us with its POISSON(x,μ,cumulative) function. If we know the mean, we can use the function to calculate the expected probability of any goal tally. Here, x is the number of goals for which we want to calculate the probability, μ is the mean or expected number of goals calculated by the Dixon-Coles model (recall that 'expected' and 'mean' are essentially the same thing), and 'cumulative' denotes a logical argument that determines the form of the probability distribution returned. If cumulative is TRUE, the POISSON function returns the cumulative Poisson probability that the number of goals events occurring will be between zero and x inclusive; if FALSE, it returns the Poisson probability that exactly x goals will be scored. For example, the probability of Aston Villa scoring exactly 3 goals calculated via this function is POISSON(3,1.264,FALSE) = 9.51%. Using Excel's POISSON function and the two teams' expected goals, as estimated by Dixon-Coles, I've calculated the Poisson probabilities for Aston Villa's and Sheffield United's possible goal tallies. The results are shown in the table below (Poisson %) up to a maximum of 6 goals. Knowing the probabilities for either team to score a specified number of goals, we can then use the multiplication rule to calculate the probabilities for any score. The correct-score probabilities are also shown in the shaded area.

	SHU	0	1	2	3	4	5	6
AV	Poisson %	20.27%	32.35%	25.82%	13.73%	5.48%	1.75%	0.47%
0	28.25%	5.73%	9.14%	7.29%	3.88%	1.55%	0.49%	0.13%
1	35.71%	7.24%	11.55%	9.22%	4.90%	1.96%	0.62%	0.17%
2	22.57%	4.57%	7.30%	5.83%	3.10%	1.24%	0.39%	0.11%
3	9.51%	1.93%	3.08%	2.45%	1.31%	0.52%	0.17%	0.04%
4	3.00%	0.61%	0.97%	0.78%	0.41%	0.16%	0.05%	0.01%
5	0.76%	0.15%	0.25%	0.20%	0.10%	0.04%	0.01%	0.00%
6	0.16%	0.03%	0.05%	0.04%	0.02%	0.01%	0.00%	0.00%

Finally, we can use the additional rule to calculate the probabilities of the three possible results: home win, draw or away win. The Aston Villa home win probability is calculated by summing the darker shaded area; the Sheffield United away win probability is calculated by summing the lighter shaded area; and the draw probability is the sum of the probabilities along the diagonal. These come to 30.24%, 45.00% and 24.59% respectively. You will note that these sum to 99.83%. The missing 0.17% will be found in scores involving 7 or more goals for either team. To calculate the fair odds as estimated by this model, we invert the probabilities. If you want you can do this for the individual correct scores, but here I will just do that for the match result. Aston Villa to win would be priced at 3.31, Sheffield United at 2.22 and the draw 4.07.

Comparing these to the best available prices from the bookmakers on the day of the match I reported above, we would conclude that there was expected value backing both Aston Villa (3.50/3.31 − 1 = 5.74%) and Sheffield United

(2.43/2.22 − 1 = 9.46%). In contrast, the draw was a negative expectation bet (3.44/4.07 − 1 = -15.48%). In the event, the game finished 0-0 (a 5.73% chance according to the model). Does that mean the model was wrong? Of course not. Yes, the model could be wrong, but a single result won't tell you that. Remember the random variables that influence the match. Luck will be the major factor determining a single result. To know whether this model was reliable and accurate, we would need to use it over hundreds, indeed probably thousands of matches, yes, really thousands. Later in the book, I will show you why.

What about our quest to predict the finishing league positions? We can run the Dixon-Coles model in the same way for all the other remaining 91 fixtures, calculating the match outcome probabilities of each one. With a total of 92 fixtures and 3 possible outcomes for each, however, the number of potential different scenarios for the league table is huge, in fact 3 to the power 92, written 3^{92}, or 78,551,672,112,789,411,833,022,577,315,290,546,060,373,041 in full. Calculating the precise probabilities of all these scenarios to find the most likely outcome for the league table would be a thankless task, even for Poincaré's infinitely powerful mind. Instead, we can turn to the Monte Carlo simulation to do the job for us. This involves a two-step process to simulate the goals scored for the remaining matches. Firstly, we will use a uniformly distributed random number using Excel's RAND() function to determine the Poisson probability. Secondly, we will invert the POISSON function to find the number of goals from this probability, given the expected goals for a team as estimated by the Dixon-Coles model. In fact, Excel does not offer a function for the inverse of the Poisson distribution. However, one is available via the Real Statistics Excel Resource Pack (you can find it via Google), which can be downloaded and installed as an Excel Add-in (and switched on via Developer > Excel Add-ins from the Excel ribbon). The function takes the form POISSON_INV(probability,mean), and calculates the smallest integer x such that POISSON(x,mean,TRUE) ≥ probability. Thus, by substituting RAND() for the probability of scoring x goals, POISSON_INV(RAND(),mean) will output a random goal tally for a team where 'mean' is the expected goals (from the Dixon-Coles model). For example, if RAND() = 0.27 for Aston Villa against Sheffield United, POISSON_INV(0.27,1.264) = 0 goals. Alternatively, If RAND() = 0.97, =POISSON_INV(0.97,1.264) = 4 goals. We can then build a Monte Carlo simulation following the methodology described in the previous chapter to produce a large number of random goal tallies for both teams for all remaining 92 matches, calculating league points for each team based on the match score. Finally, these Monte Carlo iterations allow us to calculate the expected finishing league table. My Monte Carlo simulation consisted of 10,000 iterations, and the expected finishing points for the 20 teams (the arithmetic mean of the 10,000 simulated points totals) was as follows.

Team	Expected Points	Actual Points	Actual Position	Points Difference
Liverpool	100.61	99	1	-1.61
Manchester City	79.82	81	2	1.18
Leicester City	68.49	62	5	-6.49
Chelsea	64.54	66	4	1.46
Manchester United	62.52	66	3	3.48
Wolves	58.73	59	7	0.27
Sheffield United	55.87	54	9	-1.87
Tottenham	53.46	59	6	5.54
Arsenal	52.27	56	8	3.73
Everton	51.47	49	12	-2.47
Burnley	51.09	54	10	2.91
Crystal Palace	47.68	43	14	-4.68
Southampton	45.58	52	11	6.42
Newcastle United	42.66	44	13	1.34
Brighton	40.25	41	15	0.75
Watford	37.48	34	19	-3.48
West Ham United	36.93	39	16	2.07
Bournemouth	35.75	34	18	-1.75
Aston Villa	33.78	35	17	1.22
Norwich City	28.64	21	20	-7.64

I've also included the actual finishing points, actual finishing positions and the difference between actual and expected points (a negative value denotes an underachievement with respect to model expectation). Broadly speaking, the Monte Carlo simulation predicted the finishing points of teams reasonably well; 12 of the teams were within ±1 win/loss of expectation. However, there are some notable exceptions. Norwich City, Crystal Palace, Leicester City and Watford substantially underperformed in the final 9 games of the season. It cost Leicester City a Champions League spot and Watford relegation to the Championship. Meanwhile, Southampton and Tottenham substantially overperformed relative to model prediction. These deviations from expectation could be random. Alternatively, they might have some underlying causal explanations. Perhaps poor performers might blame the lack of crowds, and in the case of Norwich might have given up trying after they were relegated with 3 games still to play. Better performers, meanwhile, might have undergone structural improvements to their game. In the case of Southampton, the humiliation at the hands of Leicester in October 2019 may have heralded a turning point. Both Tottenham and Southampton continued to perform well, and over games played since the restart of the 2019/20 campaign in June 2020 and into the 2020/21 season, were ranked 1st and 5th respectively on 26 November 2020 when I ran the model.

We can test to see if any of the deviations between expectation and actual outcome are statistically significant. Cast your mind back to the primer on statistics, and in particular my discussion of statistical hypothesis testing. Our null hypothesis would be that an actual team performance was either lucky or unlucky relative to expectation. The alternative hypothesis would be that, in fact, something else **caused** the deviation. Of course, there is a third hypothesis: my model is wrong, but we won't worry about that for now. How likely is it that Norwich, for example, will collect just 21 points, 7.64 fewer than the model predicted? We can count the number of times it happened in the Monte Carlo simulation, and hence calculate the percentage (and implied likelihood) as a fraction of the total number of iterations. It happened only 74 times, implying a probability of 0.74%. This frequency, and those of all the other points totals that were observed can be plotted in a frequency distribution.

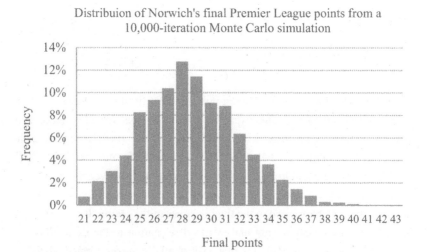

Distribuion of Norwich's final Premier League points from a 10,000-iteration Monte Carlo simulation

In fact, 21 points is the fewest possible, since this was the points total Norwich held when the Premier League was suspended. After resumption, they lost their 9 remaining fixtures. With an implied probability of less than 1% that Norwich would do so the weaker thresholds of statistical significance (5% and 1%) have been met. Hence, we might conclude that the null hypothesis has been disproved, in favour of the alternative one, where something other than chance may have accounted for their terrible performance. Of course, we should remind ourselves that this sort of conclusion is simply subjective and based on arbitrary conventions about statistical significance. Given that my Monte Carlo simulation can produce 74 occasions in 10,000 where Norwich lose all 9 games completely randomly, we should always remain open to the view that chance was the only thing at play. This sort of inference testing doesn't prove that something **caused** Norwich to lose all 9 (although that may well be the case); it simply informs you about the chance of seeing something, given nothing was causing it at all. Remember: with enough iterations, anything is possible by chance.

We could also directly calculate the probability of Norwich losing all the games from the match odds themselves. After removing the bookmaker's margin (later, I will show you how), I calculated the probability of Norwich losing each game. Then, using the multiplication rule, I multiplied these all together to calculate the probability of them losing all 9. The answer was 0.38%. That's within the same ballpark as the figure generated by the Monte Carlo simulation. For the record, the most points Norwich could have finished with is 48 (from 9 wins). The highest total they achieved in 10,000 tallies was 43. This is hardly surprising. Based on the actual match odds, the probability of 9 wins was roughly 1 in 60 million; we'd have needed 60 million Monte Carlo iterations to have a reasonable chance of notching up just one 48-point total.

How often did Manchester City, Manchester United, Chelsea, Leicester City and others finish in Champions League spots? My Monte Carlo simulation can answer that too. Unsurprisingly, Liverpool occupied 1st place in all 10,000 iterations. They were, after all, 25 points ahead when the League was suspended, and Manchester City only had a maximum of 30 points available to win. Manchester City, however, were never outside the top 4, implying they were effectively a certainty to achieve a Champions League place, although a larger Monte Carlo simulation may well have witnessed a few iterations where that would happen. For the other hopefuls, their implied top 4 probabilities were as follows.

Team	# top 4	% top 4	Implied odds	Bookmakers' odds
Leicester	9,103	91.03%	1.10	1.14
Chelsea	6,031	60.31%	1.66	1.62
Manchester United	3,710	37.10%	2.70	2.75
Wolves	809	8.09%	12.36	9
Sheffield United	240	2.40%	41.7	15
Tottenham	67	0.67%	149	15
Arsenal	27	0.27%	370	17
Everton	7	0.07%	1,429	26
Burnley	6	0.06%	1,667	N/A
Crystal Palace	1	0.01%	10,000	N/A

The remaining 8 Premier League teams failed to register a single top 4 finish in any of the 10,000 iterations. Leicester City actually finished 5th, yet the implied odds from this model for them winning a Champions League place were just 1.10. They were the big losers, with Manchester United, an outsider before the League resumed, taking their place. How do these implied probabilities compare to the bookmakers' odds that were available at the time? I've shown prices that were available just before the resumption of the League in June in the final column. Remember, when looking for a good bet, we aren't interested in finding winners – although it goes without saying that it's nice to win – we are interested in finding value. And recall, expected value is any bet where the odds the bookmakers are offering are longer than the 'true' odds. If my Monte Carlo model was accurately predicting the 'true' top 4 odds, then you can see that there was value available in bets on both Leicester City (1.14/1.10 – 1 = 3.6%) and Manchester United (2.75/2.70 – 1 = 1.9%). One of them turned out to be a winner, the other a loser. To reiterate, two bets can tell us nothing about the validity of the prediction model; for this we need many hundreds or thousands more. Incidentally, Manchester City to finish in the top 4 were available at 1.02. Given there were no occasions in 10,000 iterations where they finished outside, these odds would also appear to represent value. (1.02/1.00 – 1 = 2%).

You may have also noticed that for the less likely top 4 finishers, or longshots – Wolves, Sheffield United, Tottenham, Arsenal and Everton – there is an ever-increasing divergence between their model-implied 'true' odds and the bookmakers' odds, with the latter being much shorter. For the favourites, they are much closer. Everton, for example, would have been predicted by my Monte

Carlo simulation to make top 4 less than 1 time in a 1,000. Yet, the bookmaker was only prepared to lay 26. Given the probability that Everton had of making top 4, why wasn't the bookmaker prepared to offer me much more, should I win? There are a number of explanations for this, which readers of my previous books may be familiar with. Some of these relate to the psychology of bettors, in particular their miscalculation of low probability outcomes – humans exhibit a bias towards overestimating their likelihood – and their exploitation by bookmakers. Others relate to the greater impact of uncertainty for lower probability outcomes, and the potentially greater liabilities they create for the bookmaker. If your model is wrong by 1% about Manchester City, that's the difference between 'true' odds of 1.00 (100%) and 1.01 (99%). By contrast, if it's wrong about Everton, that's the difference between odds of 1,429 (0.07%) and 93 (1.07%). Since bookmakers are also using models to estimate the 'true' odds, there's obviously a much bigger scope for a pricing error, the longer the odds are. Far safer, then, to err on the side of caution and quote odds that are much shorter than they should be. In terms of what the bookmaker is doing, this means that when they create a margin (or vig) they are not distributing it equally across all possible outcomes but are actually placing more of its weight, or emphasis, on the longshots than the favourites when those are present in their betting market.

The disproportionately bigger deviation between the 'true' odds and the bookmakers' odds as they lengthen is known as the favourite-longshot bias. It can be found in many sports betting markets, including football, tennis and horse racing. Since longshots, compared to favourites, are priced disproportionately shorter than the 'true' chances imply, it means that you can expect to lose disproportionately more per stake betting on them blindly. That is to say, the expected payout (or return) will be less than for favourites. For example, in the home-draw-away football betting markets of the major European football leagues, betting a £1 stake on the average available bookmaker's odds on a team when they were longer than 20, between the seasons 2012/13 to 2019/20, would have lost you an average of £0.37, or more than a third. By contrast, if you'd have bet the odds that were shorter than 1.33, you'd have actually made a little bit of money without doing any predicting at all. Free money, you might think. Well, yes, in this case it would have been, but here some of that could have been good fortune. More typically, we would still expect losses on the shortest-priced favourites, but much smaller than for the longshots.

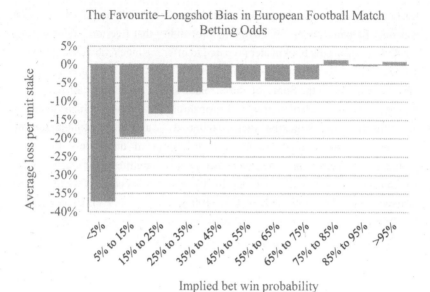

The Favourite–Longshot Bias in European Football Match Betting Odds

Implied bet win probability

Despite the less unfavourable odds this bias can offer for favourites, bettors continue to love betting on the longshots, and bookmakers continue to worry about the liabilities this creates for them, so the favourite–longshot bias persists. It is an example of what economists call a market inefficiency, when there is a structural and non-random way in which the quoted value of things (in this case the bookmakers' odds) does not reflect accurately the underlying fundamental value (the 'true' chances of football teams winning).

What about the odds for relegation? 8 Premier League teams, shown in the table below, had at least one Monte Carlo iteration where they were relegated.

Team	# relegated	% relegated	Implied odds	Bookmakers' odds
Norwich	9,714	97.14%	1.03	1.10
Aston Villa	7,417	74.17%	1.35	1.40
Bournemouth	5,176	51.76%	1.93	1.83
West Ham	3,487	34.87%	2.87	2.87
Watford	2,994	29.94%	3.34	3.25
Brighton	830	8.30%	12.05	3.75
Newcastle	321	3.21%	31.2	21
Southampton	55	0.55%	182	34

Most likely was Norwich. As we've already seen, they were indeed relegated, losing all 9 of their remaining games. The Monte Carlo simulation gave them less than a 3% chance of avoiding relegation. You could have had odds of 1.10 at one bookmaker. That would have been a steal given the short odds (1.10/1.03 − 1 = 6.8% expected value). The odds of 1.40 for Aston Villa also offered expected value (1.40/1.35 − 1 = 3.7%), but that would have proved to be a losing bet. To reiterate, however, one unexpected outcome does not invalidate a model, any more than one expected one validates it. Once again, you will notice the unfavourable pricing of the outsiders − or longshots − for relegation.

Although a small number of results cannot validate or invalidate a prediction model like this Monte Carlo simulation, all bettors who use them should remain ever-alert to the possibility of flaws. I'll say it again: the outputs of a model are only as good as the inputs that go into it. What might some of the possible flaws in this model be? An obvious one was failing to update the attack and defence strengths of teams as each round of fixtures was played. Doing so would arguably make them more relevant in terms of the most recent performance. Perhaps more generally it might be considered inappropriate to use such a large sample of fixtures to calculate attack and defence strengths, going back to the beginning of the season. Dixon and Coles attempted to solve this problem by applying a stronger weighting for more recent games. To save time, I just decided not to bother.

Another potential source of error was the disappearance of crowds; in particular, how would home teams play without their fans? In fact, once major European leagues which restarted had completed their 2019/20 season, there was shown to be a weak but obvious drop in home win percentage of about 2%. In the following season, with fans still absent, the size of this decrease grew in some divisions. In the Premier League, for example, there were in fact more away wins (153) than home wins (144) in the 2020/21 campaign, something previously unheard of. Of course, if home teams are winning less and away teams winning more, that shouldn't have much impact on final league points. What a team might lose in performance at home, they will gain away. Nevertheless, there were other reported changes, in particular, how the game was played and how the referee controlled it. These might have had an influence on the goal scoring, and hence the number of expected goals. Since the Poisson model which lies at the heart of my Monte Carlo simulation relied on expected goals, we shouldn't underestimate the possible influence that playing without crowds may have.

Perhaps the most significant potential model error lies in the assumption that team goals can be Poisson-distributed in the first place. For this to be true, goal scoring should be independent, but is that really the case? Arguably, teams which fall behind may become more motivated than they were to redress the balance. On the other hand, teams that draw level might be more motivated to push on. Whatever the dynamics at play, it surely cannot be denied that goal scoring in football will involve a considerable degree of player and team psychology. If that is the case, the idea that goals just go in at random must surely be brought into question.

Being 'well-documented' means many bettors are potentially already using the Dixon-Coles model for football match prediction. The corollary to this is the implication that the odds bookmakers quote will already reflect the information it brings. A statistical model about a football match is simply a means of quantifying information about the teams, when attempting to find the match outcome probabilities. The better the information, and the better the way it is modelled, the more valid (reliable and accurate) the probabilities will be. The bookmakers' odds are simply the public expression of their model and the information that went into it. They may change the odds if they receive new information that requires their model to be updated. That could be in the form of news about the teams, or it could be in the form of money bet by their customers, some of whom may also be using different, and possibly superior models. If a lot of money comes for one of the sides, the bookmakers may start to believe their initial model was wrong. The shortening of their odds (whilst lengthening the odds for the other team) is then a measure of the correction to their model. Odds may move many times to reflect the continual flow of new information about the match. As the total amount of information about it increases, arguably the accuracy (or what economists call efficiency) of the odds improves. This process is called price discovery, whose consequence typically, although not always, is to arrive at odds that most accurately (or efficiently) reflect the 'true' match outcome probabilities.

Being, as they are, a reflection of a collection or crowd of opinions, the odds might be regarded as an expression of the 'wisdom of a crowd'. I've discussed at length this concept in my last book, *Squares and Sharps, Suckers and Sharks: the Science, Psychology and Philosophy of Gambling*. Indeed, later I will show you how you can use it to make a sustainable profit. Some have argued that, really, most bettors are pretty dumb, backing teams on a whim, with the odds instead reflecting the wisdom of the bookmakers' odds compilers and a few other very savvy customers. Be that as it may, even if this premise is valid, it doesn't really invalidate the concept; it just reduces the size of the crowd. The significant take-home message, however, is this: if the model you are using is already reflected in the odds, because other people are using it too, it won't be good enough to help you overcome the bookmakers' margins. If you want to beat the odds and find for yourself some expected value in what the bookmakers are offering, you will need to have a prediction model that is better than theirs, and arguably also better than a whole load of their customers, too, who influence the bookmakers' odds.

Some statisticians have advocated abandoning Poisson and using other distributions to model football goals instead, for example the Weibull distribution and the negative binomial distribution, but I have no plans to go there in this book. Instead, I think it's time to move on to another Monte Carlo simulation.

The unlikeliness of Leicester City's 2015/16 Premier League title

No one, not least the supporters of Leicester City, will forget the team's remarkable winning of the 2015/16 Premier League. At a time when the big 6 teams – Chelsea, Manchester City, Manchester United, Arsenal, Liverpool and Tottenham – were beginning to establish themselves as a class above the rest, Leicester City, under the management of Claudio Ranieri, performed the unthinkable and finished ahead of them all on 81 points. Admittedly, this was one of the lowest winning totals of the Premier League in a season when all the regular big players appeared to have taken leave of absence, but the scale of the achievement cannot be underestimated. Bookmakers had offered 5,001 (or 5,000/1 in fractional format) for them to win at the start of the season. They no longer offer such long odds on any team, even though such a price was already hugely discounted via the favourite–longshot bias. What exactly were the 'true' odds of Leicester City winning the Premier League that season? One rudimentary way to estimate that would be to measure how likely it was they would have won the Premier League the season before and then assume their level of performance would broadly remain the same.

I could use something like the Dixon-Coles model I introduced earlier in this chapter to estimate the chance of Premiership teams winning their matches. I could make it more reliable by updating the attack and defence strengths after every round of fixtures, to reflect each team's ability as it waxes and wanes through the course of the season. Arguably, however, a much easier method, for this exercise at least, would be to just borrow the model that the bookmakers use to create their football match odds for every game; that is, use their odds directly as a measure of the implied probabilities. After all, bookmakers will be using similar models to Dixon-Coles to produce their odds; why try to reinvent the wheel when one has already been invented for me? What is more, their model is likely to be better than mine at estimating the 'true' match odds, because that is their job and they have access to more sophisticated data and data analysis tools than I do. Regardless, even if I did have a better match prediction model than theirs, capable of making profits from betting on the matches, it arguably won't make a huge amount of difference to the outcome here, which is to say how likely Leicester City were to win the 2014/15 Premier League the season before their triumph.

A bookmaker's match odds, in a way, are to match outcomes what xG are to goals; they strip out the luck. Whilst xG tells us how many goals we would have expected to see, given the quality and quantity of the scoring chances in a game, the match odds tell us the expected outcome in probabilistic terms, albeit before the match kicks off. At the end of a 90-minute football match, there are three possible outcomes: home win, draw or away win. If you were to assign numbers to these outcomes, you might use 1 for the outcome that happened and 0 for those that didn't. Prior to the match, however, we can use the odds to express the probability of each of these three results occurring. Remember, just calculate their reciprocal. Suppose the home odds were 2, the draw odds were 3 and the away odds 6. The home probability would be 0.5 (or 50%), the draw 0.333 (or 33.3%) and the away 0.167 (or 16.7%). We can then say that the expected amount of home win was a half, the expected amount of draw was a third and the expected amount of away win was a sixth. The actual result is just a consequence of the hidden random variables, in the same way that actual goals are. The outcome might deviate substantially from expectation, but that does not mean the former invalidates the latter, certainly not over just one game. The away team might win, but it is still perfectly acceptable to say they had a sixth of an expected win.

What if we now factor in League points for winning (3), losing (0) and drawing (1)? If the home team had a 50% chance of winning, and 33.3% chance of drawing and a 16.7% chance of losing, then their expected points can be calculated by multiplying each probability by their respective points and summing the products. Thus, the home team had (0.5 x 3pts) + (0.333 x 1pts) + (0.167 x 0pts) = 1.833 expected points (xP). Similarly, the away team had (0.5 x 0pts) + (0.333 x 1pt) + (0.167 x 3pts) = 0.833 xP. Of course, the game will either finish with 3 points awarded to one of the teams and 0 points to the other, or 1 point to each, but xP tells us the average number of points we should expect each team to win if the exact same game could be played an infinite number of times. Since betting odds are available for all 380 matches in a Premier League season, we can simply calculate the xP in this way and sum the totals for each of the 20 teams over their 38 games in a season. This will give us their expected finishing points totals, and hence their expected League positions.

We already know, however, that bookmakers' odds are not fair and the implied probabilities of the three possible outcomes sum to more than 100%. Thus, we must remove their margin before we calculate the fair outcome probabilities and the xP. To do this, we need to know how the bookmaker applied their margin in the first place. Unsurprisingly, they won't tell us, so we have to guess. A rudimentary method would apply it evenly across every possible outcome, but we also now know that this is not the case. There is a bias to the application of this margin, a favourite–longshot bias, where a bigger margin weight is applied to longshots than to favourites. Through my website Football-Data.co.uk, I have discussed at length some of the possible ways that this margin could be applied, and hence removed by reverse engineering. These include my own method that assumes the size of the margin weight is proportional to the odds (double the odds, double the margin weight), and a couple of others: the odds ratio and a logarithmic function. You can find detailed mathematical descriptions of these methodologies via my website (see the link 'Wisdom of Crowds'), in addition to an Excel 'Fair Odds' calculator that will do the margin stripping for you. There is also work in this area from the financial economist Hyun-Song Shin who was one of the earliest theorists to discuss the favourite–longshot bias and how to account for it when removing the bookmakers' margins, but his methodology is arguably better suited to horse racing, which typically has more runners and thus more possible outcomes.

My preferred method for football home-draw-away betting odds is the logarithmic function. Briefly, this assumes that the bookmakers transform their fair win probabilities for each outcome into unfair ones by means of a common exponent. An exponent is simply a number representing the power to which another number is raised, for example 3 in 2^3 ($= 2 \times 2 \times 2 = 8$). Since probabilities are less than 1, raising their power with an exponent greater than 1 would reduce them. For example, $0.5^{1.05} = 0.484$. Bookmakers want to increase these probabilities to build an overround and a margin. Thus, the exponent must always be less than 1. $0.5^{0.95} = 0.518$. Similarly, $0.333^{0.95} = 0.352$ and $0.167^{0.95} = 0.182$. Summing these unfair probabilities makes 1.052 or 105.2%. The corresponding odds are now 1.93 (home), 2.84 (draw) and 5.49 (away). You can see the longer odds have had a proportionally bigger margin weight applied to them. The actual weights are 1.035 for home (2 / 1.93), 1.056 for draw (3 / 2.84) and 1.094 for away (6 / 5.49). Simple but effective; it's called a logarithmic function, but it might just as well be called a power function, since a logarithm is just the opposite of a power. If $2^3 = 8$, then $\log_2 8 = 3$, where the number 2 is known as the base. Here, you would say log to the base 2 of 8 = 3. Similarly, if $0.5^{0.95} = 0.518$, then $\log_{0.5} 0.518 = 0.95$. Likewise, $\log_{0.333} 0.352 = 0.95$ and $\log_{0.167} 0.182 = 0.95$. To reverse engineer the application of the margin in this way we need to use logs, so perhaps that's why the name is preferred.

We should also decide which bookmaker we are going to use for this exercise. Since we want as accurate an estimate as possible of match outcome probabilities, it would make sense to use the bookmaker that quotes the most accurate (or efficient) odds. But how to tell? Over many years of odds data analysis, I have found that the best bookmaker for this task is Pinnacle.com. I will explore the reasons for this in more detail later in the book; for now, it is enough to say that their business model demands it. Most other bookmakers use a different business model to theirs, and hence quote prices slightly differently and arguably less accurately. If that is so, I hear you wonder, is it easier to find expected value from their odds? Yes, it is. Again, I will be looking at how we find it, and what the implications of exploiting it are.

Furthermore, which odds should we use? Pinnacle's first quoted odds, called the opening odds, based solely on the interpretation of their match prediction model? Or odds that have been updated after more information and money has been received? The time at which the most amount of information is available and the most money wagered on a game occurs just before the kick-off. These are called the closing odds, because kick-off is the time the betting market will close, unless the bookmaker has an option to put it into play, with odds updating as the match progresses. Arguably, the closing odds are the most accurate of all odds, at least on average. Undeniably, they are more accurate than the opening ones; I have carried out further data analysis to demonstrate this to be true. Again, more on that later.

Having removed the margin from Pinnacle's closing odds (for this exercise I used the logarithmic function), I calculated the xP for the 2014/15 Premier League season. Since we are using the match odds as the season progresses to calculate the final season xP total, in effect we are gauging how the bookmaker updated their opinion about the relative prospects of each team. A statistical method that assigns probabilities or expectations based on current information prior to observation, which are then revised post observation after new data has been collected, is known as the method of Bayesian inference. For example, a bookmaker will have an opinion about Liverpool defending the Premier League title and assign a probability to that. After being thrashed by Aston Villa 7-2, it is likely that the bookmaker will want to update the probability given the new data, most likely reducing it because they no longer believe them to be as defensively good as previously thought. A similar downgrading of Liverpool's chances occurred when Virgil van Dijk, their key central defender, was ruled out for the remainder of the 2020/21 season following injury in the Merseyside derby against Everton on 17 October 2020.

Using the method described above for calculating xP, Leicester City amassed a total of 43.78, placing them 13th in the xP table (they actually finished 14th with 41 points). Teams finishing so low in the table and with so few points (just 6 ahead of relegation), don't win the following season's Premier League, do they, particularly when they sack their manager (Nigel Pearson) who'd engineered the team's Premier League survival, have seen their best player (Esteban Cambiasso) leave, and acquired the services of a new manager (Claudio Ranieri) who'd never won a league title and had only recently been sacked as an international manager (Greece) for losing to the Faroe Isles. Thus, it would be a reasonable assumption that at best, Leicester City could be expected to achieve much the same in 2015/16 as they had in 2014/15: that is, survive relegation. Even when they sat in 5th place in October 2015, Stats.com's supercomputer was predicting a 13th place finish with 45 points.

xP can tell us where we think Leicester City will finish in the 2015/16 Premier League table, but it can't tell us the likelihood of them winning the League, or indeed the chances of finishing in any of the 20 possible positions. For that we need a Monte Carlo distribution, since calculating the probabilities of all possible scenarios for all 20 teams mathematically is impossible. It was bad enough for 92 games. Now we have 380, and 3^{380} possible outcome scenarios. I won't write this number out in full – it has 182 digits! Using a random number to simulate a match outcome in the same way I did for the last Monte Carlo exercise, I simulated the entire 2014/15 Premier League season 100,000 times. The mean xP for all teams matched almost exactly those calculated using the xP formula. The worst match was still within just 0.2% and the majority were within 0.05%. Leicester again amassed a mean of 43.78 xP and finished in a virtual 13th place. This time, however, we can see the distribution of possibilities. I've shown these for Leicester City below. The distribution, although discrete – it must be since League points are discrete – takes on the familiar shape of the continuous bell-shaped normal distribution.

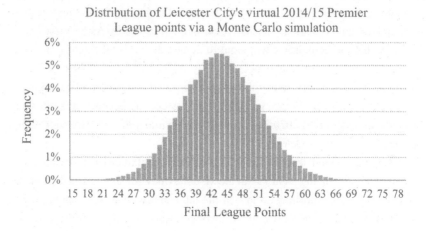

Distribution of Leicester City's virtual 2014/15 Premier League points via a Monte Carlo simulation

We can test if the normal distribution offers a reliable approximation by seeing if the data conform to the empirical rule, where 68.2%, 95.5% and 99.7% of the data fall within 1, 2 and 3 standard deviations, respectively. Here, the figures are 69.5%, 95.3% and 99.8%. This is hardly surprising since the results are simulated randomly. A normal distribution is always the telltale sign that the system under investigation is random in nature. The minimum and maximum tallies are 15 and 79 points. Indeed, 79 was an outlier; the next highest was 75. The standard deviation (recall, that is how far, on average, each score lies from the arithmetic mean) is 7.29 points. Leicester City, as we know, finished the 2014/15 season with 41 points, much less than 1 standard deviation from the mean xP and well within the most probable region of the distribution.

We can repeat this exercise for League positions, as the next chart illustrates.

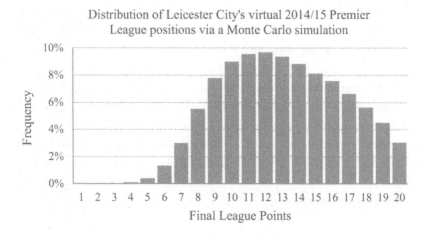

Distribution of Leicester City's virtual 2014/15 Premier League positions via a Monte Carlo simulation

Their best finishing position was 2nd – it happened 3 times in 100,000 Monte Carlo iterations. They finished 3rd a further 19 times. The probability of relegation was 13.14%. The average finishing position was 13th rounded to the nearest integer; one place higher than their actual finishing spot.

Let's review our working hypothesis: the performance of Leicester City in 2014/15 will be repeated in 2015/16. By performance, we actually mean 'expected performance' as predicted by this Monte Carlo model, using the 2014/15 match odds as the inputs. Hence, we would conclude that the chances of Leicester City winning the 2015/16 season are less than 1 in 100,000. When I first ran the model a few years ago with different odds and a different method for removing the margin, my Monte Carlo simulation had one iteration in the 100,000 where they became champions. Broadly speaking, however, my calculated xP and expected rankings are the same second time round. Thus, the predicted odds should be no shorter than 100,000. Furthermore, in 100,000 model iterations of the 2014/15 season, the team never amassed more than 79 points. Yet in 2015/16 they finished as champions with 2 more, a whopping 5 standard deviations above expectation.

We should already suspect that the probability of achieving 81 points based on this hypothesis will be less than 1 in 100,000. Since we have shown that the spread of virtual points in the Monte Carlo simulation can be approximated by the normal distribution, Excel provides a useful function to directly calculate this: NORM.DIST(x, μ, σ, cumulative). The function's parameters are described in the parentheses. x is the required value for which you want to calculate the probability, μ is the arithmetic mean of the distribution, σ is the standard deviation, and 'cumulative', as for the POISSON Excel function, is a logical argument that determines the form of the function. If cumulative is TRUE, NORM.DIST returns the cumulative distribution function or the total area in the distribution to the left of x; if FALSE, it returns the probability density function or the probability density at x. Being a continuous distribution, the interpretation of 'probability density' can be a little hard to conceptualise for those not familiar with integral calculus. Fortunately, we need 'cumulative' to be TRUE, which is far easier to comprehend. With Leicester City's xP of 43.78 and a standard deviation of 7.29 points, NORM.DIST(81,43.78,7.29,TRUE) returns an answer of 0.999999835. This can be interpreted as meaning that 99.9999835% of the points totals should fall below exactly 81, and 0.0000165% above. That's approximately 1 in 6 million. Of course, since virtual points in a Monte Carlo simulation are discrete and can only be integers, with no possibility of an infinite number of decimal points in between them, the use of a continuous data function isn't wholly appropriate, but it does at least give you a ballpark idea of how unlikely 81 points actually was, based on the expectation that Leicester City would perform much as they had the previous season. Excel does have a binomial function, BINOM.DIST(s,t,p,cumulative), for discrete data (where s is the number of successes in a series of independent trials, t, each with success probability p) but there are clearly practical obstacles to using it here. Firstly, with three possible match outcomes, we don't have a binomial proposition. We could attempt to reduce Leicester City's performances to 'wins' versus 'not wins', but each match, furthermore, has a different success probability. To use this function, the probability of success on each trial must be constant. Naturally, in situations such as these, where calculating exact probabilities and probability distributions is difficult, this is precisely the reason why we turn to the Monte Carlo simulation in the first place, to estimate them.

I re-ran the Monte Carlo simulation using the 2015/16 match odds to see what Pinnacle.com had been making of Leicester City's relative prospects compared to other teams as the season progressed. Obviously, they did not fall away as the Stats.com supercomputer had predicted; they continued to win, often by small margins and by playing counter attacking football. Consequently, Pinnacle started to reflect some of this elevated performance in the betting odds for later matches, making them a little shorter than they would have been otherwise. Evidently, however, they still regarded much of what Leicester City were doing as just lucky. By the end of the season when they were champions, their expected position was 9th with 53.13 xP, just 9.35 more than the previous season and still nearly 28 points (and the best part of 4 standard deviations) behind their actual total of 81 points. 177 of the 100,000 iterations saw them crowned champions, about one in 565. In just 20 iterations (or 0.02%) were they able to equal or better 81 points, the maximum being 86. With a standard deviation of 7.66, the function NORM.DIST(81,53.13,7.66,TRUE) returns a figure of 99.986%, meaning 0.014% (or about 1 in 7,000) would be expected above 81 points, a close match for the actual proportion returned by the Monte Carlo simulation. Even when judged by the match odds of 2015/16, let alone those of the previous season, Leicester City had massively over-achieved relative to expectation. No other team has come anywhere close to this level of deviation from expected performance, before or since.

One question remains: was this over achievement just pure chance, a once-in-a-thousand blue moons, or is there something wrong with the Monte Carlo model? After some reflection, I think the answer is a bit of both. Yes, Leicester City had been incredibly lucky, but arguably not so lucky to the tune of less than

1-in-100,000. A couple of reasons might be invoked to argue that the model is flawed. Firstly, the team's collective ability may have improved to a level that was not sufficiently being reflected in the match odds during the 2015/16 season. As such, the 2014/15 odds would not provide a reliable prediction of what to expect during the following season. And Pinnacle (along with other bookmakers) were too slow during 2015/16 to fully notice. Of course, we can only learn these things with hindsight, and hindsight is never a great way to invalidate a prediction model. Perhaps more importantly, using a random number to simulate match wins and losses may not be appropriate. Doing so implies that match results are independent, where the next one has no memory of the previous. That might be true of roulette balls but arguably it's not true of Leicester City's players, who all have memories capable of expressing emotions about match outcomes and translating those into performances for subsequent games. Consequently, possible League points may not normally distribute at all. The invalidation of independence might also account for some of the explanation, in addition to the favourite–longshot bias, for the much shorter odds for top 4 placing and relegation the bookmakers had offered compared to the odds implied by my previous Monte Carlo simulation for the 2019/20 Premier League season.

Whatever distribution League points do take, the tails could be fatter than the normal one, meaning rare events are actually a lot more likely than the normal distribution would imply. However, because the precise shape of the distribution is unknown, we cannot calculate the mean and standard deviations, and hence we are unable to calculate the true probabilities of these rare events. All we can say is that they are probably more likely than we thought they were. Was this event more likely than the odds of 5,001 implied? It's a moot point. Such events have been coined by the risk analyst Nassim Taleb as 'Black Swans' (a term that became the title of his bestselling book); they lie beyond the realm of normal expectations and probability theory. In that regard, at least, Leicester City winning the Premier League can perhaps be reasonably described as a Black Swan.

A Monte Carlo Simulation for Tennis

Suppose there is a tennis match where player A plays a single game against player B. The complementary rule tells us that if the probability that player A will win a single point is p, then the probability that player B will win a point is 1 − p. What is the probability that player A will win the game? The scoring system in tennis goes 15, 30, 40, then game. However, at a score of 40-40, or deuce, the winner of the next point gains an 'advantage'. If this player wins again, they win the game, but if they lose the score returns deuce. Like the penalty shootout, this is an example of what is known, in statistics, as a Markov chain (named after the Russian mathematician Andrey Markov), a sequence of random and independent events in which the probability of any particular sequence outcome depends only on the probabilities of each and every step in the sequence.

Calculating the probabilities of all the different ways player A can win the game will arguably present a challenge. Following the multiplication rule, player A can win to love (where their opponent fails to score) by winning the first 4 points with a probability p^4. Alternatively, they can win after 40-15 with probability $4p^4(p - 1)$. This is derived from multiplying the probability of winning 4 points (p^4) by the probability of conceding 1 point $(1 - p)$. There are then 4 possible ways to concede 1 point and still win the game to 15 (at love, at 15, at 30 and at 40). Hence, we multiply the product $p^4(1 - p)$ by 4. They could also win to 30. There are 10 possible ways to win 4 points and concede 2 so the probability is $10p^4(1 - p)^2$. Finally, there are 20 possible ways to reach deuce, where each player wins 3 points. Hence, the probability is $20p^3(1 - p)^3$. However, how do we calculate the probability of a win from here, given that the nature of the rules implies that the game could, in theory, go on forever? For those far more mathematically minded than I am, it is possible to determine this via an infinite series. I had to Google it. The probability, it turns out, is $p^2 / (1 - 2p(1 - p))$. Thus, the probability of winning via deuce is $20p^3(1 - p)^3 \times p^2 / (1 - 2p(1 - p)) = 20p^5(1 - p)^3 / (1 - 2p(1 - p))$. Thus, following the addition rule, the probability that player A wins the game is $p^4 + 4p^4(p - 1) + 10p^4(1 - p)^2 + 20p^5(1 - p)^3 / (1 - 2p(1 - p))$.

As with the penalty shootout, deuce is about the point where I typically give up with mathematical first principles. We are still only in the first game. To calculate the probability of a player winning a set, we then need to repeat this exercise all over again, factoring in the rule for winning by 2 clear games, or by tie-break if the set goes to 6-6 (which must be won by 2 clear points). We must then repeat this process for calculating the probability of a player winning the required number of sets to win the match, before their opponent manages it. By the end, the equation is going to be a monster. Let's abandon the maths and build a Monte Carlo simulation instead. The process is much the same as for the penalty shootout. For the simplest of models, there are only two significant inputs: the probability of player A winning a point when serving and the probability of player B winning a point when serving. We don't need to worry about the probabilities of winning a point when receiving, since this is the complement of the probability of the server winning. It's then simply a matter of using the Excel formulae to build in the rules of tennis point scoring and simulate the evolution of a match a large number of times. My Monte Carlo simulation had 10,000 iterations to calculate the probability of one player winning a best-of-3 sets match with a final set tie-break. The chart below shows how the probability of winning the match varies as a function of the probability of player A or player B winning a service point.

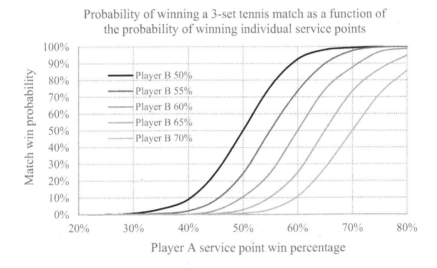

You can see, unsurprisingly, that where both players are equally rated, they each have a 50% chance of winning the match. Essentially, the contest becomes a coin toss. When one of the players has a relative marginal superiority in their service win percentage, the probability of match victory increases quite dramatically. Just a 10% superiority in service point win percentage translates in to an 85% to 90% probability of winning a 3-set match. This would rise to about 90% to 95% for a 5-set match. This is the process of accumulative advantage, where a small advantage one player holds over the other in each step is compounded into a much bigger advantage over a series of iterative steps during the course of a match. Tennis is an iteratively-played competition comprised of sometimes hundreds of points, so small differences in player ability will translate into big difference in players' match winning chances. It is for this reason that tennis frequently throws up some very short-priced favourites (1.01 or even shorter) and some very long-priced underdogs. It also provides an explanation for why the greater proportion of success, for example as measured by Grand Slam titles, is held by just a tiny proportion of the players.

Colloquially, accumulative advantage is known as the Matthew Effect. The term was coined by sociologist Robert Merton in 1968 when he described how the more eminent scientists in a team tend to get the most credit for the team's work, regardless of who did the work, and takes its name from the Parable of the Talents in the biblical Gospel of Matthew. Similar aphorisms you may have come across are 'the rich get richer, and the poor get poorer', attributed to the English poet Percy Bysshe Shelley, 'winner takes all' and the 'Pareto Principle'. Wherever there is the opportunity to apply one's advantage iteratively over many steps, such asymmetry in outcomes will be inevitable. One obvious area where this can be expected to occur is in the world of betting. You may be familiar with the expression 'the house always wins'. This is directly a consequence of the iterative nature of most gambling games. Spinning roulette wheels is an obvious example but betting every weekend on your favourite football team is too. The 'house' might only hold a 2% advantage over you in one step, but over 1,000 steps, its influence is going to accumulate significantly.

We can also use the Monte Carlo simulation to estimate the influence of relative player superiority on the chances of winning games and sets. Unsurprisingly, since a set and a game have proportionally fewer steps (points) in the iteration, the accumulative advantage is smaller. I've shown the curves for a game, set and match win probability as a function of player A's serving win percentage for the case where player B's serving win percentage is 50%.

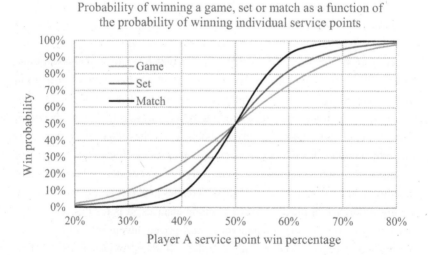

Probability of winning a game, set or match as a function of the probability of winning individual service points

My Monte Carlo, furthermore, will also estimate the probability of any specific match score (in sets) or set score (in games), the expected number of total games played in the match, and the expected game superiority of the winner over the loser. This information can all be translated into betting odds and compared to those offered by the bookmakers. Let's consider an example.

By the time Nadal and Djokovic faced each other in the 2019 Rome Masters, a best-of-3 sets outdoor clay surface match on 19 May of that year, they had gone head-to-head 22 times on that surface in their ATP careers (not counting their Davis Cup meeting). Over those matches, Nadal had a winning service point percentage of 61.28%; Djokovic's was 58.48%. Plugging those values into the Monte Carlo model and running 10,000 iterations, the following outputs were obtained.

1) Nadal wins 63.53% (implied odds = 1/0.6353 = 1.574).
   Djokovic wins 36.47% (implied odds = 2.742).
2) Nadal wins first set 59.35% (implied odds = 1.685).
   Djokovic wins first set 40.65% (implied odds = 2.460).
3) Mean total games played = 24.61.
   Iterations < 24.5 games = 51.13% (implied odds = 1.956).
   Iterations > 24.5 games = 48.87% (implied odds = 2.046).
4) Mean total games played in first set = 9.88.
   Iterations < 9.5 games first set = 48.55% (implied odds = 2.060).
   Iterations > 9.5 games first set = 51.45% (implied odds = 1.944).
5) Nadal wins 2-0 = 35.06% (implied odds = 2.852).
   Nadal wins 2-1 = 28.47% (implied odds = 3.512).
   Djokovic wins 2-0 = 16.59% (implied odds = 6.028).
   Djokovic wins 2-1 = 19.88% (implied odds = 5.030).

On the day, bookmakers offered the following (best) odds.

1) Nadal to win 1.57; expected return = 1.57/1.574 = 99.7%.
   Djokovic to win 2.50; expected return = 2.50/2.742 = 91.2%.
2) Nadal to win first set 1.65; expected return = 1.65/1.685 = 97.9%.
   Djokovic to win first set 2.50; expected return = 2.50/2.46 = **101.6%.**
3) Match under 24.5 games 1.74; expected return = 1.74/1.956 = 89.0%.
   Match over 24.5 games 2.25; expected return = 2.25/2.046 = **110.0%.**
4) First set under 9.5 games 2.20; expected return = 2.20/2.06 = **106.8%.**
   First set over 9.5 games 1.72; expected return = 1.72/1.944 = 88.5%.
5) Nadal wins 2-0, odds 2.40, expected return = 2.40/2.852 = 84.1%.

Nadal wins 2-1, odds 4.00, expected return – 4.00/3.512 = **113.9%**.
Djokovic wins 2-0, odds 5.00, expected return = 5.00/6.028 = 83.0%.
Djokovic wins 2-1, odds 6.00, expected return – 6.00/5.030 = **119.3%**.

I've highlighted the expected value bets in bold; there were 5 of them. Remember, for expected value we are looking for expected returns (the unit stake included) to be greater than 100%. Anything less will be a loss-making proposition in the long run, assuming our prediction model is correct. The average expected return for these 5 bets is 110.3%, provided we bet the same size stake for all of them. In the event, Nadal won the match 6-0, 4-6, 6-1, meaning only 2 of the 5 bets proved to be winners, the first set under 9.5 games at 2.20 and Nadal to win the match 2-1 at 4.00. Nevertheless, this would have been sufficient to return a small net profit of 1.20 units for a 5-unit outlay, or a 124% return on investment. That's more than the average expected return, but it's clear why; the biggest contribution to the profit was the bet on Nadal to win 2-1. This only had 28.47% chance of winning; the fact that it did means we had a fair degree of luck on our side. Of course, a bettor should **never** judge the validity of their prediction model by only one or a small handful of results, regardless of whether those results are favourable or unfavourable. Good and back luck (those pesky hidden random variables) dominate in the short term. However, what might be worth observing is generally how close the Monte Carlo model's implied odds were to the published bookmakers' odds. Broadly speaking that should give you confidence that you are probably doing the right things. Your task, as a modeller, is then to fine-tune what you do to build something better than the models the bookmakers are using. Here, that might mean thinking about how the two players had been performing in the earlier rounds of this tournament, how tired they might be from the amount of time spent on court, how they'd been playing the key points, or what the weather was like for the match-up and hence the speed of the surface.

With regards to one of those factors, the way players play the key points, this can throw the assumption of point independence into doubt. The validity of the Monte Carlo simulation rests on every point played being independent of the previous ones, in the same way that spins on a roulette wheel are. But arguably, the assumption of point independence is not secure because, like football players, tennis players have memories fuelled by emotion, that will subject them to all sorts of motivating factors depending on the point being played. Djokovic, in particular, is renowned for being a master of playing the key points. One only has to think of the 2019 Wimbledon Final, where he saved two consecutive match points whilst returning the Roger Federer serve, going on to claim the title. More generally, human beings are subject to many cognitive biases; one of these is loss aversion, where we are more sensitive to losses than we are to gains. It has been shown in professional golf, for example, that players are nearly 4% more likely to save par than to make birdie, even after the influence of the shot distance has been accounted for. Making birdie is considered a gain, understandably so because it is one shot better than what the golfer should be achieving. Similarly, shooting a bogey will psychologically be regarded as a loss. Thus, players try harder to avoid it. Perhaps a similar loss aversion may be at play in tennis, with players saving a higher percentage of break points than their service point win percentage would predict. Always be sensitive to possible flaws in your model assumptions. Systematic mistakes in inputs are likely to be magnified once you have arrived at the outputs, particularly in stepwise models like a Markov chain Monte Carlo simulation, in the same way that a marginally better tennis player accumulates their advantage over the course of a match.

A Monte Carlo Simulation for the NBA Finals

I'll put my cards on the table right now: I know almost nothing about NBA basketball; its rules, its history, its nuances. About the only things I know are that it's a pretty high scoring game (and seems to have got higher in the past 10 to 15 seasons), draws are not permitted, with overtime settling games where necessary, and there's a rather good Netflix series about Michael Jordan's Chicago Bulls (*The Last Dance*). Nevertheless, I wanted to have a go at using a Monte Carlo simulation to model a game, or to be more precise, a series of games. I chose the 2018/19 Finals between the Toronto Raptors and defending champions Golden State Warriors. The 2019/20 season was disrupted by the pandemic and the completion of games did not follow the format of previous seasons, with only 22 of the 30 teams, who were within 6 games of a playoffs spot when the season was suspended, invited to finish the season at the Disney Bubble in Orlando. The NBA Finals are competed over a maximum of 7 games, with the first to 4 winning. Toronto held home court advantage, meaning they would play at home in games 1, 2, 5 and 7, with Golden State playing at home in games 3, 4 and 6. If a team wins 4 games before the end of the 7-match series, the remaining games are not played. Game 1 was scheduled for 30 May 2019.

The model I used to calculate the relative attack and defence strengths of Toronto and Golden State was the same as the one I used for the football ratings model when I attempted to simulate the end of the 2019/20 Premier League season. Like football, the NBA has a home court advantage, although it's not as strong. Hence it makes sense to treat the home and away metrics separately. Again, calculating these is simply a function of comparing the two teams' average point scoring and conceding to the NBA average point scoring and conceding, and finally calculating the expected points they will score. For this task I included the pre-season games as well. For games where Toronto were scheduled to play at home (1, 2, 5 and 7) the expected points for Toronto and Golden State were 111.34 and 111.61 respectively, with a game total of 222.95. For games where Golden State were scheduled to play at home (3, 4 and 6), their expected points were 112.49, and 112.69 for Toronto. According to my model, both home and away games, and therefore the Series as a whole, were about as close to a coin toss as you could reasonably get. This is not how the bookmakers saw it; more on that shortly.

How do we translate these expected points into win probabilities? In football, the distribution of goals scored by a team can be approximated by the Poisson distribution. Points scored in NBA matches, by contrast, are more readily described by the normal (or Gaussian) distribution. Recall that Excel has a function NORM.DIST that allows one to calculate the probability of either fewer than or more than x number of points, provided you know the arithmetic mean and standard deviation. I've already quoted the means; these are just the expected points as calculated by Dixon-Coles. Excel has the STDEV function to allow you to calculate the standard deviation for a set of data. The standard deviation for Toronto's points when playing home in the 2018/19 season was 11.15. For Golden State playing away it was 12.31. For example, the probability that Toronto will score fewer than 100 points at home can be calculated in Excel by NORM.DIST(100,111.34,11.15,TRUE) = 15.45%. This is equivalent to the area under the normal curve to the left of the position marked by 100 points. Similarly, the probability that Golden State will score more than 115 points away is given by $1 -$ NORM.DIST(115,111.61,12.31,TRUE) = 39.15%. This is equivalent to the area under the normal curve to the right of the position marked by 115 points. Excel also has an inverse function with the syntax NORM.INV(p,μ,σ) which, for a given probability, p, defined by NORM.DIST(x,μ,σ,TRUE), returns the value x (where μ is the mean and σ the standard deviation). Thus, if we randomise p using Excel's RAND() function, we can randomise the output x, where those outputs will be distributed normally. If we repeat this over a large number of iterations for both teams, we've made our Monte Carlo simulation. It's then just a simple matter of counting the number of times Toronto beat Golden State (or vice versa) to calculate the implied probability (and fair odds) of either team winning a game.

The frequency distribution of simulated points for both teams where Toronto plays at home is shown in the chart below. I've used a scatter plot rather than a histogram because, with the latter, you would be unable to tell them apart. They look just like the normal distribution curve; they should, because the outputs were generated by a random variable with a normal distribution. The model suggested the teams were very closely matched. Toronto's distribution is slightly narrower and taller than Golden State's because their points standard deviation was a little smaller. In 100,000 iterations, Toronto outscored Golden State 49,444 times, implying their win probability was 49.444%, equivalent to fair odds of 2.025. Golden State's win probability was 50.556%, pricing them at 1.978.

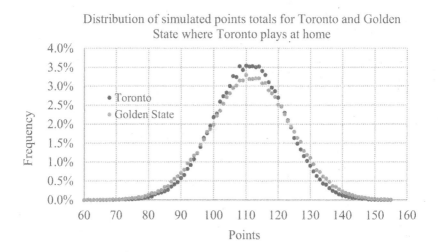

Distribution of simulated points totals for Toronto and Golden State where Toronto plays at home

In fact, these odds are pretty close to the bookmakers' fair opening odds for Game 1. With the margin removed, Pinnacle opened with 2.08 for Toronto and 1.92 for Golden State; bet365, similarly, offered 2.05 and 1.95, respectively. However, in the build up to the match, the odds for Toronto shortened quite significantly, such that by market closure and the start of the game they were favourites, with the fair odds 1.83 and 1.80 (and Golden State 2.21 and 2.25) at Pinnacle and bet365, respectively. I have no idea what new information prompted such a move. Whatever it was, it evidently proved to be reliable. Toronto won the game and indeed went on to win the whole Series 4-2.

I also ran my Monte Carlo simulation for the remaining games, up to a possible maximum of 7 in total. When Toronto played away, they had expected points of 112.69 (with a standard deviation of 11.35). Golden State playing at home had 112.49 points (with a standard deviation of 12.62). Toronto won 50.421% of these simulated games, implying odds of 1.983. Golden State had implied odds of 2.017. For the Series as a whole, Toronto won 49.922% of the simulated NBA Finals, implying their odds for victory were 2.003. Golden State would have been priced at 1.997.

In stark contrast to my model, pundits and bookmakers had made Golden State firm favourites to defend the title they had won the season before. Several days prior to Game 1 after the finalists became known, the market opened at 1.36 (fair price 1.40) and 3.25 (fair price 3.5) for Golden State and Toronto, respectively. I suspect, in line with the odds movement for Game 1, these narrowed somewhat, but I don't have the data to check. Nevertheless, with respect to the overall Series winner, my model was evidently missing something. A big clue comes from the implied prices of games 3, 4 and 6, where Golden State were at home. My model actually made Toronto marginally favourite in those games, whilst the bookmakers believed Golden State, with an opening fair price of 1.50, had twice the chance of Toronto (3.00) to win Game 3. Whilst that gap narrowed by market closing (Golden State 1.74, Toronto 2.36), this was still a long way from my model outputs. Toronto won Game 3, yet the bookmakers (and fans) still believed Golden State would start cranking up their performance as the Series progressed, pricing them at 1.49 for Game 4. In the event, that didn't happen, with Toronto winning this game as well, before finally claiming the Series in Game 6 away from home.

Why did my model diverge so significantly from the ones the bookmakers were using for Golden State playing at home? I used the whole of the preseason and regular season to calculate the attack and defence strengths, and the expected points for each team. Perhaps this time frame is too long. Much can change over the course of the season. As for my Premier League model, I gave no preferential weighting to more recent games. Another clue that my model was inaccurate came from the actual number of points it was projecting the two teams to score. With a total of nearly 223 expected for Toronto's home games, that was a whole 10 points higher than the middling line – 213 points – on the over/under betting market for Game 1, where a bet on either over or under 213 points has roughly a 50% chance of success. Based on my Monte Carlo model, the implied probability of seeing under 213 points was 27.6%, and 72.4% for over. Again, why such a large discrepancy?

There is a well-worn maxim that describes the postseason: 'The Game Slows Down.' Apparently, this is more than a mere cliché. Statistical analysis proves that the pace in the NBA playoffs does slow slightly, by about 2%, although the precise reasons for this remain somewhat of a mystery. I'm sure readers more familiar with the NBA will have their views about what they might be. This does not mean the relative quality of offence or defence changes significantly; better offences and defences, after all, make the playoffs. 'Slowing down' implies that the pace of play is slower, with possessions lasting longer, teams using more of the permitted 24-second shot clock per possession, and hence fewer possessions per 48 minutes of play (which is the length of a game). Looking at the game totals for the 2018/19 season, the average postseason game total prior to the Finals was 213.30 points, compared to a figure of 220.84 for the preseason and regular season combined. I decided to rerun the model, this time using only the playoffs points to calculate the attack and defence strengths, and the expected points, for both teams. Their sum was now considerably lower and closer to the bookmakers' total points markets. For Toronto home games, Toronto had 105.27 expected points whilst Golden State had 105.14. Again, close to a coin toss, but the bookmakers' odds were implying that anyway. For Golden State home games, by contrast, Toronto had 106.71 but Golden State had more than 4 more, with 110.89, making them favourites. By how much?

Let's run the Monte Carlo simulation again, but first, a little aside. In theory I should use the standard deviation for Toronto and Golden State's postseason game points but given the small number of games, this led to some rather unreliable figures. For example, Toronto's away points spread in the postseason was very narrow (with away scores of 98, 107, 95, 101, 101, 100, 103 and 105) having a standard deviation of just 3.81. This is almost certainly a lucky occurrence and would not be expected to continue over a much longer period of games played under 'playoff conditions'. Using this figure to randomly generate their match totals for the simulation via the NORM.INV function, however, would mean a much narrower range of outputs than would typically be expected for an NBA team. Thus, to make the simulation more reliable, I decided to stick with the same standard deviation figures I had used for both teams in the original model, that is those for the whole season. We could argue all day about exactly what figures should be used. For example, slightly smaller expected totals should probably be accompanied by a slightly smaller spread in those scores. Nevertheless, the discrepancy will be marginal and make little difference to the final Monte Carlo outputs. Whatever they should be, it makes sense for them to be around 11 to 12, since that is the average standard deviation for the NBA more generally, even in the playoffs.

So, to the results. Toronto were winning 50.443% of home games (implied odds 1.982), Golden State winning 49.557% away (implied odds 2.018). The big change, however, was when Golden State played at home. Now they were winning 59.705% (implied odds 1.675), with Toronto away winning 40.295% (implied odds 2.482). These odds are much closer to the quoted closing odds for Game 3 as I reported them earlier, although something like a 15% expected value was still available in the opening market before those shortened. You can see the difference between the two teams more markedly in the points distribution below.

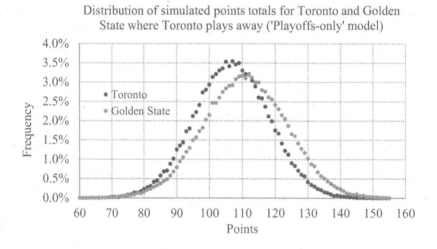

Distribution of simulated points totals for Toronto and Golden State where Toronto plays away ('Playoffs-only' model)

Since points scored by NBA teams are normally distributed, there is actually a little trick one can use to calculate the probability of one team outscoring another, and thus winning a game, avoiding the need for a Monte Carlo simulation. Provided the scoring of points by Toronto ($x_{Toronto}$) and Golden State ($x_{GoldenState}$) are independent, then the points differences between teams ($x_{difference}$) are also normally distributed, with a mean ($\mu_{difference}$) given by the difference between the teams' means, and a standard deviation ($\sigma_{difference}$) given by the square root of the sum of the squares of the individual team standard deviations. Mathematically, we would write:

$$x_{difference} = x_{Toronto} - x_{GoldenState}$$

$$\mu_{difference} = \mu_{Toronto} - \mu_{GoldenState}$$

$$\sigma_{difference} = \sqrt{\sigma_{Toronto}^2 + \sigma_{GoldenState}^2}$$

The standardised form of this distribution is then:

$$z_{\text{difference}} = \frac{x_{\text{difference}} - \mu_{\text{difference}}}{\sigma_{\text{difference}}}$$

where $z_{\text{difference}}$ is the number of standard deviations $x_{\text{difference}}$ is away from the mean $\mu_{\text{difference}}$. The probability of Toronto scoring fewer than Golden State ($x_{\text{Toronto}} - x_{\text{GoldenState}} < 0$) can be calculated in Excel using the NORM.DIST function, setting $x_{\text{difference}}$ to 0 and use $\mu_{\text{difference}}$ and $\sigma_{\text{difference}}$ as the other function arguments. Doing the arithmetic, we have:

$$\mu_{\text{difference}} = 106.71 - 110.89 = -4.18$$
$$\sigma_{\text{difference}} = \sqrt{11.35^2 + 12.62^2} = 16.98$$

Thus, NORM.DIST(-4.18,16.98,TRUE) = 0.59724 (or 59.724%). Following the complementary rule, the probability of Toronto scoring more than Golden State is then simply $1 - 0.59724 = 0.40276$ or 40.276%. Recall that the figure from the Monte Carlo simulation was 40.295%. I've drawn the frequency distribution of the 100,000 simulated points differences between Toronto (away) and Golden State (home). The mean is -4.18 points, the standard deviation is 16.98, and the area under the 'curve' to the right of 0 points difference is 0.40276, or 40.276% of the total area under the whole 'curve'. That area is equivalent to the probability of Toronto scoring more than Golden State when playing away.

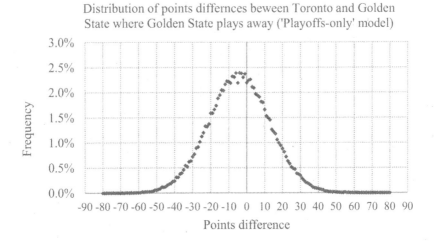

Distribution of points differnces beween Toronto and Golden State where Golden State plays away ('Playoffs-only' model)

I'd understand completely if the mathematics and terminology in this last paragraph seem a little inscrutable. When it proves to be so, that, after all, is why we use the Monte Carlo simulation.

With my updated 'playoffs-only' model, Golden State were now winning 58.783% of the 7-match Series (implied Series winner odds 1.701) with Toronto 41.217% (implied odds 2.426). These are still narrower than the published odds several days before Game 1, but, as mentioned, I suspect those published odds narrowed too, in line with the shortening of Toronto for Game 1. Nevertheless, a market opening price of 3.50 offered expected value of 44.3% (3.50/2.426 − 1) with the playoffs-data-only model and an even more generous 74.7% (3.50/2.003 − 1) with the full-season-data model. Figures like those would normally have me worrying that my model was wrong. Just possibly, however, it was the early market opinion that was in error this time, underestimating Toronto's true chances of becoming Champions, blinded by Golden State's dynastic run of five consecutive Finals (winning 3 of them between 2015 and 2018). Evidently, the price swings towards Toronto in the lead up to all but one of the games (Game 5, which Golden State had to win to continue the Series) would support the argument that Toronto were increasingly being regarded as serious contenders. They did, after all, win all three of their away games, where Golden State were supposed to be heavy favourites. Of course, I don't really know anything about the subtleties of NBA, so perhaps it's best to leave speculation about all of this to those who do.

A Monte Carlo Simulation for the US Presidential Election

It is almost certain that the 2020 US presidential election between Republican incumbent Donald Trump and Democrat challenger Joe Biden became the biggest betting market of all time. Matthew Shaddick, the head of political betting at Ladbrokes Coral Group, had estimated about £1bn would be wagered globally across the industry. I suspect that underestimates the real figure by at least an order of magnitude. The Betfair exchange alone saw approaching £2bn of matched bets. Given the level of excitement that was evidently being caused by arguably the most divisive President the United States has seen, on the night of the election I felt motivated to throw my hat into the prediction modelling ring. At this point I should declare that I had believed Joe Biden a stonewall favourite to win the election. When I backed him, the price was 1.51 on the Betfair exchange. I considered the 'true' price to be nearer 1.20, meaning that if I was correct, I was being offered around 25% expected value. Why? Whilst the polls had called the wrong result in 2016, there were a number of factors that suggested history would not repeat itself. Firstly, Biden had a bigger poll lead than Hillary Clinton, particularly in the swing States. Secondly, Biden is not Hillary Clinton; she was evidently not loved by a significant section of the American electorate. Thirdly, Biden is not Trump; for many this would prove to be an anti-Trump vote rather than pro-Biden one. Fourthly, contrary to the Trump narrative, Biden is neither a progressive nor a socialist, but rather a moderate in the Democratic Party. Fifthly, COVID-19 and the resulting economic recession may have sowed seeds of doubt amongst swing voters about Trump's competence in handling a crisis and perhaps more importantly, the direction of his moral compass implied by his failings in this regard. Finally, as culturally regressive as it sounds, perhaps it just needed a 70-something white man to defeat a 70-something white man.

A US presidential election is decided by the Electoral College, a group of presidential electors required by the US Constitution to form every four years for the sole purpose of electing the President. Each state appoints a number of electors which broadly reflect the size of the state by population. California, for example, is the largest with 55; the smallest like Vermont, Delaware and the District of Columbia have only 3. It is the Electoral College, rather than the public electorate, who choose the next President. Currently, a total of 538 electors are appointed, meaning an absolute majority of 270 or more Electoral College votes is required to elect the President. With a couple of exceptions, Maine and Nebraska, which split their votes rather than awarding all to the winner, convention has it that a state's Electoral College electors all vote according to the winner of the public vote in that state.

The prediction website FiveThirtyEight (named after the number of Electoral College votes up for grabs in a US Election) had been even more confident about a Biden win, predicting an 89% chance (with implied odds of 1.124) when they stopped updating their model on the day of the election, with Biden taking an expected 348 of the Electoral College votes (I will abbreviate hereafter with ECVs) and Trump the remaining 190. The Economist's election model was even more lopsided towards Biden, estimating a margin of victory by 356 to 182. The New Statesman model predicted 339 votes to 199 in favour of Biden. By contrast, the spread betting firm Sporting Index were predicting a Biden win with 308 EVCs. Who was right; I wanted to find out, and more importantly, attempt to correlate projected ECVs with projected winner odds. Such a job is perfectly suited to a Monte Carlo simulation.

To build a Monte Carlo simulation, I first needed an input model to predict the expected probability of either Biden or Trump winning the Election. I could build my own forecasting model. Unfortunately, I know even less about US politics than I do about the NBA. Furthermore, after 25 years of trying to build them for a football betting market, I've come to appreciate that it's actually easier to copy what the experts – the bookmakers – do. However, if we are trying to find out if the bookmakers, rather than the pollsters (and I), are wrong, we can't exactly use their betting odds, can we? We need a proxy source of data and a proxy forecast model. One method is to use the state betting market, reciprocating the betting odds to calculate the probabilities for each of the 50 States plus the District of Columbia, and sum the expected Electoral College votes (xECV) which they imply. For example, Trump was considered to have a 61% chance of taking Florida. With 29 Electoral College votes up for grabs that is equivalent to 17.7 xECV (29 x 0.61), with 11.3 going to Biden (29 x 0.39). The Betfair exchange had just such a market for all of the 50 (+1) states. I collected their odds at 23:45 on Tuesday 3 November 2020, 15 minutes before voting closed on the eastern seaboard, removed any margin that was present, and did the maths. Biden's total xECV was 307.75, with Trump gaining 230.25, essentially matching the Sporting Index spread betting market. The full set of probabilities and calculated xECVs for each state is shown in the table below, ranked in ascending order of a Trump win probability.

State	Trump win %	Biden win %	ECV	Trump xECV	Biden xECV
Hawaii	1.02%	98.98%	4	0.04	3.96
Vermont	1.58%	98.42%	3	0.05	2.95
Massachusetts	1.71%	98.29%	11	0.19	10.81
California	1.89%	98.11%	55	1.04	53.96
New York	2.11%	97.89%	29	0.61	28.39
Rhode Island	2.21%	97.79%	4	0.09	3.91
Washington State	2.48%	97.52%	12	0.30	11.70
Delaware	2.56%	97.44%	3	0.08	2.92
Maryland	2.60%	97.40%	10	0.26	9.74
Illinois	3.29%	96.71%	20	0.66	19.34
Connecticut	3.41%	96.59%	7	0.24	6.76
New Jersey	3.64%	96.36%	14	0.51	13.49
DC	3.82%	96.18%	3	0.11	2.89
Oregon	4.44%	95.56%	7	0.31	6.69

State	Trump win %	Biden win %	ECV	Trump xECV	Biden xECV
Virginia	7.86%	92.14%	13	1.02	11.98
Colorado	7.97%	92.03%	9	0.72	8.28
New Mexico	8.87%	91.13%	5	0.44	4.56
Maine	14.10%	85.90%	4	0.56	3.44
New Hampshire	19.68%	80.32%	4	0.79	3.21
Nevada	20.20%	79.80%	6	1.21	4.79
Michigan	21.42%	78.58%	16	3.43	12.57
Minnesota	21.42%	78.58%	10	2.14	7.86
Wisconsin	23.17%	76.83%	10	2.32	7.68
Pennsylvania	29.92%	70.08%	20	5.98	14.02
Arizona	45.27%	54.73%	11	4.98	6.02
North Carolina	50.87%	49.13%	15	7.63	7.37
Florida	60.96%	39.04%	29	17.68	11.32
Georgia	61.26%	38.74%	16	9.80	6.20
Ohio	70.06%	29.94%	18	12.61	5.39
Iowa	71.83%	28.17%	6	4.31	1.69
Texas	75.68%	24.32%	38	28.76	9.24
South Carolina	89.59%	10.41%	9	8.06	0.94
Alaska	90.41%	9.59%	3	2.71	0.29
Montana	90.41%	9.59%	3	2.71	0.29
Mississippi	95.31%	4.69%	6	5.72	0.28
Indiana	95.56%	4.44%	11	10.51	0.49
Missouri	95.61%	4.39%	10	9.56	0.44
Utah	95.91%	4.09%	6	5.75	0.25
Kansas	96.27%	3.73%	6	5.78	0.22
South Dakota	97.01%	2.99%	3	2.91	0.09
Tennessee	97.14%	2.86%	11	10.68	0.32
Louisiana	97.19%	2.81%	8	7.78	0.22
Kentucky	97.60%	2.40%	8	7.81	0.19
North Dakota	97.60%	2.40%	3	2.93	0.07
Idaho	98.02%	1.98%	4	3.92	0.08
Nebraska	98.02%	1.98%	5	4.90	0.10
Arkansas	98.11%	1.89%	6	5.89	0.11
Wyoming	98.89%	1.11%	3	2.97	0.03
Alabama	98.98%	1.02%	9	8.91	0.09
West Virginia	98.98%	1.02%	5	4.95	0.05
Oklahoma	99.05%	0.95%	7	6.93	0.07
Total			**538**	**230.25**	**307.75**

How do we translate these xECVs into the odds for Biden or Trump to win? Enter the Monte Carlo simulation. By using a uniformly distributed random number, in Excel the RAND() function, to simulate the result of each state, we can run the election many times and count how often Biden or Trump win. If the random number falls below a win probability for a candidate, they take all the ECVs; if above, they take none. For the purposes of this model, I assumed Maine and Nebraska behaved as the other 49. They only contribute 4 and 5 votes respectively to the total of 538, so won't make much meaningful difference to the model outcome. The first chart below shows the distribution of Biden/Trump ECV tallies from 100,000 simulated elections. Biden won 89.9% of the simulated elections, which implies true odds of 1.125, almost the same as FiveThirtyEight's expected win probability for Biden. The average ECV tally for Trump was 230.29, for Biden, 307.71, almost identical to the calculated xECVs above, as they should be. The standard deviation in ECVs was 31.95 ECVs for Biden and Trump alike (clearly so since the sum of ECVs for the two candidates on any model iteration always makes 538).

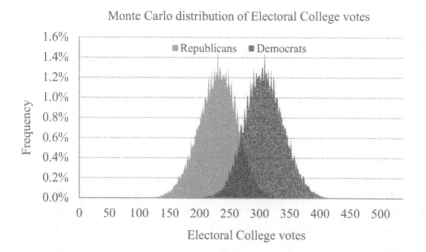

Monte Carlo distribution of Electoral College votes

The frequency distribution of both Biden and Trump ECVs closely follows the normal distribution. That is to be expected, given their randomised construction. However, there is evidently a problem with my model. FiveThirtyEight predicted 348 Electoral College votes for Biden and 190 for Trump as the best estimate in their 40,000-iteration Monte Carlo simulation. Mine was predicting 308 versus 230, yet with the same odds for a Biden victory. The discrepancy arises because my model considered the public vote, and by extension the ECVs, in one state to be independent of all other states. Unsurprisingly, that is a flawed assumption. Clearly there are common nation-level correlations at play, meaning that if one state, for example Wisconsin, votes in a particular way, another, for example Michigan, is likely to do so too. A prediction error in one state is thus also likely to be correlated in others.

The name for this directional relationship between two random variables is covariance. Covariance is the reason bookmakers will not allow you to build multiple bets (doubles, trebles and so on) from state betting markets, or in any other betting market for that matter, where the outcome probabilities are correlated. The most significant impact of a covariance between random variables – in this case win probabilities in individual states – is a much greater spread or variance in the data. The greater the variance, the less likely one candidate will beat the other. This is simply a consequence of the laws of probability. You can visualise this in the chart above. The darker region of overlap between the two distributions is equivalent to the probability of Trump beating Biden. If their distributions were taller and narrower, with a smaller standard deviation but the same means, this area of overlap would shrink. In contrast, if the distributions were shorter and wider with a larger standard deviation, the area of overlap would grow. FiveThirtyEight presumably make it their business to develop a highly sophisticated covariance model that considers the state-by-state voting correlations. Their ECV distribution had nearly double my standard deviation, at almost 60.

Undeterred, I made another attempt at building a US election prediction model, this time attempting to introduce some state covariance, in much the same way that I described earlier how fair odds might be transformed into unfair ones using a common exponent. My method was thus as follows. For every iteration in the simulation, the Betfair-implied win probabilities for Trump in each state were raised to the power of a specific exponent. For example, if the exponent was 1.1 then Trump's win probability in New York was transformed from 0.0248 to $0.0248^{1.1} = 0.0171$; for Arizona, from 0.4527 to $0.4527^{1.1} = 0.4182$; for Alabama, from 0.9898 to $0.9898^{1.1} = 0.9888$. Biden's transformed win percentages were then calculated using the complementary rule (1 – Trump's win percentage). In this way, the error in the Betfair model was quantified by the size of the transformation exponent and correlated across all states. An obvious weakness is that it's likely not all states will exhibit the same level of covariance; some will show more independence, others less, but I have neither the intellect nor the financial resources that FiveThirtyEight have at their disposal to account for these differences. Across the 100,000 Monte Carlo iterations, the size of the transforming exponent was then randomised using a lognormal distribution (where the logarithm of a random variable is normally distributed – I'll introduce this distribution more formally in the chapter on staking), with a mean of 1. Anything higher than 1 would collectively reduce Trump's win probabilities in all states, as in the example above. Anything lower than 1 (but always above 0) would collectively increase Trump's win probabilities. The point of using a lognormal rather than normal distribution is to ensure symmetry between exponents above and below 1. Excel has the function LOGNORM.INV(p,μ,σ) to perform this task. By randomising the probability argument, p, with RAND(), I could thus lognormally randomise the exponents. Then, by varying the size of the standard deviation, σ, of this distribution (I chose values between 0 and 1) I could vary the strength of the covariance. The bigger the standard deviation, the more varied the exponents, and the greater the impact of correlated errors in the implied Betfair probabilities. Yes, I know this all sounds rather convoluted, I'm sorry, and I rather suspect it would fail any statistical modelling course. Anyway, the model outputs are arguably meant to be more qualitatively informative than quantitatively valid.

The table below compares 11 different simulations, for 11 different values of my lognormal standard deviation. A figure of 0 means all original Betfair state win probabilities remain untransformed, since every exponent is 1. This is effectively equivalent to the original model, where state voting is completely independent. You can see that as the level of covariance is increased (by increasing the lognormal standard deviation), the amount of spread in the distribution of ECVs (as measured by the ECV standard deviation) increases. This is entirely predictable. Since state covariance means that states tend to vote the same way, this will lead to bigger ECV tallies for Trump or Biden, and bigger margins of victory in more of the Monte Carlo iterations. This increase in distribution spread is matched by a decrease in the chances of Biden taking overall victory, for the reasons explained earlier. Hence, his implied odds lengthen too. You will also notice that with a lengthening of price, Biden's mean ECV total (equivalent to xECV) starts to decrease, although the median ECV broadly remains unchanged. My covariance model has introduced an asymmetry into the distribution of ECVs, which increases as more covariance is applied. Trump has proportionally more elections than Biden where he scores a big win. I think this arises because, in his luckiest elections, there are more available ECVs available for Trump to overturn in Democratic strongholds like California and New York than vice versa. The stronger the covariance, the more likely it becomes that Trump can overturn these states in blocks, and the bigger his ECV tally. Some big wins will skew the arithmetic mean above the median.

Lognormal ST DEV	Trump mean ECV	Biden mean ECV	Trump median ECV	Biden median ECV	ECV ST DEV	Biden win %	Implied Biden odds
0	230	308	231	307	32	0.890	1.123
0.1	230	308	231	307	33	0.879	1.138
0.2	231	307	231	307	37	0.852	1.174
0.3	232	306	231	307	42	0.817	1.225
0.4	233	305	231	307	48	0.781	1.281
0.5	235	303	232	306	55	0.748	1.336
0.6	236	302	232	306	63	0.720	1.388
0.7	238	300	232	306	70	0.697	1.434
0.8	240	298	232	306	78	0.679	1.472
0.9	241	297	232	306	85	0.663	1.508
1	243	295	232	306	92	0.650	1.540

So which covariance is the right one? Clearly, there's a certain amount of subjectivity in answering that, but we do at least have one independent measure: the ECV standard deviation in FiveThirtyEight's simulation. Recall, this was nearly 60. Looking at the table above, the closest match to that figure is in line 7. For this simulation, Biden's mean ECV tally was 302, with the median (or middle) tally a little higher at 306. Trump's mean and median were 236 and 232. From this simulation run, Biden had a win probability of 72% with implied odds of 1.388. The frequency distribution is shown below. I've purposely maintained the same vertical axis scale so you can compare this to the original distribution, where state voting was wrongly assumed to be completely independent. Covariance increases the standard deviation, thus making the distributions fatter and shorter, although their total areas remain the same as for the independent model, adding up to 1 (or 100%). You can also see the positive skew in Trump's distribution, with a longer, fatter tail towards the right hand side, increasing the mean relative to the median, and vice versa for Biden's. The central darkest shaded area is now considerably larger, and Trump has a greater probability of winning.

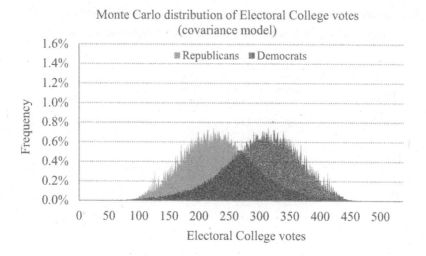

Monte Carlo distribution of Electoral College votes (covariance model)

We are now perhaps in a better position to attempt an answer to the original question: who was right about the US Election – the pollsters, who were predicting about 350 ECVs for Biden with a 90% chance of winning, or the betting models, who were projecting about 306 to 308 ECVs and around a 70% chance for victory? As I've said before, it's never a good idea to judge the quality of a prediction by a single outcome, since we never get to see the real election played out 100,000 times, like we can on a computer. The single real-world result that actually happens could well just be lucky. We will ultimately never know. Nevertheless, it's always rewarding when your model predicts the outcome accurately, and that is what has happened here. Biden won the US Election with 306 ECVs to Trump's 232, matching exactly the median in the covariance distribution above, and just 4 away from the arithmetic mean. Similarly, the figure of 308 for Biden's xECV, using just Betfair's state betting odds and no Monte Carlo simulation, is also close, far closer than FiveThirtyEight and the other pollsters. FiveThirtyEight would remind us that their projected figure of 348 is within one standard deviation of Biden's actual result, and thus well within typical error margins associated with significance testing, where a difference of at least two standard deviations is typically required before one would begin to suspect the model was invalid. Nevertheless, intuition tells me that the betting markets have done a better job at forecasting the outcome than the pollsters.

In recent times, it has become almost a mantra to claim that the betting markets offer the best political polling predictions. Whilst their wisdom can also be flawed from time to time, as was the case in the 2016 presidential election and for Brexit, there seems to be some validity to the claim. It is based on the observation that betting markets, more than any other prediction methods, are informed not only by considerable professional insight, as for the traditional polls, but also by weight of money. Money is a means of quantifying opinions. It's also required to make a livelihood. If your livelihood is earned by expressing opinions about the future, but where you only get paid if you're right, there is a certain pressure not to be wrong. This is called having skin in the game. Arguably, whilst pollsters may lose reputation and face for making bad calls, they will, generally speaking, still keep their salaries. Bettors, and in particular, professional bettors, however, depend entirely on the quality of their predictions. If they are wrong, they don't get paid, and their families don't get fed.

There is one more outstanding question that I need to answer: if the Betfair state betting market, via my Monte Carlo simulation, was implying Biden odds of 1.39, why was their main winner market offering me a price of 1.51, and an expected value of 8.6%? There appears to be some disconnect between the two markets. At least one of them must have been inefficient, that is to say, inaccurate. Granted, it seems I was wrong about Biden's true price being closer to 1.20, but if my Monte Carlo model was correct, 1.51 was still a positive expectation bet. Indeed, at the time I collected Betfair's state betting odds they were quoting 1.68 for Biden to win. Why would Betfair's winner market be at odds (pardon the pun) with their state betting market? Given the much smaller size of the latter in terms of the volume of money wagered, it's all the more puzzling that the former seems to have been less accurate. More usually, market volume correlates with market efficiency. More money means more opinions; more opinions mean more cancelling of random errors; more error cancellation means more 'wisdom of a crowd'; more 'wisdom of a crowd' means a more accurate betting price. Of course, I can't entirely rule out the possibility that either the way I transformed Betfair's state betting market into a presidential winner probability, or the state betting probabilities themselves, were wrong. Interestingly, however, if we just look at the odds for the 51 betting markets, only one, Georgia, saw the favourite (Trump) lose. In all the other closely fought States – North Carolina, Florida, Ohio, Arizona, Wisconsin, Minnesota, Pennsylvania, Texas and Michigan – the Betfair state betting market called the most likely outcome correctly.

Why wasn't Donald Trump allowed back into the White House?
Because it's forBiden. Thank you and goodnight.

P.S. That is a joke, not a conspiracy.

I think that's enough prediction modelling. I've tried to keep things as simple as possible, but I should apologise (again) if I've lost some of you along the way, or conversely if you've found much of this chapter too rudimentary. For those in the latter camp, I can strongly recommend Andrew Mack's *Statistical Sports Models in Excel*, a two-part volume that goes into much more mathematical and Excel programming detail than I wanted to do here. Andrew looks at all kinds of traditional modelling approaches, not just Monte Carlo. Anyway, time to move on. Next, we'll look at how the Monte Carlo simulation can help you understand your likelihood of winning and making a profit.

WINNING

In betting, you only know if you won or lost. You never actually know for sure if you were accurate or inaccurate in your assessment of the probabilities, at least not for individual bets. In this context, there are two categories of uncertainty. One is the uncertainty surrounding the validity of your model that is attempting to determine the probability of a certain future being realised. This is, unsurprisingly, called model uncertainty, although philosophers give it the fancier description of epistemic uncertainty, after the Greek word for knowledge. Epistemic uncertainty is due to things one could in principle know but do not in practice, either because data used in the prediction model is inaccurate or missing, or because the model knowingly or blindly ignores certain effects. My ignorance of precisely how US state voting covaries is an example of epistemic uncertainty. Essentially, this type of uncertainty, if significant or biased enough, can invalidate your prediction model. The other category is what is known as aleatory uncertainty, or more commonly statistical uncertainty, the stuff I've already alluded to on numerous occasions when referring to those hidden variables. The word derives from the Latin *aleator*, a dice player. Aleatory uncertainty is representative of unknowns that differ each time we run the same experiment, the hidden variables to which we assign the word 'random'. Repeat a process many times, for example tossing a coin, and subtle variations in starting conditions will render different outcomes. The precise causes of these differences remain unknown, the knowledge of which **cannot** be determined sufficiently.

There will be some, like Poincaré, who may argue that "cannot" is simply a reflection of limited information and processing power. If we could know perfectly all the starting conditions and had infinite processing power to model their evolution forward in time, we should be able to predict with certainty the precise outcomes. Thus, just because we cannot measure sufficiently with our currently available measurement devices does not preclude, necessarily, the existence of such information, which would reduce aleatory uncertainty to epistemic uncertainty. In practice, the complexity of systems we find ourselves trying to model makes such information gathering impossible. Furthermore, a 20th century revolution in physics that rewrote the nature of reality at the tiniest of scales demonstrated that Poincaré's belief in the possibility of perfect knowledge was a theoretical impossibility as well. In both a philosophical and physical sense, then, aleatory uncertainty really is irreducible; it really is a thing in itself; it really does make sense to talk about 'true' probabilities of outcomes even if we don't precisely know what they are, and not reduce them to a binary yes or no, true or false, win or lose, happened or didn't happen.

From this perspective there is only aleatory uncertainty in a game of dice or roulette. The precise outcome probabilities are known perfectly. Whether you win or lose is only a matter of luck (and the size of the casino's margin). In sports betting, however, the 'true' outcome probabilities are unknown (hence the quotation marks). As I've previously described, sports competitions which we can bet on are far more complex than roulette and dice. This time, whether you win or lose is also a matter of skill, more specifically whether you are better at reducing the amount of epistemic certainty than the bookmaker is. You might bet on Liverpool to win, believing them to have a 50% chance of victory. The bookmaker believes the correct probability is 45%. In truth, they have a 40% chance; both you and the bookmaker were wrong, but you were more wrong than the bookmaker and thus your expected value was negative. They win; you've had a lucky outcome but still made a bad bet. On the other hand, you correctly believe them to hold a 40% chance of victory, and this time the bookmaker believes the correct figure is 35%. They lose, an unlucky outcome but still a good bet. In reality, because the 'true' probability always remains unknown, it's difficult to figure out how much of your outcomes – both good and bad – are driven by epistemic uncertainty and how much by aleatory uncertainty. In this chapter, I'll attempt to show you how you can try to separate the influences of luck and skill and learn to tell one apart from the other. I'll say at the outset, however, that you will never be certain whether the reason you are winning is because of skill or whether it is only because of luck. As with everything else in betting, we can only answer this question with a probability. I must also tell you that, even for skilled bettors, who are superior to the bookmakers at knowing the 'true' odds, aleatory uncertainty – that is to say, luck – accounts for almost everything that will happen in the short term. Understanding how luck influences winning in betting, and the distribution of profitable returns associated from it, is the topic to which I will now turn my attention.

The Law of Large Numbers

A couple of years back my attention was drawn to a betting history that belonged to the popular online racing advisory service MyRacingTips. There were about

1,000 tips in this particular record, and they had returned about 96% of total money invested (or a 4% loss), assuming all bets were given the same stake size. Is that history large enough to judge the quality (or rather the lack of it) of this service? To answer that question, we need to know how likely it is that such a set of returns will occur relative to some independent yardstick of expectation. The most obvious one is the profit line since bettors are typically in the habit of hoping to find themselves above it. After a little bit of maths, it turned out that it was quite possible, within the bounds of statistical uncertainty we discussed earlier, that MyRacingTips had simply been unlucky. About 18% of the time, the effects of aleatory uncertainty – luck – would have seen MyRacingTips actually perform even worse, assuming that their expectation was to break even. That's far too high to be able to claim, beyond doubt, that the reason for the observed loss was a bad prediction model. Of course, being a racing advisory service, I have little doubt that their expectation was to be better than break-even. Suppose, instead, their expectation had been a 105% return from stakes invested or a 5% profit over turnover. In such a scenario there was still a 2% probability that the service could lose 4% just by being unlucky. It was called *Nap of the Day*. That means just one bet a day. Imagine betting for nearly 3 years and you still don't know if you've been unlucky or your prediction model doesn't work. There is a quicker way to find out, but I'll come to that a little later in the chapter. For now, I want to show you how I did the mathematics.

Let me take you back a few chapters to the binomial distribution for outcomes of binary propositions, for example heads/tails, yes/no, true/false or win/lose, which are figuratively described as success/failures. Perhaps you remember that the arithmetic mean of this distribution is given by the number of trials, n, multiplied by the probability of success for each trial, p. In 10 coin tosses the mean, or expected, number of heads would be 5. You won't always see 5 (indeed that won't be seen most of the time), sometimes it may be 4, sometimes 7, occasionally even only 1 or none, but the standard deviation of the binomial can tell us what the chances are of any number of heads. More generically, the standard deviation, s, in the total number of successes in a sample of n trials is given by $\sqrt{npq}$, where q is the probability of failure on each trial, and since q = 1 – p (by the complimentary rule), we have:

$$s = \sqrt{np(1-p)}$$

which can be rewritten as:

$$s = \sqrt{n(p - p^2)}$$

When Jacob Bernoulli was experimenting with his coin-toss trials, he noticed that as the number of them increased, the standard deviation in the total number of heads increased too. For example, with 10 tosses of a coin, n = 10 and p = 0.5. Hence, s = 1.58 tosses. With 1,000 tosses, s increases to 15.8. The fact that the increase is exactly 10-fold is not a coincidence. n has increased 100-fold which is 10-squared. Take a look at the formula above. s is proportional to the square root of n, so if n increases by a factor of 100, n will increase by a factor of the square root of 100 which is 10.

Yet Jacob noticed something else as well. As n increases, the size of s as a proportion of n (or s/n) starts to decrease. 1.58 as a proportion of 10 is 0.158 or 15.8%. 15.8 as a proportion of 1,000, however, has fallen to 0.0158 or 1.58%, just one tenth the size for n = 10. Instead of a standard deviation in the total number of trial successes, we now have a standard deviation in the percentage of trial successes, because we have divided by the total number of trials. Every time we toss a fair coin n times, the expectation is for half (0.5) of the outcomes to be heads, but most of the time the proportion of heads will be either fewer or more than half, with the extent to which they vary, just as for counts of heads, defined by the binomial distribution (since all we've done is divide by n). Imagine each set of 10 coin tosses as an individual sample, with the proportion of heads in each, 0.5, 0.4, 0.7 or whatever, being the sample mean. How far one of those sample means is likely to deviate from the expected mean of 0.5, sometimes called the true population mean, is known in statistics as the standard error of the mean (SE). Thus, dividing the binomial standard deviation by n, we have:

$$\frac{s}{n} = \frac{\sqrt{np(1 - p)}}{n}$$

And since $\sqrt{n}/n = 1/\sqrt{n}$, the standard error of the mean simplifies to:

$$SE = \frac{\sqrt{p - p^2}}{\sqrt{n}}$$

which is the same as:

$$SE = \sqrt{\frac{p - p^2}{n}}$$

Thus, whilst standard deviation increases proportionally with the square root of n, the standard error decreases proportionally with the square root of n.

In statistics, the standard error of the mean is more generally shown by the formula $\sigma/\sqrt{n}$ (σ divided by the square root of n), where σ, you may recall, is the standard deviation of a population of data and n is the size of the sample which is drawn from the population. Qualitatively, the standard error of the mean refers to the standard deviation of the distribution of sample means taken from a population. The smaller the standard error, the more representative the sample will be of the overall population. In the context here, the data population can be thought of as a Bernoulli distribution of heads and tails. In the limit where the number of coin tosses reaches infinity, the number of heads will be the same as the number of tails. Since the standard deviation, σ, of a Bernoulli distribution is given by $\sqrt{pq}$, where q is the complementary probability to p and thus equal to $1 - p$, we have:

$$\sigma = \sqrt{p - p^2}$$

Since p in a coin toss = 0.5, $\sigma = 0.5$. Thus, the standard error in the sample mean in a series of Bernoulli samples (or trials) is given by:

$$SE = \frac{\sqrt{p - p^2}}{\sqrt{n}}$$

Which of course is the same as:

$$SE = \sqrt{\frac{p - p^2}{n}}$$

The resulting formula is the same, we've just arrived at it via a different route. For a coin toss, this is $0.5 / \sqrt{n}$.

Perhaps it's easier to visually illustrate how the standard error of the mean decreases with increasing number of trials. Although it is more appropriate to use a histogram for displaying discrete data, I've used a curve to assist the visualisation. Remember, also, that as the number of trials increases, the discrete binomial distribution is ever more closely approximated by the continuous normal distribution. The first of the next two charts is the distribution of the number of heads in 10 coin tosses.

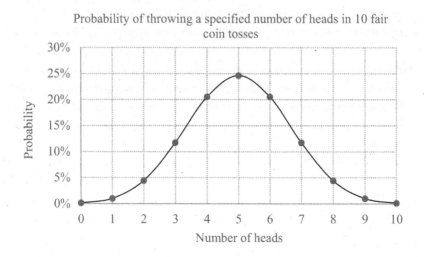

Probability of throwing a specified number of heads in 10 fair coin tosses

The second chart is the distribution for the number of heads in 1,000 coin tosses. When I drew the same distribution earlier, I intentionally restricted the number of heads axis to between 450 and 550 for a better visual representation of the curve. This time I'm deliberately showing the full axis from 0 to 1,000 to help illustrate the change in the size of the standard error.

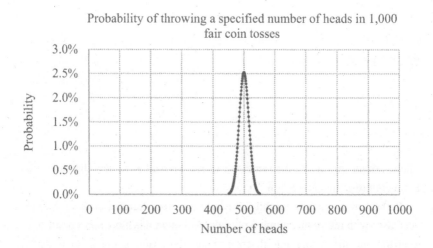

Probability of throwing a specified number of heads in 1,000 fair coin tosses

You can see that as the number of trials increase, the chances of deviating a long way from the mean decrease. In 10 coin tosses you may still see some outlier results. Seeing only 1 head out of 10, for example, has a chance of about 1%. In 1,000 tosses, however, those outliers are just too unlikely. Seeing 100 heads in 1,000 tosses (or the same 1-in-10 proportion) is so improbable as to be sure that will never happen in the lifetime of the universe. Even seeing 400 or fewer would require every person in the world alive today to toss a coin 1,000 times to expect just one person to see this happen.

What Jacob Bernoulli had observed and subsequently proved mathematically is called the law of large numbers. Originally named by Jacob as his Golden Theorem, it quickly became known as Bernoulli's Theorem before being coined, by French mathematician Siméon Denis Poisson (we met his distribution earlier) more than a century later, with the more familiar name we know it by today. It is arguably the most important statistical theorem that bettors ought to understand since the dividing line between winning and losing over the long term is sharply defined by it. According to the law, the average of the results obtained from a number of trials should tend closer towards the expected value as more trials are performed. For coin tossing, the more times we toss a fair coin, the closer the percentage of heads will be to the expected value of 50%, and the less likely it will be to deviate a specific percentage away from that expectation. For bettors, the more bets they place, the more likely it is that they will be closer to their expected winning percentage. If that expected winning percentage is not large enough to overcome the bookmaker's margin, the result will be financially painful. The longer a bettor bets for without holding positive expected value, the more inevitable it is that they will lose money. They might be lucky in the short term, but the law of large numbers is simply another way of saying that, in the end, good fortune will run out. As the German proverb goes: 'luck sometimes visits a fool, but never sits down with him.'

The speed at which the law of large numbers gets to work can be illustrated graphically. The plot below shows how the standard error in the proportion of heads for a coin toss (p = 0.5) decreases with increasing number of tosses (n). The rate of increase is described by a power law, where the quantity of a variable (in this case, the standard error) changes as a function of the power of another (in this case, the number of coin tosses). The power here is -0.5, meaning that as the number of coin tosses increase by 4, the size of the standard error decreases by the square root of 4; in other words, it halves. The mathematical function that describes this relationship is shown next to the line in the graph (x = number of coin tosses, y = standard error of the mean). Thus, $y = 0.5x^{-0.5}$ is equivalent to SE = $0.5 / \sqrt{n}$.

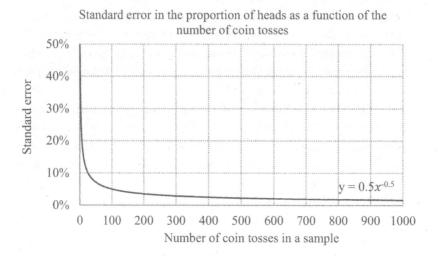

Standard error in the proportion of heads as a function of the number of coin tosses

It's a fast decline, isn't it? After just a small number of coin tosses, we can already expect that lucky outliers in the proportion of heads (or for a bettor, the percentage of wins or losses) will become a rarity. Below I've redrawn the chart with both axes logarithmic (increasing as powers of 10). Remember, a logarithm is just the reverse of a power. When you draw a power law on a chart with logarithmic axes, you will see a straight line.

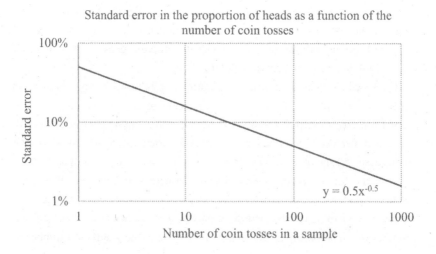

Standard error in the proportion of heads as a function of the number of coin tosses

Quite a lot of betting markets are framed as the toss of a coin, where either side in a wager has roughly a 50% chance of winning. Where one team or player is much stronger than another, a way of balancing up the chances is for the bookmaker to penalise the stronger side with a handicap. This would be points in sports like NBA and NFL, goals in football, games or sets in tennis, runs in cricket and MLB, frames in snooker and sets in darts. For example, in Game 4 of the NBA finals series between Golden State and Toronto, the bookmakers were making Golden State about twice as likely to win. To equalise both sides, they applied a 5.5-point handicap to Golden State (written as -5.5), meaning that 5.5 points would be deducted from Golden State's points total. Conversely, Toronto have a +5.5 handicap. Thus, if Golden State beat Toronto by fewer than 6 points, bets on Golden State -5.5 points would still lose. Where handicaps have been applied as whole integers, for example 5 points, if the two teams are tied after application of the handicap, the bet is settled as a 'push' where stakes are refunded without profit or loss.

Handicaps in football are obviously smaller than in NBA because there are far fewer goals scored, but similar rules apply. One interesting addition, however, has come in the form of Asian handicap betting, which has introduced quarter-goal handicaps as well. As for standard handicaps (called point spreads in America, and not to be confused with spread betting in the UK), you'll win a bet if you are at least half a goal ahead after factoring in the handicap. When there are quarter-goal or three-quarter-goal handicaps, however, you can find yourself winning or losing by a quarter of a goal. In such cases, you would then win half or lose half, where in the former, half your stake wins at the published odds with the other half returned, whilst in the latter, half your stake is lost with the other half returned. For example, when Liverpool played West Ham in the Premier League on 31 October 2020, the bookmakers quoted a -1.25 handicap for Liverpool (and +1.25 for West Ham). Since Liverpool won the match 2-1, Asian handicap bets on them were settled as half losses, whilst bets on West Ham were settled as half wins.

Handicap betting offers an alternative form of betting to fixed odds and moneyline markets (where you're just betting on the side to win) for those who don't like to take such big risks betting high-priced longshots, or who aren't attracted by the small payouts from short-priced favourites. Indeed, evidence from neuropsychology suggests that equalising the chances of binary propositions is the most attractive form of predicting futures to a human being, perhaps because it maximises the uncertainty. Things that are more certain just become boring. Would you rather watch England play Germany 100 times in a

World Cup Final or England play San Marino? Have a look at how the standard deviation for a Bernoulli distribution of a coin toss varies as we make the coin progressively less or more biased towards heads. Remember, the standard deviation, σ, of a Bernoulli distribution is $\sqrt{pq}$, and since $q = 1 - p$, therefore $\sqrt{p - p^2}$, where p is the probability of heads and q the probability of 'not heads', otherwise known as tails. The largest value for σ occurs for exactly 50-50 propositions. The function looks like a horseshoe.

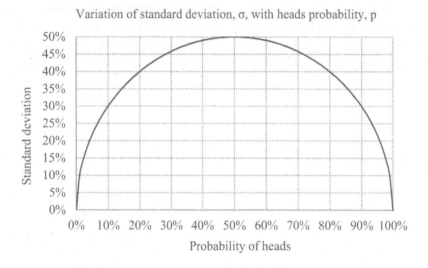

Variation of standard deviation, σ, with heads probability, p

What are the implications of the law of large numbers on staying ahead of the profit line? Let's consider an imaginary bettor who just bets in a 50-50 handicap market for fun, with no predictive skill on their side, where the outcomes are strictly binary (win or lose). Evidently, that's not the case for American point spreads (that have pushes), and even less so with Asian handicaps (which have pushes, half wins and half losses), but let's conveniently forget about those for now. Their performance will simply be dependent on luck, and the longer they bet for, the less likely it is that either good or bad luck will take them far from expectation. What is their expectation? It's obviously to win 50% of their bets. However, they will need to win more than this to avoid losing money, since the bookmaker's margin takes away a little bit of their profit each time they win. The fair price for a 50% proposition is 2.00. The more generous bookmakers may offer you 1.95 (a margin of 2.56%), meaning you make £0.95 profit for a winning £1 stake. Less generous bookmakers will offer 1.90 (a margin of 5.26%).

Let's now pose a question: what is the probability of making a profit after n bets? When betting odds of 1.95, they would need to win at least 1/1.95, or 51.28%, of their bets. With odds of 1.90, that increases to 52.63%. Thus, the question becomes: after n bets, what is the probability that they will have had at least 51.28% (or 52.63%) winners when the expectation is 50%. We can now use the NORM.DIST Excel function to calculate the probability. Strictly, we should be using Excel's binomial function BINOM.DIST, given that the win probability is the same for every bet, but it's just easier doing the calculation with the former. For larger values of n, the normal distribution is an excellent approximation for the binomial, and when your odds vary, as they do for most bettors, it becomes impossible to use binomial anyway. The only other piece of information we need for this function is the standard deviation; here this will be the standard error of the mean. The standard error of the mean for 214 bets, for example, is $0.5/\sqrt{214}$ = 0.0342 (or 3.42%). Thus, the probability that there will be fewer than 51.28% winners will be given by NORM.DIST(0.5128,0.5,0.0342,TRUE) = 0.6462 or 64.62%. Following the complimentary rule, the probability of having more than 51.28% winners will be 1 − 0.6462 = 0.3538 or 35.38%. (Calculating via the BINOM.DIST function yields a figure of 36.63%.) If betting at odds of 1.90, the function yields an answer of 22.07% (and 22.61% via BINOM.DIST).

We can perform this calculation for any number of bets, just changing the value of n in the calculation of the standard error of the mean. The chart below illustrates how quickly the probability of making a profit declines the longer our recreational bettor is betting for.

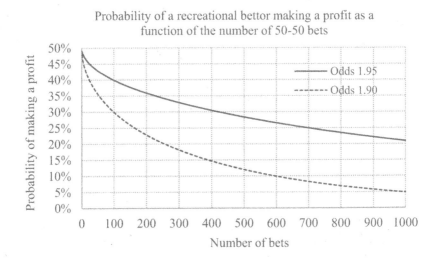

Probability of a recreational bettor making a profit as a function of the number of 50-50 bets

Clearly, it pays to find more generous bookmakers, but even with the most generous, a recreational bettor placing 20 binary handicap bets each week would have about an 80% chance of losing money by the end of a full year. That increases to 95% when the bookmaker's margin is double. There is an inevitable truth associated with the law of large numbers: recreational betting is, financially speaking, a mug's game. Of course, many people gain more pleasure from betting than merely the possibility of financial rewards, but the truth is that if you bet to be lucky, as the German proverb says, Fortuna won't keep you company for long.

Of course, the flip side is also true. If your expectation is greater than the win percentage required to break even, then the law of large numbers is not your worst enemy but your best friend. An exceptionally talented handicapper would expect to win about 55% of their bets. Hence, when calculating the standard error of the mean, remember to use $p = 0.55$ this time (giving you $0.4975/\sqrt{n}$). Here is their corresponding chart.

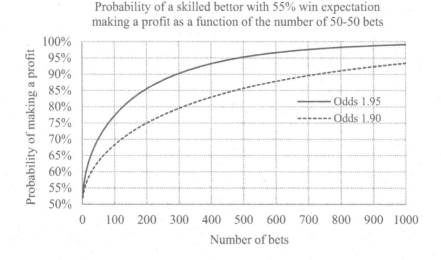

Probability of a skilled bettor with 55% win expectation making a profit as a function of the number of 50-50 bets

Perhaps you can now see that the dividing line between long term success and failure is narrow. The longer you bet, the narrower it becomes. To quote the late J.R. Miller, professional gambler and author, 'the fact is, the difference between the percentage of bets won by successful sports bettors and the percentage of bets won by chronic losers is relatively small'.

We've been calculating the distribution of win percentages due to aleatory uncertainty (luck), and the chances of exceeding (or failing to exceed) expectation, but what most bettors really want to know is how their actual betting returns might vary. Can we use the standard error of the mean to calculate these in the same way? Yes, we can; we just need to make a little adjustment to the formula, but thankfully it's a small one, and allows us to estimate the distribution of returns for any betting odds. Win percentages might be more intuitive for handicappers where odds are broadly 50-50, but those who prefer fixed odds or moneyline arguably find it easier to analyse profits (or losses). The standard error of the mean profit percentage is given by:

$$SE = o \sqrt{\frac{p - p^2}{n}}$$

where o is the betting odds (and, to recap, p is your expected win probability). All we have done is multiplied the standard error of the mean win percentage by the betting odds. By profit percentage I mean your profit over turnover, otherwise known as yield, or your return on investment (ROI) minus 100%. Returning £120 from £100 staked is a 120% ROI and a 20% profit percentage (yield). Of course, the presumption here is that all your bets have the same odds, o, but in fact this formula is quite robust when these vary. Later, with help from a real betting history, I will show you how robust. If your odds do vary, it's usually quite acceptable to use their arithmetic mean. There are, however, two important assumptions for using this formula reliably. Firstly, all bets must have the same stake size. There are things you can do when that isn't the case, but in such situations it's often just preferable to pull out the Monte Carlo simulation. Again, I'll show you how later, although hopefully you already have an idea from the previous chapters about how to perform one on your own betting futures and histories. Secondly, all outcomes must be binary: win or lose. Evidently, there's a third possibility for point spreads: the push or tie; and a further two for Asian handicap: half-win and half-loss. I'll explain how you to deal with these as well, but first let's continue with the simplest scenarios.

Perhaps you remember from earlier that your expected return for a bet can be calculated by dividing the bookmaker's odds by the 'true' odds. Let's label the expected return r and the true odds t. Since $p = 1/t$ and $r = o/t$ it follows that $p = r/o$. With a little bit of substituting and rearranging in the formula above it can be shown that the standard error in the yield for samples of n bets is given by:

$$SE = \sqrt{\frac{r(o - r)}{n}}$$

Thus, for the special case where you expect to break even, and the odds you bet are equal to the true odds (meaning $p = 1/o$ and $r = 1$), this reduces to:

$$SE = \sqrt{\frac{o - 1}{n}}$$

The next chart shows how the standard error in the yield varies as a function of your betting odds (or more precisely your win probability, $1/o$) when $r = 1$. I've illustrated the curve for $n = 1,000$ bets. Different values of n will have different curves but follow the same trajectories. The smaller the value of n, the higher the standard error, which is self-evident from the above equation.

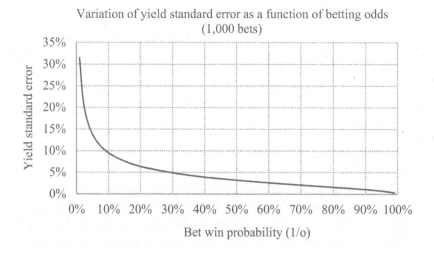

Variation of yield standard error as a function of betting odds
(1,000 bets)

Almost all bettors will never be too far from $r = 1$ over the long term. The vast majority will be a little below it, suffering the consequences of the bookmaker's margin. A few clever and hard-working souls will be marginally above it, having found the holy grail of expected value in their methodologies, letting the law of large numbers work for them. Thus, for nearly all, o and $1/p$ are typically close, and any difference has little impact on the standard error calculation. If you're feeling lazy, just use the $o - 1$ version, unless you're betting exceptionally long or short odds, or your performance follows either Yhprum or Murphy's law. (If you're wondering who Yhprum is, try spelling his name backwards.)

You can see that the longer your odds (or smaller your win probability), the larger your yield standard error, and the faster it increases in magnitude. This is just another way of saying that the influence of luck at longer odds has a much bigger impact on your outcomes, although I suppose all bettors intuitively understand this anyway. The difference to your profits when you win a bet at odds of 10 is much greater than when you win at odds of 1.10. Naturally, the bigger your sample of bets, n, the smaller the difference one additional winning bet will make, but the winning bets with the longer odds will always be making a proportionally bigger difference. Statisticians call this variance. Here, it defines the extent to which the yield from a sample of n bets with odds o can vary randomly about an expected (population) mean. Remember, in the primer on statistics, variance was defined as the square of the standard deviation. A bigger variance is just another way of saying a bigger influence from luck – those hidden random variables.

The next chart illustrates how your sample size influences the variance in your possible yields. Since we've simply transformed the standard error in sample win percentage by a factor o (the odds), the same power law relationship between the yield standard error and the number of bets applies. I've plotted this function for different betting odds, again for the case r = 1. Both axes are logarithmic, hence the straight lines.

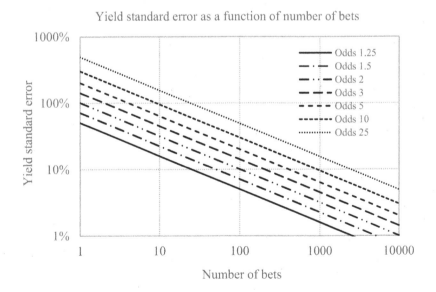

Yield standard error as a function of number of bets

You can use this chart to compare the expected amount of variance in betting yields between different odds. For example, the variance in your yield from roughly 100 bets with odds 2 is about the same as from roughly 1,000 bets at odds 10. This means that to reduce the influence of luck to an equivalent level, you would need to place 10 times as many bets at the longer odds. The difference between odds of 1.25 and 25 is even more stark, with about 100 times the variance for a particular sample size.

As for win percentage, we can now use this information to say something about our outcome expectations, either prospectively (looking forwards) or retrospectively (looking back). Looking forwards, a good betting prediction model will make estimates of the true odds, t, for an outcome. This can be compared to the bookmaker's odds, o, to determine the expected value, o/t. Aggregated over a sample of bets, n, we can then estimate the expected return, r, simply by calculating the mean expected value of all the bets in our sample. Looking backwards, we could, instead, use our betting history to provide a measure of r, assuming that what happened was the most likely to happen. This is called a maximum likelihood estimation. (There are dangers with this approach which I'll address shortly; the smaller the history, the weaker the validity of this assumption is likely to be.) To calculate the standard error, just use the formula above, entering your values of r, o and n, and finally use Excel's NORM.DIST function to calculate what you want to know. Suppose I want to know my chances of making a profit after 100 bets with odds 3.25, where I believe I have a mean expected value of 10% (r = 110% or 1.10). $SE_{yield} = \sqrt{r(o-r)}/\sqrt{n} = \sqrt{1.10(3.25-1.10)}/\sqrt{100} = 0.1538$ or 15.38%. The probability of making a profit greater than 0% is then calculated by the function 1 − NORM.DIST(0,0.1,0.1538,TRUE) = 0.7422 or 74.22%. If you prefer to think in percentages rather than decimals, Excel will cope with that. In this case you would use 100% − NORM.DIST(0%,10%,15.38%,TRUE).

We can also draw a distribution of the possible yields we could finish with. Since we're using a normal distribution function to simulate their variance, you won't be the least bit surprised to see that they follow a normal distribution. The area under the curve to the right of the vertical axis, as a proportion of the total area under the curve, is 74.28%, the proportion of possible yields that will be profitable. You can see that even with an expected value of 10% you can expect to make a loss in over a quarter of your 100-bet samples.

Distribution of possible yields with expectation = 10%,
odds = 3.25, bets = 100

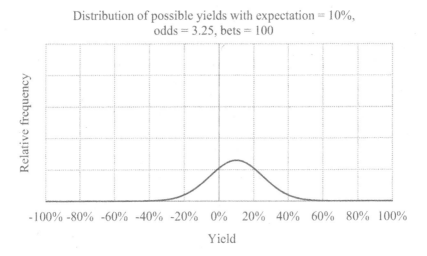

What happens after 1,000 bets? Remember the coin tosses? You should expect a narrower distribution with a smaller standard error. I've redrawn it for the larger sample. The vertical scales in the two charts are equivalent.

Distribution of possible yields with expectation = 10%,
odds = 3.25, bets = 1,000

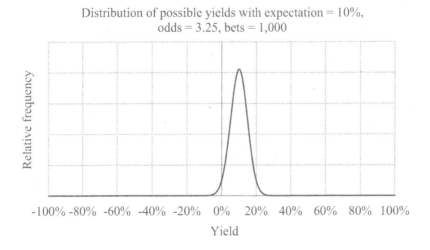

Surprise, surprise. The possible yields after 1,000 bets are now more closely grouped. The area under the curve is the same as before but it's become tighter and taller. It's a direct consequence of the law of large numbers. Notice, too, that the area of profitability has grown. To calculate it precisely, just adjust the standard error in your NORM.DIST function, which will be $\sqrt{1.10(3.25 - 1.10)}$ /

$\sqrt{1000}$. The probability is now 98.01%. If you're losing after 1,000 bets with odds of 3.25 holding expected value of 10%, you've been rather unlucky.

What happens when we change the odds? Again, given the relationship between odds and standard error, I'm sure you can predict it. Shorter odds; smaller standard error; narrower distribution; less variance. Longer odds; larger standard error, wider distribution; more variance. I've illustrated the distributions for odds of 1.5 and 10 together in the chart below, again for 1,000 bets with 10% expected value.

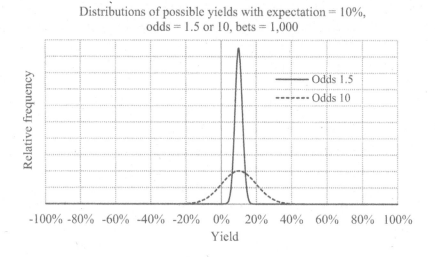

Distributions of possible yields with expectation = 10%, odds = 1.5 or 10, bets = 1,000

If you're losing after 1,000 bets with odds 1.5 holding 10% expected value, then there's probably something wrong with your prediction model. This would happen by chance about once in a million times. It's far more likely that you were never holding a 10% advantage after all. At odds of 10, by contrast, it will still happen about once in every 6 samples of 1,000 bets.

Greater variability in performances for longer odds is also the reason why records of horse racing bettors and tipsters typically appear to outperform those betting on other sports. Races generally have far more 'runners' than most sports betting markets. This means that, on average, the odds are much longer. As a consequence, there's more opportunity, through chance, for larger yields. Of course, in the public domain you tend to only see the profitable histories, those in the right hand tail of the distribution. The losers, the ones in the left hand tail, will have vanished from view. You can see simply by looking at the two right hand tails above that you're much more likely to see larger yields when the odds are longer. This does not mean they are better; rather, it just means they've taken more risk to win more reward. Risk adjusted, they will, broadly speaking, be as good (or as bad) as each other within the normal boundaries of variance.

What can we do when our bets have more than two possible outcomes? Well, now we are unable to use the binomial formula for the standard deviation, and thus unable to use $\sqrt{r(o-r)/n}$ for the standard error. Instead, we have to calculate it mean manually, but this is not so tricky. Recall that the standard error of the mean is given by formula $\sigma/\sqrt{n}$, where σ is the standard deviation in the data population. For coin tosses this was an infinite series of heads and tails, denoted by 1s and 0s. For wagers, this is an infinite series of individual bet profits and losses, where all stakes have a value of 1. For example, for fair odds of 2 the data population would be an infinite series of profits +1 and losses -1, with an expectation $\mu = 0$ and standard deviation $\sigma = 1$. Drawing a sample of 100 bets from this population would then have a standard error of 0.1. For markets like Asian handicap, however, not all of our bets will be win or lose. Assuming that all odds are still 2, ties will have profits of 0, half-wins will have profits of +0.5 and half-losses will have losses of -0.5. For such histories, just calculate the standard deviation manually. In Excel, you can simply use the STDEVP function, the standard deviation in a population of data. Since some of your profits and losses are going to have smaller absolute values, you can expect their standard deviation to be smaller too. By how much will depend upon how often you have half-wins, half-losses and ties, but given the typical rates at which these outcomes arise, you might expect a standard deviation to be about 5 to 10% smaller. Consequently, the standard error will be smaller too, and your distribution of possible betting yields narrower than for straight win-lose betting propositions with equivalent odds. Of course, you could alternatively turn to a Monte Carlo simulation, but to use one you'd need to know the probabilities of not only winning and losing, but also half-winning, half-losing and tying, and for that you would need a Dixon-Coles prediction model or something equivalent to it. You may indeed have used one to develop your predictions in the first place, in which case there's no problem.

Given a set of betting results, what is a level of probability beyond which we could be confident our model was not doing what we had expected it to be doing? 1 in a million implies almost certainly you need to start again. 1-in-6, however; well, that's not enough to rule out bad luck. Cast your mind back to my discussion on statistical testing. When the probability (sometimes called the p-value) that something happens by chance is below a subjectively defined threshold, we reject the null hypothesis that it was only chance that was influencing the outcome, in favour of an alternative hypothesis that something more systematic and non-random, in addition to chance, was going on. In the context here, that 'something else' is 'model not working as we expected it to'. To reiterate, many statisticians typically consider 5% or 1% as the thresholds below which they reject the null hypothesis. I think there are many reasons to believe these thresholds are too weak, with a greater burden of evidence required to start believing in the alternative hypothesis. I won't go into them here; the mathematics can be a bit daunting, but for those interested, Nassim Taleb (author of *The Black Swan*) offers a rigorous account. Here, it is sufficient to concur with Taleb and say that a p-value of 0.1% (or 1-in-1,000) should provide a minimum threshold. If that is accepted, then had our 1,000 wagers at odds of 10 with an expected value of 10% ended with a loss, we would not be able to conclude that something other than bad luck had 'made' this happen. Had it happened with odds of 1.25, we would come to a completely different conclusion. Because p-value thresholds are subjective, so are the conclusions we can draw when betting records beat or fail to beat them. Furthermore, you must also understand that it can never guarantee your prediction model is working (or indeed failing), nor even the probability of it doing so. On the contrary, the p-value only describes the probability that what has happened would happen by chance, assuming your model works as you had expected. Nevertheless, whilst this type of statistical testing cannot offer definite proof of the validity of your prediction model and the expected value which it implies, it does provide a useful tool with which to gain a sense of how well you are performing and whether that sits within the ballpark of expectation.

We can, of course, set our level of expectation to whatever value we choose. Here, I arbitrarily chose 10%, meaning we believe we will make a profit of £1 for every £10 staked. The centre of the distribution of possible betting yields will then be found at this value. For all the curves above, this was at 10%. Perhaps our model isn't as good, with an expectation of 5%. Changing the expectation, by changing the value of the second argument in the NORM.DIST function, will shift the normal distribution curves correspondingly. Perhaps, instead, we want to see how luck might distribute the performances of a recreational bettor, who is simply betting for fun with no meaningful effort made to outsmart the bookmaker. The expected value will then be defined by the bookmaker's overround, specifically 1/overround − 1. Suppose our reactional bettor bets exclusively 50-50 propositions with the bookmaker offering 1.95. Their expected value will be -2.5%. The chart below compares expected yield distributions after 25, 100 and 500 bets. They are now centred about a mean of -2.5%.

Distributions of possible yields with expectation = -2.5%,
odds = 1.95 bets = 25, 100 or 500

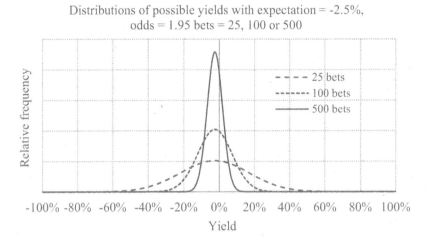

You will notice, unsurprisingly, that the longer one bets to the margin, the lower the likelihood they will have of being profitable. For these three scenarios, the NORM.DIST function implies diminishing probabilities of 44.89%, 39.88% and 28.32% respectively. Let's suppose, however, that our recreational bettor returns a profit of 15%. Change the first argument in the function from 0 to 0.15. Now, the probability of outperforming 15% where the expectation is -2.5% is 18.47%, 3.63% and 0.003% respectively. After 25 bets, we shouldn't be batting an eyelid. After 100 bets, one's attention might be drawn. After 500 bets, however, we'd have a much stronger conviction that this recreational bettor was in fact a little bit more than just lucky. However, when the bookmaker's margin is small, as often it can be in today's competitive betting market, the fact that as a bettor you can remain profitable for extended periods with only luck on your side should serve as a warning. Most bettors are in the habit of judging their predictive abilities by short term results. It's a bad habit and one you should try to avoid. I will show you why.

The Law of Small Numbers

In 1974 two psychologists, Daniel Kahneman and Amos Tversky, performed an experiment where they presented their experimental subjects with the following scenario, accompanied by a question.

A certain town is served by two hospitals. In the larger hospital about 45 babies are born each day, and in the smaller hospital about 15 babies are born each day. As you know, about 50% of all babies are boys. However, the exact percentage varies from day to day. Sometimes it may be higher than 50%, sometimes lower. For a period of 1 year, each hospital recorded the days on which more than 60% of the babies born were boys. Which hospital do you think recorded more such days?

- *The larger hospital*
- *The smaller hospital*
- *About the same (within 5% of each other)*

The birth sex of a child is a binary proposition, and counts of boys and girls will distribute binomially, assuming the same probability for every birth. Accordingly, the number of days where boys born outnumber girls by at least 6 to 4 will be nearly three times greater in the smaller hospital compared to the larger one, simply on account of the larger volatility in birth ratios. I've already shown you plenty of examples in this chapter where the smaller the value of n, the bigger the variance will be. The larger sample is less likely to stray far from 50%. Yet only 22% of respondents gave the correct answer. Evidently, thinking about the implications of sample size is not particularly intuitive.

Kahneman and Tversky called their fallacy the law of small numbers. If the law of large numbers is the most important numerical truth in betting, the law of small numbers is perhaps second only to it. Yet it's not really a law at all, but rather used more informally to illustrate a weakness in the cognitive thinking of humans. The law of small numbers describes a logical fallacy whereby an insufficient data sample is incorrectly used to infer a generalisation about the data population. A major consequence for a bettor who commits this fallacy is that they believe they are better at prediction than they really are.

The gambler's fallacy, mentioned in the opening to this book, is an example of an expression of the fallacy of small numbers. Nearly all gamblers, one would assume, understand that the colour on which a roulette ball lands is random. However, in the event of a significant excess of one colour over another during a series of wheels spins, a mistaken belief can arise that this must increase the likelihood of the opposite colour occurring more often over the next series of spins, to ensure that any unnatural short term sequence is balanced out in order for the full sequence to be considered representative of a random process. The law of large numbers, however, informs us that deviations from expectation, in this case 50% red, 50% black, can occur in any sized sample of wheel spins, but that the greater the number of spins, the greater the tendency for the percentage deviation from expectation to be smaller. Individual wheel spins have no memory. Neither do samples of wheel spins. In the extreme, no sample size, no matter how large can be used to perfectly generalise the population. We only know that the larger the sample, the more reliable the generalisation. The fallacy, in this case, is a misinterpretation of the law of large numbers (which most people have never heard of) by the law of averages (which most people will have heard of and apply incorrectly).

Another expression of the fallacy of small numbers is the hot hand fallacy, sometimes also known as the reverse gambler's fallacy. Whilst many may now be aware of the gambler's fallacy, its counterpart lies hidden as a driver of every bettor's overconfidence. The hot hand fallacy is the erroneous belief that a person who has experienced success with a random event in the short term has a greater chance of further success in additional attempts. A short term performance greater than expectation can lead to a mistaken belief that a streak is no longer representative of a random sample. For the majority of bettors, short term profits can be mistaken for evidence of predictive skill and being better at 'knowing' the future than the bookmaker, when their real expectation from their random 'coin tossing' is just paying the bookmaker's margin. Even for advantage bettors, who've secured real expected value, however, it's hard not to succumb to the fallacy of small numbers, either when winning more than their model had expected them to, or when losing more than they expected, and prematurely discarding a genuinely valid prediction model, which they had too hastily assumed to be faulty. We are all human, after all, even those who make a living from betting who are best equipped to detach their emotions from the expectations.

A consequence of the law of small numbers, well, really the law of large numbers, is that that you can never perfectly know what your true expectation is. How big must a sample of bets be to be confident that what we are seeing by way of profits is likely to be representative of our expectation? To some degree this is like asking: how long is a piece of string? The answer: it depends. Depends on what? How long it is. Fortunately, we needn't end up in quite such a tautological cul-de-sac with our original question. We have some tools. We already know that the larger the sample, the more likely it is to be representative of expectation. We also know that the longer the odds we are betting, the larger the sample we will need to form robust conclusions about the likely presence or absence of predictive skill over and above the background random variance. And finally, we have some defined thresholds, albeit subjective ones, about what probability level we will accept as reliable enough evidence to reject one hypothesis about our betting performance in favour of another. The distributions earlier should have given you a feel for what sort of sample sizes will be needed, but let's explore this a little further.

The mini-graphs below show four different possible histories for a recreational bettor after betting 1,000 binary propositions, with 50-50 outcome probabilities and with 1-unit stakes at odds of 1.95, implying a -2.5% expected value. They were produced using Excel's random number function, RAND(), to determine whether a bet wins or loses. We can calculate from the NORM.DIST function that close to 80% of these histories will finish with a loss. However, take a look at some of the intra-sample trends withing these histories, and imagine these were your records.

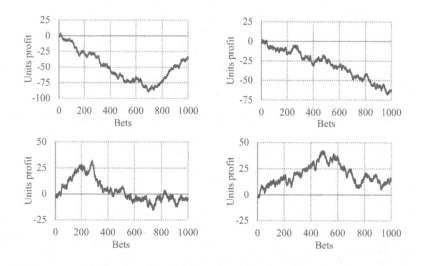

In the lower left history, you might have been forgiven for believing that after nearly 300 bets, and with about a 10% yield, you were actually rather good at betting. Similarly, in the lower right history with a yield of about 8% after 500 bets. Indeed, you might have also performed a statistical test on these records using the NORM.DIST function and concluded that if this could happen by chance only 1% of the time, then this might indicate your real expectation was better than -2.5%. Yet what follows in both records during the remainder of the history is what statisticians call regression, or reversion, to the mean. The mean, here, is the expectation of a -2.5% yield. The regression towards it is the tendency (note, not the necessity, as believed by those who commit the gambler's fallacy)

for a bet profit, or sample of bet profits, that is more extreme to be followed by one that is less extreme. To reiterate, there is no sense in which the next profit or profit sample is compensating for or balancing out the previous one. Betting profits can't know what came before or what will come after. That's why they are considered to be random variables which distribute randomly. Here, profit from the earlier part of the betting history was extreme; what followed was just mean regression. Of course, we know this to be true, because we know this bettor was defined in Excel to have a -2.5% expected yield. In reality, of course, and in the real time of betting, you won't know what is to follow, and you won't ever be sure of your true expected value. Even if the bettor's yield had been 15% after 300 bets (with a p-value of just under 0.1%), whilst I might consider the alternative hypothesis of skill more credible, we would still have little idea exactly how much skill and how much luck was contributing to the performance. It might still be a lucky record, boosted marginally by a little bit of skill. Alternatively, it might have been a rather unlucky record that was more than compensated for by a much greater predictive skill. We really have no way of knowing, certainly not with these sample sizes. Separating skill from luck in betting is a very tricky business, and you should never underestimate just how long a performance can remain extreme relative to expectation.

Let's change the odds. Now the recreational bettor is making wagers with odds of 9.75, so again with an expected value of -2.5%.

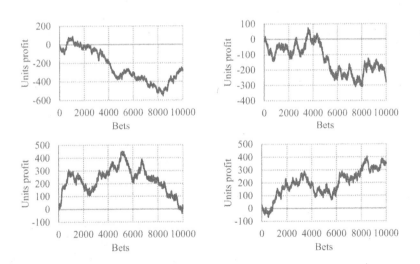

The charts look fairly similar to the earlier ones: random walks of winning and losing. However, take a look at the horizontal axes. The histories are no longer

1,000 bets, but 10,000. The bottom right history in particular should catch your attention. After 10,000 bets the yield stands close to 4%, and with the exception of a downturn between roughly 3,500 and 6,000 bets, the full history has all the hallmarks of skill. Yet we know that skill had nothing to do with this record. If a bettor presented it to you, what would you think? A NORM.DIST test will confirm that this could happen about 1% of the time, just by chance, given an expectation of losing 2.5%. Indeed, let three million people throw a 10-sided die 50,000 times, winning on 10 and paying a 2.5% commission each time they do, and one of them will likely be up by 4%. 'Sports is not dice,' you say. No, it isn't, but the variation of outcomes obeys the same statistical rules. The only difference is that in sports we don't know exactly what the true expectation is. There will always be aleatory uncertainty; the point is, does your forecast model have a better idea than the bookmaker of where the mean is?

Just consider how long a 10,000-bet history is. 10,000 bets and we can't be confident whether the bettor is just randomly tossing coins and expected to pay the bookmaker's margin. The flip side is also true. A bettor with a 2.5% advantage could just as readily be losing after 10,000 bets. Would they have even bothered staying the course? Here were the first two outputs from my random bet history generator. The first one would not be inspiring any confidence at all by the end of it.

 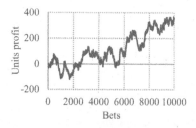

So how long is the piece of 'string'? You can see it is sometimes very, very long indeed. This may come as a surprise, but you simply cannot underestimate how easy it is, even for professional bettors, to be fooled by the law of small numbers. Lucky streaks over even sizeable samples can have you believing you are far better than you really are. Overconfidence is a pernicious and pervasive cognitive bias for nearly all human beings. The converse is also true, with loss aversion leading bettors to doubt themselves, abandoning methods early that may well have held real expected value. Humans are not robots, after all. The impossibility of knowing the true expectation for a sports bet creates the opportunity for skill, where bettors and bookmakers can compete for superiority in their accuracy of modelling it. Unfortunately, this lack of certainty also creates the perfect breeding ground for the emotions of optimism and fear, which all too easily see us depart from rational decision-making, even when we are alert to that possibility. Indeed, as someone who once played poker professionally, for whom the same rules of variance in winning and losing apply, told me, 'you'd think I'd be used to this shit by now'.

Bettors who bet just once per week, or even once per day if their odds are longer, might never find out if they are smart or just lucky. Perhaps that's as it should be if they are only betting for entertainment anyway. If you're aspiring to achieve a sustainable financial reward from this activity, however, you will probably want to, and certainly should, gain a better understanding of your possibilities based on your expectations, and whether and how soon you might need to re-evaluate them. The purpose of this chapter thus far has been to visualise and quantify these possibilities statistically; doing so can help you answer a variety of different questions. You might, for example, want to know in advance what range of profits to expect from your betting prediction model, assuming you're confident your model is valid, and the probabilities of achieving those. On the other hand, you might have a set of results and want to test them against what you thought your model would achieve, deciding from the evidence you uncover whether to accept or reject your model. Alternatively, you might want to compare those results to what the bookmakers expected you to achieve, given their odds and the size of their margin and favourite–longshot bias, to identify a signal of skill superior to theirs amongst the noise of luck. There isn't really a limit to what you can test with this approach and Excel's NORM.DIST function that is available to facilitate this testing. Whatever you are seeking to learn, however, the approach is the same: identify your expectation, based on either modelling or observation, to determine your variance of possible outcomes; then test any deviation from expectation to determine statistically whether it will arise, or will have arisen, only by chance or something more. I would always urge readers to attempt to build their own testing kits on Excel (or via other software if they prefer) since this helps with the learning process; it certainly helped me as I worked to understand the subject matter. However, for those daunted by that or who are just feeling a little bit lazy, I already have an online Excel yield distribution calculator, oven ready, as the saying goes now. As for my 'Fair Odds' calculator, you will find it at Football-Data.co.uk.

A Real World Betting Model and History

We are already a long way into this chapter and there's barely been even a whiff of the words 'Monte Carlo'. Well, it's time to address that. The formulae I've presented for understanding your possible distribution of profits (although sadly more often than not, losses) work perfectly when you are always betting the same odds, with the same stake, and with just two possible outcomes: win or lose. But as for many aspects of betting, things are rarely that simple. I've already said that the formulae are fairly robust for dealing with variable odds. Let's test that premise, comparing the outputs from mathematics with the outputs from a Monte Carlo simulation. First, however, I need to give some background to the real betting model I will be testing.

In August 2015 I began publishing football betting matches on my website for which there were opportunities to exploit inaccuracies in the bookmakers' match betting odds. I've not proved to be hugely successful at developing my own prediction models for this purpose, so when I was writing my last book, I began thinking about those who are. I'm not alone. Having studied tens of thousands of betting histories of bettors, it was obvious that hardly any of them had been particularly successful either. Plotting their performances in a distribution, adjusting for the length of history and betting odds, and accounting for the bookmaker's margin, they were indistinguishable from a distribution that would arise from tossing coins. I'll show you some of them later. The implication was clear: very few bettors have predictive skill superior to the bookmakers'; where bettors are winning, they are doing so because of luck only. This means that the bookmakers must have the best prediction models, reflected in the accuracy (or efficiency) of their betting odds, and potentially I could use them to make a profit.

Not all bookmakers are equal, however. Broadly speaking they fall into three categories. Firstly, there are what are termed the sharp bookmakers. These set the sharpest and most accurate (or efficient) betting odds; you may recall me saying earlier that they have to because their business model demands it. If their odds did not accurately reflect the 'true' probabilities of outcomes, they would not be in business long. Which bookmakers have the sharpest odds? Pinnacle.com has a long-established reputation, but there are now other brands including Bookmaker.eu, Betcris.com and Dafabet.com. However, depending on your jurisdiction you may be unable to use them if they have not been granted a licence to operate by the gambling regulator. In the UK, for example, none of these sharp brands is available to bettors.

Secondly, there are what are termed recreational or entertainment bookmakers. These bookmakers are sometime also called 'soft' bookmakers, because they set soft prices in comparison to the sharp bookmakers, which can be exploited by bettors for an expected profit. This is not to argue, however, that soft bookmakers aren't as good at predicting 'true' probabilities. Almost certainly they are, or they would be if they needed to be. Rather, my argument is that they **choose** not to set the most accurate prices, instead focusing on and marketing price value which forms the basis of their alternative business model. BetVictor, for example, was for several years promoting the slogan 'best prices most often for the Premier League'. Other soft bookmakers include the famous UK high street brands Ladbrokes, William Hill, Coral, Betfred and Paddy Power, in addition to the online-only giant bet365. All European brands, including the likes of Unibet and bwin, can legitimately be considered recreational bookmakers too. For these bookmakers, sports betting is considered to be more like a form of entertainment rather than a skills contest. You might then ask, if soft bookmakers set soft prices that are more easily beaten, how can they remain in business? The short answer is that they restrict the betting of those who have figured it out, as I will show you shortly how to. Fortunately, that's still only a small minority, which perhaps validates their view that betting **is** regarded by the majority as a form of entertainment, rather than a form of earning a living. I'll come back to this topic in the final chapter.

Finally, there are what are known as exchanges, where, in theory at least, there is no bookmaker as such, just a market facilitator who brings customers together who have opposing views about the likelihood of betting outcomes and is paid a commission for their troubles. In practice, exchanges, particularly the less popular ones, will seed their own markets to increase liquidity and attention, thereby introducing their own liabilities. Betfair is the most popular exchange, but others include Betdaq, Smarkets and Matchbook. Unlike the sharp bookmakers, all can be accessed within the UK. Thus, in theory, with bettors setting (or laying) their own odds, there is no need for the exchange to worry about being beaten; they'll be paid on winners' profits regardless, and for binary-proposition bets there's always one winner. Consequently, the activity at an exchange takes the form of a competition and is thus more akin to the betting at a sharp bookmaker. Indeed, in some senses a sharp bookmaker acts more like an exchange much of the time, aiming to maximise turnover and taking their cut via the profit margin, knowing that whilst aleatory variance may bring losses in the short term, the expected accuracy of their odds over the longer run makes their profitability inevitable. This is the law of large numbers.

If Pinnacle have more accurate odds then Ladbrokes or William Hill, for example, I can use them to calculate the expected value of a bet. Since 2001 I've been collecting a lot of football betting odds data for many of Europe's domestic football leagues. Having such a lot of them allows me to test a hypothesis: the ratio of Ladbrokes' betting odds (or those of any other soft bookmaker for that matter) to Pinnacle's betting odds is equivalent to the expected value, once we have removed the margin from Pinnacle's odds. If Pinnacle's implied fair price (margin removed) is 1.50 and Ladbrokes offer 1.55, the expected value is $1.55/1.50 - 1 = 0.0333$ or 3.33%. Alternatively, if Pinnacle's fair price is 3.20 and Ladbrokes offer only 3.05, the expected value is -4.69%.

Essentially, we are testing an antecedent hypothesis from which this one is derived: Pinnacle's odds (without their margin) are, on average, a good measure of the 'true' odds. How can we prove this? One way is to see how often teams that have a 50% probability of winning, as predicted by Pinnacle's odds, actually end up winning. If they win 50% of the time (and similarly for other probabilities), that implies the odds do reliably capture the 'true' chances. For the data that I have collected, I have plotted the correlation below.

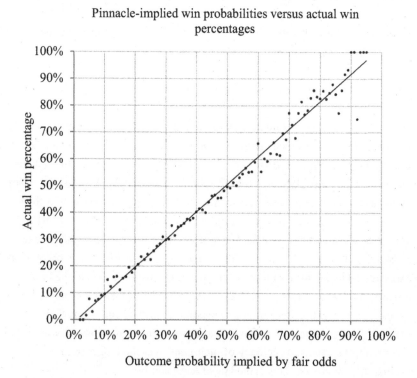

Pinnacle-implied win probabilities versus actual win percentages

The data has a 1% probability resolution. A perfect correlation between expected win probabilities on the horizontal axis and actual win percentages on the vertical axis should look like a straight line with a gradient of 1. Does it? I think you'll agree that it's pretty close. Pinnacle's odds provide an excellent measure of the 'true' chances of football teams winning, drawing and losing. We can accept the antecedent hypothesis.

What about the derivative hypothesis? From a large set of home-draw-away odds data (35,570 domestic league matches across Europe) I calculated the ratio of the published odds from four leading recreational bookmakers to those of Pinnacle's fair odds (their margin removed), yielding a total of 426,840 price ratios. By subtracting 1 from the price ratio, we have a figure for the expected value. These are then separated into subgroups with a resolution of 1% (for example -5%, -4%, -3%, -2% and so on); for each subgroup I calculated the actual yields one would have achieved betting the published recreational odds from 1-unit stakes. These data pairs are shown in the correlation plot below. I've shown the most data-populated points (accounting for 95% of the total dataset), since ratios considerably above or below 1 (where there were big price differences between the two bookmakers) had far fewer matches, and hence will show a much greater degree of variability, distorting the underlying trend.

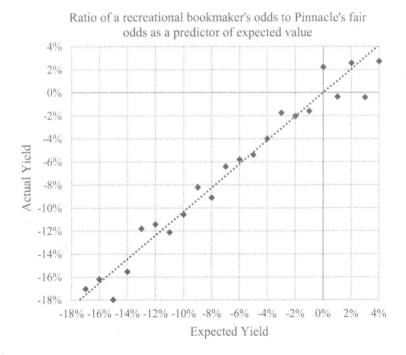

Ratio of a recreational bookmaker's odds to Pinnacle's fair odds as a predictor of expected value

The correlation really is excellent, with the trend an almost perfect 1 to 1 relationship. When a recreational bookmaker's odds are 10% shorter than Pinnacle's fair price, on average your expected value will be -10%. If they are 5% longer, it will be +5%. Understandably, there is more negative expected value, simply because of the bookmakers' margins. Remember, to find positive expected value with this methodology, a recreational bookmaker's price with their margin included has to be longer than Pinnacle's price with their margin removed. In my data sample, that happened only 5.7% of the time, but using more recreational bookmakers would increase that proportion. We can also test the reverse hypothesis: that the ratio of Pinnacle's actual price to a recreational bookmaker's fair price (the margin removed) is a good predictor of expected value. It's not; take a look.

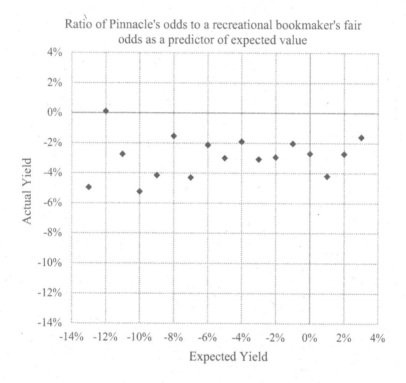

Ratio of Pinnacle's odds to a recreational bookmaker's fair odds as a predictor of expected value

Regardless of what a recreational bookmaker implies the 'true' price to be, you will be losing around 2.5% betting Pinnacle's prices, equivalent to their margin. The conclusion is clear: on average, you cannot trust the accuracy of the odds of a recreational bookmaker, but you can trust Pinnacle's and use them to exploit the former.

I have called this betting methodology the Wisdom of the Crowd, being as it is based on the way Pinnacle use their customers, in contrast to a recreational bookmaker, to help find the most accurate betting odds. Really, this is a bit of a misnomer. I should have called it the Wisdom of the Pinnacle Crowd, given that the wisdom is largely coming from their expert traders who set the opening odds and a few sharp customers who help them shape their evolution with the money they put down, but let's not split hairs. More importantly, how has the methodology been performing since I first published it? The next chart shows the betting history since I started posting the matches online in August 2015. Stakes are the same for all bets (1 unit).

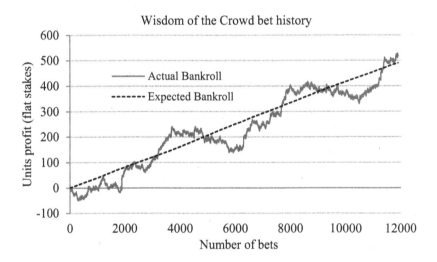

We obviously only bet when the expected value is greater than 0%. In this case I built in an additional safety buffer of 2%, meaning only bets with expected value greater than 2% would be included. Obviously, this limits the number of betting opportunities, but reduces the risk if the methodology doesn't work quite as it should. There are two lines. The first is the actual evolution of the bankroll over time. You can see there's a lot of variability, reflecting the shorter-term variance due to good and bad luck. Indeed, it may further reinforce my warning about the law of small numbers. There are two distinct episodes where consistent losses accumulated over episodes lasting more than 2,000 bets. I'd wager that almost everyone who began following this methodology at the start of those episodes would have told me I'm on a hiding to nothing before we'd arrived at the end of them. The actual profit evolution is compared against the expected accumulation of profits, as calculated from the cumulative summing of the expected value of each bet – the dashed line. For example, if the expected value is 5%, the expected profit is 0.05 units from a 1-unit stake. Shortly, I will statistically prove that my hypothesis should be accepted, but here, visually, you should already have confirmation.

In terms of betting systems, this is probably my best work. Sadly, it's not particularly novel. Many bettors before me have known that it's easier to exploit recreational bookmakers than it is to beat the sharp ones. Nevertheless, it's a robust analysis in that it has confirmed one can use Pinnacle to define a 'true' betting price in a football match betting market and use them to predict and quantify expected profits betting elsewhere. Other online services have since taken my work and developed it for use with other sports; I've given them a shoutout in the final chapter. I cannot vouch for whether they have tested the hypothesis with the same rigour that I have. If in doubt, acquire the data yourself and test.

Some words of warning. You should refrain from searching for expected value at other sharp bookmakers, and the exchanges. Whilst different bookmakers will very often have different prices, on average they will prove to be more or less matched in terms of their price accuracy. Differences are likely to be random; sometimes Sharp A will actually be sharper than Sharp B, sometimes the other way around. You'll never know which since the differences are not systematic, as they are between a sharp bookmaker and a recreational bookmaker. Of course, you can use another sharp bookmaker to provide the measure of 'true' odds, but make sure you test the hypothesis with their data first. Secondly, it is inevitable that recreational bookmakers will want to stop you using this methodology, and you can expect to experience restrictions if they believe you are exploiting them. As mentioned, I'll explore the reasons for why they do restrict advantage bettors, and the measures you can take to reduce the risk of it happening, in the final chapter.

As of writing, there have been 11,894 bets. Odds were hugely variable, ranging from 1.1 for the shortest price up to 67 for the longest. The mean and median odds were 3.89 and 3.15, respectively. The former is unsurprisingly larger because longer odds will positively skew it. The expected yield was 4.12%, which has been marginally surpassed by the actual yield of 4.35%. Using the formula for the yield standard error I showed earlier, we have $r = 1.0412$, $o = 3.89$, $n = 11,894$ and therefore $SE_{yield} = 1.58\%$. This tells us that if the possible performances are normally distributed, about 68% of them will fall between 4.12% ±1.58%, or 2.54% and 5.70%, and 95% within 4.12% ±3.16%, or 0.96%

and 7.28% (the empirical rule). Using NORM.DIST(0%,4.12%,1.58%,TRUE) we can calculate the probability of failing to make a profit to be just 0.46%. The theoretical distribution of possible yields is shown below.

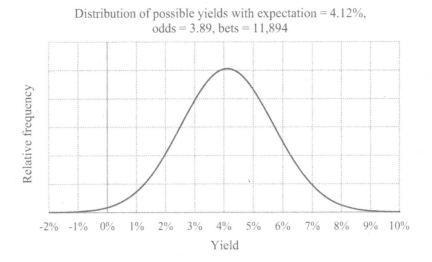

Distribution of possible yields with expectation = 4.12%, odds = 3.89, bets = 11,894

We can also use the NORM.DIST function to test for the probability of achieving or bettering the actual yield of 4.35%. The answer is 44.06%. This tells us that the actual observed yield lies well within the margins associated with aleatory uncertainty. Remember, I'd previously defined anything above 0.1% as not worthy of consideration in this respect. Even the much weaker threshold 5% is a long way off. We have essentially performed what statisticians call a goodness of fit test, to see how well the observations fit the model expectation. Hence, we have confirmed the validity of the hypothesis that the ratio of a recreational bookmaker's football betting price to Pinnacle's fair price will be an excellent predictor of expected value with which to make profits.

How reliable is the yield standard error function, however, given the huge range in the betting odds? The formula works best when all odds are the same. I said it was robust enough to handle a spread of different prices, using instead the average odds in the formula, but we should test this proposition. To do that, I will run a Monte Carlo simulation. For each bet, I have again used the RAND() function to determine the outcome, defining its probability by Pinnacle's fair price. Thus, if they have 4.00 with their margin removed, the expected win probability is 25%. We would then output the result using IF(RAND()<0.25, "Win", "Loss"), and calculate the profits accordingly, in this case +3 for a win and -1 for a loss. Repeating for every 11,894 bets we have one Monte Carlo iteration. I ran 100,000 of them for my simulation. The distribution of the 100,000 yields is shown below, superimposed on the original normal distribution created with the NORM.DIST function.

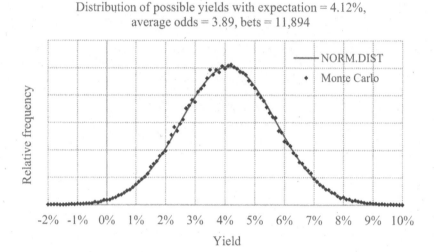

Distribution of possible yields with expectation = 4.12%, average odds = 3.89, bets = 11,894

It's an incredibly close match. Yes, there are departures from the normal distribution curve, but these are random, not systematic. The larger the number of Monte Carlo iterations, the smaller these random deviations would be. The broader conclusion, however, is that using the average odds of a betting sample to calculate the yield standard error (and its use within Excel's NORM.DIST function), even for a sample with a wide range of odds, offers a very robust short cut to performing a Monte Carlo simulation, provided the stakes are all the same. (I'll be looking at the implication of variable stakes for the mathematical short cut in my chapter on staking.) It is worth noting that 43.75% of these 100,000 yields were higher than the observed yield of 4.35%. The function predicted 44.06%. Furthermore, 439 (or 0.439%) of them were less than 0%. That compares to 0.46% as calculated via the function. Just pause for a minute: that's roughly a 1-in-200 chance that nearly 12,000 bets placed with an expected value of over 4% could lose money. It's unlikely but not impossible, and the mathematics say it can happen without having to doubt the validity of the Pinnacle-true-odds methodology. If it had happened to you, do you think you would start to doubt it or could you tell me, hand on heart, that you'd become 'used to this shit by now'? Variance in betting is truly a monster.

Some of you may still be doubting that variance or luck can have so much influence on a betting history. Perhaps you might still be thinking that these normal distributions are just theoretical; they might look nice but in reality, betting yields will just not distribute like this. Let me show you why you should abandon such thinking. From the 11,894 individual bet profits and losses, I created random samples of 100 bets – 100,000 in total – and calculated their yields. These are not yields predicted by the normal distribution, these would be actual yields for those randomised samples. I've plotted their frequency distribution below, alongside the normal distribution that would be predicted based on the full history's actual yield (4.35%) and average odds (3.89).

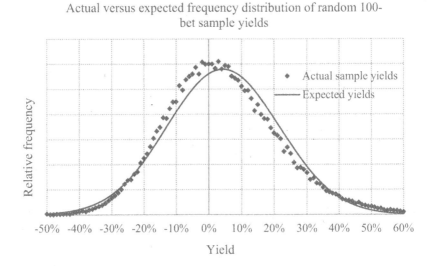

Actual versus expected frequency distribution of random 100-bet sample yields

It's a close match, although not perfect. In fact, the actual yields distribute with a slight positive skew, with a slightly longer, fatter right-hand tail and a slightly shorter, thinner left-hand tail. Consequently, the median yield (2.99%) is shifted slightly to the left of the mean yield. The reason? With highly variable odds, long ones can significantly skew profits when they win. A sample of 100 bets is not enough to reduce the distribution asymmetry to the point where it would become visually indistinguishable from the normal curve. One concept that is important in statistics is that even if a random variable – in this case individual bet profits and losses – is not normally distributed, a sample of its means **will be** approximately normally distributed, and the larger the sample, the closer the approximation. Remember the equation for calculating the standard error of the mean? It's σ/√n. The standard deviation in the 11,894 profit and losses in my history is 1.768. Thus, the standard error for 100-bet sample yields should be $1.769/\sqrt{100} = 0.1769$ or 17.69%. The actual standard deviation in my 100,000 100-bet samples was 17.64%. And the standard error predicted using the formula $\sqrt{(r(o-r))/n}$ (where r = 1.0435, o = 3.89 and n = 100) is 17.23%. The latter is slightly lower because the positive skew in the actual distribution increases the variance ever so slightly.

There may still be some who would argue that all this is to be expected because I've randomised the 100-bet samples. Let me guess what you're thinking. 'If you look at them as they happened, in sequence, you will not see the same random distribution. Whilst roulette spins don't have memories, perhaps events in sports run in streaks, and therefore so will betting outcomes.' Let's test this premise. Instead of randomised 100-bet samples, I've now calculated the yields for consecutive running 100-bet samples; for example bets 1 to 100, 2 to 101, 3 to 102 and so on up to 11,795 to 11,894, that is a total of 11,795 samples. See how their frequency distributes.

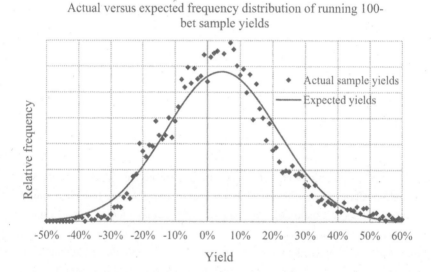

Actual versus expected frequency distribution of running 100-bet sample yields

I hope I've managed to convince you that luck really does play a big part in what happens in betting. Bets really don't have memories.

The Closing Line

'Reality Dose. When it comes to tracking picks and trying to get advice from all the countless talking heads out there, remember one thing: if you're not beating the closing line by enough to overcome the bookmaker's vig, you're not gonna win long term. Your bets suck.' These words come from professional sports bettor Gadoon Kyrollos, known to his followers on Twitter as Spanky. He has quite a back story. I would urge you to Google him. What does all of this mean?

In American sports betting, line betting, or point spread betting as I've referred to it earlier, is the more popular brand of betting. Recall, it's a type of handicap betting, where one side in a bet is handicapped relative to the other, to roughly equalise the win chances. When bookmakers need to change things to reflect some significant news about a betting market, or to respond to a disproportionate interest from bettors on one side, they will move the line rather than change the odds. Toronto against Golden State in Game 1 of the 2018/19 NBA Finals, for example, moved from an opening line of +1.5 points (the underdog) to -2 points (the favourite) by the close. The final line available at the time a sporting contest begins is called the closing line. In other types of betting market, it is the actual price that is shifted, not the line. In football home-draw-away markets, for example, there is no line to move. You are simply betting on one outcome to happen at the quoted price. Nevertheless, the same concept applies, for which we might use the term 'closing odds' or 'closing price', although I think 'closing line' has a nicer ring to it, even if we are using it to refer to a price rather than a line. Since the word 'moneyline' is used for such bets in the US, I think it's a reasonable concession. More importantly, however, what's so special about the closing line?

I have already made the case that the accuracy of a price (or a line) is largely dependent on three things. Firstly, the quality of the bookmakers' prediction model, and their willingness to reflect the 'true' probabilities in their odds and lines. Pinnacle, as I've argued, are more willing to do this than the recreational bookmakers. That's the reason why you can find expected profit from the latter, but not the former, when comparing them. Secondly, the flow of news. As more things become known about participants in a sporting contest, the better the forecast probabilities should become. News is information, and the more you have of it, the more it is theoretically possible to reduce your epistemic uncertainty to aleatory randomness. More (and better) information means a superior prediction model. Finally, the volume of money wagered by the bettors. To a degree, bookmakers will prefer it if they can eliminate their liabilities by balancing action on either side of a bet, such that whatever the result, the bookmaker will profit, the size of which is dictated by their margin. This should not be viewed as a law of bookmaking, however, but more like a loose aspiration. In some markets, it would be completely impossible to achieve anyway, given the cognitively-biased behaviour of the majority of bettors. For example, close to two-thirds prefer to bet 'over' in total points or goals markets, probably for no other reason than loss aversion. Betting the 'over' means you always start the match with a loser. If enough points or goals are scored, it's transformed into a winner. It seems this is preferred to the reverse. It hurts more, emotionally speaking, to see an 'under' bet scuppered. If bookmakers attempted to move the odds (or the lines) to reflect the disproportionate volumes on either side, they would quickly become completely inaccurate and exploitable by those of a sharper disposition. That's not something a sharp bookmaker, in particular, can afford long term. For some selected markets, they may actually prefer to set inaccurate odds (or lines). Given most bettors' propensity for irrational judgements, it can be possible for the bookmaker to gain an expected profit that is greater than that predicted by their margin alone. Obviously, on a market-by-market basis this creates liabilities for them, but they know the law of large numbers will look after them in the long run. It's not something that I believe a sharp bookmaker would do systematically, however, as the evidence from Pinnacle's football odds suggests.

The corollary of the last two factors is that later lines and odds, reflecting more information, and more money, should be more accurate (or efficient) than earlier ones, at least on average. Since the closing line is the last one, theory tells us that it should, on average, be the most accurate of all. This is not to argue that it will perfectly reflect the 'true' outcome probabilities every time. Rather, the epistemic uncertainty should be smaller than at all earlier times. There are quite sophisticated techniques to measure the informational deficit between two sets of odds, and to test the relative accuracy of one set against the other. These include scoring rules like Brier score and rank probability score, Shannon entropy and maximum likelihood estimation. However, it's far quicker, and arguably more informative, for me to show you how closing odds compare to earlier ones visually via the method I described a little earlier. Let's calculate an odds ratio and see how well it predicts hypothetical betting returns. I have a large dataset of opening and closing Pinnacle football match odds (10 seasons with 158,092 matches and 474,276 home, draw and away odds after data cleansing) for just this task.

First, let's assume that Pinnacle's opening price is a valid reflection of the 'true' price, after their margin has been removed. If this hypothesis is true, then the closing to opening price ratio will predict the returns when betting the closing price. For this task I've also removed the margin from the closing price, so these returns are purely hypothetical. Bets are made with 1-unit stakes. As before, expected yields are sub-grouped at a resolution of 1%.

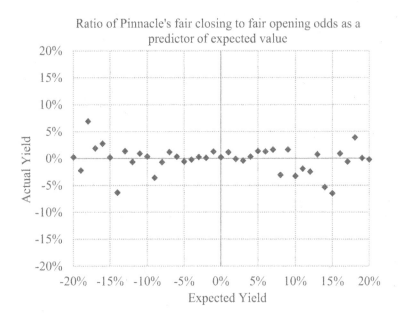

Ratio of Pinnacle's fair closing to fair opening odds as a predictor of expected value

There's no correlation at all. Discounting random variance in the chart above, the closing to opening price ratio fails to predict anything at all. No matter how much shorter or longer a closing price is relative to its earlier opening one, your average expected value when betting a closing price is 0%, or about -2.5% once Pinnacle's margin is included. Just to be clear, however, I am not arguing that every closing price is a bad bet, rather that, at the model resolution I've sub-grouped the data – one chart point per 1% expected yield subgroup – on average, there is no expected value to be found. A more sophisticated prediction model that can drill down into the individual matches that contribute to each data point and identify variables that are systematically associated with one particular outcome or another will be better able to determine a more accurate figure for a bet's expected value. Some of the data points contain tens of thousands of betting odds ratios, but it is via this sub-grouping that we can eliminate the influence of randomness and uncover the more general relationship. The absence of any in the chart provides a clue that the closing price appears to be more accurate, but let's test this by swapping things around. Does the opening to closing price ratio predict returns from betting the opening price?

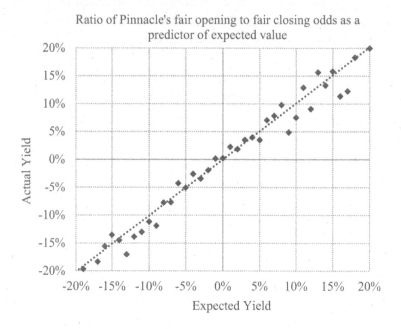

Evidently, the answer is an emphatic yes. Again, this is not to insist that every opening to closing price ratio is a perfect predictor, just that they are so on average at this data resolution. Furthermore, in real time you'd obviously never know whether a closing price is going to be shorter or longer than the opening one, so it's impossible to use this information to identify expected value. This was not the point of the exercise, however. Rather, it was to verify that closing odds are more accurate than the opening ones, presumably for the reasons I identified. Furthermore, given that expected and actual yields correlate almost perfectly (one-to-one), this implies that the closing odds provide a valid measure of the 'true' outcome probabilities, at least, on average, at my data resolution.

Armed with this information, we can confirm Spanky's declaration. On average, if you can beat a sharp bookmaker's fair closing odds, or their published ones by more than their margin, you should have found yourself expected value which can earn you a profit over the long term. If you can't, well, then you suck, or at least you should only be betting for fun. Perhaps more importantly, however, the accuracy of the closing line as a measure of 'truth' provides an independent benchmark to determine whether your betting shows any evidence of expected value. The expected value that you hold over the fair closing line is, unsurprisingly, called the closing line value. Using the NORM.DIST function to calculate the probability of your yield outperforming a threshold, or a Monte Carlo to count the number of times it might happen, can offer clues as to the presence or absence of any relative forecasting skill over and above the bookmaker's. However, these methods suffer two major drawbacks. Firstly, they don't confirm (or deny), absolutely, the existence of skill, but just statistically define the likelihood of your performance, assuming no skill is present. Secondly, such information, as we learnt earlier, can take an extraordinarily long time to acquire. In my experience, bettors are typically impatient creatures. Can the closing line benchmark offer a speedier route to this sort of knowledge?

At the time of writing, I have 2,966 European domestic league matches in my odds database from the current 2020/21 season (1 August to 23 December 2020). This contains two sets of home-draw-away match odds – pre-closing and closing – from Pinnacle and four recreational bookmakers (bet365, bwin, Interwetten and BetVictor). Having removed the margin from Pinnacle's pre-closing, 952 expected value bets were identified where the pre-closing odds at the four recreational bookmakers were longer than Pinnacle's margin-free odds, following the Wisdom of the Pinnacle Crowd methodology I described before. I'm not interested in their actual return. I've already proved that over the long term this methodology works. For the record, the expected yield from these 952 bets was 1.72%. Here, I want to find out how many of these recreational odds shortened by closing, by how much on average, and how likely it is that could happen by chance in my sample. My hypothesis is that because the recreational bookmakers were offering this expected value, on average we should witness a shortening by closing, as bettors move in to exploit the opportunities.

My prediction was confirmed. The average pre-closing to closing price ratio for this sample was 1.0394, implying the former was 3.94% longer on average. Of the 952 bets, only 196 (or 20.6%) actually lengthened, the other 756 (79.4%) either remained unchanged or shortened. That's a good start, but couldn't this have just happened by chance? We can find out by running a Monte Carlo simulation. From the 2,966 matches, I have a total of 44,336 pre-closing to closing price ratios. The average ratio was 1.0018. From this population I randomly selected 952 ratios and calculated their average, repeating this 10,000 times, and counted the number that were greater than 1.0394, the average ratio in my actual sample. There was none. Indeed, the highest, 1.0169, was not even close. I've plotted their frequency distribution below.

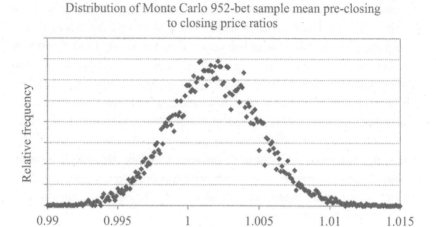

Distribution of Monte Carlo 952-bet sample mean pre-closing to closing price ratios

If I can't randomly pick a sample of 952 price ratios with a mean of 1.0394 in 10,000 Monte Carlo iterations, how many would I need before I would find one? My computer isn't powerful enough to attempt it. 10,000 iterations took me 30 minutes to run. In fact, I would need about 4 nonillion; that's 4 followed by 31 zeros. To perform this simulation in a sensible timescale would require a Matrioshka brain, a hypothesised computational power of such magnitude that it has an entire star as its energy source. Fortunately, I don't need to run the simulation; I can just use Excel to calculate the standard deviation in the data plotted above – it was 0.00316 – and count by how many of them my sample mean of 1.039 exceeds the population mean of 1.0018. You may recall that this is a z-score. The z-score for my sample mean is 11.8. Plugging this into a p-value calculator returns a probability of 0.00000000000000000000000000000027. It is somewhat of an understatement to say that this surpasses all significance testing thresholds, whether 5%, 1%, 0.1% or whatever more stringent level you would prefer. Suffice it to say, stuff like this cannot happen by chance; it is, to all intents and purposes, statistically impossible. The conclusion must then be that something caused my sample of 952 bets to have a mean price change ratio far beyond what could have happened by chance. The obvious candidate is that as the expected value made available by the recreational bookmakers was exploited, they were forced to shorten their prices.

I suppose none of this is rocket science. Intuitively, it's probably obvious to most of you by now that such a price shortening would be expected from a betting methodology such as this. The more relevant point, however, is the speed at which we've identified a signal (with a causal relationship between input and response) against the background noise of randomness. Typically, for betting systems with a mean expected value of 1.72%, I would need many thousands of wagers to demonstrate any meaningful statistical evidence of skill against bookmakers' margins. By using price movements instead, I could achieve this in as few as 65 bets. To show you how, take a look at the distribution again above. With a mean of just over 1, you can see it's slightly skewed towards the right-hand side. It's not a normal distribution, but it's not far off. In fact, the best distribution to describe these price movements is the lognormal distribution, where the logarithm of the price movements will be normally distributed. However, because the size of the standard deviation is so small relative to the mean, the normal distribution provides a good approximation. Knowing this, we can sidestep the Monte Carlo simulation altogether and simply calculate the standard error of the sample mean (SE), for any sample size of bets. Remember, the formula is given by $\sigma/\sqrt{n}$, where σ is the standard deviation in the data population. Here, the population is the 44,336 price changes, and the standard deviation in the price ratios is 0.09854. With $n = 952$, SE = 0.00319, exceedingly close to the figure from the Monte Carlo simulation. Fewer bets (smaller n) will increase the standard error of the sample mean price ratio, decrease the z-score and increase the probability of seeing 1.039. The chart below shows how the p-value changes exponentially as n changes linearly, assuming an observed mean of 1.039. For clarity I've show the p-value axis as a logarithmic one, so the relationship appears as a straight line.

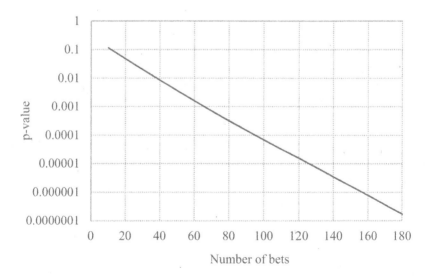

How are we acquiring information about the presence of a real causal mechanism in a betting methodology so quickly? The answer is variance. To be more specific, the variance in expectation, measured here by the proxy indicator of price movement (according to the hypothesis that prices change in response to information and money), is far, far smaller than the variance in results. Results come in 1s and 0s, or +1s and -1s for profits and losses. Expectation, here, is measured in much smaller percentage increments. Hence, deviations from the mean are much narrower; when we find one that stands out from the crowd, it's much easier to claim that it cannot have arisen by chance alone. As I demonstrated earlier with the Pinnacle opening to closing price ratio, the best proxy measure we have of expectation is the closing line, and your ability to beat it. Measuring the amount by which you do so can give you a much faster conclusion to the question: do I hold expected value? All good bettors, like Spanky, understand this. Don't waste so much of your time looking at your results, even though it is useful to know by how much they can vary. Nearly always, in the short term at least, they will simply reflect how lucky you've been. Instead, focus on whether your prediction methodology brings useful information to the betting market that is capable of moving the odds. If you can move them by more than the bookmaker's margin on average, you will have become an advantage bettor.

For every action there is a reaction, as Turkish said in the film *Snatch*. (I think Sir Isaac Newton once said something similar too.) For every bettor who eulogises about the merits of the efficiency of the closing line, there's another waiting and wanting to debunk it. Sadly, the vast majority of those bettors who do are using their results to counter the hypothesis. 'If I'm winning, who cares about the closing line?' As I've argued, that's largely a waste of time; results usually take too long to prove anything much at all. Occasionally, however, I do come across a betting history which appears, on the face of it, to buck the trend. One of them that I am familiar with comes from the professional tennis tipster Nishikori, not to be confused with the Japanese tennis professional, although presumably the choice of name is not a coincidence. By the spring of 2021, his record was showing a 9% yield from over 3,400 picks placed with the sharp bookmaker Pinnacle. Yet, on average, over this period, Nishikori had moved the odds only enough to cover their margin. Instead of losing 2 to 3% betting at the closing line, you'd actually be making about 6%. What are we to make of the hypothesis that the closing line is efficient in view of data like this?

There are a number of possible explanations. Let's look at them in turn. First of all, 'efficient' really means efficient on average. Think back to the evidence I presented for Pinnacle's closing line efficiency in their football match odds. The data resolution was 1%. Within each 1% range I was analysing many hundreds, thousands, or sometimes tens of thousands of odds and counting the winners. For example, if we group all the bets together with 'true' odds of 2.00, do half of them win? If the answer is yes, then this implies efficiency. But what is happening within that subgroup? The fact that half win and half lose only tells us that the random influences of aleatory uncertainty have evened up lucky and unlucky outcomes, leaving the signal of a 50% win rate. Aleatory uncertainty to one modeller, however, may be epistemic to another, if they are armed with a superior model capable of deconstructing unknowns and demonstrating causal connections between variables and their influences. Viewed in this light, definitions of what aleatory or epistemic mean then depend on the knowledge capabilities of the prediction modeller: an uncertainty is aleatory if the modeller thinks it cannot be practically reduced in the near term without superior modelling techniques and epistemic otherwise. Indeed, Poincaré would go as far as to say that there is no such thing as aleatory uncertainty at all, provided we have a powerful enough means of acquiring enough knowledge to reduce all aleatory uncertainty to causal determinism. All this being the case, better modellers may be capable of finding predictive variables which, once known, would move some of the odds in the 50% win probability category to a different one. Given that the bookmaker has put them there, the existence of such odds would then necessarily imply that they were mistakes, or inefficiencies to give them their technical term. If the modeller can systematically spot those inefficiencies in a way the bookmaker is unable to, then this can give them the advantage they are looking for, yet leaving the larger pool of odds, from which they came, still looking like they are efficient, on average. The fact that Nishikori says he does all his modelling intuitively, in his head, without serious computational quantification makes this all the more remarkable.

On its own, however, this argument doesn't really stand up to scrutiny. We may accept that efficient means efficient on average, and that mistakes in individual odds do exist. However, if there are bettors capable of exploiting those mistakes, shouldn't the bookmakers be aware that they are doing so? Via artificial intelligence, they can easily profile bettors and see if their bets correlate with shorter prices by closing. If sufficient volume of money is being wagered, they can then choose to mark their account. Perhaps, then, this implies Nishikori, and his subscribers, are not betting in sufficient volumes to force such a reaction, and the small amount that they move odds is not sufficient to trigger a manual investigation into their activity. Alternatively, if they are, they are doing so via agents or brokers meaning their volume might be harder to differentiate from the rest that comes with theirs. I've heard it on authority that this explanation would be unlikely; Pinnacle, for the most part, can still track sharp activity coming via a third party, unless it's arriving by stealth; being a public tipster like Nishikori would hardly qualify for that.

In 2021 Nishikori's closing line value ticked up. This coincided with a decision to begin issuing picks later when larger stake limits are available. Typically, the later the market, the larger the limits, with the largest available at closing when the bookmaker has potentially secured the greatest level of protection against liabilities. Later money, then, usually means smaller price movements. It is thus surprising to see a significant increase in Nishikori's closing line value. As of 18 March, I've counted 61 picks (on his Twitter feed where he posted the closing price) since the start of 2021. 54 of them shortened, with an average movement of 7%. After accounting for Pinnacle's margin, this is still short of what the closing line value hypothesis would predict, but the gap is narrowing. Perhaps this is evidence, after all, that Pinnacle have finally recognised Nishikori's expertise.

Of course, the weight of money on its own does not always correlate with the size of a price move. The largest bets aside, a lot of what might be called 'public money', or 'square' or 'dumb' if we wanted to be a little more derogatory, might cause little reaction at all. Indeed, as Spanky has said, *'in most cases public money is ignored by most bookmakers. A very sharp old-time bookie once told me "I just stick public bets in my pocket like they don't exist."'* A lot of dumb money might present a liability for the bookmakers, but if they are confident about the accuracy of their line, they might be prepared to hold it. Yes, you lose some and you win some with such a strategy, but the law of large numbers offers protection in the long run. Balanced action might be an aspiration, but if taking positions against dumb money increases the profit margins, well, then why not take them?

On the other hand, a little bit of sharp money might cause a much bigger reaction, provided, of course, the bookmakers have identified the source as sharper than they are. That, of course, is easier said than done. For the bookmakers to react, they would need to believe that they've made a mistake; but how can they be sure when the 'true' odds can never be known, particularly whilst they may continue to believe their own prediction models will be superior? Over time they might look at the bettor's results, but we've already seen how long that might take to force a change of opinion. If Pinnacle are not reacting to Nishikori in the way his results suggest they ought to be, we must conclude that they still do not fully recognise his information as a much better measure of 'true' probabilities than their own. Sharp enough, as of 2021, to move the line by 7% perhaps – that much is clear, and it's certainly not chance – but not sharp enough to move it by 12%, as would be predicted by the closing line value hypothesis, assuming Nishikori's actual yield of 9% is not lucky. For the bookmaker, trying to ascertain the 'true' price is a balancing act between weighting the relative merits of their prediction model, the information their sharper customers bring (and determining who the sharper customers might be), and the volume of money brought to their market by both sharps and squares alike. This process can be as subjective as it can be quantitative; I once tried to model it, probably very badly. Bookmaking is as much an art as it is a science. We can only have varying degrees of belief about who might be more accurate, and who less so. However, one thing is clear: if Pinnacle are mistaken in their judgment about Nishikori, then this implies his plays remain inefficient by closing. In this instance, then, using the closing line to measure your expected value will be misleading, as it evidently appears to be for Nishikori.

Despite Nishikori, there must surely be some customers for whom the closing line **does** more accurately predict their expected value, right? Indeed, Pinnacle's head of trading, Marco Blume, is not one to shy away from talking about his sharpest customers, 'clients', as he calls them, who help him to shape his lines after he has opened them. Is it really credible to argue that all of Pinnacle's 'clients' could be responsible for inefficient closing lines like Nishikori, and yet the closing line, on average, be as efficient as it demonstrably is? Someone must be making Pinnacle's closing lines more efficient than the opening ones, even if it isn't currently Nishikori for the bets he advises. You can't have 'efficient on average' if every price is individually inefficient, can you? Well, actually, you could via a cognitive bias known as price anchoring, but it would be a stretch to believe that its influence was so widespread as to singularly account for what's being proposed, and it's not worth a lengthy detour to talk about it here. It would certainly not meet the principle of Occam's razor, where the simplest explanation is more likely. It might sometimes also be conceivable that the best 'clients' putting down the most money could cause an overreaction to a line or a price, as the bookmakers scramble to defend their liabilities, particularly in markets where their stake limits are smaller and for which they have less understanding, or where proven tipsters with large followings seed the market with large volumes quickly. In such cases, then, the closing line value is equally unreliable since it will not necessarily reflect the 'true' line. In the biggest markets, however, this is not likely to be common, with the exception, perhaps, for the biggest and sharpest bettors, but in truth there aren't very many of those.

Why, then, do I believe that there are sharp bettors for whom the closing line value provides an accurate measure of their expected value? Put simply, it's because I've seen betting records where it is, and that **cannot** happen by chance. One example is illustrated below. It's a history from a professional bettor who places considerable emphasis on making a large number of bets – mostly football (both the European and American versions), basketball and tennis – for the purposes, as he puts it, of slaying the 'variance monster'. This sample of 14,743, for which closing odds were available, comes from bets made in 2019 only. The average odds were 2.053 and the average expected closing line value was 2.48%. Whilst the bettor didn't bet with 1-unit stakes, I've analysed the record as such.

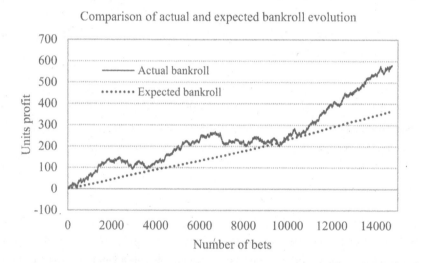

Comparison of actual and expected bankroll evolution

In fact, the yield from this sample, at 3.94%, was better than expected, although for the most part the actual bankroll tracked the trend that would have been predicted by his closing line value pretty closely. The deviation from expectation by the end of 2019, however, is not one that I would regard as statistically significant, and thus no reason to throw out the closing line value hypothesis. Using my yield distribution calculator, the actual performance sits at roughly the 96th percentile, meaning it would be bettered 4% of the time by chance, assuming the closing line value hypothesis to be true. Since I would demand a minimum of 99.9% before having doubts about the hypothesis, I'm quite happy that the performance in the final 4,000 bets is just a matter of good fortune.

What of Nishikori's actual performance? 3,400+ tips and a yield of over 9%. Given the amount that he's exceeding expectation by, his record is arguably already long enough for Pinnacle to consider him as worthy of 'client' status. Relative to an expectation of Pinnacle's margin, Nishikori's actual record could be expected to happen by chance alone (assuming no predictive talent on his part) about once in 34 million times. Even relative to Pinnacle's closing line, it is close to 1-in-100,000. That should be enough to rule out luck as the only explanation, so why haven't Pinnacle done it? Perhaps in 2021 they finally did. The fact that it might have taken so long is testament to Pinnacle's adherence to the principle of expected value, a total disregard of outcomes as a sign of anything other than chance, and complete faith in their own modellers. They do consider the information that Nishikori brings to their market as having some value in shaping that 'true' probability but as of 2021, still only about half what would be expected. Hence, I am still left wondering why? I can offer three more possibilities.

The first is that Pinnacle have to consider not just Nishikori's information but the information of other sharp bettors. Nishikori won't be right about the 'true' price all the time, and sometimes there'll be another sharp bettor betting the other side to him. Pinnacle are then faced with a decision: whose information do they pay more attention to? Sometimes Nishikori might be right, sometimes the other sharp bettor, but Pinnacle must assume that they are both bringing information on average. Hence, any movement, one way or another will be muted, until such time as Pinnacle have a clearer view about the relative abilities of both sharp bettors. Sounds plausible? Hmmm, I don't know.

The second is that Nishikori has access to insider information. Nishikori has unsurprisingly denied this since profiting from insider information in a sports betting market is illegal, and on that I must trust him. Whilst we should note from his profile that *'he prefers not to make his identity public because he's somehow related to the professional tennis world'*, this does not imply he has access to insider information. However, it might very well mean access to knowledge that would not typically be reflected in Pinnacle's betting models, and the models of their 'clients' also betting on the events that Nishikori advises. Hence, when he brings money to the market, it may not be obvious to Pinnacle what information that represents. Marco's job is to figure out what information a 'client' brings to his market. If he can do that, he can update his own model and no longer needs to pay the 'client' for their information, in the form of expected profits. You can listen to Marco on one of his podcasts describe the frustrations he experiences when he just can't figure it out. Perhaps he's not yet figured Nishikori out, or if, finally, he has, it took him a long time.

The final possibility is that Pinnacle are actively seeking an inefficient price. Rather than making a mistake, it **is** their intention to leave expected value at the closing line. Expected value, of course, is in the eye of the beholder. Sharp bettors often see the source of expected value in completely different places to square bettors, who typically don't see any value at all, just an illusion of some via their cognitive biases. As mentioned earlier, squares display a preference for betting the 'over'. If enough of them do, the bookmakers can actually shift the line to increase their expected profit, provided the squares don't notice. For example, if 60% of the money is placed on 'over' in a 1.95/1.95 totals market where the true probabilities are 48%/52%, the bookmakers will see their expected profit increase from 2.5% to 3.3%. The sharps betting the 'under', where 'true' odds are 1.923 (1/0.52) will have been given free value but provided the larger amount of square money doesn't notice what's been done, it's a cost the bookmakers will arguably be willing to pay. Given the biases that we suffer, most of us will be readily fooled by this deception.

Some of the volume on the other side to Nishikori's bets might also be arbitrage money. An arbitrage, or arb for short, occurs where a bettor can bet on all possible outcomes and make a profit no matter what the result. Obviously, that can't happen at just one bookmaker; remember, they are businesses, not charities. Arbs can, however, be created by using more. Suppose a two-way proposition is priced 2.05/1.90 by bookmaker A, and 1.90/2.05 by bookmaker B. Betting both 2.05s guarantees a profit of 2.5%. As noted earlier, recreational bookmakers like to advertise value prices. Whilst they are intolerant of bettors who attempt to routinely exploit their generosity, that doesn't stop the bettors trying. Pinnacle only need ensure that the price offered on the other side to Nishikori's bet is long enough to allow the arbitrage opportunity to exist. If they can achieve that by shortening that price by more than their usual margin, then why not, if that is the price that's attracting the majority of the volume? So long as the recreational bookmaker insists on being more inefficient than Pinnacle, and so long as the arb money continues to flow, Pinnacle will have little incentive to push the line towards the 'true' number. Consequently, expected value will persist on the side bet by Nishikori, potentially even as late as the closing line. Hence, it will fail to give us a reliable picture of Nishikori's true expected value.

Nishikori, then, may be betting in markets that Pinnacle is intentionally biasing to increase their expected profit margin. Is there any evidence for this? Well, possibly. I have previously attempted to measure the efficiency of tennis matches, using a sample of 136,722 odds from ATP, WTA, Challenger and Futures tournaments played between May 2015 and July 2019, in the same way I explained for football earlier; remove the margin from the closing odds, calculate a ratio of the opening to fair closing price and investigate whether this number correlates with actual returns. The correlation is reasonable but weaker than for football. This doesn't necessarily imply any inefficiency that is present is intentional. Rather, it might just mean that tennis as a sport is less well understood by bookmakers than football. I suspect that won't be true of the highest level ATP and WTA game, but perhaps more so for Challengers and Futures, where much lower volumes of money are wagered, and hence a more disproportionate influence by sharp bettors could sometimes void the usefulness of the closing line as a proxy for the true number.

Firstly, however, Nishikori doesn't tip on Challengers and Futures, only the most liquid ATP tournaments. Secondly, and perhaps more importantly, what inefficiency might be indicated by my analysis is not enough to account for the disparity between Nishikori's closing line value and actual yield. Even in 2021 the difference is still about 5%, after Pinnacle's margin has been taken into account. Consider for a minute what a 5% inefficiency would mean. If it were a consequence of an intentional bias introduced by the bookmaker to exploit public money, in a 50-50 market this would be equivalent to shifting the win probabilities to 46%/54%, with all the usual suspects failing to notice. Common sense tells me that's unlikely. Cognitive biases might be strong enough to blur the distinction between 49% and 50%, perhaps even 48%, but increase the manipulation a little more, and bettors' behavioural judgements would likely snap to a new equilibrium, with fewer of them backing the side being manipulated by the bookmaker. With regard to arbs, it would require soft bookmakers to be systematically offering some seriously ridiculous value to allow Pinnacle to get away with it.

On the face of it, Nishikori seems far more than just lucky, but if that is true, Pinnacle should be recognising this more than they do. Maybe in 2021 they finally are, and all this discussion is rather redundant. Perhaps, additionally, at the end of the day, there are simply occasions where your expected closing line value matters, for example where you are attempting to incorporate public information faster than the bookmaker; and then there are other occasions, niche, low-volume markets, for example, or where you are accounting for something that the market isn't trying to account for, when it doesn't. Perhaps, on the other hand, it's even simpler than that. Perhaps Nishikori just happens to be so much better at what he does than Pinnacle. If he knew what his 'true' number was, we could test such a premise, but sadly all his forecasting is done intuitively, so that will have to remain a conjecture. Of course, if Nishikori **really is** so much better at what he does than Marco, or to be more precise, if Marco knows it, I rather suspect Marco would be offering Nishikori a job.

I'm afraid I've reached the limit of my thought process about Nishikori. I suspect all the reasons I've discussed here to account for his lack of closing line value may be at play in some small way, including a little bit of good luck too. I think there is nothing in betting more likely to stir vigorous debate amongst serious bettors than the significance of closing line value. I've done my best to encourage this debate here, but the bottom line is I don't know why Nishikori doesn't move the closing line by more than he does, and in large part that's because I've never experienced life as a bookmaker. I've presented the evidence; I must leave you to draw your own conclusions. I know a man who has, and who is arguably better placed than I am to make a judgement about all of this. His name is Matthew Trenhaile; you can often listen to his views about bookmakers, betting, markets and closing line value on his Insider Betting podcasts available via several platforms and read his insightful blogs on the medium.com platform. Having been a trader for both bookmakers and betting syndicates, I am sure that he would provide a valuable insight into the puzzle that is Nishikori. Maybe it's not a puzzle at all. Maybe it's just another uncertainty that defines betting.

Irrespective of the validity of the hypothesis of closing line efficiency, the fact that there are bettors who beat the closing line is an important observation for the following reason. Given that we've proven it's so unlikely to happen by chance alone after even a small sample of bets, when it does, you can be sure that something is making that happen. If nothing else, this provides a signal to the bettor that they are being noticed in some way. That doesn't necessarily mean the bookmaker is reacting directly to their money; it could mean that the bettor has access to information which the bookmaker did not at the time the bettor struck the bet, but which by market closing had become incorporated into the price because other sharp bettors had access to that information as well. This signal is important because it provides an independent measure of the impact the information you hold has, directly or indirectly, on the market. Should the hypothesis of closing line efficiency hold water, by extension it will also provide a signal of your expected value. The professional bettor 'Danshan', who has developed his own betting app for use on the crypto betting exchange Fairlay, and who is the owner of the betting history I showed you a few pages earlier, calls it his 'cliff edge detector'. Danshan's bible is the efficient closing line hypothesis; anything that deviates from it is just variance, nothing more, nothing less, or insider information which is unavailable to the bookmaker if the deviation is too large to be reasonably explained by variance. We can debate all night and all of the following day the relative merits of Danshan and Nishikori's positions, but what is not in doubt is the usefulness of the closing line as some kind of detection system for the sustainability of your advantage. Your closing line value might not correlate perfectly with your 'true' expected value but if you have any of the former, we have to find some explanation for it, even for the little bit that Nishikori has; it can't be random, and Nishikori's closing line value is most definitely not random, it's just not as much as the hypothesis would predict. The most likely explanation is that your money brings information to the market, and if it's bigger than the bookmaker's margin, there's a decent chance that you have found expected value. The corollary is that if you lose your closing line value, you may well have lost your edge. The fact that you can learn this so quickly is the most valuable aspect of your cliff edge detector. Betting is so often like walking along the edge of a cliff; the line that divides positive and negative expected value is narrow. You want a detection system that will tell you when you're overstepping the edge and save you before you crash to the bottom. Just watching your profits and losses will, for the majority, end with a nasty mess.

Perhaps we can reconcile Nishikori's and Danshan's positions like this: if you don't move the line, that doesn't necessarily imply your prediction model holds no expected value; if, however, you do, it's virtually certain that it does.

Roll with the Punches

So J.R. Miller was right. What separates professional bettors and chronic losers is really rather small. It is the compounding of your expected value via the law of large numbers that will determine which side of the divide you find yourself. He also had something else to say about winning. *'The novice thinks you should have more money each day. [In fact], 19 out of 20 days you will be below your bankroll high.'* Miller was specifically talking about a 55% win expectation in point spreads. How did he arrive at this conclusion? We can run some Monte Carlo simulations to find out.

Let's consider first a hypothetical case: one 50-50 bet proposition with fair odds of 2.00. What is the probability my bankroll will show a new high after this bet? Obviously, the answer is 50%, since if I win, my bankroll will be higher than it was before, and if I lose it will be lower. What about after a second similar bet? There are four possible outcomes: win-win, win-lose, lose-win and lose-

lose. In the first I see a new high twice. In the second, just once, and in the third and fourth, a don't see any at all. Thus, the probability has dropped to 3/8th or 37.5%. With three bets, there are now 8 possible win-lose sequences and 24 possible opportunities for reaching a high, but only 8 of them will see it happen, reducing the probability further to one third or 33.33%. As the number of bets increases in the betting history, the probability of seeing the bankroll reaching a new high at any point during it will continue to diminish, but at an ever-decreasing rate. I spent a morning attempting to derive the relationship from mathematical principles but had to abandon the quest; it was just too complex for me to visualise, so I let Monte Carlo provide the approximation. The chart below shows the relationship for fair odds, and also where you may hold either negative or positive expected value (EV). I performed 10,000 iterations for each scenario, up to a maximum history of 1,000 bets.

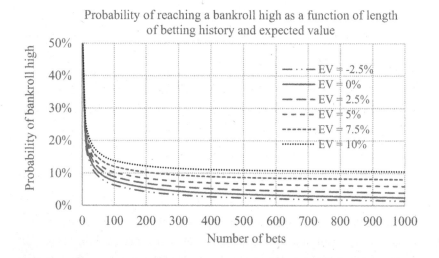

Probability of reaching a bankroll high as a function of length of betting history and expected value

You can clearly see that after just a handful of bets, your probability of witnessing another bankroll high after the next bet is small, even where you hold profitable expected value. The relationship between the length of your betting history and your chances of seeing a new high is approximated by a power law.

J.R. Miller was right again. Nearly all of the time you are going to be below your bankroll high. The scenario that most closely matches his 55% win percentage is EV = 5%. After 100 bets, your probability of seeing a bankroll high is about 10%. After 1,000 bets that's fallen to about 6%. And after 10,000 it's a little over 5%, pretty much in line with what he had suggested. Below are four example histories of 1,000 1-unit bets, where the bettor holds 5% expected value at odds of 2. There were just 66, 25, 41 and 107 occasions respectively when the bankroll reached a new high. Alongside each one is a schematic illustrating their timing. There are some considerable gaps between some of them.

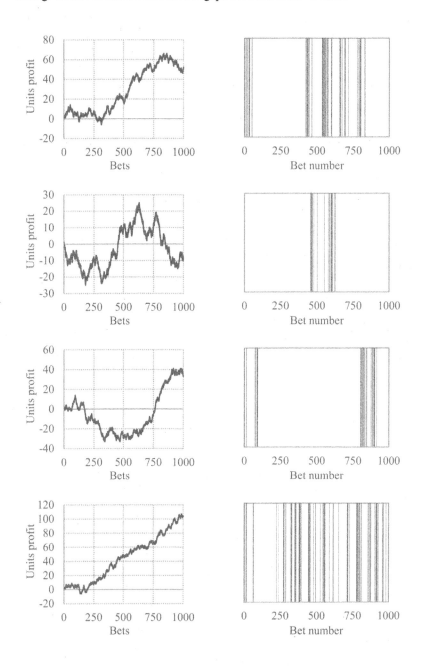

Those figures should tell you that there's quite a range of possible outcomes about the expected figure. We've already seen there's quite a variance in possible yields over 1,000 wagers. Understandably, the luckier iterations in the simulation will see a larger number of bets where a new bankroll high is achieved; the correlation is strong, as the next figure illustrates.

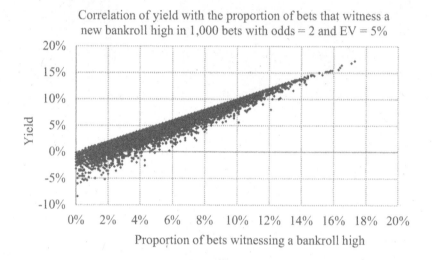

Correlation of yield with the proportion of bets that witness a new bankroll high in 1,000 bets with odds = 2 and EV = 5%

Yet even the luckiest of the 10,000 Monte Carlo iterations, with a yield of 17.2%, actually only witnessed a bankroll high in 173 of the 1,000 bets. The distribution of the proportion of bets witnessing a bankroll high is shown below.

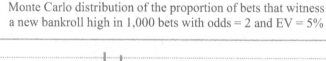

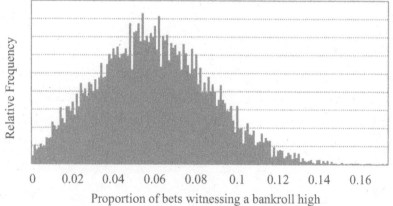

Monte Carlo distribution of the proportion of bets that witness a new bankroll high in 1,000 bets with odds = 2 and EV = 5%

To reiterate, nearly all of the time you are going to have less money than you had at some earlier time. Given that we are averse to losses, we can readily appreciate how psychologically challenging this may be. Without defence mechanisms to guard against the negative emotions that will undoubtedly arise, bettors may become liable to making irrational decisions in an attempt to correct a problem that doesn't actually need correcting. Throwing out positive expected values methods, or worse still, chasing previous losses by increasing stakes, would be two obvious errors of judgement. On the contrary, get used to having less than you once did. The law of large numbers will incrementally increase your bankroll highs little by little; just accept that there can be long intervening periods waiting for the next one to arrive. Or to put it another way: learn to roll with the punches.

We've looked at 50-50 betting propositions. What happens when the win probability changes? Take a look. Each 10,000-iteration simulation in the chart below again assumes the bettor holds an expected advantage of 5%.

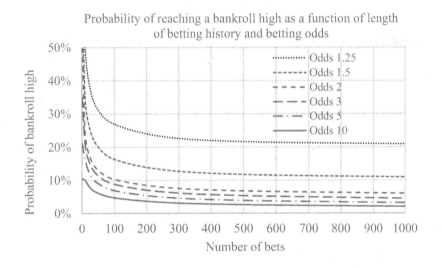

Probability of reaching a bankroll high as a function of length of betting history and betting odds

The lower the probability of winning, the lower the probability of reaching a new bankroll high. Again, it's a variance thing, although it's probably perfectly intuitive anyway. If you win less often, you reach a new high less often. Nevertheless, it's well worth being aware of the probabilities. A bettor who bets odds of 10 with expected value 5% will see new highs on average just 20 times in 1,000 wagers. Of course, advantage bettors who prefer longer odds are likely to hold more expected value than those who prefer shorter odds, again simply because of variance, although remember, this does not imply they are statistically superior. Making 1,000 bets at odds of 1.25 with a 5% advantage will be profitable 99.97% of the time. For an equivalent probability when betting odds of 10, your advantage would be 37.5%. Despite that, you'd still only be witnessing new highs 70 times in 1,000, compared to over 200 betting odds of 1.25. In the chart below, I've summarised how the likelihood of witnessing a new bankroll high during 1,000 wagers changes as a function of your expected value, for the six different odds. The longer your odds, the less impact a superior expected value will have.

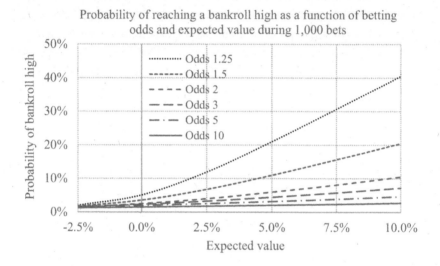

Probability of reaching a bankroll high as a function of betting odds and expected value during 1,000 bets

If you like the feel-good factor of winning and seeing your bankroll grow higher and higher more regularly, long-odds betting is probably not for you. Indeed, in terms of attaining new highs, average odds of anything over about 2 are going to present a challenge to anyone who really dislikes long periods without seeing them. I took the trouble to test my Wisdom of the Crowd history I discussed earlier in the chapter. It has average odds of 3.89. From a 1,000-iteration Monte Carlo simulation, the expected percentage of bets witnessing a new bankroll high during the 11,894-bet history was 2.50%. The expected average number of bets between highs was 42. Of course, their distribution will be highly asymmetric, with some terrifyingly large gaps indeed. The highest was 10,327, whilst the average largest was 2,590. Imagine that, yet all the while holding a 4% advantage over the bookmakers' odds. For the record, the actual history witnessed new highs in 2.53% of bets, with an average gap between them of 40, the largest being 2,588. These figures are almost identical to the Monte

Carlo predictions. Such data tells me there will have been many an advantage bettor, and not necessarily the unluckiest ones, who will ultimately choose a different career path simply because of a failure to understand the expectations associated with winning, and the psychological challenges such a failure will present. Finding an advantage in sports betting is hard enough; few bettors manage to achieve it over the long term beyond the influence of luck. Yet even proven winners will have to moderate their expectations of profitability. The psychology of losing is perhaps the most important reason why aspiring bettors will ultimately fail; so it is losing to which I will now turn my attention.

LOSING

Winning a bet is a nice feeling. Losing, however, is considered by cognitive psychologists to be at least twice as painful, psychologically speaking, as winning is enjoyed. Occasionally, a bettor's response to losing, particularly a run of losses, can lead to reckless behaviour, either betting more often or betting more money, in an attempt to recover their losses. One of the causes is a self-serving bias, where success is ascribed to internal factors like one's own abilities and hard work, but where failure is ascribed to external factors like chance. 'I win because I'm clever, I lose because I'm unlucky' so the logic goes. 'Bad luck won't last, right? That's the law of averages. I'll up my stakes to take advantage when it turns.' Somewhat bizarrely, sharp bettors may experience a kind of reversed self-serving bias, with an excessive attribution of negative outcomes to internal causes. Underperforming expectation and a blindness towards the law of small numbers can lead to irrationally and prematurely questioning the efficacy of a good betting system. It's much easier to doubt yourself after a series of consecutive losses than a series of consecutive wins, even though in statistical terms they may have similar occurrence probabilities. This is the psychology of loss aversion. It probably won't encourage readers to learn that a reversed self-serving bias has been linked to depression and schizophrenia. As always, the cure is to ignore your results, at least in the short term, and make use of proxy measures of expected value like the closing line to tell you whether to trust your methodology. In addition to that, a solid grasp of the expectations of losing should turn what might come as surprises to many bettors into mere frustrations at the fickleness of bad luck, noted and then filed away in the recesses of the mind where they are unable to wreak havoc with one's emotions.

The Expectation of Losing

Consider someone who's clever enough, on average, to just overcome the bookmaker's margin. If the bookmaker's odds are efficient, then their expectation will be to break even. The odds they are betting are, on average, the 'true' odds, which reflect the 'true' probability of a result. What is the probability such a bettor will lose k consecutive bets, where k is some integer number above zero? It's easier to first think about the probability of winning k consecutive bets. If the 'true' odds of winning are o, then the probability of winning is 1/o. Following the multiplication rule, the probability of winning two bets, both with odds o, is 1/o multiplied by 1/o, or $(1/o)^2$. For a sequence of k bets, the probability would be $(1/o)^k$. We also know from the complementary rule that if the probability of winning is 1/o, the probability of losing in binary propositions (with only two possible outcomes, win or lose) will be $1 - 1/o$. Rearranging, this is the same as:

$$\frac{o - 1}{o}$$

Thus, the probability of losing k consecutive bets, each with odds o is:

$$\left(\frac{o - 1}{o}\right)^k$$

For example, the probability of losing 3 consecutive bets with odds of 4 will be $(3/4)^3 = 27/64$, or 42.19%.

Of course, no sequence of bets happens in isolation. A sequence of losses (and wins for that matter) will occur within a much large history of bets. Suppose the total number of bets in that history is n. What, then, is the probability of having a losing sequence of k bets with odds o at some point in that series of n bets? In fact, the mathematics needed to answer this question are not trivial, and beyond what would be appropriate for a book like this. However, we can frame the question in a slightly different way; the mathematics then becomes much easier. Instead, let's ask how many times we can expect to suffer k consecutive losses in a sample of n bets with odds o. Suppose o = 2, n = 10 and k = 3; consider how many ways it is possible to put 3 consecutive losses into a sequence of 10 bets. You can have 3 consecutive losses on the first, second and third bets, the second, third and fourth bets, the third, fourth and fifth bets, and so on up to the eighth, nineth and tenth bets. That's 8 possible ways, or more generically n − (k − 1), or n + 1 − k. The number of times you can expect to see something is the probability of seeing it multiplied by the number of ways of seeing it. Hence, the expected number of times we will see at least k consecutive losing bets − let's call this e_k − in a series of n bets will be given by:

$$e_k = (n + 1 - k)\left(\frac{o-1}{o}\right)^k$$

For o = 2, n = 10 and k = 3, e_k = 1. There are 8 ways of seeing something that has a $1/8^{th}$ probability of occurring. If the odds are 3, e_k = 2.37. Obviously, you can't have 0.37 of a 3-bet losing streak, but this is an expectation, in the same way that the expected value of a die roll is 3.5. When k is much smaller than n, we can approximate this formula by

$$e_k \approx n\left(\frac{o-1}{o}\right)^k$$

since n + 1 − k is roughly n. The squiggly equals sign implies approximately equal to. For o = 2, n = 1000 and k = 3, e_k via this approximation is 125, compared to 124.75 via the full expression of the formula. e_k is proportional to n, so if the number of bets in your series doubles, so too does the expected number of losing sequences of length k. This will be true for any value of k and o. I've drawn a summary chart below to show how e_k varies as a function of k for several different values of o where n = 1,000. You could draw any number of these for different values of n.

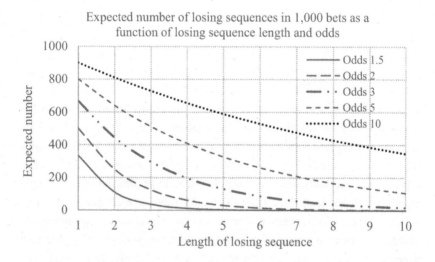

Expected number of losing sequences in 1,000 bets as a function of losing sequence length and odds

Obviously, the longer the losing sequence, the less likely it is of seeing it. e_k decreases exponentially with a linear increase in k, since it is inversely proportional to the kth power of the bet-lose probability. Plotting these curves with a logarithmic vertical axis will then display the relationships as straight lines. That is to say, the logarithm of e_k is inversely proportional to k.

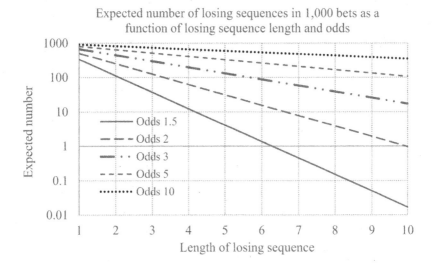

Expected number of losing sequences in 1,000 bets as a function of losing sequence length and odds

What is the longest losing sequence of bets we can expect to see, on average, in a series of n bets with the odds of winning o? If by 'on average' we are implying the arithmetic mean, then for this proposition, $e_k = 1$. If we repeated the series of n bets many times, sometimes we would see such a losing sequence more than once, other times we wouldn't see it at all, but the mean would be 1. Thus, when n is much larger than k,

$$n\left(\frac{o-1}{o}\right)^k \approx 1$$

Rearranging, we have:

$$n \approx \left(\frac{o}{o-1}\right)^k$$

And rearranging again:

$$k \approx \log_{\left(\frac{o}{o-1}\right)} n$$

where $\left(\frac{o}{o-1}\right)$ represents the base of the logarithm. Doing that sort of mathematics in your head is going to be problematic, but doing it in Excel is easy, using the function LOG(number,base). For example, if we have 1,000 bets with odds of 2, k, for $e_k = 1$, the expected longest losing sequence will be approximated by $\log_2 1000$. In Excel this would be =LOG(1000,2). The answer is 9.97. The nearest integer to this expected value is 10, for which $e_k = 0.968$. Sometimes we'll see more than one 10-bet losing streak, other times we won't see any. I ran a 100,000-iteration Monte Carlo simulation to find the distribution. I've plotted it below.

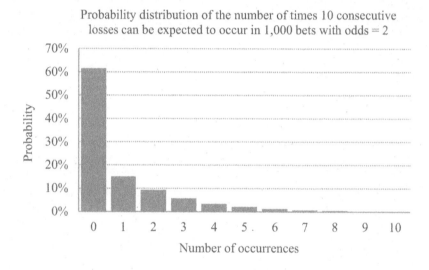

Probability distribution of the number of times 10 consecutive losses can be expected to occur in 1,000 bets with odds = 2

Incidentally, the average number of 10-bet losing streaks per 1,000-bet iteration was 0.969, almost exactly the same as that predicted by the mathematics. The highest in any iteration was 21, with the frequency of occurrence decreasing exponentially. In fact, the chances of seeing 10 or more are about 38.5%. Similarly, whilst 10 consecutive losses would typically be the longest losing sequence we would see, that doesn't mean there won't sometimes be longer ones. Remember, 10 (or to be more precise 9.97) is just an expectation for the longest on average. The next chart shows the probability distribution (based on the Monte Carlo output) of the actual longest losing streak in the 100,000 iterations. The longest was 27, but it only happened once. Anything above 15 has less than a 1% probability.

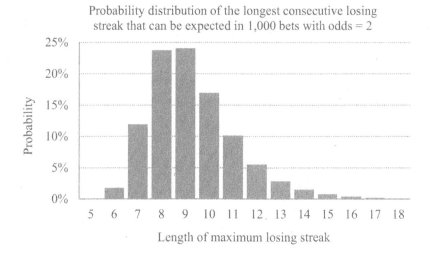

Probability distribution of the longest consecutive losing streak that can be expected in 1,000 bets with odds = 2

Even 10 consecutive losses at odds of 2 is considerable and might challenge the confidence of a lot of bettors. Fortunately, because k is approximately proportional to the logarithm of n, it won't grow quickly. To double k, we'd need to square n. Thus, we'd need a series of about 1 million bets before we might expect to see a losing streak of 20. Obviously, for longer odds, the length of losing streaks will grow; that's hardly surprising. For odds of 5, for example, we'd expect to see a losing streak of 31 during the course of 1,000 bets, but the doubling-squaring rule still applies, no matter what the odds. The chart below shows how the expected longest losing streak (k, for $e_k = 1$) varies as a function of the number of bets (n) drawn logarithmically, for a number of different odds.

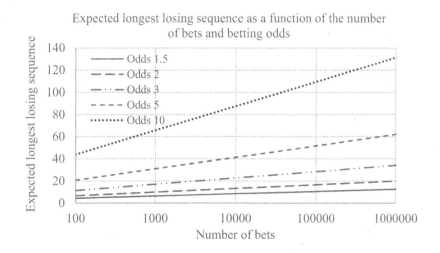

Expected longest losing sequence as a function of the number of bets and betting odds

Remember of course, 31 is just the expectation. It's always possible to see longer. In another Monte Carlo simulation with 100,000 iterations, I found one losing streak of 77. Standing on its own that has just a 1-in-290 million chance of occurring, but about 1 in 100,000 bettors making 1,000 wagers with odds of 5 will be unlucky enough to see it, assuming they can last that long.

There is an important consequence of the logarithmic relationship between k and n: the frequency of losing runs (and winning runs, for that matter) is far more dependent on luck than expected value. Sharp bettors will see almost the same frequencies of losing streaks as square bettors. Let me show you why. All the charts I've shown in this section have assumed that the odds are 'true' and fair, meaning the expected value is 0%. Let's instead consider two bettors, one square who's expected value, dictated by the margin, is -2.5%, the other sharp, who's expected value is +2.5%. If the 'true' odds were 2, implying a true win percentage of 50%, the difference between these two bettors in terms of prediction success would be 2.5%. The square bettor would have an expected success rate of 48.75% whilst the sharp bettor would have an expected success rate of 51.25%. Translating these values into odds, we have 2.051 and 1.951. For a series of 1,000 bets, the expected longest losing streaks for the square and sharp bettor are then 10.33 and 9.61. If you were just looking at losing streaks, you'd hardly notice the difference between the two bettors. I've plotted the probability distribution for the longest losing streak for the two bettors below, this time using a line rather than a histogram to aid the comparison. When bettors have expressed annoyance at my suggestion that almost everything that happens in betting is chance, perhaps this will help illustrate why I am right.

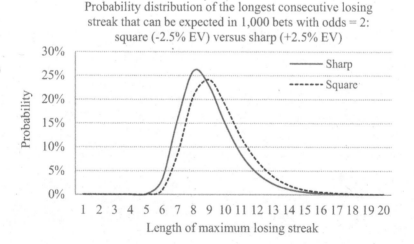

Probability distribution of the longest consecutive losing streak that can be expected in 1,000 bets with odds = 2: square (-2.5% EV) versus sharp (+2.5% EV)

Expectation is one thing, but when the probability distribution is so skewed it's not so helpful at telling us the probability of seeing and exceeding any particular losing streak length. My mathematics are not up to the job, so as you've probably guessed, we can use the Monte Carlo simulation to help us again. The next chart shows the cumulative probability, inferred from the simulation by counting the maximum losing streaks, of seeing a losing streak equal to or greater than k during a series of 1,000 bets with odds of 2. Alongside the curve for the break-even bettor (0% EV), I've also shown those for the sharp (+2.5% EV) and square (-2.5% EV). Again, you can see that the differences are small, with most of the distribution nothing to do with predictive ability at all.

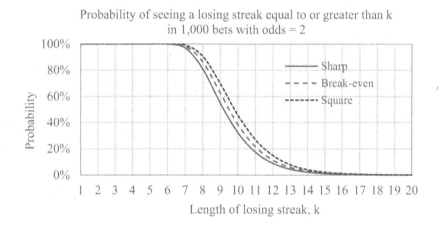

I've drawn another one for different betting odds for a break-even bettor.

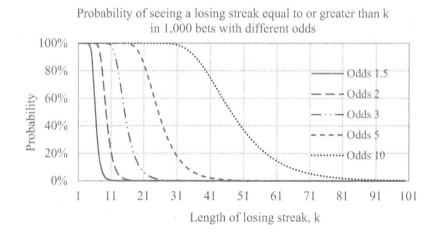

What happens if we change the size of the betting history? We would predict that as the size of the history grows, so will the probability of exceeding a particular losing streak length. The expected number of times we will see k consecutive losing bets, e_k, is proportional to the number of bets, n, but it's not clear if that will be true for the probabilities. Again, the Monte Carlo simulation will provide the answer; I've plotted five different curves for five thresholds of k and betting odds of 2. Different odds would show a different set of curves, but always the probability of seeing a specific losing streak will increase with increasing size of bet history.

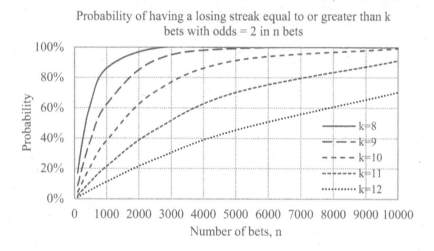

Probability of having a losing streak equal to or greater than k bets with odds = 2 in n bets

All these probability curves are idealised because I have assumed all bets have the same odds. But there's nothing stopping us using the Monte Carlo simulation for a real betting history where the odds may well vary, and sometimes quite considerably. My Wisdom of the Pinnacle Crowd history is an obvious example. Let's subject it to a Monte Carlo simulation with 100,000 iterations. The table below shows the expected number (e_k) of times we would see losing streaks for k = 5, 10, 15 and 20 bets respectively. These are compared to the actual number of times that they were witnessed in my record. It's a reasonably close match. Presumably, the actual numbers of losing streaks are slightly lower than the expected figures because the actual betting history, with a yield of 4.35%, represents a slight overperformance relative to expectation (4.12%). Until this point in the betting history, I hadn't yet seen a losing streak of 20; the largest was 19.

k	Monte Carlo e_k	Actual number	$e_k = n\left(\dfrac{o-1}{o}\right)^k$
5	1,174.92	1,110	1,150.02
10	120.41	97	111.18
15	12.93	9	10.75
20	1.39	0	1.04

According to the Monte Carlo simulation the probability of seeing a losing streak of 19 or more was 54.3%, and 39.5% for 20 or more. The fact that a streak of 19 was seen but not one of 20 is further confirmation that what happened was broadly the same as what could have been expected to have happened.

The fourth column in the table shows the expected numbers of losing streaks calculated with the mathematical approximation, but how did I use it when all the odds are different? Since $o - 1 / o$ is the probability of losing, I know what that is for each of my bets. Calculating an average for all 11,894 of them and then its reciprocal, I have what is called a harmonic mean for my betting odds. A harmonic mean can be expressed as the reciprocal of the arithmetic mean of the reciprocals of the given set of observations. That's a bit of a mouthful, but easier to describe with an example. If I have five bets with fair odds 2, 3, 5, 10 and 25, their reciprocals (or implied win probabilities) are 1/2, 1/3, 1/5, 1/10 and 1/25. Their average is 0.2347, whose reciprocal, 1/0.2347 is 4.261. You can see that the harmonic mean will place more weight on the shorter odds. For my betting history, whilst the average fair odds were 3.98, the harmonic mean odds were 2.679. Using this figure for o in the function for e_k we calculate the figures shown in the table. The similarity between those and the figures from the Monte Carlo simulation confirms we can still reasonably use the mathematical approximation if we're feeling lazy or just want a quick ballpark idea about expected losing streaks. We can also use the function $k \approx \log_{\left(\frac{o}{o-1}\right)} n$, where $o = 2.679$ and $n = 11{,}894$, to calculate the expected longest losing sequence. The answer is 20.09. Again, we're in the right ballpark. Further confirmation, if it were needed, of the conformity of the actual data to mathematical expectation comes from the plot below of the variation of the number of actually observed losing streaks as a function of the length of the streak. I've drawn the vertical axis logarithmically. If the actual data follow a straight line, that implies they are agreeing with the mathematics closely. I've let Excel draw the best-fit exponential trend line through the data. I haven't bothered to show the line predicted by the function; it's almost identical.

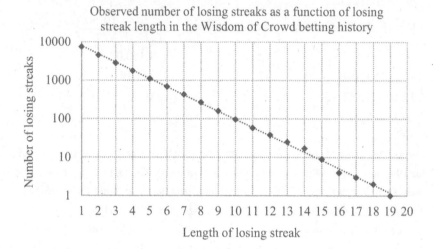

All of the mathematics for losing streaks, of course, can be used in exactly the same way for winning ones. The only difference is the probability. Now, for the expected number of times a winning streak of length k (or longer) will occur in a series of n bets with odds o, we have:

$$e_k = \frac{(n - k + 1)}{o^k}$$

which approximates to:

$$e_k \approx \frac{n}{o^k}$$

when n is much larger than k. For $e_k = 1$, we now have:

$$n \approx o^k$$

And hence:

$$k \approx \log_o n$$

where o is the base of the logarithm.

You may be wondering what the point is to all this retrospective analysis of losing streaks in a betting history. There are actually two. Firstly, by comparing what has happened to what we should expect to happen we gain further insight into how closely our prediction model is performing to expectation, and thus how valid it is. As with using the yield standard error, where we find large and statistically significant deviations from expectation, it might be time to throw out the prediction model; where we don't, we gain reassurance. Secondly, it provides an insight into what you can expect to happen in the future. A professional bettor will want information about their expected yield and about the probability of experiencing deviations from that yield over specified sample sizes; they may also want to know the likelihood of experiencing losing streaks, so that when they come, they will not be a surprise, and be much better prepared to deal with them psychologically. Knowledge, as the saying goes, is power.

Losing streaks, where all consecutive bets lose, however, are really just the tip of the iceberg. Losing 10 bets in a row with odds of 2 is clearly an unpleasant experience, but there are many more which will prove to be unprofitable. Losing 9, 8, 7 or 6 in 10 will see the bankroll lower than it was at the start of that series, and there are a lot of ways that can happen. If the mathematics for calculating the probabilities of losing streaks was difficult, it gets a whole lot messier when attempting to calculate the probabilities of drawdowns. It can be done, but I have no intention of entering that space. For the next task, the Monte Carlo simulation becomes an essential companion.

The Expectation of Drawdowns

In the same way that it is useful to know about the probability of losing streaks, it is useful to know about the probability and distribution of drawdowns. Knowing what to expect from your betting system can save you a lot of grief in the long run, either from mistakenly abandoning a method that you believe has stopped working, or from failing to abandon a method that isn't actually working as you believe it to be. Even sharper bettors can underestimate the likelihood of drawdowns in betting; when they experience a large one, their assumption will often be that their system or model, if they are using one, is no good. Methodologies holding real expected value, however, can suffer some quite large drawdowns. Here, I want to take a look at how large.

The concepts of drawdown and maximum drawdown (MDD) are familiar within the world of financial investment. Investopedia defines drawdown and maximum drawdown respectively as the peak-to-trough (percentage) decline during a specific recorded period of an investment and the largest peak-to-trough (percentage) decline before a new peak is achieved. With a little tweaking, we can transfer these concepts to the world of betting. Instead of percentage, I will limit myself here to units of loss, where every bet has a 1-unit stake. An example will make things clear. Let's suppose I start with a bankroll of 100 units. I make 5 bets, each of 1 unit at odds of 2. The first 3 of them win, whilst the 4th and 5th bets lose. My bankroll evolves as follows: 100 > 101 > 102 > 103 > 102 > 101. There is no drawdown after the first 3 bets since all of them won. After the 4th bet, a loser, the bankroll is now 1 unit lower than it was after the 3rd bet. The drawdown is 1 unit. After the 5th bet, another loser, the bankroll is now another unit lower, and a total of 2 units lower than it was at its previous high point. Thus, the drawdown after the 5th bet from the previous high point is 2 units. In the sequence of 5 bets, then, the maximum drawdown is 2 units. Suppose I have 10 bets and the bankroll evolves as follows: 100 > 99 > 98 > 97 > 98 > 97 > 98 > 97 > 96 > 95 > 94. The drawdowns are: -1, -2, -3, 0, -1, 0, -1, -2, -3, -4. Hence, the maximum drawdown is -4. You can probably guess that the longer the betting sequence, the more likely it will be to see a larger maximum drawdown, but what is the relationship? A Monte Carlo simulation will help find the answer.

Modelling a bettor with an expected value (EV) of 0%, making up to 1,000 bets at odds of 2 and stakes of 1 unit, I ran 100,000 Monte Carlo iterations, outputting the maximum drawdown after 25, 50, 100, 250, 500 and 1,000 bets. The average, and thus, expected maximum drawdowns (let's abbreviate with xMDD) across these 100,000 iterations are plotted in the chart below.

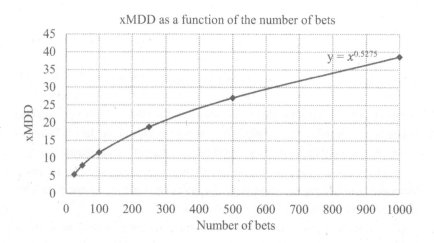

The Monte Carlo simulation indeed confirms that xMDD grows as the number of bets increases, but at a decreasing rate. I asked Excel to plot the best-fit trend line through the data points. This was a power function, with y, the xMDD roughly proportional to the square root of x, the number of bets. I've shown the power function's equation in the chart, which you could use to predict the xMDD for larger betting histories. For example, a history of 5,000 bets would, according to this equation, have an xMDD = $5,000^{0.5275}$ = 89.4. I can confirm this relationship is described by a power function or power law, by replotting the chart with both axes logarithmic. We should see a straight line, and we do.

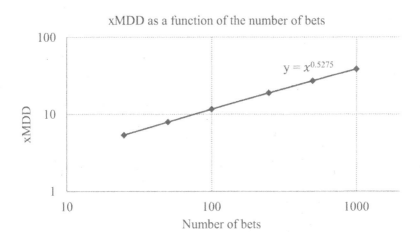

How does the expected maximum drawdown change for sharp bettors holding positive expected value, or for that matter, square bettors who should expect to lose an amount predicted by the bookmaker's margin? The larger the EV, the lower the xMDD. For EVs of -2.5%, 0%, +2.5%, +5%, +7.5% and +10% these were 51.0, 38.6, 30.0, 24.2, 20.3 and 17.5, respectively, over the course of 1,000 bets. The relationship between EV and xMDD is shown below.

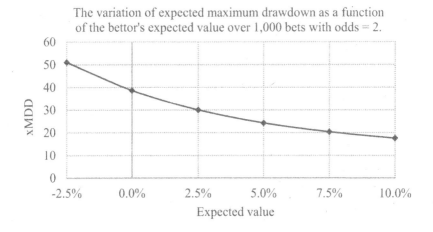

Knowing the xMDD is handy, but if we don't know how MDDs distribute, we can't say very much about the likelihood of seeing more or fewer. To be clear, the word 'maximum' here does not mean the largest possible drawdown. It simply means the largest we would typically expect to see in a specified number of bets, that is to say, what we would see on average (where 'average' is the arithmetic mean). From the frequencies of simulated MDDs over 1,000 bets with odds of 2 in the 100,000 iterations, I plotted an implied probability distribution, for the 0%-EV bettor, along with the other five at 2.5%-EV intervals, from -2.5% (roughly the size of a sharp-bookmaker's margin in popular betting markets) up to +10%, equivalent to a very sharp bettor indeed at these betting odds.

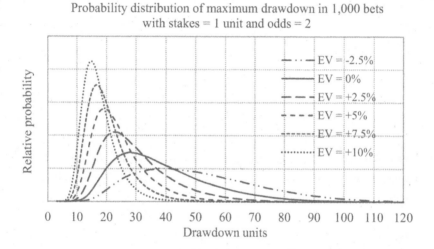

Probability distribution of maximum drawdown in 1,000 bets with stakes = 1 unit and odds = 2

In addition to a lower xMDD, bettors with superior EV will also show a narrower distribution in MDDs. All the distributions show positive skew; hence all xMDDs lie to the right of the distribution modes (their peaks). The proportion of MDDs above the xMDD for all distributions is around 40%. Understandably, the weaker your expected value, the larger a maximum drawdown you can expect to see, but the range (and thus variance) of possible maximum drawdowns grows too. For the 10%-EV bettor, the range of MDDs was 6 to 69 (standard deviation of 5.6). By contrast, the bettor losing to the bookmaker's margin showed a range of 10 to 173 (standard deviation of 20.6). Let's replot this chart with a logarithmic horizontal axis. Now the distributions are roughly symmetrical. The implication is that maximum drawdowns distribute roughly lognormally, that is to say, the logarithm of the maximum drawdown would distribute normally.

Probability distribution of maximum drawdown in 1,000 bets
with stakes = 1 unit and odds = 2

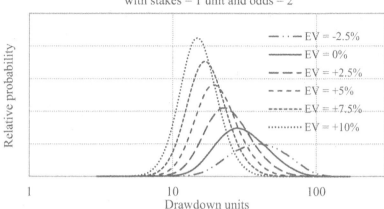

It's worth noting here that, in terms of drawdowns, the gain offered by an extra 2.5% expected value is actually quite small. In fact, nearly one third of the time, the bettor with such an advantage over the other can actually expect to see a larger maximum drawdown during the course of 1,000 bets, such are the vagaries of chance. Even a 5% advantage will still see larger maximum drawdowns around 20% of the time.

How do different odds affect the maximum drawdown distributions? Take a look below. I've plotted curves for bettors holding an expected value of 5%, but you could choose any you liked if you run your own Monte Carlo simulations.

Probability distribution of maximum drawdown in 1,000 bets
with stakes = 1 unit and EV = 5%

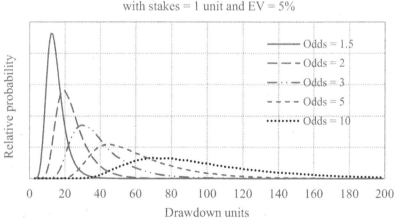

Again, distributions show positive skew, again with about 40% of MDDs above the xMDD. Unsurprisingly, longer odds mean larger expected maximum drawdowns and greater variability. xMDDs for odds of 1.5, 2, 3, 5 and 10 were respectively 14.7, 24.2, 38.9, 60.2 and 96.9. Odds of 10 showed nearly 60 times the variance in MDDs compared to odds of 1.5. The largest drawdown for the former was 370 units. Evidently, you'd need to be starting with a bankroll of a lot more than 100 units to accommodate it, given your expected profit is only 50 units over the 1,000-bet series. At these odds, a starting bankroll of 100 is just not going to cut it; over a third of the time your maximum drawdown will be as large. You might know that you hold an advantage, but if you don't model your expected drawdowns, you could overestimate an appropriate stake size, putting your bankroll at risk. With a set of Monte Carlo outputs, you can easily calculate the probability of matching or exceeding any particular drawdown, giving you valuable information about possible downside risks and how to accommodate them safely. Replotting the horizontal axis logarithmically reaffirms that the distribution of MDDs approximates a lognormal one.

Probability distribution of maximum drawdown in 1,000 bets
with stakes = 1 unit and EV = 5%

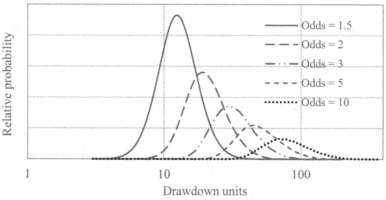

Drawdown units

I should admit that running a 100,000-iteration Monte Carlo simulation to collect the data I have presented here took over 5 hours. Of course, for any aspiring bettor, that really isn't such a burden; you could always just leave one running overnight. However, Miguel Figueres, an expert in Artificial Intelligence, tennis bettor and owner of the prediction service WinnerOdds.com has built an Excel tool that will calculate the expected maximum drawdown for a sample history in the twinkling of an eye. It's superb, allowing you to very quickly compare and contrast different scenarios of bet sample size, odds and expected value. It also includes a Monte Carlo simulator capable of up to 10,000 iterations. If you want more, like I did, you will need to build your own. It's worth noting that because the calculator has been developed using a continuous probability function, whereas the Monte Carlo outputs provide discrete data, there are very slight differences in the figures, in the same way we see small differences between the binomial (discrete) and normal (continuous) distribution probabilities. As for the normal approximation to the binomial, however, this only becomes a significant problem for small bet samples, or where the number of bets is comparable to the size of the odds. For example, the calculator outputs a figure of xMDD = 11.9 for 10 bets at odds of 10 (EV = 0%), which is clearly an impossibility. These quirks notwithstanding, Miguel's drawdown calculator is a fabulous little tool for the aspiring bettor to keep in their armoury. It also works well with variable odds. I compared the xMDD it calculated for my Wisdom of the Crowd history to the one outputted by a Monte Carlo. The figures were 115.3 and 113.7, respectively. It even accommodates a variable staking plan, provided you know the average stake and the stake-weighted odds. Again, I tested the calculator with a variable stakes Wisdom of the Crowd history. The xMDD was 71.9, compared to a figure of 74.3 produced by the Monte Carlo. You will find Miguel's calculator on Valuebettingblog.com, by Googling 'valuebettingblog drawdown calculator'.

The Risk of Ruin

Every bettor faces the prospect of losing everything that they have financially available to bet with. For the most part, however, bettors, even recreational ones who hold no expected value, bet sensibly and sustainably enough that this does not mean losing more than they can afford to. By ruin, then, I mean the loss of the whole bankroll that was set aside for the sole purposes of betting, which if lost in entirety would not impact on the daily lives of them and those around them. Of course, should such a loss occur, there is always the danger that the bettor repeats the mistakes, under the illusion that they can turn things around. Fortunately, rates of such behaviour, what we might reasonably describe as addiction, are fairly small. Most reputable data that has studied the problem around the world puts national rates of gambling addiction at below 1%, although there is an increasing body of evidence that suggests a considerable larger proportion might be classified as at-risk. For those who might be, and perhaps more importantly for those who aren't and who, furthermore, may be capable of finding expected value, it's worth exploring a little the likelihood of ruin, as I have defined it here. In particular, we will see how the probability of ruin changes the expected profit calculation.

As we've already seen, even sharp bettors with expected value can experience some quite considerable drawdowns. If one of those, or a combination of consecutive drawdowns, is larger than your bankroll at your previous high point, by definition you will have gone bust. Consider the first period in my Wisdom of the Crowd history. Where would you have been starting with a bankroll of 50 units, staking 1 unit per bet, after 300 bets?

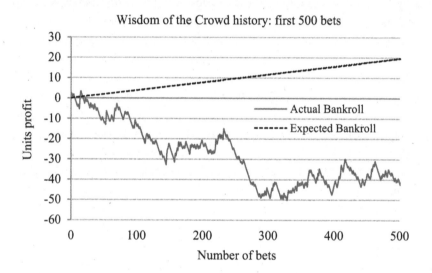

Betting stakes equivalent to 2% of a starting bankroll might seem excessive to some; to others, however, they would be considered quite small. If that includes you, I will say now: moderate your expectations. In this respect, what follows in the next few pages will hopefully help to change them a little.

What was the probability of ruin by 300 wagers here? Ruin would be equivalent to an actual loss of -16.7% (-50/300). If we assume the expected yield was +3.88% from average odds of 3.69, the figures at this time, my yield distribution calculator tells me that I should expect it to happen 1.6% of the time. That's small, and evidently the start to this history was considerably unlucky, but not so unexpected as to be impossible given an expectation of 3.89%. Even if the methodology is working as it should, misjudging what is appropriate to put at risk in an attempt to gain a financial reward could spell the end before you've even really got going. This history covered just six calendar weeks. However, it's actually worse than this. Let me try to explain why.

In his book *Skin in the Game*, Nassim Taleb offers a thought experiment about the logic of risk-taking. I have adapted it very slightly. 100 bettors go to the races each day for 100 days to wager a certain set amount each. Some may lose, some may win, but we can infer at the end of each day roughly what expected value the bettors held, within the standard margins of uncertainty, and their collective probability of success. Now assume that bettor number 28 goes bust. Will bettor number 29 be affected? No. Tomorrow, they will be replaced, and there will still be 100 bettors. Now instead suppose only you go to the racetrack 100 days in a row, starting with a set amount. On day 28 you go bust. Will there be day 29? No. Nor day 30, 31... 98, 99 and 100. You will not be replaced. It is the end of the line.

The probability of success from the collection of bettors does not apply to you. Taleb called the first set ensemble probability and the second one time probability (since one is concerned with a collection of people – a theoretical expectation – and the other with a single person through time – a true expectation). When you see performance claims of expected yields from bettors and tipsters, including the ones I have made for my own betting methodology, treat them with caution; they are theoretical expectations. They are conflating ensemble probability and time probability. Even if these predictions are valid, they are only theoretically so. In fact, no person can achieve the expected yields in a real betting market unless they have infinite pockets. In some of the possible histories, the bettor will go bust. They will not be afforded the opportunity to carry on to the end of the 100 days. There is no 'next day' after ruin. Any theoretical returns attributed to the period after going bust should actually be discounted. Thus, following Taleb, true expected returns will be divorced from their theoretical counterparts.

Perhaps the easiest way to explain this is by means of an example. Consider a bettor with expected value of +5% betting odds of 2; that's a very solid advantage, comparable to some of the best professional handicappers. They start with a bankroll of 100 units and will aim to place 1,000 consecutive bets with stakes of the same size but want to know what size to use. We can use our yield calculator to estimate the risk that all 100 units will be lost by the $1,000^{th}$ bet. Suppose the stakes were 5 units. Losing 100 in 5,000 units staked is equivalent to a -2% yield. What are the chances of this occurring, given an expected value of +5%? It's a little over 1%. This is the theoretical expectation for failing after 1,000 bets. We haven't, however, considered how we got there. There are all sorts of ways to arrive at a loss of greater than 100 units, and for some, 100 units will have been lost long before we arrived at the 1,000th bet. On paper, there's no problem with that, since we're just interested in the expectation of losing more than 2% after exactly 1,000 bets – the ensemble probability. In the world of real money, however, once 100 units is lost, there's no opportunity to recover. That's it. No next day. What, then, is the time probability of losing 100 units within 1,000 bets? We need a Monte Carlo simulation to find out. I ran one with 10,000 iterations. It happened 1,236 times, or 12.36% of the time. That's a considerably greater failure rate than implied by the theoretical expectation.

It should come as no surprise that the bigger the stake size that is chosen, the greater the likelihood of failure, but the rate of increase in the (time) probability of failure during 1,000 bets, the true risk of ruin, is much greater than it is for the theoretical (ensemble) probability of failure at the 1,000th bet. I've drawn a chart below for bet stakes from 1 to 10 units comparing the theoretical risk of failure and the true risk of ruin.

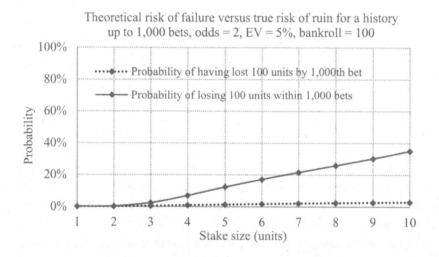

If you have deep enough pockets, then the true risk of ruin is not going to concern you terribly much. You'll just ride out the drawdowns and let the law of large numbers, and your expected value, work its magic over the longer term. For you, the theoretical probability of failure is then the only metric that you'll really care about. However, if that were the case, there'd be little point worrying about what stake size to choose in the first place, since your theoretical risk of failure doesn't change very much. Even if you used all of your initial bankroll of 100 units for each bet, knowing that you would just reach into your pocket and find another one every time you lost, your theoretical risk of having lost more than 100 units after the 1,000th bet would still only be about 5%. Such bettors, of course, are as theoretical as their risk of failure. For everyone else, it's the risk of ruin that is going to matter much more. Hopefully, this example has helped illustrate just how important it is to consider it.

Whilst your expected yield won't change, a greater risk of ruin will naturally have an impact upon your expected profits. If some of your possible histories end before the 1,000th bet, a proportion of bets that would otherwise have contributed towards them will now not exist. The next chart shows what impact this has. Again, the Monte Carlo scenario is for a bettor with +5% expected value, betting up to 1,000 bets at odds of 2. Should they lose 100 units or more at any time, their betting is over for that iteration.

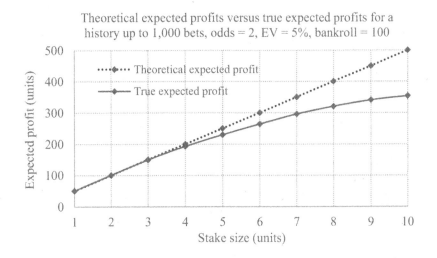

Theoretical expected profits versus true expected profits for a history up to 1,000 bets, odds = 2, EV = 5%, bankroll = 100

With these data, it should now be clear why I caution against the use of an overly aggressive stake size. Of course, larger stakes can deliver more profit, but as for every form of gambling, including gambling with positive expected value, to achieve greater rewards you have to take more risks. Whilst it's just my subjective and rather risk-averse viewpoint, I would argue that any sensible strategy at least attempts to keep the true risk of ruin as close as is practically possible to the theoretical failure probability, and that these should be kept below 1%. For odds of 2 and an expected value of +5%, that would mean stakes no larger than 2 units for an initial bankroll of 100. The longer your odds or the weaker your expected value, the smaller that stake will need to be. I ran further Monte Carlo simulations to investigate how your risk of ruin will change as a function of your betting odds, again for an expected value of +5%. The four mini-plots below compare the theoretical failure probability at the 1,000th bet – the dashed lines – to the true ruin probability within 1,000 bets – the solid line – for odds 1.5, 3, 5 and 10.

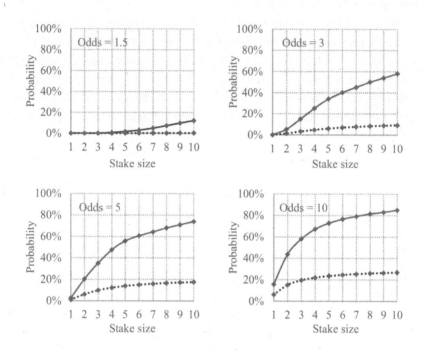

Arguably, stakes of even 1 unit for a 100-unit bankroll are unacceptably high when betting at longer odds, unless you hold a much larger expected value. Even with expected value of 10%, at odds of 10 you'll still be facing a true risk of ruin of around 9% (over 1,000 wagers) betting just 1-unit stakes. Certainly, with anything much larger it's more or less inevitable that you will go bust far quicker than the theoretical yield distribution calculator might have led you to believe. Of course, for some of you 1,000 bets might represent a long period of time, but for others hoping to slay the variance monster with a much faster turnover of wagers, that might only represent a few weeks of activity. As you saw with my Wisdom of the Crowd history, had I been betting 2 units with a starting bankroll of 100, I'd have gone bust in a little over a month. The theoretical risk was 1.6%, but the true risk of ruin was in fact double that.

What happens to the true expected profit as we change the odds? The theoretical numbers will track the same line I drew earlier, since the expected value hasn't changed; +50 units for 1-unit stakes, 500 units for 10-unit stakes. It's quite different for the true expected profit; the larger the stake the lower it is, but the reduction is much more dramatic the longer the odds. That's hardly a surprise given the risk-of-ruin curves I've just shown.

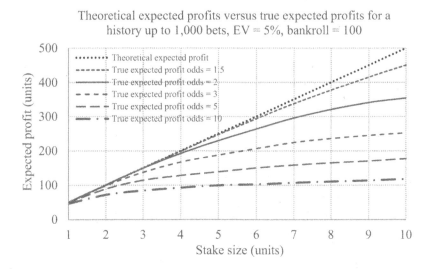

Indeed, overestimate an acceptable stake size for betting odds of anything longer than about 5 and the Monte Carlo results imply you're giving up the majority of the profit you had hoped to achieve by using larger stakes in the first place. Evidently, longer-odds bettors must then reduce their stake sizes to manage their risk of ruin, but in doing so they will also be reducing their theoretical expected profit as well. Consider the following comparison. Assuming a 100-unit bankroll, a bettor with an expected value of 5%, betting odds of 2 with 3-unit stakes, has about a 2% risk of ruin within 1,000 bets. This rises to 35% when betting odds of 5. It can be reduced back to about 2%, provided the stakes are lowered to 1 unit, but now the true expected profit is three times smaller. If this is so, why even bother betting longer odds at all? The obvious reason is because the greater variance allows for the greater possibility of superior expected value; recall that successful horse racing tipsters typically exhibit better yields than their football betting counterparts (although the unsuccessful ones provide a mirror image). Given the greater variance, a 5%-EV bettor at odds of 2 is roughly equivalent to a 10%-EV bettor at odds of 5; you can use my yield distribution calculator to confirm. To ensure the latter keeps their risk of ruin to around 2%, their stakes must be no larger than 1.5 units. With these, what is the true expected profit over

1,000 bets? Just shy of 150 units – broadly the same as the even-money bettor staking 3 units per bet. The lesson? Don't worry so much about your odds; it will likely make little difference to your true expected profits for a given protection threshold against the risk of ruin.

For those feeling a little deflated by all this talk of failure, I have a little bit of good news: the longer your history, the slower the growth rate in the risk of ruin, provided, of course, you really do hold expected value. This is probably self-evident anyway; as your bankroll grows in size, it would obviously take longer to lose 100 units. Beyond a certain size of history, it will effectively become impossible to go bust; the law of large numbers will have done its work. When that will occur will depend on your odds, your stakes and your expected value. I've compared the trajectories for 6 bettors with different expected values, betting odds of 2 with 5-unit stakes having begun with 100 units.

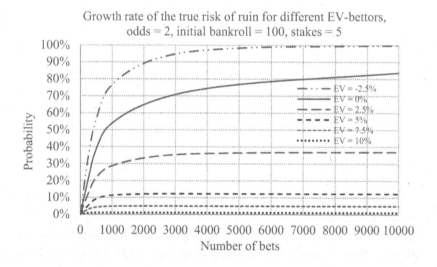

Growth rate of the true risk of ruin for different EV-bettors, odds = 2, initial bankroll = 100, stakes = 5

Essentially, almost all the risk of ruin falls in the early part of your history. This makes it all the more important to be sure you have quantified the numbers accurately. Don't let a failure to accommodate some bad luck prematurely end what might otherwise have proved a success in the long term. Of course, if you do go bust earlier than you thought, bad luck is not necessarily the only explanation. Arguably, it will be far more likely that you never held the expected value you thought you had. For expected value 0% and below, those trajectories head quickly and inexorably towards 100%, and there will be nothing you can do to prevent that. Ruin for bettors without expected value is an inevitability.

Warren Buffett, an American investor and business tycoon famed for outperforming the financial markets for decades, once said, 'in order to succeed, you must first survive.' It's a self-evident truth, but often overlooked during the business of calculating expected profits. Failing to consider the risk of ruin means they become divorced from the expected value. Nassim Taleb puts it even more starkly than that. 'The presence of ruin does not allow cost-benefit analyses.' Fortunately, I think a Monte Carlo simulation can go some way to countering his pessimism. Nevertheless, my simulations have revealed that to hold the probability of ruin to a level (perhaps 1%) where expected value and expected yield will still mean roughly the same thing, we cannot entertain stake sizes much beyond 1% of an initial bankroll, and smaller still if betting at longer odds. The fact that I was using considerably larger stake sizes to quantify the risk of ruin was to more easily illustrate the relationship between the two variables. Of course, stakes do not have to remain the same fixed size, nor indeed the same fixed proportion of your initial bankroll. Their size can instead be a proportion of an evolving bankroll, not just the starting one. As it grows, your stakes grow with it; as it shrinks, so do the stakes. Such money management will theoretically save you from going bust, although this does come at a cost. I'm saving this topic for the next chapter. Until then, there's one loose end I'd like to tie up first. I've already referred to it a couple of times.

The Variance Monster

Losing money is an inevitable consequence of betting; you won't win every time. Aspiring to make an income from betting is thus quite different to earning an income from a regular salary, which is paid repetitively and with certainty (job security aside) over a fixed return period, for example daily, weekly, monthly or annually. The bettor, by contrast will experience variation in the amount that they receive over similar return periods because of the uncertainty inherent in the betting markets. Given human beings' psychological aversion to losing, this variation can feel like an emotional rollercoaster, the impacts of which all serious bettors will want to minimise. What is the best way to achieve this? There are perhaps two main schools of thought on this, although, really, they represent two ends of a scale. Following a sales idiom, the first might be described as 'stack 'em high, sell 'em cheap'; lots of bets with low value, offering a steady drip of profits over the long run. Its counterpart might be likened to a niche market, where the mark-up for the seller would be greater but on a far smaller number of products. Here, the bettor spends more time looking for bets with larger expected value, but consequently places fewer of them. I want to investigate how these two strategies compare.

Hopefully, you will remember that the variation in your expected performance will be a function for your betting odds, your expected value and the number of bets you place over a specified time horizon. Let's first consider the last of these variables. For a given advantage and odds, how does your expected performance vary as you increase or decrease the number of bets you place? Let's recap: the standard error in your possible yields, which are normally distributed around your expected one, is inversely proportional to the square root of the number of bets. This means that if the number of bets, n, increases 4-fold, the standard error will halve. If n increases 25-fold, the standard error will decrease 5-fold. Knowing the standard error around your expected yield allows you to easily calculate the probability of returning a loss over those n bets, and Excel has the NORM.DIST function to help you. I've drawn the distribution of possible yields for two bettors, betting odds of 2 and holding expected value of 2%. The area to the left of the vertical axis – the profit line – as a fraction of the total area under the curve is equivalent to the probability of making a loss over n bets. For the first bettor, n = 100, whilst for the second bettor, n = 1,000. We might suppose that these are the number of bets placed in a month. Following the sales analogy, the first, being more selective, might be the 'Harrods' bettor, the second, the 'Walmart' variety, although this is probably stretching things a bit; 100 bets in a month is still quite a large volume for some bettors. If that is you, just exchange 'month' for 'year'.

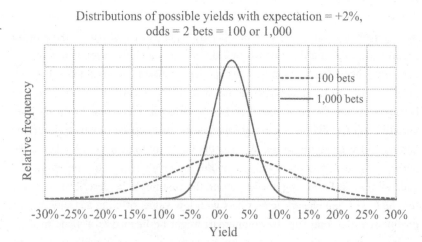

Distributions of possible yields with expectation = +2%, odds = 2 bets = 100 or 1,000

The area under the dashed curve to the left of the profit line is larger than the equivalent area under the solid line. Using the NORM.DIST function, the two areas are equivalent to probabilities of 42.1% (for the 'Harrods' bettor) and 26.4% (for the 'Walmart' bettor) respectively. Strictly, I should use the BINOM.DIST function to calculate the probabilities, since for bets with the same odds, the possible yields will distribute binomially. However, as previously argued, it's just easier to use the normal function, and a reasonable approximation for anything other than the smallest of samples. For scenarios where the odds vary, using the binomial becomes impossible anyway. In this instance, the binomial probabilities are 38.2% and 25.3%. Thus, the 'Walmart' bettor can achieve the same expected profit of 2 units by using one tenth of the stakes size of the 'Harrods' bettor (and hence reduce any risk of ruin) yet expect to lose just once in every four months compared to about 2-in-5. More generally, the theoretical probability of making a loss as a function of the number of bets (and the betting odds) is shown in the following chart. For this purpose, I'm ignoring the influence of ruin I discussed in the previous section.

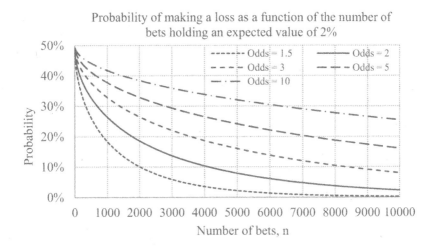

Probability of making a loss as a function of the number of bets holding an expected value of 2%

Despite their superiority with respect to the probability of loss after a month, even the 'Walmart' bettor, particular one who prefers longer odds, has a reasonable chance of losing, despite such a large number of bets. An expected value of 2%, of course, is not so far above the profit line. But hold on a moment. The 'Harrods' bettor bets fewer times precisely because they're fussier, waiting for the superior value rather than purchasing any old bargains. I gave them the same 2% expected value I'd given the 'Walmart' bettor. Instead, let's give them a 20% expected value. With both bettors betting 1-unit stakes, they will both have an expected profit of 20 units. What do the distributions look like now?

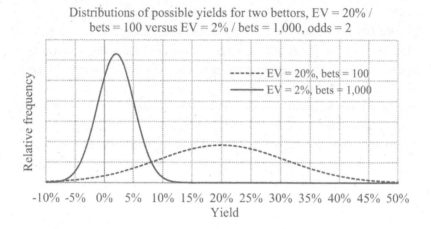

Distributions of possible yields for two bettors, EV = 20% / bets = 100 versus EV = 2% / bets = 1,000, odds = 2

The relative likelihood of a monthly loss has flipped, with the 'Harrods' bettor having just a 2.1% chance of seeing red (binomial 1.7%). For the same expected profit, the 'Harrods' strategy would appear to be by far the more sensible one. They haven't slain the 'variance monster' – the shape of the distribution is almost the same – but they've pushed it so far to the right of the profit line it no longer matters. As a further generalisation, I've illustrated how the probability of loss varies as a function of expected value and betting odds, in this instance for a sample of 1,000 bets. Again, I'm ignoring the influence of ruin.

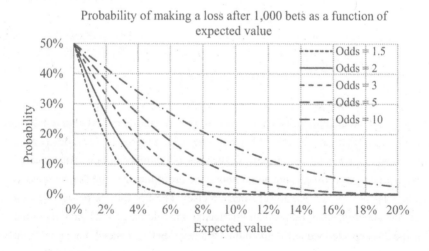

Probability of making a loss after 1,000 bets as a function of expected value

You can see from this exercise there are two ways to reduce your expected probability of making a loss over a specified period: 1) increase the number of bets; 2) increase your expected value. In the first instance the effect will be to significantly reduce the standard error in your possible yields, and thus reduce the impact of variance or uncertainty in your performance. Losing is painful, and for an advantage bettor, the variance monster is responsible for nearly all of it. If you slay the monster, by reducing the variance, you ease the pain because losses – in this case, monthly losses – occur less often. In the second instance, however, that monster has little impact. We might liken it to a hurricane that's hundreds of miles offshore; it's just as big but having almost no impact. Of course, if you're a 'Harrods' bettor and end up being wrong about your expected value, that hurricane will make landfall precisely where you're having your day at the beach. On the other hand, if your judgement proves to be sound, it's clear that variance is not really the whole story, and not the metric that should consume all of our attention. Rather, it is the expected yield per unit of variance, or risk, that will matter. In the world of finance, this metric is known as the Sharpe Ratio.

The Sharpe Ratio (SR) has become the most widely used method in the financial markets for calculating the risk-adjusted return. Its popularity is probably overly justified, given that the assumption of normally distributed returns is very often invalid. Nevertheless, I think we are arguably on safer grounds in believing that betting returns will more readily distribute this way. To calculate it, you simply subtract the risk-free rate of return from your actual return and divide by the standard error in your possible returns. Those of you with a good memory or a solid understanding of statistics might recognise this as equivalent to the standard score or z-score of a normal distribution. To all intents and purposes, that is exactly what the Sharpe Ratio is. It simply counts the number of standard deviations (or standard errors in this case) your observed return is above or below the mean value of what is being observed. In the world of finance, this mean is typically the risk-free return, or what you could achieve by taking no risk at all. That might be a government bond yield or a market tracker benchmark. Of course, in reality those investments are not entirely risk-free either, but we needn't trouble ourselves with that here. In the world of betting, one obvious risk-free benchmark would be a 0% yield, achievable by not betting at all. The worst you can do is break-even; mind you, that's the best you can do, too, but then of course you're not taking any risk. Another benchmark might be your return defined by the bookmaker's margin. Yes, you are still taking a risk by betting, but there is no long term uncertainty in a strategy that just involves betting blindly. You know you will lose; there is essentially no risk of that not happening. Here, I will concern myself with the profit line benchmark; after all, that is the yardstick by which most bettors measure themselves.

What Sharpe Ratios do our two bettors hold? The 'Walmart' bettor with a 2% expected yield from 1,000 odds has a standard error (SE) of 3.16%. You will recall that this is calculated using,

$$SE = \sqrt{\frac{r(o - r)}{n}}$$

where r is your expected return or expected yield + 1 (in this case 102% or 1.02), o is the average betting odds and n is the number of bets. Hence, relative to the profit line, the Sharpe Ratio is 2% / 3.16% = 0.63. By contrast, the 'Harrods' bettor with a 20% expected yield from 100 bets has standard error of 9.80% and a Sharpe Ratio of 2.04. This confirms what the NORM.DIST function had already found: Our 'Harrods' bettor holds a superior risk-adjusted return, or profit per unit risk taken. Although they have a greater variance compared to the 'Walmart' bettor, this is more than compensated for by the much greater yield. There is, however, a significant assumption with this thought process: that we can actually find sufficient numbers of bets where 20% expected value is available to exploit, relative to what's available at 2%. In my example here the ratio is 1:10. This might work well on paper, but can it work in practice? Can we actually find enough 'Harrods' value to secure this far superior Sharpe Ratio? We need some way of finding out.

Whilst it's obviously impossible to know the 'true' probability of outcomes, and thus the 'true' expected value of a bet, the closing line, as I have argued, provides a useful proxy measure. Yes, it may be true that there are occasions, as the tipster Nishikori would remind us, where this is not as reliable as we would like. For my purposes, however, and following my analysis of the Pinnacle football match odds betting market, I will assume it to be sufficiently accurate, on average, at a suitably narrow win percentage resolution. Following this assumption, we can say that the size of a prior price movement provides a proxy measure of the expected value that existed before the move took place. Further to this, we can then argue that where the size of that movement is greater than the size of the bookmaker's margin, this would be indicative of profitable expected value. For example, if the size of the move was 5% and the bookmaker's margin was 2.5%, the size of any theoretical expected value that might be implied to have existed will be 2.5%. In this way we can then look at how much prices typically move in a betting market to gauge how much profitable expected value may be available for bettors to discover, provided of course they are skilled at predicting the moves before they occur.

For this purpose, I've looked again at the Pinnacle dataset I used to demonstrate the supremacy of Pinnacle's closing price over their opening one. The size of the price move naturally depends on the length of the initial price. Longer odds typically show larger moves. A 1% win probability (odds = 100) moving to a 2% win probability (odds = 50) has a price move ratio of 100 / 50 = 2. By contrast, 98% (odds = 1.02) to 99% (odds = 1.01) has a price move ratio of just 1.01. In my dataset, prices of around 2 (I included those between 1.95 and 2.05 to make a large enough sample of 13,388) showed a standard deviation in the opening to closing price ratio of 8.3%. Their distribution of movements is shown below. The average was 1.0005. (For the record, excluding draws, which exhibit systematically less price movement, the average opening to closing odds ratio increases proportionally with the logarithm of the odds. Odds of 5, for example, move with a standard deviation of about 14%; for odds of 10, it's about 18%.)

Distribution of opening to closing price ratios for Pinnacle's football match odds around 2

It is the ratios above 1 that will interest here, or to be more precise those greater than the size of Pinnacle's margin. Not the book margin, however, but the margin weight applied specifically to the odds. Remember, because of the favourite–longshot bias, longer prices receive more margin weight than shorter ones. Taking this factor into account, I calculated the margin weights for all 13,388 odds. Then, dividing the price move ratio by the margin weight we arrive at a proxy measure for the expected value that might have existed in the opening price. The distribution of these expected values, with a standard deviation of 8.3%, and mean of -1.8% is shown next.

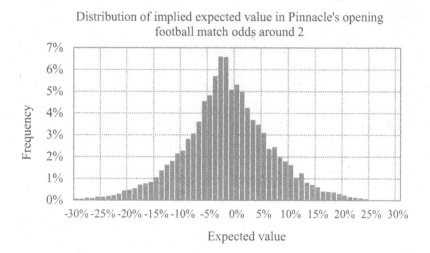

Distribution of implied expected value in Pinnacle's opening football match odds around 2

You might be surprised by how much theoretical value was available in the opening prices, assuming of course the closing ones were, on average, accurate. As many as 39% of them held expected value according to this methodology, although this falls to 30% for all football match odds as a whole. Whilst longer odds do show more price movement, the margin weight the bookmaker builds into them is disproportionately even bigger.

Of course, finding out that there's plenty of expected value available is quite a different matter to knowing how to find it systematically. Finding 1,000 bets out of 13,388 with an average expected value of 2% will obviously not happen randomly. If the standard deviation in the expected value is 8.3%, the standard error in the average expected value for 1,000 bets will be 8.3% / $\sqrt{1,000}$, or 0.26%. With an arithmetic mean of -1.8%, the z-score for achieving this by chance, assuming the distribution above is normal, will be 14.5, with a probability of 1 in a 100 quattuordecillion (or 1 with 47 zeros). I'm not sure the expected values are distributed normally, and they don't obey the empirical rule within statistical margins of error (71.5%, 94.4% and 99.3% of the data are within 1, 2 and 3 standard deviations of the mean). Nevertheless, for my purposes here, it's an acceptable assumption to make. In fact, we aren't interested in the likelihood of this happening by chance; we know even the 'Walmart' bettor must be skilled. Instead, the z-score provides an approximate measure for comparing the abilities of two bettors. If they have the same z-score this would imply they have roughly the same ability. Thus, if the 'Harrods' bettor has the same z-score as the 'Walmart' bettor, we can determine the likely number of bets they will find with an average expected value of 20%, given that the 'Walmart' bettor can find 1,000 with an average of 2%. Since,

$$z = \frac{(EV - \mu)\sqrt{n}}{\sigma}$$

where EV is the average expected value of the bettor's sample of bets (2% for the 'Walmart' bettor, 20% for the 'Harrods' bettor), μ is the average population expected value for the 13,388 prices (-1.8%), σ is the standard deviation in the 13,388 expected values (8.3%) and n is the number of bets in the sample, we can rearrange to find n.

$$n = \left(\frac{z\sigma}{EV - \mu}\right)^2$$

If z is 14.5 for an expected value of 2% over 1,000 bets, it will also be 14.5 for an expected value of 20% over about 30 bets. To put it another way, we can expect our 'Harrods' bettor to find about 3% of the bets that the 'Walmart' bettor will find, given this betting market, odds and price movement variability. Now, with a smaller sample of bets, their standard error in possible yields has increased (17.9%), with a concurrent decrease in their Sharpe Ratio to 1.12. Whilst this is still superior to our 'Walmart' bettor, they cannot expect to make the same profit whilst betting the same stake sizes. With 30 bets instead of 100, their expected profit will now be 30 x 0.2 = 6 units, as opposed to the 20 units expected by the 'Walmart' bettor making 1,000 wagers with 2% expected value. Which strategy do you now feel is superior? It's swings and roundabouts, really, and depends on whether you want a better Sharpe Ratio or more expected profit.

Whilst I'm not aware of any comparable metric in the financial world, we could multiply the Sharpe Ratio by the expected profit to provide some sort of comparison: xProfit.SR. The dot between xProfit and SR signifies a multiplication. This product for the 'Walmart' and 'Harrods' bettors is 12.7 and 6.7 respectively, suggesting the former strategy is twice as good. However, this assumes that the utility gained by a Sharpe Ratio increases linearly, such that a Ratio of 2 is twice as good as a Ratio of 1; it is not at all clear that would be true.

Furthermore, the 'Harrods' bettor could simply treble their stakes to achieve a similar expected profit. Naturally, increasing stakes can then have an impact on the risk of ruin which I have ignored for this thought experiment, although with an expected value of 20% at odds of 2, this is unlikely to pose much of a problem for all but the largest of stakes relative to the size of an initial bankroll.

Just for fun, let's run with this xProft.SR product as a meaningful statistic. Using the same set of Pinnacle open to close price movements and the same z-score methodology I've described, I've calculated the expected number of bets bettors targeting different average expected value can expect to find, relative to the 2%-EV bettor who can find 1,000. The vertical axis is logarithmic.

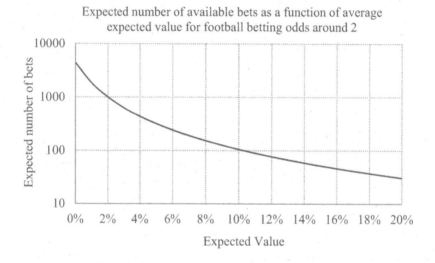

Expected number of available bets as a function of average expected value for football betting odds around 2

The expected value–expected bets function is approximately described by a power law, with a rapid decrease in availability as the bettor seeks ever greater expected value. The next chart below shows how the Sharpe Ratio and the xProfit.SR product vary with expected value. It seems that in a football match betting market with betting odds of around 2, you can expect your Sharpe Ratio to increase as your expected value increases, although the rate of improvement will slow. In contrast, the xProfit.SR metric reaches a high point for a strategy with an expected value close to 4% and appears to represent the best trade-off between expected profit and Sharpe Ratio. I wouldn't necessarily read too much into this statistic; I don't think it has any sound mathematical basis. Remember, this was just for fun. The broader message is this: try to maximise your Sharpe Ratio whilst not conceding too much expected profit in the process, and if you do increase stakes to compensate for that, make sure you've thoroughly analysed your expected increase in your risk of ruin.

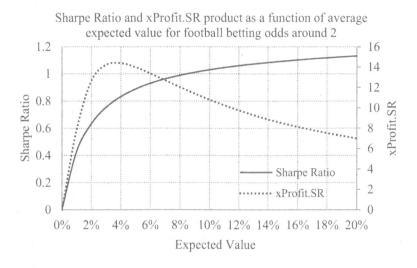

Of course, for different betting markets, different odds and different price movements, the number of available bets with a particular expected value will also be different. Nevertheless, we can probably anticipate that the relative availability between different expected values will vary according to similar power functions, with far less availability as the expected value increases. I suppose most serious bettors intuitively knew this anyway, but I think it's useful to have it quantified mathematically. It should, at the very least, provide a tool for aspiring bettors to help them decide what kind of bettor they want to be: a 'Walmart' bettor who slays the variance monster, a 'Harrods' bettor who works much harder to find the smaller niche, higher-end value, or somewhere in between. At the end of the day, I suppose you should choose what works best for you. Slaying the variance monster is important, but evidently it is not the only thing that should concern you when developing your method of taking on the bookmaker. Of course, in addition to wondering how many bets you will place, you will also want to think about what stakes they should have. Earlier I considered how changing the stake can influence your risk of ruin. I now want to turn to the business of staking more generally and investigate how different money management approaches compare against each other.

STAKING

After expected value, staking is perhaps the single biggest reason why bettors fail. It's probably the main reason why even some advantage bettors will fail too. No staking plan can turn a losing bettor into a winning one; if you think it might have, you've just been lucky. Sadly, this is not the same the other way around. I've already touched a little on the importance of thinking about the size of your stakes in relation to the size of your betting bankroll. The bigger they are as a proportion, the greater the risk that you will lose the pot you've set aside for the purposes of betting, whether recreationally or more professionally. In this chapter, however, I want to investigate further the influence of different staking methodologies on your theoretical probabilities of different outcomes, and how those compare. Nevertheless, always remember that these findings are theoretical and should be set against the more important risk of ruin. As for any analysis that I've introduced to you in this book, I would always encourage you to run your own Monte Carlo simulations. In this context, that might mean defining a bankroll and testing different staking methodologies for the risk of ruin. Here, however, I will just concern myself with the theoretical probabilities and ignore the possibility of ruin. Hopefully, most of you would be sensible enough to scale your stakes in such a manner that your risk of ruin would be less than 1% over significant timescales anyway.

Beyond behaving randomly or on a whim, there are arguably only four systematic reasons why one might choose to vary a stake size: win probability, expected value, bankroll size and loss recovery. Strictly speaking the fourth one is not so much a staking plan, more a game of Russian Roulette. The other three mainstream approaches all have their pros and cons. As for everything in gambling where uncertainty rules, there is always a trade-off between risk and reward. You will never create something advantageous from zero risk; all you can do is shift the probability distributions.

Unit-Loss versus Unit-Win

Thus far, every betting scenario or Monte Carlo simulation I have discussed has used what are termed flat stakes, or level stakes. Here, every stake is the same.

For modelling and mathematical simplicity, it is easier to define such a stake by 1 unit. Of course, you don't have to, and obviously when comparing level staking strategies, for example to investigate the risk of ruin, you might use 2 units, 5 units, 10 units and so on. When you do, the standard deviation in your profits and losses will simply be a multiple of those stake sizes, although the standard error in your yields will be the same, since obviously yield is profit divided by stakes. We could also name this staking method 'unit-loss', since when a bet loses, you lose the same stake no matter what the betting odds.

Instead of choosing to lose the same stake each time you lose a bet, you might instead opt to win the same profit every time you win a bet. We could call this staking method 'unit-win'. There's absolutely no work involved in calculating unit-loss stakes; they are all the same. How do we calculate unit-win stakes when the odds vary? The formula is really quite simple, at least for those who are happy to use European decimal odds. For odds, o,

$$\text{unit-win stake} = \frac{1}{o-1}$$

For example, for odds of 2, 4 and 7, the relative stake sizes would be 1, 1/3 and 1/6 units. Obviously in terms of monetary value, you don't have to use these figures, these are just relative ratios. If you wanted the total stakes to be equivalent to 3 units that you would otherwise place using a unit-loss strategy, you would simply scale these appropriately by multiplying each stake by a factor of the number of bets divided by the total unit-win stakes. Here, this would be 3 / (1 + 1/3 + 1/6) = 3 / 1.5 = 2. Your unit-win stakes would then be 2, 2/3 and 1/3 (making a total of 3 units). You should clearly be able to see how much more stake-weight is placed on the shorter odds. The bet with odds of 2, for example, has 6 times the stake-weight of the bet with odds of 7, since $1/(o-1)$ for the former is 6 times greater.

Given what you already know about the distribution of possible yields for different betting odds using a unit-loss staking methodology, can you predict how a distribution for unit-win staking will compare to it? We should assume that since greater stake-weight is placed on the shorter odds, such a distribution should be taller and narrower. I've plotted the outputs from a 100,000-iteration Monte Carlo simulation to compare the two staking plans. Each betting history had 1,000 bets: 200 with odds of 1.5, 200 with odds of 2, 200 with odds of 3, 200 with odds of 5 and 200 with odds of 10. Total stakes for both plans were 1,000 units. Every bet held an expected value of 5%.

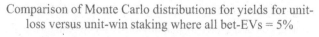

Comparison of Monte Carlo distributions for yields for unit-loss versus unit-win staking where all bet-EVs = 5%

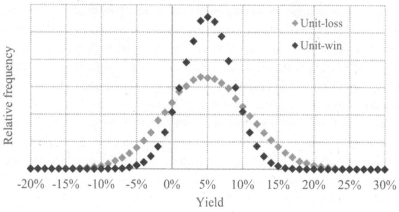

Hopefully, you will agree this is an entirely predictable result. The relative weights given to odds of 1.5, 2, 3, 5 and 10 are 51.80%, 25.90%, 12.95%, 6.47% and 2.88%. Since the expected value is the same for all bets, these figures also represent the relative contributions the different odds make to the total expected profit. Multiplying each odds by their respective weight and summing gives us a stake-weighted average odds of 2.29. This is considerably shorter than the arithmetic means of $(1.5 + 2 + 3 + 5 + 10) / 5 = 4.30$. Hence, the variance and standard error in possible yields will be smaller, and the distribution taller and narrower. The most significant consequence of this will be a lower risk of loss over the 1,000 bets. In my Monte Carlo simulation, 19,524 of the unit-loss iterations finished with a loss, compared to only 8,037 for unit-win. If unit-win staking is less risky than unit-loss staking (because more weight is placed on the shorter odds), and furthermore, so little expected profit is contributed by the longer odds (in this example the odds of 10 contribute just 2.88%), one might wonder what the point is of betting on longer odds at all. Just ditch them and bet the shorter odds only. I will address this point shortly, but before I do, I'd like to look at whether it is still possible to use my approximation formula for the yield standard error to save us the trouble of running the Monte Carlo simulation.

The chart below shows again the Monte Carlo frequencies for the unit-win staking, together with the normal distribution curve predicted by my approximation function for the yield standard error. To remind you, this is given by $SE_{yield} = \sqrt{r(o - r)/n}$, where r (1.05) is your expected return (or expected yield + 1), o (4.30) is your average odds and n (1,000) is the number of your bets.

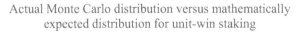

Actual Monte Carlo distribution versus mathematically
expected distribution for unit-win staking

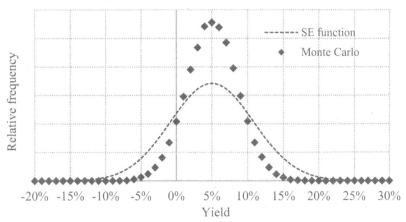

The normal curve predicted by my SE_{yield} function unsurprisingly matches the Monte Carlo distribution for unit-loss staking. This is because the function assumes all stakes have equal weight. Evidently, we can no longer use this function to short-cut the Monte Carlo process. Or can we? What if we changed the figure for the average odds? What if instead we used the stake-weighted average odds, 2.29, for the value of o? Have a look.

Actual Monte Carlo distribution versus mathematically-
expected distribution using stake-weighted average odds for
unit-win staking

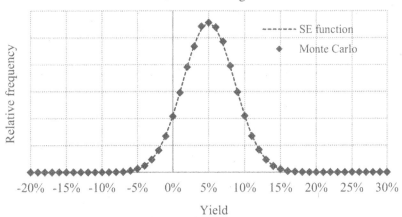

Clearly, my function still provides an excellent approximation for the expected distribution of possible yields; you just need to make sure you are using the appropriate average odds.

Something about this thought experiment comparing unit-win and unit-loss staking doesn't seem quite right. As mentioned, it's almost as if there's no point to betting long prices, since in the scenario I have described, they contribute so little towards an overall expected profit whilst annoyingly increasing the likelihood of loss over a specified number of bets. This argument would be recursive, such that, in the limit, you would end up simply betting the shortest possible odds of 1.01, or 1.001, or 1.0000001, if the bookmaker offered such prices. However, herein lies a clue to the flaw in my scenario. How can you have expected value, and hence an expected yield, of 5% when your betting odds are 1.01? If you won 100% of bets placed at a price of 1.01, your yield would be 1%. It cannot be more. For odds of 1.05, your maximum yield is 5%, for odds of 1.5, 50%, odds of 2, 100%, and for odds of 10, 900%. The longer the odds, the greater the range of possible yields. We need to investigate further how their likelihood varies.

The Symmetry of Likelihood

Suppose you bet a team with an 80% chance of winning, and 'true' odds of 1.25. Suppose, also, the bookmaker wrongly believes the win probability is 75%. They're running a promotion and have no margin. Their odds are 1.333 (or 1/0.75). Accordingly, your expected value is 6.667%, calculated by 1.333/1.25 − 1 or 0.80/0.75 − 1. Now consider a second scenario: the bookmaker publishes margin-free odds of 6.667, believing the win probability to be 15%, but you know the 'true' win probability is 20%, implying 'true' odds of 5. This time your expected value is 33.33%, calculated by 6.667/5 − 1 or 0.20/0.15 − 1. The difference in expected win percentage between your estimate and the bookmaker's is the same in both scenarios, 5%, but the expected value is 5 times larger in the second one. It seems that in terms of expected value, equivalent errors are punished more heavily, the longer the odds are. Of course, this is a significant reason why bookmakers are wary of making mistakes on longer prices, and hence an argument for why they introduce a favourite–longshot bias into their price setting, when determining their margin. What is more of interest to us here, however, is how likely it is that these errors will be made.

Suppose the first scenario is repeated 100 times. What is the likelihood of failing to make a profit, given that your expected yield is 6.667%? One way we could express this likelihood is by the number of standard deviations your expected yield, 6.667% in this instance, deviates from 0%, the bookmaker's expectation of your performance, since they are offering you fair odds and believe those odds to be 'true'. This, of course, is our friend the z-score, and as a reminder, goes by the formula,

$$z = \frac{x - \mu}{\sigma}$$

Here, x is your expected yield (or $r - 1$, where r is your expected return), μ is 0, the bookmaker's expectation, and σ is your standard error in your distribution of possible yields for samples of 100 bets. Using my formula for the standard error as a function of odds, o, expected return, r and bets, n, we have,

$$z = (r - 1)\sqrt{\frac{n}{r(o - r)}}$$

Let's do some arithmetic. With r = 1.0667, o = 1.333 and n = 100, we find z = 1.25. For the second scenario, r = 1.333 and o = 6.667; z is still 1.25. Whilst your expected yield has increased 5-fold, so has the standard error in your possible 100-bet sample yields, meaning the likelihood of achieving such a yield, from the perspective of the bookmaker, is the same. Provided you can find the bookmaker's errors in their estimation of a 'true' win probability, you should expect to see larger expected value, and higher yields, the longer the odds.

The reason for this likelihood symmetry can be found at the heart of the binomial standard deviation, which forms the basis for all the mathematics I have covered on likelihood estimation for binary outcomes. Recall that this is given by $\sqrt{npq}$, where n is the number of bets, p is the win probability and q the complementary lose probability of a bet, and equal to $1 - p$. For my first scenario, p = 0.8 and hence q = 0.2; thus, the standard deviation in the number of wins would be $\sqrt{100 \times 0.8 \times 0.2} = 4$. 75 wins, being 5 fewer wins than 80, is 5/4 or 1.25 standard deviations away from our expectation. In the second scenario, p = 0.2, and hence q = 0.8. Now, the standard deviation will be $\sqrt{100 \times 0.2 \times 0.8}$. The answer is also 4, and it's fairly obvious why; the values for p and q have just swapped, but their product remains the same. In fact, p multiplied by q is symmetrical about $p = 0.5$; therefore, so is $\sqrt{npq}$. I showed this symmetry earlier in the book to describe the variation of the standard deviation in a Bernoulli distribution, $\sqrt{pq}$, as a function of p; you may remember it looked like a horseshoe. The variation of the binomial standard deviation $\sqrt{npq}$ as a function of p will look exactly the same; all we've done is multiple by $\sqrt{n}$.

Now we have an explanation for why tipsters who advise on horse races, which typically have much longer odds, tend to show superior yields to tipsters who advise on sports. Their superiority is just an illusion. Adjusted for variance (or risk), they are arguably not any better at all, at least in terms of a likelihood estimation. Really, tipsters should be graded by their z-score, not their yield. The z-score adjusts for the risk contained with the length of the betting odds. Essentially, it's performing the same task as the Sharpe Ratio in finance. Of course, the flipside to profits is losses. Whilst skilled operators who bet longer odds may show large positive yields, unskilled ones, at the mercy of variance, are much more likely to suffer larger negative yields too. Again, that doesn't imply they are worse; they will likely have similar negative z-scores to their sports betting equivalents. All of this discussion is really just another way of interpreting how a bettor's distribution of possible yields will vary as a function of their betting odds. The longer the odds, the wider the distribution, and the larger the range of possible yields, either positive or negative, depending on the bettor's expected value.

We can use the z-score equation above to determine what expected value (EV) a bettor might hold for different odds, given a constant z-score, as their odds change. We just need to rearrange the equation in terms of r, the expected return. Unfortunately, that is easier said than done and the solution is nasty, even for those with a mathematical orientation. As always, n = number of bets, o = odds and z = z-score.

$$r = EV + 1 = \frac{2n + z^2 o + \sqrt{(2n + z^2 o)^2 - 4n(n + z^2)}}{2(n + z^2)}$$

I absolutely promise this is the worst equation I will show you. There's no need to attempt to interpret it beyond understanding that as you change o, whilst holding z and n constant, you will see how r, and therefore EV, will change as well. Just let Excel do the work for you. It is rather arbitrary what values of z and n you should choose, although it's probably best to pick meaningful values so you have meaningful outputs for your EV-odds relationship that will reflect possible betting performances. Let's stick with my thought-experiment figures from earlier, namely n = 100 and z = 1.25. I've plotted the relationship between the odds and expected value for this scenario below. Alongside this curve, I've plotted two more for z-scores of 0.5 and 2. The larger the z-score, implying a potentially more skilled bettor, the steeper the curve trajectory.

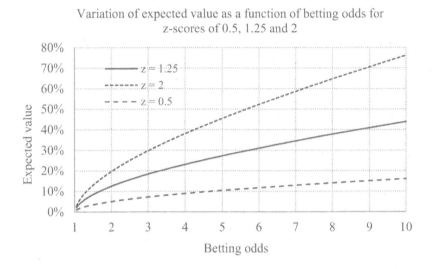

Variation of expected value as a function of betting odds for z-scores of 0.5, 1.25 and 2

If you are interested in experimenting with these relationships further but remain daunted by the mathematics, I've built another simple Excel calculator (also available at Football-Data.co.uk), just for this purpose. Always remember, however, it is not designed to tell you what expected value you can hope to achieve, let alone tell you whether you might be a skilled bettor. Rather, it's designed to give you a flavour of how longer odds will typically be accompanied by better value, should you be skilled enough to find any in the first place.

Let's return to the model for unit-win staking. Now we know that the expected value for a bet is not likely to be the same for all odds, how will this strategy compare to a unit-loss strategy? Recall, for my original model I considered five different betting odds: 1.5, 2, 3, 5 and 10, with an expected value of 5% for all. Let's suppose instead that only the odds of 1.5 hold the 5% value. What EVs can we expect for the other odds? Using my EV-odds function, they are 7.25%, 10.53%, 15.32% and 23.97% respectively. Now let's re-run the Monte Carlo simulation and see what happens. The distribution is shown below, again alongside the distribution for the unit-loss staking strategy.

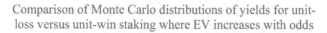

Comparison of Monte Carlo distributions of yields for unit-loss versus unit-win staking where EV increases with odds

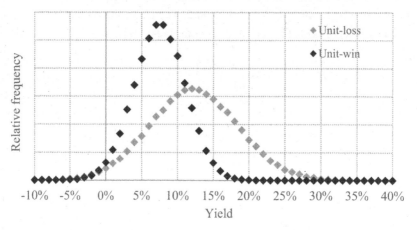

Again, the standard error for the unit-win strategy is smaller than that for unit-loss, resulting in a taller, narrower distribution, and again for the same reason. However, the main difference is that it is shifted significantly to the left, with the mean yield only 7.51%, compared to 12.40% for unit-loss. 12.41% is, in fact, the average expected value where all stakes are the same, so why has unit-win underperformed so dramatically? It's the stake-weighting again; the longer odds have the smaller stakes, but it is the longer odds which have the greater expected value. Consequently, more stake-weight goes to the bets with the lower expected value. The expected stake-weighted average value is 7.52%, matching the output of the Monte Carlo simulation.

Let's draw the mathematical distribution, using figures $r = 1.0752$ and $o = 2.29$ for the SE_{yield} function, and compare it to the Monte Carlo output. Once again, we are assured that, provided we use the correct weighted-average values for the odds and expected return, the SE_{yield} function will do an excellent job of approximating the distribution of possible betting performance for a unit-win staking strategy. The function predicts a probability of failing to profit in the 1,000 bets of 1.90%, close to the actual frequency of 1,965 (1.965%) Monte Carlo iterations in the simulation which did so. This is now more than for the unit-loss strategy, which has a predicted figure of 1.89%, again almost matching the observed 1,870 iterations (1.870%).

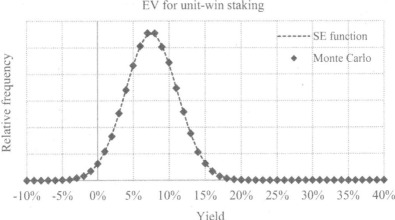

Actual Monte Carlo distribution versus mathematically-expected distribution using stake-weighted average odds and EV for unit-win staking

The unit-win strategy may have narrowed the distribution of possible outcomes, but at the expense of the expected mean, so much so that it is now marginally more likely to fail, relative to unit-loss. Is there a way to preserve the benefits of a narrower distribution, yet at the same time prevent the expected yield from regressing towards the profit line? Yes.

The Kelly Criterion

If longer odds, on average, hold more expected value, then why not take advantage of that by betting larger stakes? Well, why not indeed. That is precisely what a 'Kelly stake' will do. Developed by John Kelly while working at AT&T's Bell Labs in 1956, the mathematics of the Kelly Criterion are beyond what we need concern ourselves with here, involving what are known as utility functions. Utility is just an economic way of saying 'usefulness'. Gaining money has an economic utility, but how much? Following the mathematics of Daniel Bernoulli (Jacob's nephew), Kelly proposed we express a logarithmic utility with respect to profit, such that the percentage of the change will matter more to us than the absolute difference. For example, if everything you own is worth £1,000, increasing it by £1,000 is going to make much more of a difference than if you were already worth £1,000,000. For the latter, an increase of £1,000,000 would have the same utility as an increase of £1,000 for the former. Kelly also proposed that rather than seek to maximise the expected value of wealth, we seek to maximise the expected value of the logarithmic utility function.

Whilst the mathematics of the Kelly utility function might be frightening to most, the formula for the Kelly Criterion which is derived from it, and which defines the appropriate stake size, is relatively straightforward. For expected value, EV, and odds, o,

$$\text{Kelly stake} = \frac{\text{EV}}{o - 1}$$

Like unit-win staking, the Kelly stake is also a function of the betting odds, again inversely proportional to the odds minus 1. However, unlike unit-win, Kelly is additionally proportional to the size of your expected value. Understandably, therefore, a prerequisite to being able to use Kelly staking is that you know what your expected value is. That, furthermore, requires you to know the 'true' probability of your bet winning. For aspiring bettors, we might hope that this is always the case anyway.

Strictly speaking, Kelly was concerned with the growth of wealth; thus, the Kelly stake is actually a percentage of one's existing capital. If a bet wins, the capital grows; if it loses, the capital shrinks. The next Kelly stake is then a percentage of the new capital. By taking into account both the expected value of a bet and the risk associated with winning it, the Kelly Criterion provides a mathematically precise way to compute optimal bet sizes that maximise the overall growth of a bankroll, rather than maximising your yield (or profit over turnover), assuming, of course, your wealth utility function is logarithmic. I will be taking a much closer look at percentage staking later in the chapter. For the time being, however, I will treat the Kelly stakes in the same way as I have those for unit-win and unit-loss. That is, they do not change with respect to the size of your capital, and are thus not influenced by betting outcomes that precede them, but rather remain fixed with a constant average size of 1 unit. Many advocates of Kelly staking still find a full Kelly stake to be too risky. I will show why when I re-examine it again later in the context of percentage staking. They argue that a logarithmic utility function is too aggressive for most bettors who suffer from the bias of loss aversion. Instead, fractions of Kelly are proposed. Nevertheless, stakes are still calculated in the same way, and are proportional to EV / (o − 1).

How does Kelly staking compare to unit-loss over my hypothetical 1,000-bet history? For this model scenario I will use the same expected values that I defined via my z-score function. Thus, for odds 1.5, 2, 3, 5 and 10, and expected values of 5%, 7.25%, 10.53%, 15.32% and 23.97%, using the Kelly formula we have stakes of 1.72, 1.25, 0.91, 0.66 and 0.46 units, once I have scaled them to ensure their average is 1 unit. Compare these to 2.59, 1.29, 0.65, 0.32 and 0.14 units for the unit-win strategy. The Kelly stakes are comparatively larger for the longer odds than they are for unit-win stakes, and smaller for the shorter odds, because a new influence is coming from the size of the expected value, acting in the opposite direction to the influence of the odds, that doesn't feature in unit-win staking. For example, the ratio of Kelly stakes for odds of 1.5 and 10 is just 3.75, compared to 18 for unit-win. Again, I ran 100,000 iterations and plotted the distribution of yields.

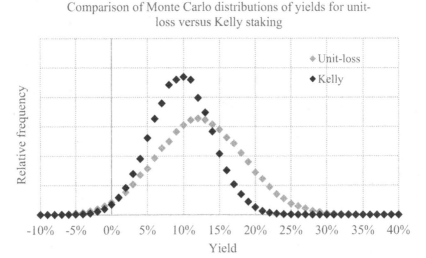

Comparison of Monte Carlo distributions of yields for unit-loss versus Kelly staking

Compared to the unit-win distribution, Kelly staking shows an improved expected yield. The average in my simulation was 9.68%, which is close to the theoretical expectation of 9.67%. This is hardly a surprising result given Kelly has increased the stake-weight of the higher value bets. Nevertheless, it still underperforms the expected yield for unit-loss. Despite greater stake-weight for the higher value bets, the influence on stake-weight by the length of the odds is still greater. Hence, the stakes for longer odds are still smaller than for bets on the shorter odds, meaning there is still proportionally more stake-weight on the lower value bets, although not as much as for unit-win. Unit-loss, by comparison, has the same stake for all bets, long and short odds alike. Of course, Kelly staking is not designed to maximise your yield, but rather your expected profit growth. We can't investigate that here because my stakes are not bankroll percentages.

As mentioned, this will follow later in the chapter. Nevertheless, the standard error is still smaller than for unit-loss staking and given the improvement in expected yield compared to unit-win, has a lower probability of loss after 1,000 bets than for unit-loss. 1,059 of the Monte Carlo iterations witnessed losses. Remember, the figure for unit-loss was 1,870. Thus, it would seem that Kelly staking offers an excellent compromise between the more aggressive unit-loss staking, which seeks greater returns but with increased risk, and the more risk-averse unit-win staking, which seeks to minimise the likelihood of failure, but must forgo some expected profit by doing so.

Finally, let's see how the Monte Carlo distribution for this hypothetical Kelly strategy compares to the mathematically-predicted one using the SE_{yield} function to approximate the standard error in the yield. Stake-weighted odds are 3.14, whilst stake-weighted expected value, as mentioned, is 9.67%.

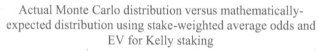

Actual Monte Carlo distribution versus mathematically-expected distribution using stake-weighted average odds and EV for Kelly staking

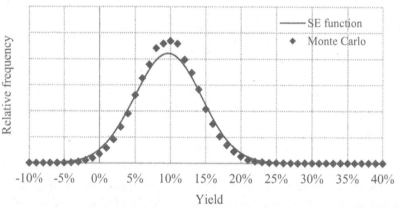

It's a reasonable match, but not as close for unit-win or unit-loss. The standard error is actually slightly smaller for the Monte Carlo distribution (4.23%) compared to the figure calculated from $SE_{yield} = \sqrt{r(o-r)/n}$ (4.73%), resulting in a marginally narrow, taller distribution. I think the reason for this is cross-correlation between expected value, odds and stake size. To test this idea, I reversed relationship between odds and expected value, so that the shorter odds had more value, not less. This time the Monte Carlo distribution was a little wider and shorter in comparison to mathematical expectation. Given that odds of a specific length in my hypothetical history all held the same expected value, arguably this magnified the influence of the cross-correlation. Of course, the betting history was built by means of a thought experiment. A real-world history would likely show much greater random variation of expected value, and I would expect to see better agreement between the two distributions.

Theoretical betting histories constructed by thought experiment are all very well, but wouldn't it be wise to test our staking plans against some real data? Yes, and I will with my history from the Wisdom of the (Pinnacle) Crowd methodology, as I did for unit-loss staking earlier. Before I do, however, there is one final unit staking strategy I would like to introduce to you: unit-impact.

Unit Impact

In Volume 21, Issue 6 of the *Journal of Sports Economics* (August 2020), Andrés Barge-Gil and Alfredo García-Hiernaux of the Complutense University of Madrid published a paper addressing how a profitable bettor should stake under conditions where estimates of 'true' outcome probabilities are unknown. They called it 'unit-impact' staking. Good forecasters should always be attempting to model 'true' probabilities. That, after all, is how you calculate your expected value for a bet. Indeed, whether a bettor, aspiring to be consistently profitable, should even be active where they are unable to perform such modelling successfully is arguably questionable. Nevertheless, we should acknowledge that, on a bet-by-bet basis at least, 'knowing' the 'true' odds, and hence one's 'true' expected value, is shrouded in uncertainty, both epistemic and aleatory. Consequently, having some general means of estimating expected value can prove helpful. I've already presented one way where we can estimate it, or to be more specific, how it might vary with the betting odds, by means of the z-score. Unit-impact staking offers another. Let's see how it works and investigate what sort of yield distribution it will reveal.

Whilst unit-loss and unit-win, respectively, hold the size of a bet loss and win constant, regardless of the betting odds, the unit-impact staking method holds constant the difference in the bankroll between winning and losing. In contrast to unit-win, for which the stake is calculated from the reciprocal of the odds – 1, the unit-impact stake is proportional to the reciprocal of the odds. For example, for odds of 2 and 5, the reciprocals are 0.5 and 0.2. Thus, if the stake for odds of 2 was £100, it would be £40 for odds of 5 (since 100 x 0.2/0.5 = 40). If a bet at odds of 2 wins, your bankroll will increase by £100. If it loses, it will decrease by £100. The net impact between winning and losing is £200. Now consider the bet at odds of 5. If it wins, the profit is 4 x £40 = £160. If it loses, your loss is £40. Again, the net impact is £200 between winning and losing. Barge-Gil and García-Hiernaux were looking for something less aggressive than unit-loss, but less risk-averse than unit-win, but under conditions where your 'true' expected value for every bet is unknown, making the Kelly stake calculation impossible.

I've subjected unit-impact staking to the same thought-experiment betting history as for unit-loss, unit-win and Kelly. Of course, in my model, I actually **do** know the expected values for every bet, because I nominated them myself using the z-score method, but what is of interest is how unit-impact compares to the other staking plans. I've shown the Monte Carlo distribution as a line this time to aid clarity.

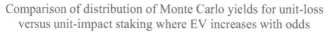

Comparison of distribution of Monte Carlo yields for unit-loss versus unit-impact staking where EV increases with odds

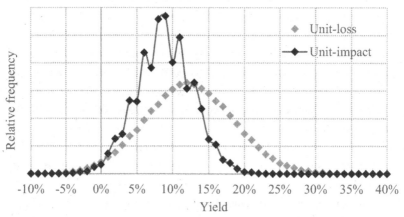

When I first saw the yield distribution for unit-impact staking, to say the least, it came as a bit of a surprise. After scratching my head for some time, and having ruled out simulation input error, I realised that the reason for this multimodal distribution was to be found in the very nature of the staking method itself. With unit-impact staking, for a given set of odds, some yields are less likely, whilst others are more common, relative to other staking plans. Why? Because the potential difference in a yield between after a bet wins or loses is the same no matter what the odds. For example, consider just two bets; the first has odds of 1.25, the second, odds of 4. There are four possible outcomes (loss/loss, loss/win, win/loss and win/win). With unit-loss there are four possible yields (-1, -0.375, +1 and +1.625), but for unit-impact there are only three (-1, -0.048 and 0.905).

Whenever there is only 1 winner, whichever bet it is, the yield is exactly the same (-0.048). For four bets, two with odds of 1.25 and two with odds of 4, there are 16 possible win-lose permutations. For unit-loss there are 9 possible yields but for unit-impact only 5. Essentially, every bet has the same stake-weighted odds, in this little example 1.905, in my Monte Carlo model 2.778. With my chosen odds of 1.5, 2, 3, 5 and 10, some yields effectively became impossible. Whilst that will be less common for more natural betting histories with a larger number of different odds, the same logic will still apply. My chart above has a yield resolution of one data point per percentage of yield. If I increase this to 10, I now find that dozens of yield-values have zero counts.

Multimodality aside, how does unit-impact staking compare to the other plans? In my chart I've compared it to unit-loss. Much as for unit-win, it underperforms in terms of expected yield (8.85%), again for the same reason – more stake-weight on the shorter odds with the lower expected values. It's better than unit-win (7.52%), but inferior to Kelly (9.67%). In terms of risk aversion, the opposite is true, with 1,246 model iterations (1.246%) falling below the profit line. Given the nature of the staking plan and the expected yields I used, this is all as would be expected. Are we still able to use the $SE_{yield} = \sqrt{r(o - r)/n}$ function to estimate this probability? We're on shakier ground, given the significant departure of the Monte Carlo distribution from perfect normality. Whilst the broader shape is still present, the standard deviation in the 100,000 yields (3.88%) is a little lower than that predicted by my approximation (4.29%), which consequently predicts more profit-failures (1.95%) than actually occurred.

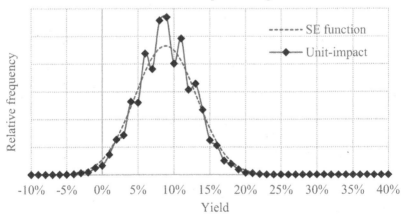

Comparison of distribution of Monte Carlo yields for unit-loss versus unit-impact staking

Of course, whenever you are in doubt about the reliability of a mathematical function to make estimates about your range of possible yields, running a Monte Carlo simulation is always a safe bet, if you'll excuse the pun. After all, if it was good enough for Stanisław Ulam and the Manhattan Project, it should be good enough for you and me.

Let's pause to take stock of how the four staking plans compare with each other in terms of expected profitability and risk of loss. For this purpose, I will use my idealised curves predicted by my standard error function. Whilst I recognise that for Kelly and unit-impact staking at least, there are divergences from normality, they are not significant enough to detract from the broader comparison.

Comparison of yield distributions for unit-loss, unit-win, unit-impact and Kelly staking

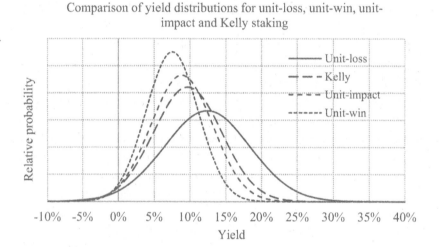

The fact that these four plans performed as they did in relative terms to each other was entirely dependent on the odds I specified and the expected value I awarded those odds. With different numbers, we might see a subtly different relative order to those distributions, but broadly speaking we can summarise as follows. Unit-loss seeks to maximise expected profit, but takes more risk to do so, whilst unit-win seeks to minimise risk, giving up some profit in the process. Unit-impact and Kelly represent compromises between the two, and in the case of Kelly, is seeking to maximise logarithmic utility. Whichever staking plan you choose to follow, you will always be faced with this trade-off, as you are with any aspect of betting, whether to choose long odds or short ones, or to bet larger or smaller. Kelly staking is arguably the most logically sensible strategy for most serious bettors to follow, provided they know (or a least believe they know) what their expected value for each bet is, since it makes no assumptions about the relationship between expected value and betting odds. By contrast, the other staking plans do, which is why they will underperform, relative to Kelly, in terms of profit and risk expectation combined. It's worth spending a little time explaining here what I mean.

Reinterpreting Different Staking Plans as Kelly-Variants

Barge-Gil and García-Hiernaux proposed that when there is uncertainty about your 'true' expected value for individual bets, unit-impact offers a useful approximation, given typical relationships between expected value and betting odds, and showed it to be superior to unit-loss and unit-win. Each of these staking plans can be reinterpreted as variants of the Kelly Criterion. Since this stipulates that a stake size is proportional to the expected value (EV) divided by the odds (o) minus 1, for unit-loss we have,

$$\frac{EV}{o-1} \propto 1 \qquad\qquad \text{therefore} \qquad\qquad EV \propto o - 1$$

The symbol $\propto$ implies the left side of the equation is proportional, rather then equal to, the right side. If the left doubles, the right doubles too. For unit-win, we have,

$$\frac{EV}{o-1} \propto \frac{1}{o-1} \qquad\qquad \text{therefore} \qquad\qquad EV \propto 1$$

Lastly, for unit-impact, we have,

$$\frac{EV}{o-1} \propto \frac{1}{o} \qquad\qquad \text{therefore} \qquad\qquad EV \propto \frac{o-1}{o}$$

Reinterpreting unit-loss in terms of Kelly sees the expected value grow in direct (linear) proportion to the rate at which odds $-$ 1 grows. This would imply a very rapid progression. Betting a stake of 1 unit at odds of 2 and odds of 10 implies that the expected value for the bet at odds of 10 should be 9 times that of the expected value of the bet at odds of 2. You probably already know intuitively that this is nonsense; such implied expected value at long odds will simply not exist. Of course, proponents of Kelly staking would say this provides an argument against unit-loss; it takes excessive risk on low-probability outcomes. By contrast, the implied expected value for unit-win is constant; it is the same no matter what the odds. Again, we've already seen this is highly unlikely to be true. Kelly-advocates, similarly, would argue that this time, too much emphasis is placed on the high-probability outcomes. Finally, expected value for unit-impact increases with increasing odds at a rate proportional to the ratio $(o - 1) / o$. As o increases, so will this ratio but at an ever decreasing rate as it tends towards a figure of 1. Since for $o = 2$, $(o - 1) / o = 0.5$, this means that the maximum possible expected value will only be double what it is for odds of 2. Does that seem intuitively valid? Barge-Gil and García-Hiernaux said they tested it against a real-world database of bets and concluded they had found empirical justification for unit-impact staking. I decided to do the same.

We can plot these EV-odds relationships for each staking plan on a chart to see how they compare. I did exactly this a few pages earlier by using the symmetry of likelihood and the z-score function as a means of identifying a possible relationship between the two variables. Having reinterpreted unit-loss, unit-win and unit-impact, I now have three more possible relationships. Which one best fits some real-world data? Using Pinnacle's betting odds (margin-removed) as a measure of the 'true' odds for a bet, any price available with another bookmaker will theoretically offer expected value, the size of which is given by that price divided by Pinnacle's fair price and subtracting 1. As I've previously described, this is the basis of my Wisdom of the (Pinnacle) Crowd methodology. In real time, via Football-Data, I only provide notifications for matches with expected value greater than 2%; the buffer is just an additional risk management measure, although the size of the buffer I chose is rather arbitrary. Analysing a larger data set of European domestic league football matches back to the 2012/13 season I found 55,237 odds where the best-priced bookmaker was offering expected value greater than 0%. As such, this was the best available expected value for that particular match outcome, following this particular methodology, and at that particular time when the odds were observed. The average odds for this history were 3.30, whilst the average expected value (and therefore expected yield from unit-loss staking) was 2.20%. In the event, the actual yield that would have been achieved was 1.77%, implying a slight underperformance relative to expectation, but well within statistical error margins that would otherwise have me questioning the methodology. The actual yield was at the 25th percentile, given a yield standard error of 0.65% for this sample size, not close to the 0.1[th] percentile that would have me worrying. Dividing the odds into sub-groups with a 1% win-probability resolution, I plotted the average expected value for each sub-group, alongside my EV-odds curves for my four staking plans: unit-loss, unit-win, unit-impact and unit-z (for want of a better name).

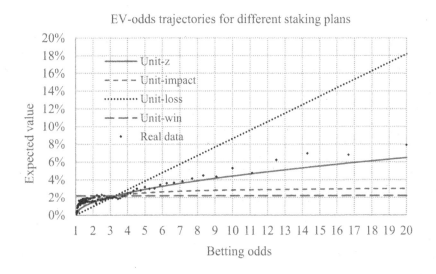

The curve that best fits my real data is one derived from unit-z staking. As predicted, the trend for unit-loss is too steep, whilst the trend for unit-win is just flat and completely unrealistic. Similarly, the trend for unit-impact flattens too quickly to be representative of what best expected value is available in a football match betting market at different odds. It is too insensitive across a broad range of odds. I would expect the same to be true of other betting markets. For example, for markets with larger number of runners like racing, with higher odds and where higher yields are more common for reasons I've explained, the unit-impact curve implies much larger yields at shorter odds than would typically be expected. Granted, my unit-z curve does not provide a perfect match; you can see in the second plot below, where I've zoomed into the shortest odds, that it provides a much weaker fit. Nevertheless, it's the best of the four and would be thus the most reliable method for estimating expected value if you didn't otherwise know it by other means, particular for the longer odds. Of course, I did know it by other means, so really this whole exercise is rather academic.

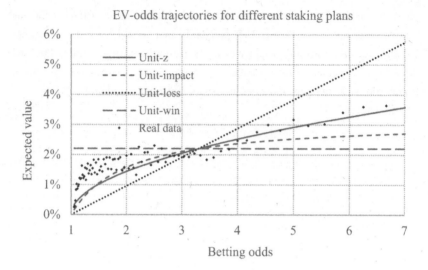

To use this methodology to estimate your expected value, you need some reference point of what your expected value is on average. In my chart above, this point comes from the average odds and the average expected value and is the point at which all curves cross each other. How do you acquire that information, however, without knowing what your expected values are specifically for every bet? You might turn to your actual betting yield to offer you a measure, but how can you be sure that this hasn't just arisen because of luck? As you surely know by now, to be able to distinguish between luck and true expected value can require some large betting histories. The lesson, as always, for any aspiring bettor, then, is to make sure you have a way of 'knowing' your expected value for every bet, even if that means acknowledging the uncertainty inherent in the number. Despite this observation, I still think that, if nothing else, reinterpreting different staking plans as Kelly-variants, and whether any of them actually correlate with real-world data in a meaningful way, is a useful educational exercise that can contribute to an understanding of what is actually going on in a betting market.

The z-score describes the likelihood of a betting yield arising by chance. Why, then, would it have anything to do with expected value, which we typically associate with skill? Indeed, it is true that a z-score does not tell you the likelihood of expected value being true, only the likelihood that a yield might happen given that it's not. The smaller the probability, the more inclined we will be to throw out the hypothesis that luck is the only explanation for observation. Nevertheless, even for a sharp bettor who holds genuine expected value, the rules of probability still apply. The distribution of possibility and likelihood is still, broadly speaking, the same as it is for a square bettor, since other things being equal, the standard errors will be almost the same. The only difference is that their distribution mean (the centre of the normal curve) has been shifted to the right of the profit line. This being the case, sharp bettors and square bettors alike will exhibit a greater variance in outcomes when their bet probabilities are lower, that is to say, their odds are longer. Distributions of possible yields will be broader and shorter for long odds, taller and narrower for short odds. The only difference between the square and the sharp is the position of the mean; negative for the former, positive for the latter. Thus, regardless of the true underlying skill of the bettor, the z-score provides the most intuitive means of describing the relationship between expected value and betting odds. It's what we would expect given the rules of probability. The fact that it appears to offer the best match to observed data is all the more reassuring.

Of course, in terms of maximising profit whilst minimising risk, a staking plan will only ever be as good as the expected value that resides in the odds, and more specifically how closely your staking plan fits with the expected value–betting odds relationship. When I compared unit-loss, unit-win and unit-impact, I did so under the assumption that the true expected values varied according to the z-score function. As such, the Kelly distribution would be equivalent to one for unit-z staking, because the relationship between odds and expected value was defined by it. Just for fun, how would they compare if, instead, the relationship was defined by unit-loss, with expected value proportional to odds − 1?

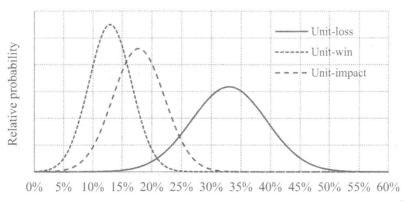

Yield distributions for different staking plans when expected value is proportional to odds - 1

The expected value for unit-loss is now 33%, since that is the average for odds of 1.5 (5%), 2 (10%), 3 (20%), 5 (40%), and 10 (90%). The unit-win and unit-loss plans still take less risk but give up so much profit expectation as a consequence, because of the stake-weight bias towards shorter odds. If expected value really was proportional to the odds − 1, then Kelly distribution would now be equivalent to the unit-loss distribution, and unit-loss staking would represent the optimal trade-off between risk and reward. Of course, expected value does not vary with odds like this in real betting markets; this exercise is merely to illustrate the relative merits of different staking, and the conditions where they are most suitable.

How about when unit-win is the most optimal staking plan, where expected value is constant no matter what the odds? I've held it at 5%.

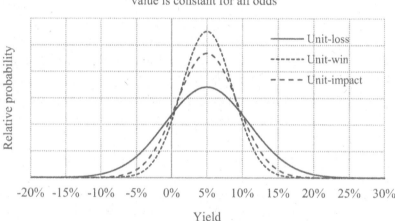

Yield distributions for different staking plans when expected value is constant for all odds

Unsurprisingly, all expected yields are the same − 5% − since all bets have 5% expected value. Unit-win, however, has the narrowest distribution and the smallest chance of loss because the stake sizes are appropriately sized to minimise the risk. The shortest odds have more stake-weight than both unit-impact and unit-loss, thus reducing the variance in the distribution. If expected value was constant for all odds, the Kelly plan would be equivalent to unit-win.

Finally, unit-impact. With expected value varying as a function of odds − 1 / odds, the unit-impact plan will offer the optimal risk-reward trade-off.

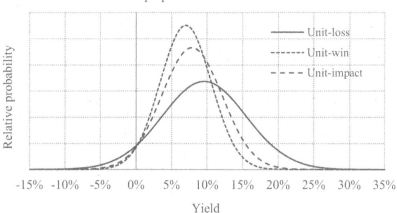

Yield distributions for different staking plans when expected value is proportional to odds - 1 / odds

In this scenario, unit-loss still has the largest expected yield (9.60%) but has the greatest probability of loss (5.3%). Unit-win has the lowest probability of loss (1.1%) but has the lowest expected yield too (6.99%). The best compromise is unit-impact, precisely because that's how the expected value–betting odds function has been defined for this scenario. Expected yield is 7.9% and loss probability is 4.2%. To reiterate the point: a staking plan will only ever be as good as it is expected to be, given your expected value and the way it varies with the betting odds.

Of course, it might be the case that you don't have a Kelly utility function. Rather, perhaps you are comfortable with a greater risk of loss over a specified length of betting history, preferring to seek potentially greater reward as compensation. For you, unit-loss might typically, although not necessarily, be preferable. Placing the same weight on a bet regardless of the odds will naturally mean a bigger distribution of possible outcomes, but that means profits as well as losses. The inherent danger with more aggressive staking plans comes in the risk of ruin. I haven't analysed that here, but we can be confident that the wider the theoretical distribution of yields, the greater the risk of ruin, and the more likely it is that your actual risk of failure will deviate from these normal distribution probabilities. To accommodate this, you might reduce the size of the unit-loss stake. That won't change your expected yield, but it will reduce your absolute expected profit. In managing your risk of ruin, you may then find that other staking plans become superior. Really, staking is just a matter of swings and roundabouts. Whichever way you manage your staking, risk and reward will be engaged in an eternal struggle. Your only job with respect to money management is to decide what sort of tolerance you have for the former against how much desire you have for the latter. No two people are equal, although it's probably true to say that Kelly offers the most mathematically rigorous compromise, even if human emotions will often have us deviating from that.

Uncertainty in your Expected Value

No money management plan is going to be successful if you haven't secured real expected value. However, would you believe me if I told you that, provided you're correct, on average, about your expected value, errors calculating it on a bet-by-bet basis won't matter? Well, such a surprising result is true. You can test this with a Monte Carlo simulation.

Consider again my hypothetical 1,000-bet history, with five different odds (1.5, 2, 3, 5 and 10) and five different expected values for bets with those odds (5%, 7.25%, 10.53%, 15.32% and 23.97%). In reality, we'll never have such precision in 'knowing' what our expected values are for our bets. Both aleatory and epistemic uncertainty reduce that quest to the impossible. More realistically, our 'true' expected values will distribute about a mean value. For example, for the odds of 1.5, the mean expected value is 5%, but some expected values will be more, and some will be less, although we'll never know which, since the 'true' outcome probabilities are impossible to know. To model this, I assumed that the 'true' expected values of bets were normally distributed about their mean. Furthermore, I chose a standard deviation of two times the mean to quantify the shape of this distribution. Thus, for odds of 1.5 with a mean expected value of 5%, the standard deviation in the 'true' expected values is 10%. For odds of 10 with a mean expected value of 23.97%, the standard deviation in the true expected values is 47.94%. With such a standard deviation, 30.85% of true expected values will actually be less than 0%. Of course, that will be balanced by 30.85% being more than two times the mean. Take a look at how this affects the distribution of yields for the Kelly staking plan. Remember, the expected mean is 9.67%. Just to be clear, you are looking at two different distributions here, not one with a best fit trendline. I've had to show one as a scatter and one as a line, since if they were the same, you would be unable to tell them apart. We see the same result no matter what the level of uncertainty in the specific expected values.

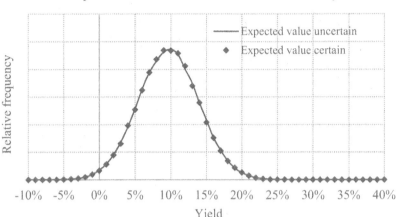

Comparison of Kelly Monte Carlo distribution where expected values are known with or without certainty

Given the inherent randomness in betting, this should provide great comfort to those worrying about errors. So long as your errors are random and cluster about a mean that you know with high precision, over reasonably-sized bet histories they will have no impact. Kelly staking is often regarded as risky on the grounds that it's so difficult to know your true expected value for a bet. So long as you're correct on average, it doesn't matter. The same is also true for the other staking plans I've considered: unit-loss, unit-win and unit-impact.

Comparative Performance of Staking Plans for a Real Betting History

Let's conclude this investigation into unit staking with a look at how these different money management plans might have comparatively performed with my real betting history: Wisdom of the (Pinnacle) Crowd. Below, I've shown four mini-charts comparing the actual (solid line) and expected (dashed line) profit trends for each staking plan. I've purposely kept the same scale for the vertical (profit) axis so that you can compare the four staking methods. In terms of actual performance, unit-loss, unit-win and unit-impact are broadly speaking performing on a par with each other, with Kelly staking outperforming all of them. Yields for the four staking plans were: unit-loss = 4.35%; unit-win = 4.03%, unit-impact = 4.27%; Kelly = 6.06%. Similarly, the Kelly plan has the highest expected yield (4.44%) but it's much closer to the other three (unit-loss

= 4.12%, unit-win = 3.56%, unit-impact = 3.74%) than for the actual performance.

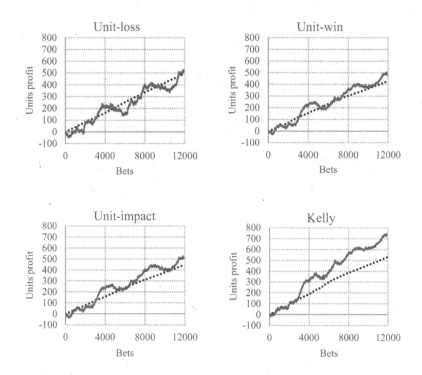

All four actual performances overachieved relative to expectation, but that was greatest for Kelly staking. The fact that Kelly was predicted to perform better than unit-loss staking is interesting, however. For my hypothesised 1,000-bet history earlier, unit-loss was seen to produce the highest expected yields, at the expense of a greater risk of loss. Kelly, by contrast, offered a compromise between risk and reward. How is it possible, here, for Kelly to show a greater expected yield than for unit-loss, yet still show a lower risk of loss? The explanation can be found when we consider the variability of the expected values. In my hypothesised model, bets with the same odds were awarded the same expected values. In reality, however, this is unlikely to be the case. Where there is variation in expected value for bets with the same odds, the stake-weighted average for those odds will always be larger for Kelly than for unit-loss. Why? Because for unit-loss, all stakes are the same; for Kelly, bets with greater expected value will have larger stakes. For example, the average expected value for 5 bets with the same odds holding expected values of 1%, 2%, 3%, 4%

and 5% will be 3% for unit-loss. For Kelly staking, however, the stake-weighted average expected value will be 3.667%. This stake-weighting influence acts in the opposite direction to the influence introduced by the variability in the odds. If that influence, on average, is greater, we may see expected yields for Kelly that are greater than those for unit-loss, and yet still with a smaller distribution standard error; a win-win scenario. Whether this will happen will very much depend on the nature of your betting history, specifically the odds and the expected values for each of the bets. It's not something that could be predicted in advance since obviously you won't know all of these figures at the outset.

Despite the overperformance relative to expectation, none was beyond typical statistical confidence limits that might otherwise have us questioning the validity of the betting model, even for the Kelly plan. Below, I've shown where the actual yields lie within their expected distributions, by means of a vertical line. Monte Carlo outputs are represented by scatter plots, whilst the curves signify the normal distribution approximated using my function for the standard error in the yield. As for my hypothesised betting history, there is excellent agreement between the two, although unit-impact again exhibits the multi-modal distribution.

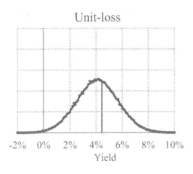

Unit-loss

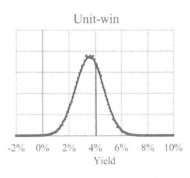

Unit-win

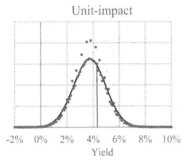

Unit-impact

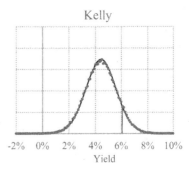

Kelly

Finally, see how the four distributions compare together. For simplicity and clarity, I've used the function-calculated curves rather than the Monte Carlo scatter plots, although we should remember that for unit-impact at least, there is a divergence between the two.

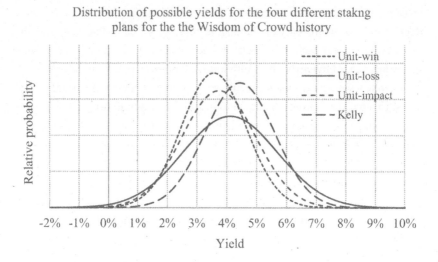

Distribution of possible yields for the four different stakng plans for the the Wisdom of Crowd history

With the widest distribution and largest standard error, unit-loss should typically allow you to achieve the highest yield if you are lucky. The trade-off is it can deliver the lowest yields if you're unlucky instead. If you prefer to take less risk, adjusting your stake size to take account of the odds with unit-win or unit-impact will help in that respect. And if you want the best of both worlds, then provided you know your expected value, at least on average, Kelly staking offers mathematically the best possible compromise.

Proportional Staking

All of the staking plans I've talked about thus far have been what might be called fixed staking plans. Of course, that's not strictly true because the size of the unit stake will vary according to the length of the odds, or the amount of expected value you hold, or a combination of the two. Nevertheless, by 'fixed' we mean fixed relative to the size of the bankroll you first started with. Two bets with the same odds and same expected value will always have the same number of units risked on them, although of course what a unit means to a bettor in terms of actual money will vary according to their available wealth and capacity for risk-taking. However, this need not be the case. If the second of these two bets occurred at a time in the betting history of the bettor when their accumulated wealth from all previous betting was double what it was at the time of the first bet, then why not stake twice as much? In doing so, we would be linking the size of the stake to the size of the existing bankroll at the time the bet is struck. Such a strategy is typically referred to as proportional or percentage staking, since the percentage size of the stake is proportional to the size of the existing bankroll. All other things being equal, if the bankroll is twice as large, the stake will be twice as large; if the bankroll is 5 times as small, the stake will be 5 times smaller. What size the percentage will be is up to the bettor, although the Kelly Criterion, as I mentioned earlier, provides a handy way to help define it.

There are two obvious benefits to proportional staking. The first is that, in theory at least, you can never go bust. Your risk of ruin is zero. If your bankroll has halved, your stakes will now be half the size too. If it halves again, so will the stakes. If you lost every single bet you ever placed, progressive stake sizes would become smaller and smaller, but never reach zero. Of course, in practice, the size of your bankroll would be so small that the difference between this and ruin is nothing more than a mathematical technicality. The second major benefit to staking proportionally is that it allows your bankroll to grow faster than it otherwise would betting fixed units. This is a consequence of compounding – the reinvestment of the previous bet's winnings into the next one – and the same influence that sees your bank savings grow if you are lucky enough to have any, and indeed lucky enough to find a bank right now that would even pay you a meaningful rate of interest. Of compound interest, the physicist Albert Einstein famously said, "[It] is the eighth wonder of the world. He who understands it, earns it... he who doesn't... pays it."

All of this sounds too good to be true, right? Zero risk of ruin (theoretically) and yet a way to harness the most powerful force in the universe to make our wealth grow. Of course, when something seems too good to be true, it usually is, and proportional staking is no exception to this rule. As I am sure you are tired of me saying, gambling is always a trade-off between risk and reward, or cost and benefit. What is the cost to proportional staking? Stay with me and you will find out. It's not a deal-breaker but it's important that you understand it and why it is so; then you can choose, subjectively, whether the rewards and benefits outweigh the risks and costs.

Let's build a Monte Carlo simulation to compare the expected returns from fixed unit staking on the one hand and proportional staking on the other. This one is really simple: just 1,000 wagers at odds of 2, with a 5% expected value. The Kelly stake for such a bet will be 5 units or 5%, depending on the staking plan we are following. For the first, all 1,000 bets will be 5 units. For the second, all bets will be 5%, the first of which is 5 units if we start with a bankroll of 100 units. Thereafter, exactly what the stake size will be in units will be dependent on how the bankroll has grown or shrunk as a consequence of previous winning and losing bets, but it will always be 5%. My Monte Carlo simulation had 100,000 iterations and the chart below shows the frequency distribution of the final bankroll after 1,000 bets. I have ignored ruin. For unit staking, it is possible to lose 100 units, but when that happened, I allowed the betting to continue to 1,000 bets. Obviously for proportional staking, theoretical ruin is impossible.

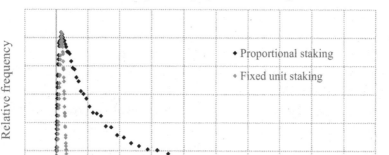

Monte Carlo distributions of final bankrolls for fixed unit staking versus proportional staking

You'll need to look closely to see the distribution for the unit staking, with the light-grey scatter. The average final bankroll is 349.9, a whisker off the expectation of 350, whilst the standard deviation is 157.8, again almost identical to that predicted by my yield standard error function (157.9). The highest final bankroll was 990 which occurred twice. With about a 1-in-40,000 probability of occurring, that's about right for a 100,000-iteration Monte Carlo simulation.

The distribution of final bankrolls for proportional staking is completely different. By contrast, it has a strong positive skew, with lots of smaller bankrolls but a few extremely large ones, far larger than the largest unit staking bankroll. Indeed, I've not even shown the largest ones in the chart above. If I had, you wouldn't have been able to see the unit staking distribution at all. The largest proportional staking bankroll was 211,299.72 units. In one sense, it's probably not surprising that you will see larger bankrolls with proportional staking when you hold positive expected value, because you are typically betting more units. Nevertheless, the huge disparity between the two plans and the size of the distribution asymmetry that arises from proportional staking should illustrate just how powerful the influence of compounding is. The mean final bankroll was 1,205.3; this is considerably bigger than the median bankroll of 349.2 because the few super-sized bankrolls in the simulation are positively biasing the arithmetic mean. For proportional staking, the median is arguably a better average to use, since it is closer to the bankroll you are likely to see most often. In fact, in this Monte Carlo simulation, only 21,356 of the 100,000 Monte Carlo iterations finished with bankrolls above the arithmetic mean or expected bankroll. The fact that the median was almost the same as the mean bankroll for unit staking is merely just coincidental. If I had used different input parameters, for example 2.5% expected value and stakes, that would not have happened.

Whilst it's obvious that we are staking more absolute units with proportional money management, it's not obvious how this impacts the yield. Consider just the first two bets; let's suppose the first is a winner and the second a loser. For unit staking, we win 5 units and then we lose 5 units. The net is 0 and hence the yield is 0% too. For proportional staking, however, we win 5 units from the first, but now lose 5.25 units from the second, since the second stake was 5% of 105, or 5.25 units. There is now a net loss of 0.25 units and hence a yield of -0.25 / 10.25 = -2.44%. That's not all. Suppose instead the first bet lost and the second bet won. For unit staking the yield is still 0%. For proportional staking, however, whilst the net loss is still the same – 0.25 units – the yield is different because the total stakes are different. This time, the second stake was 4.75 units, or 5% of 95 units. The yield is -0.25 / 9.75 = -2.56%. Exactly what yield you have is path-dependent, that is to say dependent on the order of winning and losing, and smaller than for unit staking. For 2 bets with 2 possible outcomes each there are 2^2 or 4 possible paths – lose/lose, lose/win, win/lose and win/win – and 4 possible yields. For 10 bets there are 2^{10} or 1,024 possible paths and 1,024 possible yields. By contrast, for unit staking there are only 11. For 1,000 bets there are $2^{1,000}$ possible yields. Excel is just able to output this number; anything much bigger and it refuses. The number is approximately 1 with 301 zeros following it. More generally, the number of possible yields from proportional staking for a binary bet that only has win or lose outcomes will be 2^n, where n is the number of bets. With so many possible yields when n is anything larger than a relatively small number, I really would have no idea how to define the probability distribution for proportional-stake yields from mathematical first principles. For unit staking, by contrast, the number of possible yields is only $n + 1$. Defining the probability distribution of yields depends only on the number of wins and losses because the yield is not path-dependent. Hence, it's simply a matter of using the binomial distribution, or the normal approximation if n is larger than say 10, or when the odds for the bets differ, as we have already seen. As you know by now, if the mathematics are too difficult, use a Monte Carlo simulation.

What is the expected yield for 1 bet with an expected value of 5%? It should be intuitively obvious, but let's calculate it mathematically; multiply each possible yield by its probability and sum the products. Winning and losing, respectively, have probabilities of 0.525 and 0.475. Since their yields are +1 and -1, the expected yield will be $0.525 - 0.475 = 0.05$ (or 5%). What about 2 bets? As I've explained, for proportional staking, what yield you will see is path-dependent. Let's look at the possible paths and their probabilities. Again, summing their products will give us the expected yield for 2 bets.

Path	Result 1	Result 2	Yield	Probability	Product
1	Loss	Loss	-1	0.2256	-0.2256
2	Loss	Win	-0.2564	0.2494	-0.0064
3	Win	Loss	-0.2439	0.2494	-0.0061
4	Win	Win	+1	0.2756	0.2756
Total				**1**	**0.0375**

The answer is 0.0375 (or 3.75%). This is lower than the expected yield for unit staking, which, being independent of the path, will always be 5%. Why is it lower than 5%? For proportional staking, there is an asymmetry between losses and gains. For the second path, the second stake (4.75 units) is smaller than the first loss (5 units). Thus, despite a win, it will not be enough to recover the original loss, and the net yield will be below 0%. Similarly, for the third path, the second stake is larger than the first win. Since it is lost, the net yield will again be below 0%, and therefore, so too, will the expected yield. For unit staking, paths 2 and 3 have yields of 0%. Systems that are path-dependent are called non-ergodic; the expectation depends on the route taken through time. Football league ranking and points are examples of non-ergodicity; where a team finishes a season depends, to a significant extent, on when they score and concede their goals. In the 2016/17 season for the English Football League 2, Carlisle and Blackpool finished 6th and 7th with 71 and 70 points, respectively. Both had scored 69 goals, but Carlisle, despite finishing one place higher, conceded 68 goals, 22 more than Blackpool. Teams only receive 3 points whether they win 1-0 or 10-0, and 0 points if they lose by the same score lines.

For an ergodic betting history, by contrast, the expectation is the same no matter what path through time is followed. You may recall my discussion earlier about the risk of ruin, and the distinction I made between ensemble probability and time probability. For bettors following unit staking, the risk of ruin means expectations are actually non-ergodic. True expectations are dependent on the pathway through time bettors take. Of course, sensible staking for a sharp bettor who holds expected value can reduce the risk of ruin to negligible levels. The ensemble probability and time probability are then almost the same, and the system almost ergodic. Expectations with proportional staking are non-ergodic. As Taleb might say, it then makes it much harder to do cost-benefit analysis. Following the method above, I've done it for the first 10 bets of my 1,000-bet history. I've plotted path-dependent expected yields in the chart below.

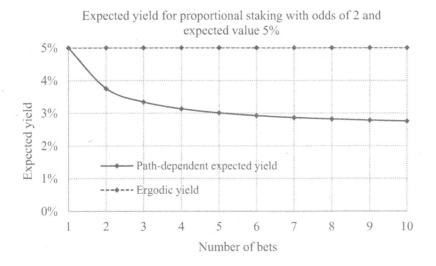

Expected yield for proportional staking with odds of 2 and expected value 5%

I could have gone a little further, but by 21 bets I'd have run out of Excel worksheet rows to help me do the mathematics, never mind 1,000 of them for which I'd need a spreadsheet many tens of orders of magnitude bigger than the visible universe. Nevertheless, it's fairly self-evident that the expected yield trends towards a limit roughly half of the ergodic yield. Using a Monte Carlo simulation, the average yield for 1,000 bets was 2.49%. How do they distribute? Take a look.

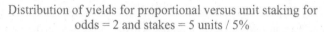

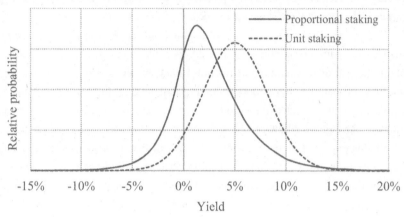

Distribution of yields for proportional versus unit staking for odds = 2 and stakes = 5 units / 5%

The area under the curve to the left of the profit line tells you the probability of making a loss. For unit staking, the size of that area as a proportion of the full distribution is about 5.4%. For proportional staking, it's 21.4%. The reason? For proportional staking, it takes more bets, on average, to recover previous losses. Furthermore, the bigger the loss, the larger the extra number of bets needed to recover; the problem is exponential. It takes an 11% growth to recover a 10% loss, but a 100% growth to recover a 50% loss. See how the number of bets required to return a bankroll to 100 units compares for unit staking (5-unit stakes) and proportional staking (5% stakes).

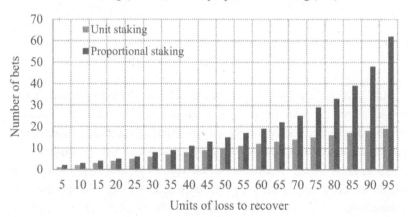

Number of bets (odds = 2) to return to 100 units for unit staking (5 units) versus proportional staking (5%)

Obviously, losses for unit staking will accumulate faster than for proportional staking, since for the latter, as the losses accrue, the stake size decreases. However, because of the asymmetry between losing and gaining, those losses accrue faster than they can be regained. With this scenario, it will take 14 more losing bets than winning ones to halve the bankroll, but 15 to recover it. It would take 45 more losing bets than winning ones to cut a bankroll by 90%, but 48 to restore it.

This is the trade-off for proportional staking: your expected bankroll may be greater, sometimes much greater; but your expected yield, and consequently your probability of profit, will be lower, compared to unit staking. Indeed, sometimes you may find that the median bankroll, as a measure of the most likely to be seen, will be less than what you started with; more than half of the distribution of yields will be unprofitable. The trade-off is even more significant for longer odds. Have a look at the one for odds of 5.

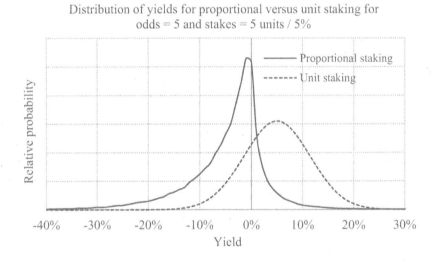

Distribution of yields for proportional versus unit staking for odds = 5 and stakes = 5 units / 5%

Whilst the expected final bankroll is the same as for odds of 2, the median is much reduced. Indeed, it's only 10.7, compared to 349.2 when the betting odds are 2. Over 77% of the Monte Carlo iterations saw the bankroll close with less than it had started with; this despite an expectation of multiplying it by more than a factor of 12. The variance and asymmetry in the distribution of final bankrolls are now huge; the largest was nearly 65 million units, the smallest just 0.00002 units. The average yield is now -4.5%. For longer odds, the asymmetry and impact of non-ergodicity is even greater, as revealed in the next chart.

Expected yields from 1,000 bets with 5% proportional stakes

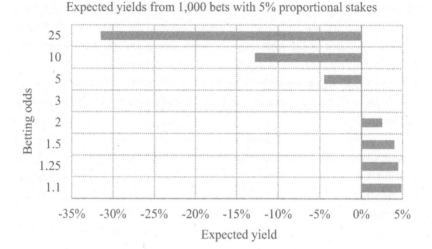

Of course, the solution to the problem of non-ergodicity of proportional staking yields and the asymmetry of bankrolls is partly provided by Kelly. If you follow it, you wouldn't be risking 5% stakes, holding 5% expected value, betting at odds of 5. You would reduce those to 1.25%. Your expected yield is again now roughly half the expected yield for unit staking, namely 2.5%, as it was for 5% stakes when betting at odds of 2. Now the probability of making a loss is about 33%, instead of 77%. As always, however, there is a trade-off. Reducing the size of the stakes to reduce risk of losing also reduces the size of the expected final bankroll. Instead of over 1,200, it is now only 186, with a median of just 136. Swings and roundabouts. Kelly, of course, is designed to provide you with the best possible trade-off between risk and reward, provided your utility function for accruing wealth is logarithmic.

Rather interestingly, the appropriate Kelly percentage for any odds will have an expected yield from proportional staking of about half the expected value. If your expected value is 20% betting odds of 10, betting Kelly stakes of 2.22% will have an expected yield of about 10%. Furthermore, betting twice the appropriate Kelly stakes will show expected yields of about 0%, and median final bankroll of roughly the same as you started with. This is the case of odds of 3 in the chart above. A 5% stake with 5% expected value is twice the size of the appropriate Kelly stake. Stakes of 20% for odds of 1.5 also hold an expected yield of 0%; so too odds of 5 with 2.5% stakes, and odds of 10 with stakes of 1.11%. More generally, you can see how the expected yield for proportional staking varies as a function of the stake percentage and the betting odds. Here, I have shown the curves for an expected value of 5%.

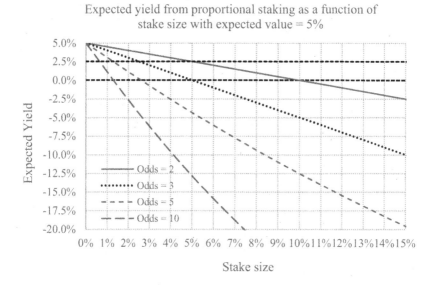

Expected yield from proportional staking as a function of stake size with expected value = 5%

The intersection of the curves with the dotted line at a yield of 2.5% is roughly the size of the appropriate Kelly stake. The intersection point with the 0%-yield line is double-Kelly. There is some interesting, if rather complex, mathematics behind this relationship. I don't intend to review this in detail, but I will look again at the implications of betting larger stakes than the Kelly recommendation, and in particular what your expectations will be with a size that is twice the Kelly stake.

Bankroll Growth

If the size of the yield is path-dependent for proportional staking, that is not the case for growth. Proportional money management, after all, is about increasing the rate at which your bankroll will grow rather than increasing the absolute size of your yield. In particular, the maximising of the expected value of the logarithm of wealth (rather than wealth itself) by The Kelly Criterion is equivalent to maximising the expected geometric growth rate. Why doesn't the order of wins and losses matter with respect to bankroll growth? Again, a simple example will help to clarify.

A bettor makes 20 bets at odds of 2 holding an expected value of 10% and a Kelly stake of 10%. If the first bet wins, their bankroll will now be 110% (or 1.1) times the original bankroll. If it loses, it will be only 90% (or 0.9) times the original bankroll. The same is true after each sequential bet. Consequently, after 20 bets, if the bettor has had the expected number of 11 winners, we can easily calculate the growth in their bankroll (BG) as follows:

$$BG = 1.1^{11} \times 0.9^9 = 1.1054$$

It doesn't matter what order the wins and losses come in. The bettor could start with 11 winners and finish with 9 losers; or they could start with 9 losers and finish with 11 winners; or they could have any other of the 167,960 total possible ways of arranging this combination of winners and losers. They will still finish with 110.54% of what they started with. If you don't believe it, try it yourself in Excel for just 2 or 3 bets instead of 20. No matter the order of wins and losses, the final bankroll growth, BG, will be the same. More generally, for n bets at odds of 2, with a stake percentage of s (expressed as a decimal), and number of winners, w,

$$BG = (1 + s)^w (1 - s)^{n-w}$$

whilst for any odds, o,

$$BG = (1 + (s(o - 1)))^w (1 - s)^{n-w}$$

If the odds were instead 3, BG would be 2.8786 for 11 winners and 9 losers, and 1.2144 for 8 winners and 12 losers. In my hypothetical 1,000-bet history, how many winners did the Monte Carlo iteration with the largest bankroll of 211,299.72 units have? BG = 211,299.72 / 100 = 2112.997 and s = 0.05. Through a little bit of trial and error I can quickly find w. The figure is 589.

Knowing the expected value (EV) allows one to calculate the expected rate of bankroll growth (xBG) as follows:

$$xBG = (EV. s + 1)^n$$

The dot between EV and s signifies a multiplication, that is to say the product of the expected value multiplied by the stake. In my simple example, the bettor holds a 10% (or 0.1) expected value. Consequently, the expected (or mean) bankroll growth will be given by $((0.1 \times 0.1)+1)^{20} = 1.01^{20} = 1.2202$. More generally, for Kelly staking, $s = EV / o - 1$. Consequently, for a Kelly stake,

$$xBG_{Kelly} = \left(\frac{EV^2}{o-1} + 1\right)^n$$

A bettor holding expected value of 10% would typically win 11 out of 20 bets at odds of 2. Doing so, as we've seen, would grow their bankroll by a factor of 1.1054. How is this less than the expected bankroll growth of 1.2202? Remember, 'expected' is equivalent to the arithmetic mean. We already know from the Monte Carlo distribution earlier that this figure is heavily skewed by a few exceptionally large bankroll growths. Larger growth figures will contribute disproportionately more to the mean. For example, for 20 bets at odds of 2, the largest possible, from 20 winners, would be 6.7275, although it only has a (binomial) probability of 0.00064%. Multiplying the bankroll growth by its probability for each of the 21 possible outcomes (0 winners through to 20) and then summing will give us the expected bankroll growth. The answer is 1.2202, or 122.02% of what you started with, the same as via the equation above. The figure of 110.54% we obtain from an expected number of 11 winners with a corresponding 9 losses is, in fact, the median. It represents the halfway point in the distribution of different possible values of bankroll growth, but because that distribution is positively skewed, it will be smaller than the mean or expected bankroll growth.

With a little bit of algebra, I can actually determine the equation for the median bankroll growth, median(BG), in terms of the expected value, or to be more precise, the expected return, r, which is $EV + 1$. Since:

$$EV = \frac{w_e(o-1) - (n - w_e)}{n}$$

where w_e is the expected number of winners, I can show that:

$$r = \frac{w_e o}{n}$$

and hence the expected number of winners is expressed by:

$$w_e = \frac{nr}{o}$$

Substituting this expression for w_e in place of w in the equation for BG above, we have:

$$\text{median(BG)} = (1 + (s(o - 1))^{\frac{nr}{o}}(1 - s)^{n(1-\frac{r}{o})}$$

And since for Kelly staking, $s = EV / o - 1 = (r - 1) / (o - 1)$, I can prove that:

$$\text{median}\left(BG_{\text{Kelly}}\right) = \left(\frac{r(o - 1)}{o - r}\right)^{\frac{nr}{o}} \left(\frac{o - r}{o - 1}\right)^{n}$$

Plugging $r = 1.1$, $o = 2$, and $n = 20$ into this equation gives an answer of 1.1054, exactly as calculated before for the expected number of 11 winners. Note that this equation only has relevance for values of $r > 1$. Where $r < 1$, the Kelly stake is negative, clearly an impossibility, but this negative disappears within the equation so that a result is still given. Indeed, $r = 0.9$ will give the same answer as 1.1.

For simplicity, let's define $EV^2/(o-1) + 1$ in the equation for the expected Kelly bankroll growth (xBG_{Kelly}) as the Kelly bankroll growth factor, F, the factor by which a bankroll is expected to grow after each bet. Here, for example, with an expected value of 10% at odds of 2, $F = 1.01$, meaning, on average, a bankroll will be 1% larger after the bet than before it. F is a little bit like a banking interest rate; the only difference is the time period. Following this, we then have:

$$xBG_{\text{Kelly}} = F^n$$

As we know, a power or exponent is just the opposite of a logarithm. The logarithm of a number is simply the power to which the base must be raised to give the number. For example, 5 winning bets at odds of 2 with a 10% stake increase the bankroll by a factor $1.1 \times 1.1 \times 1.1 \times 1.1 \times 1.1 = 1.1^5 = 1.6105$. This is equivalent to $\log_{1.1} 1.6105 = 5$, where 1.1 is the base of the logarithm and 5 is the number of winners. 1.1 is simply the growth factor for a winning bet. Similarly, we can rewrite the equation above as:

$$n = log_F xBG_{\text{Kelly}}$$

where F is the base of the logarithm. Since the Kelly stake is designed to maximise the logarithm of the growth rate in the bankroll, this equation should not come as a surprise. For bets with the same odds and expected value, the logarithm of the expected bankroll growth is proportional to the number of bets. Double the number of bets and you will double the logarithm of the expected bankroll growth.

It's perhaps easier to illustrate the logarithmic relationship between winners (or more correctly-speaking, the excess number of winners over losers) and bankroll growth visually. I've drawn it below for my 20 hypothetical bets at odds of 2 and a stake of 10%, showing the bankroll growth as a function of the number of winners. The chart on the left shows the bankroll growth as a linear scale; for the chart on the right, I've redrawn it as a logarithmic scale.

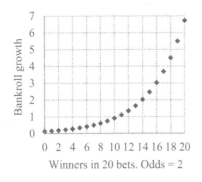 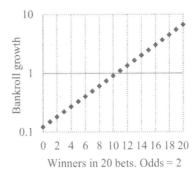

Similarly, for the expected bankroll growth for Kelly staking, the solid lines below show how xBG_{Kelly} varies as a function of the number of bets, n. Again, notice the logarithmic relationship. What are the dashed lines? I'll come to that shortly.

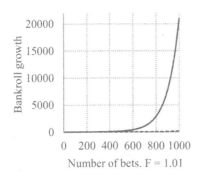 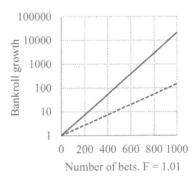

The left chart, in particular, illustrates nicely the power of exponential compounding. No wonder Einstein thought it the most powerful force in the universe. With a growth factor of 1% per bet, you can expect to turn a £1 bankroll into almost £21,000 within just 1,000 bets. Of course, finding regular expected value of 10% at odds of 2 is no easy task. Furthermore, the solid lines represent only the arithmetic mean path your betting history would follow, not the most likely one; remember the distribution asymmetry and the weighting towards super-sized bankroll growth. In contrast, the median path will follow a much shallower trend. In this example, the median bankroll would be only 149.66 times the size of the starting one, or £149.66 if you started with £1. I've shown these in the charts above as dashed lines. Notice, in particular, in the left hand chart with a linear (rather than logarithmic) bankroll growth axis, it's barely even perceptible in contrast to the expected path. Whilst the mean Kelly bankroll growth is proportional to the nth power of the Kelly bankroll growth factor, F, where n is the number of bets, the median Kelly bankroll growth can be closely approximated by:

$$median(BG_{Kelly}) \approx \left(\frac{F + 1}{2}\right)^n$$

From this, we can approximate the ratio of the mean to median Kelly bankroll growth as:

$$\left(\frac{xBG_{Kelly}}{median(BG_{Kelly})}\right) \approx \left(\frac{2F}{F + 1}\right)^n$$

Whilst around 140 times smaller than mean bankroll in this example, a median bankroll of £149.66 is still far superior to the bankroll of £20 you would expect to achieve from unit staking, starting at £1 and staking £0.10 per bet. What, then, is the catch? As I demonstrated via my analysis of yields, although you stand to win more via proportional staking and the power of compounding that it offers, the trade-off is the greater probability of losses, on account of the greater amount of time spent recovering from them. For my scenario here, the probability of loss after 1,000 wagers is 5.6%. For unit staking it is less than 0.1%. Exactly how I calculated the first figure will soon be revealed.

Take another look at my logarithmic mini-plot above for the 20 bets at odds of 2 with stakes of 10%. Look closely at the point for 10 winners: it sits just below a bankroll growth of 1. Since a figure of 1 is equivalent to breaking even, or an expected yield of 0%, evidently this scenario has resulted in a loss. The explanation is the same as before: it takes an 11% growth to recover a 10% loss, but if all stakes are 10%, the wins won't completely compensate for the losses. The bankroll growth factor for a win and a loss – or, indeed, a loss and a win, since the order, as explained, doesn't matter – is given by $1.1 \times 0.9 = 0.99$. For 10 wins and 10 losses, then, it will be $0.99^{10} = 0.904$. The larger the number of bets, the bigger the loss. After 200 bets and 100 winners, your bankroll would be $0.99^{100} = 0.366$, and after 2,000 bets and 1,000 winners it would be just 0.0000432 of what you started with, or £1 if you'd started with £23,164. Your expected (mean) bankroll will still be 1 if your expected value is 0%, but it's so unlikely to happen. Only 1.25% of possible histories in this scenario would be profitable. This should illustrate nicely why the median is a much better metric to measure your expectations when staking proportionally.

For the equivalent stake size, the disparity is even more pronounced for longer odds. Betting at odds of 4, 5 unit-stake winners and 15 unit-stake losers would break even. With proportional stakes of 10%, the final bankroll after 20 bets would be $1.3^5 \times 0.9^{15} = 0.764$; after 200 bets (with 50 winners), 0.0682; and after 2,000 bets (with 500 winners), you'd have turned Jeff Bezos' wealth into about 30 pence. The power of compounding, unsurprisingly, works both ways. Of course, if you actually knew your expected value was 0%, you wouldn't be betting 10% stakes, indeed you shouldn't be betting seriously at all; I've just provided this example to emphasise the downside to proportional staking. Perhaps more importantly, however, if you aren't yet sure whether you do hold any true expected value, proportional staking is a method of money management that is arguably best left alone until you do. You may not go bust but without expected value, even luck is unlikely to reward you. Indeed, even when you do hold some, getting your stakes wrong can turn an otherwise successful strategy into a puzzling failure. With that in mind, it pays to know the probabilities of that happening. It would be nice to be able to calculate those via a mathematical function, in the same way that I showed it was possible for unit staking. Let's find out if it can be done.

Bankroll Distributions for Proportional Staking

With unit staking your bankroll growth is proportional to the number of winners and it distributes normally. For proportional staking, we've seen that it's actually the logarithm of bankroll growth which is proportional to the number of winners.

Can you guess how that distributes? Let's replot the asymmetric Monte Carlo distribution I showed a little earlier – 1,000 wagers at odds of 2 with a 5% expected value and 5% Kelly stakes – but with a logarithmic axis.

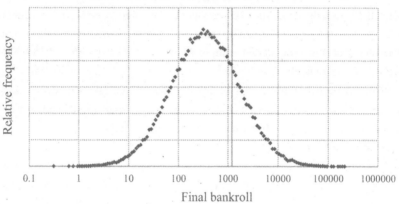

Monte Carlo distribution of the final bankroll for proportional staking with logarithmic axis

It has the distinctly familiar look of the normal distribution. In fact, this distribution is lognormal, but because the horizontal axis is logarithmic, it takes the shape of a normal one. Like the normal distribution, the lognormal distribution is a continuous probability distribution of a random variable. However, whilst for the normal distribution it is the variable itself that is normally distributed, for a lognormal distribution it is the logarithm of the variable that is normally distributed. The mean of this distribution is shown by the vertical black line. Given the preceding mathematics I've shown you, hopefully this won't have come as a surprise. Percentage growth or a percentage contraction is exponential in nature. That is, with each bet, a bankroll grows by a factor of 1 plus the percentage stake, or contracts by 1 minus the percentage stake. Multiplying these factors together in a series of bets creates a power (for example, $1.01^{100} = 2.705$), the exponent of which is equivalent to the logarithm ($\log_{1.01} 2.705 = 100$, where 1.01 is the base). Since the bankroll growth is proportional to the growth factor raised to the power of the number of winners, the logarithm of the bankroll growth will be proportional to the number of winners itself. Furthermore, since the number of winners will distribute normally (to be more precise binomially, but I've explained numerous times why I use the normal approximation), so, too, will the logarithm of the bankroll growth.

How do the mean and median bankrolls for this distribution compare to the figure calculated from my equations? Recall, the mean final bankroll was 1,205.3 and the median 349.2. With EV = 0.05, r = 1.05, s = 0.05, o = 2 and n = 1,000, for the mean we have:

$$xBG = ((0.05 \times 0.05) + 1)^{1000} = 12.1445$$

Since the starting bankroll was 100 units, the final expected one will be 1,214,45 units. For the median bankroll, we have:

$$median(BG) = (1 + (0.05(2 - 1)))^{\frac{1,000 \times 1.05}{2}}(1 - 0.05)^{1,000\left(1-\frac{1.05}{2}\right)} = 3.4922$$

Thus, the final median bankroll will be 349.22 units. Both sets of figures match closely. Graphically, the median occurs at the centre of the lognormal distribution above, whilst you can see that the mean is to the right. Recall that for positively-skewed distributions, the mean will always be greater than the median.

Excel has the NORM.DIST function to output normal distribution probabilities, for example when we would like to know the likelihood of beating, or failing to beat, a particular yield with unit staking. It would be useful to have a similar function to use with a lognormal distribution, that could calculate the probabilities of exceeding, or failing to exceed, a particular bankroll growth. Fortunately, Excel has one: the LOGNORM.DIST function. The full syntax is LOGNORM.DIST(x,μ,σ,cumulative), where x, the random variable whose logarithm distributes normally, is a specific bankroll growth threshold value (for example 1 for break-even or 2 for doubling), μ and σ are the arithmetic mean and standard deviation of the natural logarithm of x, and 'cumulative', as for Excel's other distribution functions, is a logical argument that determines the function's form. Setting it to TRUE returns the cumulative distribution function or the total area in the distribution to the left of x. Essentially, it does the same as the NORM.DIST function but with the natural logarithm of x rather than x itself. To use it, however, we need to calculate the natural logarithm of the Monte Carlo bankrolls. Before I do that, however, I need to briefly explain what a natural logarithm is. Apologies if you know it, or if you find I am repeating material I've already covered.

All logarithms have bases. The base is the number raised by an exponent to make a power. For $10^2 = 100$, 10 is the base and 2 is the exponent. Similarly, 2 is the base in $2^3 = 8$. The natural logarithm of a number is its logarithm to the base of the mathematical constant e, or Euler's number, named after another 18th century Swiss mathematician Leonhard Euler, who was trying to solve a problem about compound interest originally proposed 50 years earlier by Jacob Bernoulli. The number is irrational, meaning it cannot be expressed as a fraction. Another irrational number is pi, or π. It is approximately equal to 2.7183 but being irrational will have an infinite number of decimal digits, although it is known to over a trillion decimal places. Jacob had wondered what would happen to some money in a bank if the time period of interest payment was reduced. Typically, we might expect interest to be paid annually. If it were paid at 100%, a very generous bank indeed, your money would have doubled. It's equivalent to a winning bet with odds of 2. Instead, suppose the bank pays 50% but every 6 months instead of 12. That's now equivalent to two winning bets at odds of 1.5, with the winnings from the first reinvested into the stake for the second. Now your bank will be 1.5 x 1.5 = 2.25 times what you started with. Keep going; suppose now the bank pays 100/12%, or 8.33% every month. That's like 12 consecutive winners at odds of 1.0833. Now your bank will be 2.613 times its original size. What about 365 days paid at 100/365% or 0.274%, or 365 bets at odds of 1.00274? The growth factor is now 2.714. As the number of bets, n, increases, so does the bank growth factor, but at an ever-decreasing limit. As n tends towards infinity, the growth factor will tend towards the number e. Whilst its discovery may have come from a whimsical thought experiment, Euler's number has become one of the most important and widely used mathematical constants, not least in the mathematics of exponential growth (or contraction) which describe the betting histories for proportional staking as well. It features in the equation for the probability function for the normal distribution. Indeed, it appears in arguably the most beautiful equation of all, Euler's identity, along with four of the most significant numbers in mathematics, π, the imaginary number i (or $\sqrt{-1}$), 1 and 0.

$$e^{i\pi} + 1 = 0$$

I know none of this tangential thinking has anything to do with betting and Monte Carlo simulations, but I will always take the opportunity to talk about Euler's identity if one is presented. Perhaps I should get out more.

The natural logarithm of x is written as $\log_e(x)$ or more usually as $\ln(x)$, where 'l' abbreviates logarithm and 'n' abbreviates natural. Excel has the $\ln(x)$ function to calculate them for you. I calculated the natural logarithm of the final bankroll for all 100,000 iterations in my Monte Carlo simulation and plotted them below.

The distribution is essentially equivalent to the one above with the logarithmic axis; the only difference is I've applied the logarithmic transformation earlier.

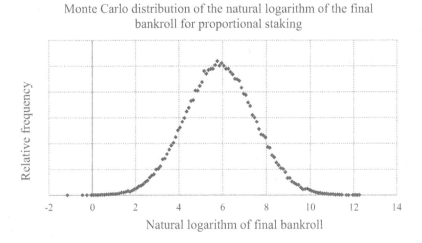

Monte Carlo distribution of the natural logarithm of the final bankroll for proportional staking

The mean of Ln(bankroll) for this distribution is 5.855 and its standard deviation 1.579. I can now calculate the probability of having less than I started with (LOGNORM.DIST(100,5.855,1.579,TRUE) = 21.44%), the probability of doubling my money (1 − LOGNORM.DIST(200,5.855,1.579,TRUE) = 63.77%) or the probability of finishing with more than the arithmetic mean (1 − LOGNORM.DIST(1205,5.855,1.579,TRUE) = 21.62%). One might wonder what the point is of going to all the trouble of transforming the Monte Carlo bankrolls into logarithms to then perform these calculations, when we can simply count the number of iterations where the final bankroll was less than 100, more than 200 or more than 1,205. Doing so yields figures of 21,447, 63,616 and 21,356, closely matching the percentages calculated using the LOGNORM.DIST function. Indeed, in this case, there probably isn't much point since you've had to run the Monte Carlo simulation in the first place. Nevertheless, I wanted to show you the process because we can use my equation for the median bankroll growth, together with the equations for the lognormal distribution, to calculate these probabilities from first principles. Let's go through the steps.

1) Calculate the median bankroll growth.

Let me repeat once again the equation for calculating the median bankroll growth for proportional staking, when the stake percentage (s), odds (o) and expected value (r − 1) remain constant.

$$\text{median(BG)} = (1 + (s(o - 1))^{\frac{nr}{o}}(1 - s)^{n(1-\frac{r}{o})}$$

For n = 1,000 bets at odds of 2 with stakes of 5%, holding an expected value of 5%, the figure is 3.4922.

2)   Calculate the mean of the bankroll growth's natural logarithm.

For a random variable that is distributed lognormally, the median is equal to e^{μ}, where e is Euler's number and μ is the mean of the variable's natural logarithm, not the mean of the variable itself. Consequently, μ is equal to the natural logarithm of the median of the variable. Here, the variable is the bankroll growth, and the median is 3.4922. Consequently, the mean natural logarithm of bankroll growth, μ, will be ln(median(BG)) = ln(3.4922) = 1.2505.

3)   Calculate the standard deviation of the bankroll growth's natural logarithm.

For a random variable that is distributed lognormally, the mean is equal to

$$e^{(\mu+\frac{\sigma^2}{2})}$$

where σ is the standard deviation of the variable's natural logarithm, not the standard deviation of the variable itself. Here, the mean is the expected bankroll growth, xBG. We already have another equation for the mean or expected bankroll growth:

$$\text{xBG} = (EV.s + 1)^n$$

With EV = 0.05, s = 0.05 and n = 1,000, xBG = 12.1445. We also have:

$$\mu = \ln(\text{median(BG)})$$

Hence, rearranging for σ, we have:

$$\sigma = \sqrt{2(\ln(\text{xBG}) - \ln(\text{median(BG)}))}$$

Following the logarithm quotient rule, this simplifies to:

$$\sigma = \sqrt{2\ln\left(\frac{xBG}{median(BG)}\right)}$$

Since xBG = 12.1445 and median(BG) = 3.4922, σ = 1.5788.

4) Finally, use the function LOGNORM.DIST(x,μ,σ,TRUE) to calculate the probability of a bankroll growth exceeding, or failing to exceed, a chosen threshold.

The function mean, μ, is your figure calculated in step 2 (in my example 1.2505), whilst the standard deviation, σ, is your figure calculated in step 3 (in my example 1.5788). x is your chosen threshold, for example 1 for break-even, 2 for bankroll doubling and so on. For example, for 1,000 bets at odds of 2, stakes of 5% and expected value 5%, the probability of making a loss is given by LOGNORM.DIST(1,1.2505,1.5788,TRUE) = 21.416%. This is almost identical to the actual Monte Carlo proportion of 21.447%. The probability of surpassing a bankroll doubling is given by 1 – LOGNORM.DIST(2,1.2505,1.5788,true) = 63.796%, again almost the same as the figure from the Monte Carlo simulation, 63.616%.

This mathematics might be more than some of you can cope with. If it is, then you can always run a Monte Carlo simulation to estimate the success and failure probabilities for different scenarios of odds, stakes, expected value and the number of bets. However, for those who are comfortable with the equations for proportional staking, they offer a very quick alternative to the Monte Carlo simulation, in the same way that my function for estimating the standard error in betting yields did so for unit staking. Granted, this 'first principles' method won't visually illustrate the distribution, but as for unit staking, I've built a rudimentary proportional staking calculator that does this job. Again, you will find it on Football-Data.co.uk. I've used this calculator to test a number of scenarios. Let's have a look at some of them, and see how changing the different variables o, s, EV and n will change the shape of the lognormal distribution and the associated probabilities of different types of success and failure.

We already know that the number of bets is proportional to the logarithm of the expected and median bankroll growth. Let's have a look at how that plays out across the full probability distribution. Below, I've compared the distributions for 100, 1,000 and 10,000 bets, where o = 2, EV = 2.5% and s = 2.5%.

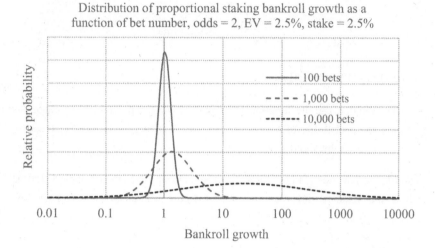

Distribution of proportional staking bankroll growth as a
function of bet number, odds = 2, EV = 2.5%, stake = 2.5%

The influence of exponential growth of bankrolls via proportional staking is obvious to see. Expected bankroll growth is 1.064 for 100 bets, 1.87 for 1,000 bets and 517 for 10,000, whilst for the median bankroll growth the figures are 1.032, 1.37 and 22.8. Accompanying the exponential increase in the expected and median bankroll growth is a colossal increase in the variance of possible bankrolls, with the realistically largest and smallest ones differing by as many as six orders of magnitude over a history of 10,000 bets. Remember, the horizontal axis in the chart above is logarithmic, not linear. If it were, the distribution for 100 bets would be narrower than the width of the finest human hair on the page you are reading. Whilst the law of large numbers reduces the probability of failure as the number of bets increases, the range of possibilities increases dramatically. Such is the power of compounding. This is in stark contrast to the range of possible yields from unit staking, which narrows significantly as the number of bets increases.

How does the distribution vary as a function of your expected value, all other things (stake size, odds and the number of bets) being equal? Naturally, we should expect both the mean and the median bankroll growth to increase exponentially as expected value increases. How will the shape of the distribution change? Whilst increasing the expected value transforms the distribution towards greater bankroll growth, the size and shape remain unchanged. Notice that the median bankroll growth for a break-even expected value falls below 1. I've already covered the explanation for why.

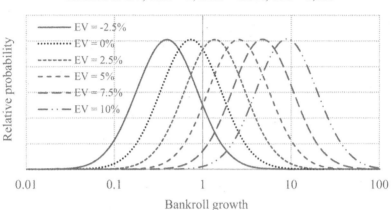

Distribution of proportional staking bankroll growth as a
function of EV, odds = 2, stake = 2.5%, bets = 1,000

What about the influence of the betting odds? I've compared five different
scenarios where the odds are 1.5. 2, 3, 5 and 10. EV = 2.5%, stakes = 2.5% and
the number of bets is 1,000 for each.

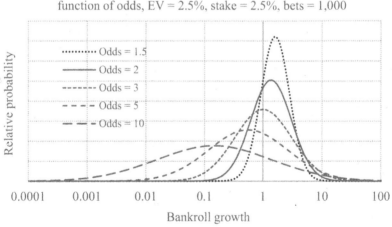

Distribution of proportional staking bankroll growth as a
function of odds, EV = 2.5%, stake = 2.5%, bets = 1,000

For each scenario, the expected bankroll growth is the same: 1.87. The median,
however, decreases with lengthening odds. Indeed, for anything longer than odds
of 3 with these scenario parameters your median will actually be equivalent to a
loss. Longer odds obviously have the potential to deliver some massive bankroll
growth. However, because variance has increased, there is also the potential for

some truly disastrous performances, even though you are holding expected value in your bets. Since the distribution is asymmetric, as the variance increases, the median must decrease if the mean is to remain the same. The same will be true for any number of bets. This is not to argue that odds longer than 3 will always show a median bankroll growth less than 1; there is something particular about my chosen parameters that I will explore in more detail shortly. You may recall earlier that when the stake increased above roughly twice the size of the theoretical Kelly stake, the expected yield fell below 0%. For odds of 3 with a 2.5% expected value, the Kelly stake is 1.25%, half of what I have used in my scenario here. Let me show you the distributions when the stake size is twice the appropriate Kelly percentage. Again, the number of bets is 1,000 and EV = 2.5%.

Distribution of proportional staking bankroll growth when stake = 2 x Kelly, EV = 2.5%, bets = 1,000

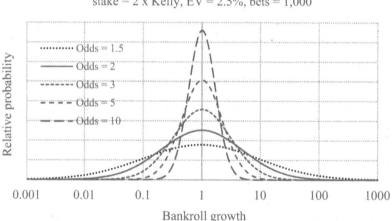

The longer the odds, the narrower the distribution. That is to be expected because, as the odds lengthen, the stakes shrink in size. This, however, is not the reason for showing you this chart. Rather, it's to illustrate the size of the median bankroll when the stake size is twice that recommended by the Kelly Criterion. It's around 1, no matter what the betting odds. Anything larger and the most likely betting history will involve a loss. Of course, your expected bankroll growth is still larger than 1, but it's a much lower-probability history given the asymmetry of the distribution. Don't forget, you are looking at a logarithmic scale and a lognormal distribution, not a normal one.

Let's take a look more generally at how the distribution changes as we change the size of the Kelly fraction, that is, the size of the stake relative to the recommended Kelly size. We have seen that 2 x Kelly associates with a median bankroll growth of 1, in other words breaking even, despite holding expected value. What about fractions less than 1? The following probability distributions compare full-Kelly staking (stake = 2.5% with EV = 2.5% at odds = 2) to half-Kelly (stakes = 1.25%) and quarter-Kelly (stakes = 0.625%). The history is again 1,000 bets.

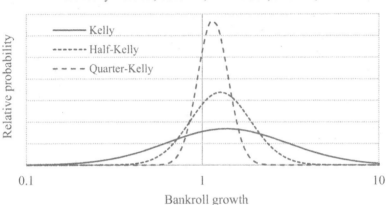

Distribution of proportional staking bankrolls as a function of the Kelly fraction, odds = 2, EV = 2.5%, bets = 1,000

Whilst the median bankroll growth for fractional-Kelly staking is, unsurprisingly, smaller than for full-Kelly, it's not a deal-breaker. For my scenario parameters, the full-Kelly median is 1.37; for half-Kelly and quarter-Kelly, it is 1.26 and 1.15, respectively. It is true that the mean is reduced significantly more for fractional Kelly. Full, half- and quarter-Kelly mean bankroll growth is 1.87, 1.37 and 1.17. Remember, however, that the mean bankroll is a lower-probability occurrence because of the underlying bankroll growth distribution asymmetry. More importantly, fractional-Kelly reduces the probability of failing to make a profit, with the area to the left of 'bankroll growth = 1' progressively smaller as the Kelly fraction is reduced. For full-Kelly, the probability of loss-making after 1,000 bets is 34.6%. For half- and quarter-Kelly, this falls to 27.7% and 24.5%. For bettors with larger expected value, there are proportionally bigger gains to be had in terms of risk management by employing fractional-Kelly staking. With an expected value of 5% (1,000 bets at odds of 2), full-Kelly staking comes with a 21.4% probability of finishing with less than you started with. Half-Kelly, rather coincidentally, given the size of the fraction, cuts this in half to 11.7%; meanwhile the median bankroll growth has only fallen from 3.49 to 2.55. No matter the scenario or how small a Kelly fraction you choose, your probability of ending with less than you started with will always be larger than it is for unit staking. However, that is the risk you are taking, via proportional staking, in attempting to grow your profits. In betting, there is never a free lunch.

Reducing the chance of failure by giving up a little bit of bankroll growth seems a reasonable price to pay, at least for bettors who don't share Daniel Bernoulli's rather aggressive logarithmic utility function. Joe Peta, the former Wall Street market maker and hedge fund stock trader, and head of Performance Analytics at Point72 Asset Management, puts it like this. 'The problem with using Kelly is that no matter what you calculate your expected return to be, your variance will be ridiculously [and] uninvestably high.' That much is obvious when you look at the distributions above set against the backdrop of the logarithmic bankroll growth axis. When the probability of increasing your bankroll 6-fold is about the same as seeing it shrink by a factor of 3, you can appreciate the problem you're dealing with. There is just such a large range of possibilities. This is just for 1,000 bets; imagine the variance for much longer histories. Kelly staking may provide the optimal trade-off between risk and reward for fully-rational agents; most human beings, however, are far from that, perennially affected by loss aversion and the fear of failure. Sometimes, Kelly can throw up some frighteningly large stakes. Whilst there's no denying they maximise the efficiency of the growth in your bankroll, they have the capacity to challenge the nerve of even the most emotionless bettor. A game from Spain's La Liga provides us with a clear example of this. On 10 September 2016, Real Madrid played Osasuna at home. The true price via my Wisdom of the Crowd methodology was 1.076. One bookmaker was offering 1.13, with an expected value of 4.96%. Consequently, the suggested Kelly stake was 38.2% of your bankroll. Fancy it? No, nor me. Fortunately, it won. However, another with a similarly eyewateringly large Kelly stake was not so fortunate. Paris Saint-Germain played Caen at home on 20 May 2017: true price 1.211; best price 1.35; expected value 11.47%, Kelly stake 32.8%; they drew. Understandably, this is not the sort of drawdown that most bettors can tolerate from just one bet. Using fractional-Kelly is arguably a reasonable solution to that problem.

What about other fractions larger than 1? I've already covered the implications of double-Kelly. What about something even larger? The next chart compares full-Kelly with '2 x Kelly' and '4 x Kelly'. For illustrative purposes I've treated these separately from Kelly fractions less than 1, because of the huge differences in variance. Note that both horizontal and vertical scales are now different to those used in the first chart. Hence, whilst the curves for full-Kelly are, in fact, exactly the same (the solid lines), the one in this chart looks different to the one above.

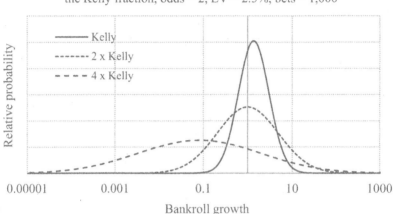

Distribution of proportional staking bankrolls as a function of the Kelly fraction, odds = 2, EV = 2.5%, bets = 1,000

Two important features should be noted. Firstly, as the size of the fraction increases above 1, the median regresses to the left. Full Kelly offers the optimal median bankroll growth; that's hardly surprising since it's designed to be an optimally efficient method for maximising bankroll growth. Notice, however, how quickly things become bad. For '4 x Kelly', whilst your mean (expected) bankroll is now 12.14 (compared to 1.87 for full-Kelly), your median is just 0.08, and nearly 79% of the time you'll finish with less than you started with. If you were mad enough to indulge in '8 x Kelly', your median bankroll would be just £1 having started from nearly £5 million, and more than 99% of possible histories would be unprofitable. Secondly, the variance in multiple-Kelly staking is off the scale; for '4 x Kelly' it's more than 61 million times greater than for quarter-Kelly for this scenario. If the variance monster was frightening for unit staking, the one accompanying multiple-Kelly staking should have your hair turning grey. The lesson: **don't** overestimate your expected value; if you do, you can expect a high probability of failure and accompanying head-scratching why that has happened.

I decided to combine the two charts above into one below, just to illustrate how significant the change in variance is as we increase the size of the Kelly fraction, from less than 1 to more than 1.

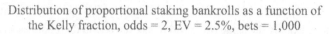

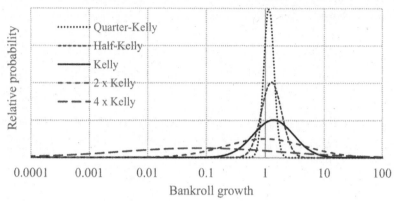

Distribution of proportional staking bankrolls as a function of the Kelly fraction, odds = 2, EV = 2.5%, bets = 1,000

Sadly, it's not yet possible to show animations in books made of paper. With this in mind, I've uploaded one to Football-Data.co.uk (with my Excel calculators) illustrating how the probability distribution for bankroll growth changes as we progressively increase the Kelly fraction from 1/4 through to 4. This is equivalent to increasing stakes from 0.625% to 10%. Despite the illustrative difficulty in combining all these probability distributions, I hope that you can broadly follow both the position of the median and the size of the area to the left of the 'break-even' line, as the Kelly fraction changes. The bigger the Kelly fraction, the greater the probability of ending with less than you started with. Here's a chart showing you how that probability changes, for this particular betting scenario, as the Kelly fraction changes. The Kelly fraction scale is logarithmic.

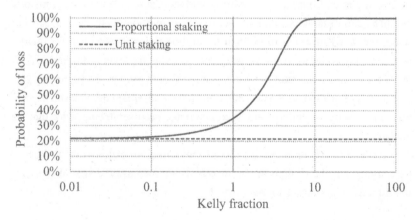

Probability of loss as a function of the Kelly fraction

Different scenarios with different odds, expected value and numbers of bets will have different curves, but the general shape will be broadly similar, and as already mentioned, the probability of loss will always be greater than for unit staking, regardless of the stake size. Of course, whilst large multiples of the Kelly stake are accompanied by such a low probability of success, no serious bettor is ever going to knowingly bet such stakes. Nevertheless, overestimating your expected value amounts to the same thing, even though this will be done unwittingly. Perhaps you might have believed your expected value was 10% and therefore your appropriate Kelly stake for odds of 2 would be 10%. If your true expected value is, in fact, 2.5%, you are then effectively betting with '4 x Kelly'. More usually, a bettor's perception of expected value is an illusion; their true expected value will be around -2.5%, with a bookmaker's margin of equivalent size. No staking plan is going to save you from that.

In the next chart, observe how the median bankroll for my betting scenario varies with the size of the Kelly fraction. The maximum occurs for Kelly fraction = 1, which obviously is the size of the full Kelly stake. Fractions both smaller and larger than 1 see lower median bankroll growth but fractions larger than 2 have a median bankroll growth less than 1 or break-even (shown in the chart with dashed line).

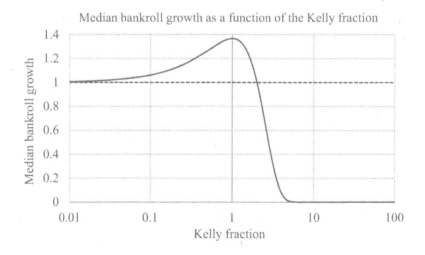

Median bankroll growth as a function of the Kelly fraction

You may recall that when stakes were twice the appropriate Kelly stake, expected yields were about 0%. We've arrived at the same finding via a different route. The same is true for all other odds, as I illustrated earlier showing the probability distributions for five different odds when the stake was double the Kelly size.

The mathematics that describes this function are, to my eye, fiendishly complicated, although, to be fair, I'm not much of a mathematician. For those of you brave enough to want to learn more, Edward O. Thorp, the American mathematician, author of *Beat the Dealer* (which mathematically proved that the house advantage in blackjack could be overcome by card counting) and hedge fund analyst, has written a paper titled *The Kelly Criterion in Blackjack, Sports Betting, and the Stock Market*, which can be easily found via a quick Google search. The chart below reproduces a small section of the previous one, but with a linear Kelly fraction scale.

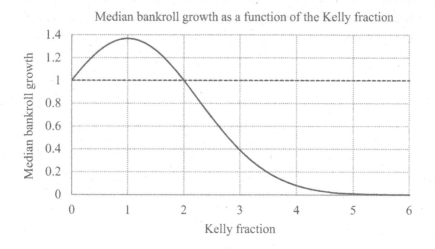

I have one more set of Kelly scenarios I want to share with you before I test whether the mathematical functions that I've described for proportional staking can reproduce outputs from a Monte Carlo simulation for more variable real-world betting histories. You might well feel you've had enough of them by now, but this one, and the conclusion that springs from it, is really something. The next chart compares the probability distributions for five different odds, 1.5, 2, 3, 5, and 10, again for 1,000 bets with a 2.5% expected value and appropriate full-Kelly stakes (respectively 5%, 2.5%, 1.25%, 0.625% and 0.278%). In contrast to unit staking, the variance decreases as the odds lengthen. This happens because the stake size decreases significantly. Nonetheless, the mean and median bankroll growth is larger for shorter odds, and sufficiently so such that the probability of finishing with less than you started with is progressively smaller. For odds of 10 that is 44.8%; for odds of 1.5, by contrast, it falls to 28.6%.

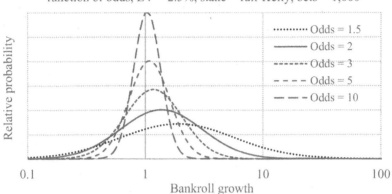

Distribution of proportional staking bankroll growth as a function of odds, EV = 2.5%, stake = full-Kelly, bets = 1,000

If this is so, what is the point of betting longer odds if your bankroll growth is smaller and the probability of bankroll contraction larger than for shorter odds? This is the same argument I presented against unit-win staking, and as then it is recursive. However, as previously explained, it is unrealistic to believe different odds will have the same expected value. In terms of likelihood and availability, longer odds will typically have more opportunities for larger expected value. Let's again use the same z-score function I developed earlier to define what expected values different odds will take. If we hold odds of 2 at an expected value of 2.5%, then odds of 1.5, 3, 5 and 10 will have expected values of 1.75%, 3.57%, 5.09% and 7.75%. With these figures, full-Kelly stakes readjust to 3.5%, 1.78%, 1.27% and 0.862%, with odds of 2 still at 2.5%. Take a look at what happens to the probability distributions. I've maintained the same vertical axis scale.

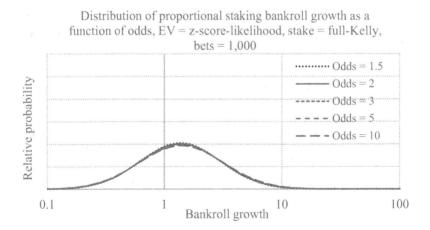

Distribution of proportional staking bankroll growth as a function of odds, EV = z-score-likelihood, stake = full-Kelly, bets = 1,000

What a remarkable finding. Essentially the Kelly distributions for all odds are identical. What tiny differences exist arise, I think, because of something called discretisation: the process of transferring continuous probability functions into discrete counterparts. The normal and lognormal distributions are continuous. Betting profits and losses, by definition, however, are discrete, even when the histories run into thousands of bets. My equations for both the standard error in unit staking yields and the mean and median bankroll growth for proportional staking are based on discrete variables: r, o, s, n and EV. I'm then asking Excel to interpret these via its normal and lognormal continuous functions to draw these charts. Slight deviations from true probabilities, true expected yields and true mean and median bankroll growth will be inevitable, in the same way that for small bet histories, the (continuous) normal distribution provides a less reliable approximation to the (discrete) binomial distribution. Despite discretisation, I think we are safe to draw the following conclusion. Given the likelihood of the availability of expected value for different odds, it is arguably irrelevant what odds you choose to bet at if you follow a Kelly staking strategy. Whether you are targeting hot favourites in tennis or long underdogs in horse racing, your Kelly bankroll growth probability distribution will broadly be the same. Who knew? The same is true for unit staking with respect to the distribution of absolute profits (not yields). The chart below shows the probability distributions for absolute profits (not yields) where the stakes are units (not percentages).

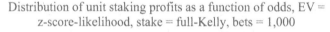

Distribution of unit staking profits as a function of odds, EV = z-score-likelihood, stake = full-Kelly, bets = 1,000

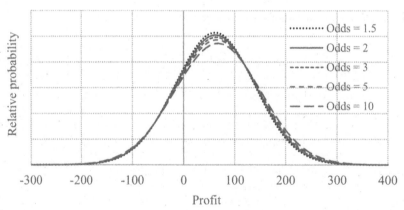

Testing the Functions against Monte Carlo with a Real Betting History

The reliability of the mathematical function that I produced to describe the probability distributions of yields from unit staking plans (unit-loss, unit-win and Kelly) was demonstrated by comparison to Monte Carlo outputs. I'd like to perform a similar reliability check for my proportional staking functions. For this task I will again use my Wisdom of the Crowd betting history, which has a considerable spread of odds and expected values. I will compare the same four staking plans as before, but this time, instead of units, I am using percentages of the existing bankroll at each bet. For example, where unit-loss risked the same number of units on each bet, percentage-loss risks the same percentage of current bankroll. Similarly, percentage-win seeks to win the same percentage for each bet, whilst percentage-impact seeks to hold constant the percentage difference in the bankroll between winning and losing. Kelly, of course, is now the proportional staking plan it was originally designed to be. Given the history is nearly 12,000 bets, I've opted to apply a fraction of 0.25 to all four staking plans to ensure the range of Monte Carlo bankrolls is manageable and the variance not too astronomical. For the Kelly plan, for example, it then becomes a quarter-Kelly.

Actual bankroll growth figures for percentage-loss, percentage-win, percentage-impact and Kelly were respectively 13.89, 16.56, 18.85 and 74.42. The Kelly plan was the star performer. It was also the big overachiever relative to expectation. I've had to increase the scale relative to the other three plans to show it in the chart. Expected (mean) bankroll growth for the four plans in the same order were 25.09, 16.27, 18.64 and 32.24. The four mini plots that follow compare the actual (solid line) and expected (dotted line) performances for the four plans.

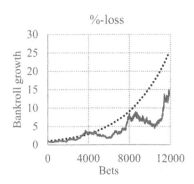
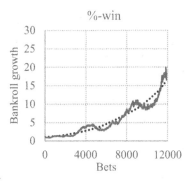

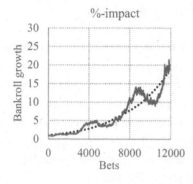

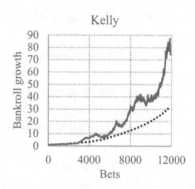

Remember that the expected trend is actually equivalent to the lognormal distribution mean, not the median, so even the percentage-win and percentage-impact plans have actually been quite lucky. Only percentage-loss appears to have underperformed relative to expectation.

The more important question is whether the bankroll growth probability distributions associated with each of these plans can be predicted adequately using my mathematical functions. First, let's calculate the expected (mean) and median bankroll growth for each of the four staking plans using the functions I published earlier. We still have the same stake-weighted mean expected values and mean betting odds as those used for the unit staking plans. For percentage-loss, percentage-win, percentage-impact and Kelly respectively, the stake-weighted mean expected values are 4.12%, 3.56%, 3.74% and 4.44%, whilst the stake-weighted mean odds are 3.89, 2.35, 2.78 and 2.56. With these figures, the expected (mean) bankroll growth figures are 25.10, 16.27, 18.65 and 32.28, almost identical to the expectations calculated from the 11,894-bet history. The median bankroll growth figures are 11.77, 11.45, 11.72 and 21.47. In fact, the actual bankroll growths for all four plans are larger than these median figures, even for the percentage-loss staking plan, which initially looked like it had underachieved. According to Excel's LOGNORM.DIST probability function, the actual percentage-loss performance sits on the 55th percentile, meaning only 45% of histories would be expected to perform better. For percentage-win, percentage-impact and Kelly, their performances sit respectively on the 67th, 69th and 92nd percentiles. None of these, even Kelly, represents a statistically significant deviation from the median bankroll, meaning that I still trust my underlying betting methodology.

Finally, let's see how these function outputs compare to those derived from a 100,000-iteration Monte Carlo simulation. The mean bankroll growth figures for percentage-loss, percentage-win, percentage impact and Kelly respectively are 24.96, 16.21, 18.57 and 32.12, closely matching the figures derived from the mathematical functions. The same is true for the median bankroll figures, which are 11.71, 11.50, 12.38 and 20.79. Despite the large variation in my history's betting odds, expected values and stake sizes, the mathematical functions still provide a reliable approximation to a Monte Carlo simulation. Take a look below at just how reliable. Monte Carlo outputs are represented by the scatter plots, whilst the distribution curves have been built using the mathematical function.

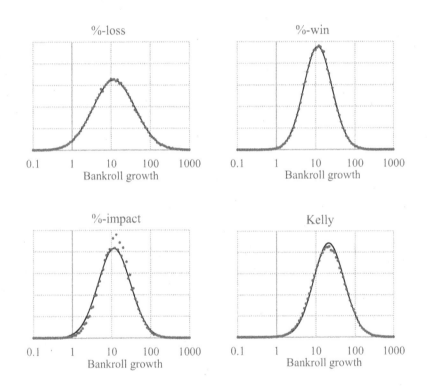

Lastly, let's compare the four probability distributions and the probability of loss. Kelly again offers the best of both worlds by maximising growth at the same time as minimising the risk of finishing with less than you started with. Indeed, with this quarter-Kelly strategy, the function predicts a probability of just 0.03% that the bankroll would have contracted after these 11,894 bets. In the Monte Carlo simulation, it happened 53 times (or 0.053%). For the percentage-loss plan, by contrast, the predicted probability is 2.26% (it happened 2,084 times, or 2.084%).

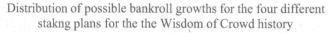

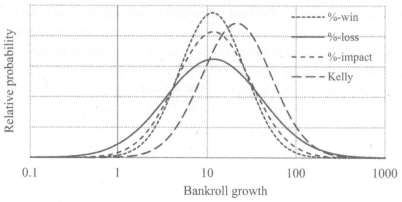

Distribution of possible bankroll growths for the four different staking plans for the the Wisdom of Crowd history

There is one major caveat with all of my discussion on proportional staking, and the mathematical functions I've developed to predict their lognormal probability distributions. To be able to calculate a new stake in terms of the actual units risked, the previous bet must have been settled. Throughout my discussion, including for the analysis of my real Wisdom of the Crowd history, I have assumed that all bets are sequential, and none is active simultaneously. No such problem is experienced with unit staking, since the size of the stake remains fixed relative to the size of the initial bankroll (or some other reference figure), not the current one. For Kelly staking, in particular, which is designed with the intention of maximising the growth rate of the bankroll, this can present a problem. Fortunately, however, there are mathematical solutions. I don't intend to cover these here. However, for those keen on using Kelly money management with simultaneous bets, Pinnacle.com provide a useful resource describing a methodology to calculate Kelly stake percentages for bets placed at the same time, indeed even bets placed on multiple outcomes in the same betting market. It is easily found by Googling 'Pinnacle real Kelly criterion'. For those with a stronger mathematical skillset, the poker player Dan Abrams, writing on his own website Playingnottolose.com (*Applying the Kelly Criterion to an event with existing bets*), explains why even negative expected value bets can be suitable for a Kelly strategy where the bettor is hedging against existing bets. His material is well worth a read, as is his Twitter timeline @DoctorRazzWSOP.

Progressive Staking

I've almost come to the end of my chapter on staking. I could make a strong case for ending it now. For one thing, if you've come this far, I dare say you are rather tired of seeing so many probability distributions for so many different staking plans. Perhaps more importantly, what I will describe next should arguably be thought of as less a staking plan, and more a bettor's version of Russian Roulette. Nevertheless, I'm including it anyway, if for no other reason than it perfectly illustrates the path dependent (non-ergodic) reality a bettor inhabits, and the issue of ruin. At the beginning of this chapter, I identified four main reasons how (and indeed, why) one might choose to systematically change a stake size. I've covered the first three: win probability, expected value and the size of your existing bankroll. That leaves the final one: loss recovery. Really, 'loss recovery' is a euphemism for 'loss chasing', which is probably also a euphemism for 'bettor's ruin'; in my opinion, that would be a far more apt name. Let's get the disclaimer out of the way now, so there can be no doubt in your mind as to what my opinion is: **chasing losses is a fool's game**.

The basis of a loss recovery plan is that a stake is increased for the next bet if the previous one lost, with a view to recovering what was lost in addition to what is hoped to be won from the new bet. If that bet loses too, the next stake will be increased still further. Such money management is frequently described as progressive, with the way the stake size changes following a defined progression that is path-dependent through a series of losses and wins. Perhaps the only limit to the number of possible progressions that could be employed in an attempt to recover previous losses is a bettor's imagination, and new versions with fancy names designed to lure the unsophisticated bettor to follow them are dreamt up all the time. Some of the more historically familiar progressive staking plans include the d'Alembert system, named after the 18th century French mathematician Jean le Rond d'Alembert (and sometimes referred to as the pyramid staking plan), the Fibonacci staking plan, named after Fibonacci's number progression, and the Labouchère system, originally cooked up by the Victorian politician, writer, publisher and gambler Henry Labouchère. I've no intention of filling my pages with methodological descriptions of these systems that serve no other purpose than to indulge the overconfidence of an unsophisticated bettor. For the curious amongst you, there is always Google to find out how they work. I will, however, make one exception – the Martingale. This is perhaps the most famous, or rather infamous, of progressive staking plans, probably on account of the ease with which it can be explained and implemented if you are foolish enough to do so. Furthermore, the conclusions that I will make from analysing the Martingale staking plan can arguably be extended to all other progressive systems as well.

The name 'Martingale' is familiar to practitioners of probability theory and finance as a sequence in which the conditional expectation of the next value of a random variable is equal to the present value. We don't need to concern ourselves with the mathematics of such a sequence. Of more interest is the historical origins of the term in the context of playing games of chance. There is considerable uncertainty about when and how the word first appeared, although the French mathematician Roger Mansuy has provided a rather enchanting and didactic review in his 'Histoire de martingales' in the journal *Mathematical Social Sciences* (volume 169, 1st March 2005) to shine some light on the topic. Roger suggests the term may have first found its way into common parlance via the 4th edition of the *Dictionnaire de l'Académie française*, the official dictionary of the French language, in 1762, in which it was noted that 'to play the martingale is to always bet all that was lost'. Such a description encapsulates the Martingale strategy perfectly. The stake for the next bet is sized such that it will recover the **whole** loss of the bet preceding it, as well as all losses for all consecutive losses preceding the current one. Through an attempt to recover 'all that was lost', Martingale is the most aggressive of all progressions.

The term 'Martingale' became associated with betting strategies that were in popular use in 18th century French society. The simplest of these strategies was designed for a game in which the gambler wins the stake if a coin comes up heads and loses if it comes up tails. The strategy had the gambler double the bet after every loss, so that the first win would recover all previous losses plus win a profit equal to the original stake. A similar progression can be applied to other 50-50 propositions like roulette black-red or odd-even, and sports bets where the probabilities have been equalised by means of a handicap. The stakes continue to double after every consecutive loss until a win; the next stake is then reset to the original size. If the target profit for a winning bet is 1 unit, the initial stake size, and the size following a win, can be calculated using the reciprocal of the odds − 1 (just as for the unit-win staking plan). For 50-50 propositions, the odds are 2, so the initial stake is 1 unit. Stake-doubling after losses can lead to some frighteningly large stakes. The rate of increase is exponential. After 3 losses, the 4th stake will be 8 units; after 5 losses, the 6th stake will be 32 units; and after 10 consecutive losses, the 11th stake would be 1,024 units.

We needn't restrict ourselves to just 50-50 propositions. With odds of 3, the first stake will be 0.5 units. If it is lost, to win it back (0.5 units) and make a net profit of 1 unit, our target profit is now 1.5 units, so we need a stake of 0.75 units, or 1.5 multiplied by the first stake. Should that lose as well, the third stake will be 1.5 multiplied by the size of the second stake, or 1.125. More generally, the rate of the Martingale progression, M, of the increase in stake size after a loss for bets of odds, o, is given by:

$$M = \frac{o}{o - 1}$$

For odds of 1.5, for example, the rate of progression is 3, meaning the exponential growth in stake sizes after consecutive losing bets is even faster. Furthermore, with initial stake $1 / (o - 1)$, the stake of the kth bet following $k - 1$ consecutive losses, will be given by

$$\frac{M^k}{o}$$

whilst the total accumulated loss from k consecutive lost bets following a win is:

$$M^k - 1$$

The rationale behind the Martingale staking plan is that eventually a bettor will win. With infinite wealth and an infinitely generous bookmaker (or indeed casino) willing to accommodate any stake size, it works. For 50-50 propositions, for example, on average every 1 of 2 bets will reward you with 1 unit of profit, meaning that your bankroll can slowly accumulate. Having infinite wealth means that the occasional catastrophic drawdown, whose probability decreases exponentially with increasing size, poses no existential threat. Of course, we might rightly wonder why anyone with infinite wealth would bother to gamble in the first place. In contrast to this fantasy, the real world presents many challenges. Aside from the obvious ones that no bettor possesses infinite wealth, nor any bookmaker infinite generosity, advocates of Martingale will routinely underestimate the likelihood of catastrophic losing sequences, spurred on by an overconfidence in their abilities that is almost never warranted. Indeed, if such overconfidence were warranted, they would have no need for Martingale. Why sabotage any real expected value when the law of large numbers will nurture it for you? Before I quantify the extent of that sabotage, however, I'd like to show you why the promised returns form Martingale are all illusory anyway.

Suppose we're offered the chance to bet three times on the outcome of a fair toss of a coin. The proposition is binary with two equally possible outcomes. For three coin tosses there are $2^3 = 8$ possible permutations (P) of heads (H) and tails (T), which are shown in the third column in the table below. We've decided to bet on heads for all three coin tosses. Since heads and tails are equally likely, the odds for the bet are 2. To make a profit of 1 unit from winning the first bet, we should stake 1 unit. If we win, we stake another unit on the second bet, and so, too, the third, if we win the second bet. If we lose a bet, we double the stake according to the Martingale progression for odds of 2. Given our bets and the outcomes for each of the 8 permutations, I've shown the stakes, profits and total in the following three columns. Since the probability of heads or tails is ½, then the probability of any permutation is $(½)^3 = ⅛$ or 0.125. The expected profit for any permutation is the permutation's profit multiplied by its probability. These are shown in the final column and summed for the total expected profit for all possible permutations.

P	Bet	Outcome	Stakes	Profits	Total	Chance	xProfit
1	H, H, H	T, T, T	1, 2, 4	-1, -2, -4	-7	0.125	-0.875
2	H, H, H	T, T, H	1, 2, 4	-1, -2, +4	+1	0.125	+0.125
3	H, H, H	T, H, T	1, 2, 1	-1, +2, -1	0	0.125	0
4	H, H, H	T, H, H	1, 2, 1	-1, +2, +1	+2	0.125	+0.25
5	H, H, H	H, T, T	1, 1, 2	+1, -1, -2	-2	0.125	-0.25
6	H, H, H	H, T, H	1, 1, 2	+1, -1, +2	+2	0.125	+0.25
7	H, H, H	H, H, T	1, 1, 1	+1, +1, -1	+1	0.125	+0.125
8	H, H, H	H, H, H	1, 1, 1	+1, +1, +1	+3	0.125	+0.375
Total			36		0	1	0

The total is zero. According to the law of large numbers, the best we can hope for over the long term is to break even, just as we would for unit staking. If the game is unfair and you've been unable to find any expected value, in such circumstances your total expected profit will be negative. Have a look at the comparable table for unit staking below. The total expected profit is again zero.

P	Bet	Outcome	Stakes	Profits	Total	Chance	xProfit
1	H, H, H	T, T, T	1, 1, 1	-1, -1, -1	-3	0.125	-0.375
2	H, H, H	T, T, H	1, 1, 1	-1, -1, +1	-1	0.125	-0.125
3	H, H, H	T, H, T	1, 1, 1	-1, +1, -1	-1	0.125	-0.125
4	H, H, H	T, H, H	1, 1, 1	-1, +1, +1	+1	0.125	+0.125
5	H, H, H	H, T, T	1, 1, 1	+1, -1, -1	-1	0.125	-0.125
6	H, H, H	H, T, H	1, 1, 1	+1, -1, +1	+1	0.125	+0.125
7	H, H, H	H, H, T	1, 1, 1	+1, +1, -1	+1	0.125	+0.125
8	H, H, H	H, H, H	1, 1, 1	+1, +1, +1	+3	0.125	+0.375
Total			24		0	1	0

Take a closer look at the two tables. The Martingale strategy has increased the number of times we can expect to make a profit, relative to unit staking, from 4 to 5. Unfortunately, this is at the expense of one large expected loss. All Martingale has really achieved is a change in the distribution of risks. The trade-off for gaining one extra outcome with positive expectation is another with a much greater negative expectation, relative to the equivalent outcome for unit staking. This risk asymmetry is the source of the inherent danger associated with the Martingale strategy. Increasing the number of coin tosses exponentially increases the number of permutations. For 5 coin tosses there are $2^5 = 32$ possible permutations. For 10 coin tosses there are $2^{10} = 1,024$ possible permutations. By the time we get to 20 coin tosses, I run out of Excel rows in a worksheet to help me calculate the individual expected profits for each permutation.

As the number of permutations increases, so does the proportion of them that hold positive expected profit. For 4 coin tosses, 11 of the 16 (68.75%) are profitable; for 5 tosses, the figure is 23 out of 32 (71.88%); and for 10 tosses, it's 866 out of 1,024 (84.57%). Yet as the proportion of profitable permutations increases, so does the risk asymmetry. The mini-plots below compare the possible expected profits for Martingale staking versus unit staking. The first two are for 5 coin tosses. There are more different possible expected profits for a Martingale strategy (12) compared to unit staking (6) because the time-order in which they occur matters. Outcomes using Martingale are non-ergodic or path-dependent. Furthermore, whilst for unit staking the negative and positive expected profits are symmetrical, there is marked asymmetry for Martingale. The second two are for 10 coin tosses. Notice that whilst the difference between possible positive and negative expected profits for unit staking has shrunk (indeed, it's barely possible to make out the histogram), the opposite is true for Martingale. There are now far more possible expected profits (39 for Martingale compared to 11 for unit staking) and a far greater asymmetry between negative and positive expectation for different permutations.

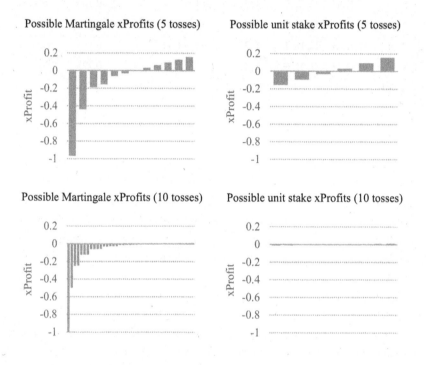

Possible Martingale xProfits (5 tosses)

Possible unit stake xProfits (5 tosses)

Possible Martingale xProfits (10 tosses)

Possible unit stake xProfits (10 tosses)

In Wonderland, with infinite wealth and infinite bookmaker generosity, none of this redistribution of risk matters. On planet Earth, the redistribution is such that it will dramatically interfere with the likelihood of ruin, and given enough time, that interference is all but inevitable. Let me show you why.

If we continued to bet on the toss of a fair coin, whilst our expected (mean) profit would theoretically always remain zero, our median profit will be close to half the number of units staked, or more generally for any betting proposition n / o, where n is the number of bets, o the odds for each bet, and 1 unit is the target profit per bet. After 10 coin tosses, on average 5 will have won. After 1,000 tosses, there will typically have been around 500 winners. Provided a catastrophic drawdown along the way hasn't happened, we might reasonably expect to have made a profit of close to half the number of bets, since here the odds are 2. But how likely are those drawdowns? I've already covered the mathematics of losing streaks. You may recall that for a series of n bets we should expect to see one losing streak of length k, whose size is approximated by:

$$k \approx \log_{\left(\frac{o}{o-1}\right)} n$$

where o / o − 1 is the base of the logarithm. And since o / o − 1 = M, the Martingale progression factor for odds o, this becomes:

$$k \approx \log_M n$$

For odds of 2, the base is 2. Let's consider 1,024 bets, which is 2^{10}. Since $\log_2(1,024) = 10$, we can expect to see at least 1 losing streak of 10 bets, for an accumulated loss of 1,023 units. However, it's worse than that. If we lose 10 consecutively, we still need to find the 11th stake to continue the Martingale series. This will be 1,024 units, implying that the minimum bankroll we would need to have had 11 bets prior to this would be at least 2,047 units. Imagine this catastrophe occurred right at the end. We might expect to have accumulated a profit of close to 512 units. To be able to accommodate a spend of 2,047 units however, this would mean starting with 1,535 units to be hopeful of covering this eventuality. Of course, there's no telling when such a losing streak would occur. It might not happen at all, or instead it might happen 2 or 3 times, or worse still, you might be unlucky enough to see a losing streak of 11 or 12 (assuming you had enough capital to cover them), but, on average, we can expect to see about one of length 10. If it occurred earlier, 1,535 units as a starting bankroll would be insufficient to avoid complete ruin. Arguably, you really need to start with 2,047 units just to cover the possibility that it happens at the beginning. Assuming your bookmaker permits increasing stakes in this manner, would you be comfortable risking £2,047 just to win around £512 in the form of £1-profits, or £20,470 for 512 £10-profits, when there's a reasonable chance of disaster?

The longer you bet for, the greater the likelihood that you will see longer losing streaks. Given the equation above, for odds of 2, as you double the number of bets, you increase by one the length of the losing streak you can expect to see once on average. Every time that happens, you must double the capital that you need to prevent ruin, since for every additional consecutive loss, you double the following stake. If you anticipate playing Martingale for 8,192 bets, you should expect to see at least one losing streak of 13. You would need 16,383 units in risk capital, just for the prospect of winning 1 unit every time you bet, yet that's not enough to protect against the bad luck of a losing streak of 14 or more. Yes, you are likely to have some winnings to set against that risk, but they will never be enough. Even if your losing streak came at the end, your likely profit will only contribute one quarter towards the capital you need to have in reserve to guard against such risk. This ratio is the same for any length of betting sequence.

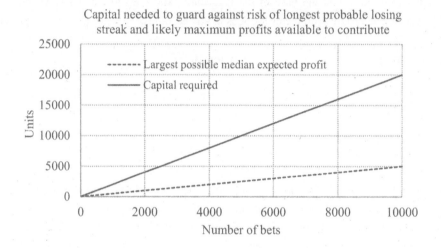

Capital needed to guard against risk of longest probable losing streak and likely maximum profits available to contribute

If you think that's bad, it's even worse for longer and shorter odds. This ratio of 4:1 is the smallest possible, given the scenario of targeting 1 unit profit per bet. In fact, the ratio is symmetrical about a win probability of 50%. The ratio for win probabilities of 20% and 80%, with odds of 5 and 1.25, is 6.25. For win probabilities of 95% (odds = 1.053) and 5% (odds = 20), the ratio is 21.05.

Whilst there is symmetry in the ratio of likely capital needed versus likely profit available to contribute, that is not true for the risk capital itself. With a strategy of targeting 1 unit profit per bet, shorter odds require a larger initial stake size. Odds of 20, for example, need a stake of 0.053 units. By contrast, odds of 1.053 require a stake of 19. Whilst it's far less likely to lose, when it does, the Martingale progression means almost immediate chaos. For odds of 1.053, the progression factor is 20. If the first stake is 19 units, the one following a loss will be 380 units, and if you're unlucky enough to lose 2 in a row at these odds the third stake will be 7,600 units! If you play Martingale at these odds with the appropriate progression factor for 1,000 plays, set aside 20,000 units, with the hope of winning 950, to cover something that you can expect to see once. For odds of 20, you'll need just 1,050 units but with a likelihood of winning only 50. Martingale always looks good in theory until you quantify what is likely to happen to you. When you do that, you can see that you are forced to have huge sums of reserve capital just to win what amounts to tiny sums in comparison. If you are lucky enough to possess such capital in the first place, you don't really need to indulge in Martingale to increase it a little bit more.

What, then, is the probability of ruin using Martingale? For this, we need to run a Monte Carlo simulation, since for any series of bets beyond a small sample, the number of permutations quickly becomes impossibly large to handle mathematically. Evidently, this is going to be determined by the amount of risk capital you are prepared to hold, the odds you bet and the length of history you hope to be betting for. With a target of 1 unit per win, the longer your odds the less risk capital you will need, since both your initial stake size and stake increase progression factor are smaller. The trade-off, of course, is that your Martingale strategy will make less absolute profit, assuming you don't go bust. For my Monte Carlo, I've picked a risk capital of 1,000 units where the profit target per bet is 1 unit. For odds of 2, that should cover 9 consecutive losses, so long as you don't have such a streak in your 50 bets. For odds of 1.5 and 3, it would be 5 and 16 consecutive losses, respectively. This size of risk capital is somewhat arbitrary, but perhaps represents an upper limit of what your psychology can cope with and what most bookmakers will accept. If you think you have the stomach, and the capital, to risk more, you can run another Monte Carlo simulation. My chart below shows how the probability of ruin increases the longer you bet for. Ultimately, ruin is all but inevitable; it's not so much if, but when, it happens.

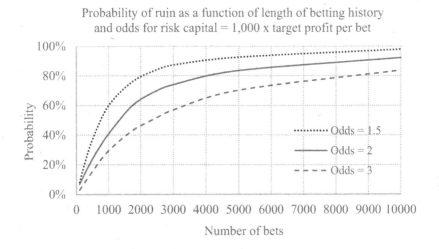

Probability of ruin as a function of length of betting history and odds for risk capital = 1,000 x target profit per bet

Finally, I've used a Monte Carlo simulation to estimate the size of risk capital you will need to keep the probability of ruin below thresholds of 25%, 50% and 75% as a function of the length of the betting history. Since for odds of 2 the loss from the longest expected consecutive losing streak doubles as the length of the betting history doubles, this relationship is linear for any probability threshold.

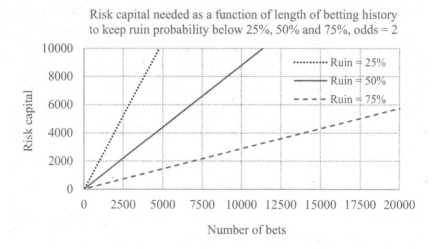

Risk capital needed as a function of length of betting history to keep ruin probability below 25%, 50% and 75%, odds = 2

You might reframe the 50% ruin probability as equivalent to a 50-50 bet. Unfortunately, the expected value for this proposition is truly awful. For example, for 1,000 bets at odds of 2 with a target of 1 unit per win, you'll need a risk capital of about 825 units for a 50% chance of losing it before your series has completed. Your likely profit, should ruin be avoided, is just 500 units. In effect, you're being offered odds of 1.61 with a 50% win probability, and thus an expected value of -20%, despite every individual bet in this scenario being fair. Entertainment aside, why bother going to the lengths of betting up to 1,000 times with such a poor-value proposition, when you could just as easily stake the full 500 units on a single bet at odds of 2 with a far smaller expected value disadvantage. Of course, this is not to encourage you to stake larger bets, simply to illustrate the absurdity of following a Martingale strategy if your motivation is finding expected value.

For shorter odds, the risk capital required for a 50% ruin probability in 1,000 bets is much greater. For odds of 1.50, for example, it would be about 1,725 units. With a target profit of 1,000 / 1.5 = 667 units, your effective odds are 1.39, with expected value -31%. The shorter the odds, the more negative the expected value. For odds of 1.25, it falls to about -35%, and to -45% for odds of 1.1. The limit is

-50% since that is the worst possible for a 50-50 proposition. By contrast, for longer odds, the risk capital required for a 50% ruin probability in 1,000 bets is much smaller, and the disadvantage in the effective expected value smaller too. With odds of 3, the required risk capital is about 425 units, the target profit 333 units, the effective odds 1.78 and the expected value -11%. For odds of 5, the expected value is about -5.5%. The longer the odds, the less you give up in expected value, but the less target profit you will make if ruin is avoided. By the time you get to odds of 20, you're close to getting expected value of 0%, but your target gain is now so small as to make it hardly worth the bother. Of course, this assumes you can find such long odds to bet that are fair (or better). As you should know, the longer the odds, the larger the margin weight the bookmakers build in, and any unfairness in the odds you are betting is going to conspire against you, increasing your probability of ruin, and conversely increasing the amount of risk capital you would need to reduce its probability.

All of this is really just a different way of presenting the age-old trade-off of risk and reward. If you want more, you have to take more risk, or accept a bigger disadvantage, to get it. Whilst it might offer a roller-coaster of excitement and fear, by reinterpreting the Martingale strategy in this way, I have shown it to be truly a flawed methodology. Its weakness lies in its path-dependent and hugely asymmetric profit expectations, and the inherent dangers posed by losing streaks. Yes, it is true that if you hold real expected value in your odds, you can turn Martingale into a positive expected value proposition. 1,000 Martingale bets at odds of 2 holding expected value of 10% are equivalent to an even-money proposition with +50% expected value, since the risk capital required falls to 250 units. That sounds attractive, but nearly all of you reading will never find such an advantage. For mortals like me, the variance in losing streaks is just too great to really consider Martingale as anything other than a bit of fun. It should never be regarded as a serious strategy for a serious bettor. Furthermore, if you are astute enough to find 10% expected value in the first place, other strategies like Kelly (or fractional Kelly) staking, or simply making multiple or permutation bets from your singles, are more effective methods of growing your bankroll without significantly changing your risk of ruin.

TIPPING

The world of online betting has spawned an entirely new and secondary industry of online tipping or touting, as it's more commonly known in the US. It brings with it a whole new set of hurdles the bettor must overcome, if they are to gain any success from it. The primary motivation for a tipster is to make an additional income from their betting expertise, on top of the one they can derive from their own betting. There are two primary advantages. Firstly, selling a regular subscription helps to smooth the variance in their earnings. You already know what impact the law of small numbers can have. Secondly, it might indeed replace a primary income from betting which has been limited or lost entirely due to restrictions by the bookmakers. Critics will frequently point out that no bettor with any real expected value would ever need to sell it, implying that those who do must be engaged in either wilful or blind charlatanism. I prefer to adopt a less extreme position, leaving open the possibility that a few tipsters at least will not fall into this sweeping categorisation. Nishikori, whom we met earlier, is one of them. The primary motivation for the bettor buying advice is to make a profit that they would otherwise be unable to engineer themselves, either because of a lack of forecasting skill, or simply because of a lack of time to find out if they could really have one. Whilst winning with wits and beating the system is, for many, the attraction to betting, for others, earning a profit is quite sufficient in that regard. There are, however, a number of pitfalls that await the unsuspecting customer of betting advice. It is for this reason I've devoted a chapter to tipping, and in particular to finding out how the Monte Carlo simulation can help us see the wood from the trees.

Are Most Tipsters Simply Tossing Coins?

I spent 14 years following, analysing and reporting on the performances and fortunes of those who give betting advice to others. There was one main conclusion to be drawn: tipsters are little or no better than the average bettor, who, in turn, is, on average, no better than would be expected if they were just tossing coins. I've written at length in my previous book, and also in this one on the topic of the closing line, why this should be so. Briefly again, for a dynamic market where the value of your information lasts as long as it remains private, it couldn't really be any other way. Once you reveal your information to the market in the form of a bet, your information becomes public. If the bookmaker recognises your information as useful, their market price will adjust accordingly. Since the arrival of new information about the true probability of an outcome is largely random, the evolution of the market will be largely random too. It is thus only those bettors, and tipsters, who can systematically find access to new information that the rest of us are unable to, who will be able to systematically maintain an advantage over the market and hold expected value in the odds which they bet. It may be true that some betting markets contain biases, reflecting the biased behaviours of bettors whose money creates them, but typically these biases remain small. Where they are exploitable by those savvy enough to understand and be aware of them, it's simply a matter of time before any opportunities disappear. As the economist's joke goes: 'I thought I saw $100 lying on the ground, but I must've imagined it; if it had been there, someone would've picked it up.' Betting, like tennis, is an iterative, relative-skills competition, where the smallest of advantages in the way you have access to information that others do not can accumulate, over many bets, into much bigger advantages via the law of large numbers. Betting, therefore, is a game of winner takes all. Only a few are really good enough to win systematically; the rest of us will simply be tossing coins to pay their salaries.

It's a pretty sobering conclusion which is typically denied, but when you analyse the data, it's difficult to draw any other. If you were to look at the world of online tipsters and touts, however, you would likely draw a completely different one. There are literally thousands upon thousands of bettors giving or selling advice in the form of tips, the majority with profitable performance records, and hundreds more 'supermarkets', where you can browse the performances of a large collection of tipsters, all of them telling you how much you could have won, if only you'd been brave enough to consider their services. I'm not here to tell you that being profitable from betting isn't possible. My chapter on winning should have already shown you just how likely it is. Many bettors, and many tipsters, do win; the far more important question is what, if anything, is causing that? I've already explained how you can use statistical significance testing to assess the likelihood of your, or anyone else's, betting profit having arisen by chance, or alternatively something other than chance. If it's the latter, it could be sustainable; if the former, it will regress to the mean, with the mean being defined by the bookmaker's margin. We also know that the shape of a data distribution will give us clues as to whether the underlying explanation for it is random or otherwise. Let's look at a performance distribution for a large collection of tipsters.

Different tipsters have different preferences, with different staking, betting odds and betting history lengths. We need some way to standardise them so that we can aggregate their performances within a single distribution. The tool for this task is, once again, the z-score. Let's recap: the z-score measures the number of standard deviations (or standard errors) an observed return falls above or below expectation. Since the equation for the standard error in possible returns, r, from a number of bets, n, with average odds, o, is:

$$SE = \sqrt{\frac{r(o - r)}{n}}$$

and the equation for the z-score is:

$$z = \frac{(observed - expected)}{SE}$$

we have:

$$z = \frac{(observed - expected)\sqrt{n}}{\sqrt{r(o - r)}}$$

For the special where the expected yield is 0% (or expected return 100%, that is to say break-even), the equation for the z-score becomes:

$$z = \frac{(r - 1)\sqrt{n}}{\sqrt{r(o - r)}}$$

The z-score provides a risk- and length-adjusted likelihood estimate for an observed return relative to expectation. Positive z-scores imply overperformance relative to expectation, negative z-scores underperformance. By converting performances to z-scores, we compare them within a single distribution.

What sort of z-score distribution do you think a sample of tipsters might exhibit? If all of them were equally sharp and performing to the same level, we might see a distribution something like the left chart below. You should now be familiar enough with the aleatory nature of betting outcomes to know that such a distribution would be highly unlikely unless all tipsters were tipping exactly the same bets. Even for sharp tipsters, they can expect to suffer or benefit from varying degrees of good and bad luck. It's far more likely that the z-score distribution would look more like the chart on the right. The dashed line represents the expected distribution of z-scores, whilst the solid line shows our distribution of sharps. On average, our collection of tipsters is sharper than would be expected, where the expected performance, for example, is defined by the bookmaker's margin. Individual performances, however, are still subject to aleatory uncertainty about that sharper mean.

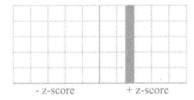
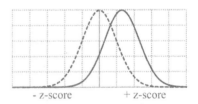

Below I have shown the z-score distribution for 2,690 real performances from the tipster supermarket Pyckio.com. The data, from 2015, include over 1 million tips, which showed an aggregated yield of -2.02% from unit-loss staking. Given the on odds and the size of the margins for all these bets, the expected yield was -2.36%. If this was just one tipster, then there's about a 1-in-4,000 chance that they would have exceeded expectation by as much as they did. As a collection of 2,690 tipsters, however, see how their distribution of z-scores compares to one that is generated randomly. A z-score of 0 is equivalent to yield of -2.36%.

Tipsters' z-score distribution versus random distribution

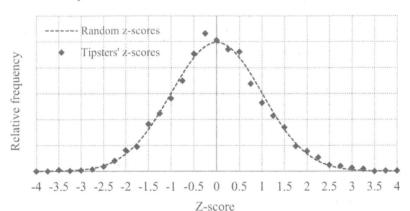

Not only do the tipsters' z-scores distribute normally, with no statistically significant deviation from the empirical rule, but the mean of their distrubtion, z = 0.012, is almost exactly the same as for the random distribtion (z = 0). If the outcomes for this collection of tipsters had been determined by tossing coins, you would not be able to tell any meaningful difference between the two performance distributions. This does not imply that all tipsters were effectively tossing coins. However, for the distribution shape and mean to match those of a random one as closely as this, that can only happen if the number that were actually doing something more than would be expected by chance alone is very small, and too small for them to be revealed here. I know some must exist, because I've seen the closing line value of betting histories that cannot possibly happen by chance. Furthermore, Pinnacle's head of trading, Marco Blume, would have little need to talk of his 'clients' if they didn't. Nevertheless, their proportion is arguably small; it's hard to put a precise figure on it, but I think it is likely to be less than 1 in 100. One proxy measure might be the proportion of customers paying Betfair Exchange's premium charge. The company quote a figure of less than 0.5%. Another might be the proportion of restricted sports betting customers. In January 2018 former Skybet CEO Richard Flint revealed at a Parlimentary debate that they were restricting 3%. Richard was careful to point out that customers were not restricted for winning. Of course, it's quite easy to be winning, that is to say, profitable, with luck, at least in the short term, but good luck regresses to the mean, and no bookmaker is going to restrict the accounts of customers who they know are just lucky. Whilst no mention of why customers were restricted was made, the presumption must be that it was for those holding expected value. I've had my own betting accounts closed where my expected value was profitable, despite the actual balance showing significant losses. Of course, it's much easier to beat the odds of a recreational bookmaker who's intentionally offering value as a marketing gimmick than it will be to beat the sharper markets of Betfair's exchange and Pinnacle's sportsbook. After all, I'm no betting sharp and I've shown you how to do it via the Wisdom of the (Pinnacle) Crowd.

Yet if so few tipsters (and bettors, for that matter) are sharp enough to hold real expected value, how is it that the world of online tipping appears far rosier?

Survivorship Bias

Sir Winston Churchill is often (wrongly) associated with the famous aphorism 'history is written by the victors'. Whilst there is no definitively documented instance in which he is known to have uttered these words, its implication is clearer. History is not grounded in facts, rather it's the winners' interpretation of them that prevails. The victors can force their narrative on the people. It's probably a bit of a stretch to liken betting tipsters to political and military leaders, but the way in which winning tipsters set the narrative about sports betting exhibits similarities, even if the way it is set is without intention or direction. The point here is that we tend to only read the stories told by the winners; once tipsters lose, they often disappear from the storytelling, and if you were not following their story to the point at which they did, you may never even know that they were once a part of it. The winners survive, the losers perish and disappear. Failed tipsters will often remove all trace of their past performance, so that when they start again it's as if they had never existed. Tipster supermarkets also tend to remove tipsters who are no longer active. By far the most common reason for a cessation in activity is failure. If nearly all of these tipsters are winning and losing through luck alone, this survivorship bias towards winners can easily create the impression that the tipsters you see possess some remarkable forecasting talent, encouraging you to place far more faith in their abilities than is truly warranted.

Survivorship bias is the logical error of concentrating on the people or things that 'survived' some process, whilst inadvertently overlooking those that did not because of their lack of visibility. Survivorship bias can lead to overestimating the chances of success because failures are ignored. Its name was first coined during the Second World War when a free-thinking Hungarian mathematician named Abraham Wald solved the problem of where to put additional armour plating on the Allied bombers that were experiencing heavy losses. Initially, engineers assumed that, through an examination of the bullet holes of returning aircraft, those areas that showed the highest concentration of bullet holes – along the wings, around the tail gunner and down the centre of the fuselage – needed the extra reinforcement. It didn't work. The mistake, which Wald saw instantly, was that the holes revealed where the planes were strongest, since these were ones actually making it back, that is to say, surviving. By contrast, no one had previously given any thought to the planes that were lost. Counterintuitively, Wald suggested putting extra armour plating where the bullet holes weren't. The engineers' original error was so significant, statisticians decided to give it a name: survivorship bias, or the tendency to include only successes in statistical analysis.

When attempting to measure the probability of success in domains of uncertainty like sports betting, it's no good just studying the sample that has succeeded. If we do, we risk turning causality on its head. Rather than suppose that success is caused by skill, survivorship bias ensures that we perceive the winners to be skilful because they have been successful. The problem here is that inference is drawn from outcomes, not the forecasting processes themselves. Where aleatory uncertainty plays a significant role in what happens, there is only a weak connection between the forecasting process and the result, which only reveals itself slowly via the law of large numbers. If all you care about is results, you're liable to draw erroneous conclusions, particularly if you are also fooled by the law of small numbers. On the contrary, don't look only at the winners and infer that skill must have caused them; study the forecasting process to see whether it consistently leads to success. To do this, you have to be able to see all the winners and losers, and what they are doing. In the world of online tipping, we are rarely afforded such an opportunity.

In my last book *Squares and Sharps, Suckers and Sharks: the Science, Psychology and Philosophy of Gambling*, I wrote in some detail about many examples of survivorship bias. It would not be appropriate to go over this material again here. Instead, I would like to show you how a Monte Carlo simulation can reveal how easy it can be to be fooled by it. Let's build one with a simple scenario. A tipster supermarket advertises the 'talents' of bettors wishing to sell their betting advice. Unknown to the supermarket, and to the customers buying the advertised picks, all tipsters are tossing coins. That is to say, they have no skill beyond being able to find a best price in a market which, on average, let's say, is good enough to give the customer expected value of 0% and an expected yield of 0% before the costs of paying for the advice. On day one of the supermarket's launch, it has one advertised tipster, and with every new day, one new tipster is added to their platform. Every day, each tipster advises one pick with a unit-loss stake (1 unit), and they are given 100 days from the day they start to demonstrate their 'skill'. Beyond 100 days, any tipster who is showing a yield of less than -5% on any day is removed from the platform, since they have been deemed insufficiently skilled to be allowed to remain in the supermarket. Our Monte Carlo simulation can help answer the following questions.

1) How many tipsters are remaining in the supermarket on the nth day?
2) How many of those remaining tipsters are profitable on the nth day?
3) What is the aggregated yield for remaining tipsters on the nth day?
4) Does this population of tipsters look sharp?

After the first 100 days, there will be 100 tipsters in the supermarket since none will have yet reached the time threshold where any possible elimination is activated. We can estimate the probability that the first tipster will be eliminated on day 100 using the NORM.DIST function and my equation for the yield standard error, SE. Recall, this is a function of the odds, o, and the expected return, r, and for the special case where our expected value is 0% (and hence $r = 1$), is given by $SE = \sqrt{(o-1)/n}$, where n is the number of bets. Hence, for 100 bets, the mean yield standard error will be $\sqrt{(o-1)}/10$. For odds of 2, for example, $SE = 0.1$ or 10%. Thus, the probability of elimination for any tipster after their first 100 days will be given by NORM.DIST(-5%,0%,10%,TRUE) = 30.9%. More generally, as the number of bets, n, increases, the probability of elimination after the nth bet on the nth day will slowly decrease via the law of large numbers, since the standard error is also decreasing with increasing n. Systems that display an increasing survival rate with time are said to exhibit what is colloquially known as the Lindy effect, named after the New York delicatessen, where comedians and actors would gather to discuss their performances, reasoning that the greater their past exposure, the greater the likelihood of future work. I've shown how the elimination probability on the nth day evolves with increasing n for 3 different betting odds beyond day 100 in the chart below. The longer the odds, the greater the likelihood of elimination, understandably so since the variance in the distribution of possible yields is greater.

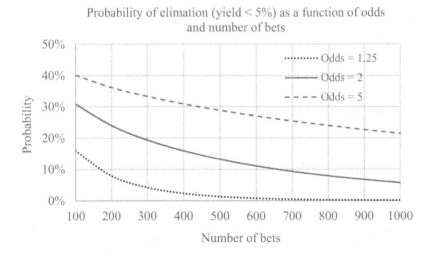

Probability of elimation (yield < 5%) as a function of odds and number of bets

Calculating the probability of one particular tipster being eliminated on any particular day is one thing. Determining the percentage of surviving tipsters amongst a collection of them is altogether a far more complex task. Different tipsters have different history lengths. Furthermore, every day we are adding a new one to the collection. Mathematically, this would be an almost impossible task. A Monte Carlo simulation, however, will easily answer my four questions.

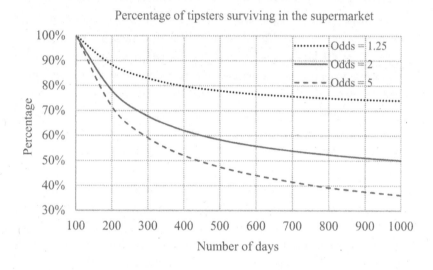

Percentage of tipsters surviving in the supermarket

Since the elimination rate of tipsters is faster for longer odds, the proportion of surviving tipsters in the supermarket drops faster. However, for all odds, as time passes, the earlier tipsters who manage to survive face an ever-decreasing chance of elimination. Hence, since new tipsters are being added continuously at the same rate (one per day), the decline in survival rate slows. For odds of 2, for example, around half of tipsters are still surviving by day 1,000.

What proportion of the surviving tipsters are profitable? A tipster surviving beyond 100 days is permitted to continue until their yield drops below -5%. Arguably, that's quite a lenient threshold. Would you be attracted to a tipster with a -4.5% yield after 1,000 picks? Probably not. Nevertheless, with even this level of lenience, look at how the profitability rate of the surviving tipsters evolves over time. At day 100, the expectation is that 50% of the tipsters will be profitable. Those who are, have been lucky; those who are not, have been unlucky. Thereafter, the proportion of surviving tipsters who are profitable increases, but at an ever-decreasing rate, until an equilibrium level, defined by the balance between survivors and new intakes, is reached.

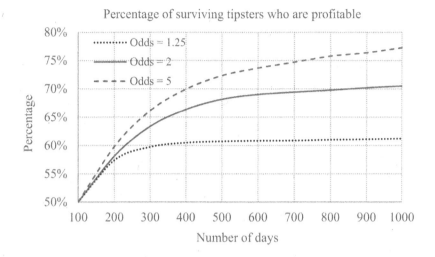

Percentage of surviving tipsters who are profitable

The longer the odds, the greater the proportion of survivors who are profitable, and the higher this equilibrium level will be. Again, this is a consequence of the greater standard error. Bad luck kills off proportionally more tipsters betting longer odds. For those who manage to survive, however, the rate at which the standard error declines with increasing number of bets is greater, meaning proportionally more of the lucky ones will remain profitable.

Thirdly, if we add up all the profits and losses made by all surviving tipsters on the nth day, and divide by the total number of bets they have advised, what will be the aggregated yield? Take a look at how it evolves as the days progress.

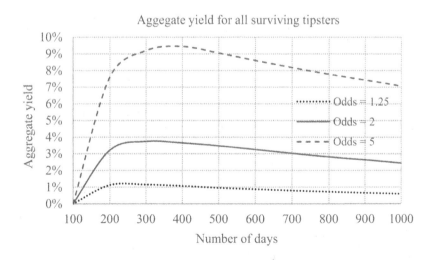

Aggegate yield for all surviving tipsters

The aggregated yield is always above 0%, although over time there is a gradual decline towards it, as would be predicted by the law of large numbers for those surviving in the supermarket. The initial spike between 100 to 300 days is a consequence of the larger standard error for even the oldest tipsters who are still relatively young, and hence a faster elimination rate and a greater bias towards the profitable survivors. The longer the odds, the greater the aggregated yields, again because of the greater standard error and elimination rate of the unlucky tipsters.

Finally, the last question: does this population of tipsters look sharp? We can use the z-score metric to find out. Given that every tipster's performance is assumed to be a consequence of chance only, their expected z-score will be 0. I asked my Monte Carlo simulation to calculate the average z-score for surviving tipsters throughout the 1,000 days. See how it evolves.

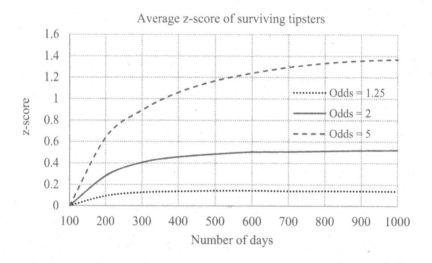

Where the odds are longer and the elimination rate greater, the bias towards lucky survivors is stronger, and hence the z-scores are higher. The chart below compares the distribution of z-scores for surviving tipsters on the 1,000th day (for odds = 2) with one where no tipsters are eliminated and there is no survivorship bias. Whilst a z-score of 0.52 (the average at day 1,000) for an individual tipster would not be considered statistically significant and sufficient evidence of forecasting talent above chance, as an average for a collection of hundreds of tipsters, the difference is hugely significant. For the samples in this distribution, the likelihood that you would see such a difference without the influence of survivorship bias is around 1 in sextillion (22 zeros).

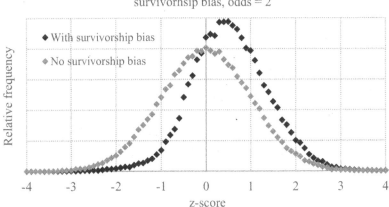

Distribution of 1,000th-day z-scores with and without survivorhsip bias, odds = 2

If the elimination threshold is raised, for example to a 0% yield, the survivorship bias becomes even stronger. For odds of 2, the proportion of surviving tipsters by day 1,000 is just a quarter. The proportion of those survivors who are profitable, however, is now 80%, whilst the aggregate yield is nearly 5%. Of course, it's unlikely that a tipster supermarket would terminate the contract of an unprofitable tipster after just 100 picks; nor is it likely that the tipster would quit after such a short period. Even the most statistically illiterate tipsters and tipster supermarkets will surely understand something of the law of small numbers, even if subconsciously. Nevertheless, it does illustrate the dangers of only counting the winners and failing to look at the losers.

Consider, for an additional moment, what you are seeing in these charts. Here's an example: for a tipster supermarket accumulating one new tipster per day, tipping average odds of 5 (not uncommon in horse racing), a two-year track record may show around 300 active tipsters, 225 of them profitable, with an aggregated yield of 8%. All this from a collection of coin tossers who hold an expected value of 0% and possess absolutely no forecasting skill whatsoever beyond knowing how to use an odds comparison. This is the illusory power of survivorship bias. Arguably, it's so powerful that it may even be deluding the supermarket owners themselves. Whilst it will not be in their marketing interests to maintain the records of eliminated tipsters on their platform by removing their records, they may be completely unaware of exactly how much bias they could be introducing to their tipster performance reporting. Here's the lesson for anyone considering a purchase of tips from a tipster supermarket: ask to see **ALL** of their data, for all of their tipsters, both past and present, winners and losers. If they haven't kept them, or won't give them to you, they're not to be trusted. Simply find another one who will, or better still, improve your own betting forecasting skills. Doing that, after all, is free.

Testing the Credibility of a Tipster's History

Despite the overwhelming evidence that very few tipsters are worth their salt, they will always provide a niche for those unable or unwilling to do their own prediction forecasting. Losing money because of blindness to survivorship bias is one thing. Losing it because of fraud is quite another, and an altogether more unsavoury way to go broke, even if the outcome is broadly similar. Through my verification work, I had the pleasure (or misfortune, depending on your point of view) to work with hundreds of tipsters over an extended period of time. It is my considered opinion that the vast majority of them were honest, even if blind to their own absence of skill. Albert Venn Dicey, the British jurist and constitutional theorist, once said, 'a man's interest gives a bias to his judgment far oftener than it corrupts his heart.' I agree with him. In my second book, *How to Find a Black Cat in a Coal Cellar: the Truth about Sports Tipsters*, there were only a small handful of stories which featured the interests of a scammer. Despite their rarity, however, they do exist. Some are easier to spot than others. Typical techniques for uncovering online scammers may involve comparing the domain ownership of the tipster's website to the ownership of any 'independent' verification service which they refer to as a claim of honesty and transparency. Tipsterconnection.com, for example, marketing itself as an 'independent verification service' has, in the past, been associated with tipsters which have identical domain registration numbers and even Google Analytics account IDs to their own. In case they are reading, I still hold the evidence. Anyone with more than the most rudimentary of understanding about aleatory uncertainty in betting, of course, would immediately know from the absurdly high strike rates, some as high as 90% from many thousands of 50-50 propositions, that all these data are invented for the purposes of committing fraud. If bookmakers were really this bad at pricing sporting events, and the process of bettor price discovery just a figment of an economist's mind, then the whole industry wouldn't even exist in the first place. However, sometimes it's not so easy to tell, so I do want to consider what statistical methods might be available to us to help determine the credibility of a history of picks. I will review three.

The first is probably the most obvious: does the tipster move the betting line or betting price? Without wishing to reopen the conundrum that is the tennis tipster Nishikori, I think we can accept that a genuinely skilled tipster advising picks that hold real expected value, and who has real subscribers betting those picks, can, in some way, be expected to correlate with a movement that cannot be explained by chance. The beauty of using evidence of price movement is that, as previously explained, it is independent of results and provides an almost immediate source of information. If a tipster claims a history of thousands of picks with large double digit yields, it is inevitable that there will be some record of price movement associated with those picks, assuming that they were genuine.

Consider the football advisory service Fixedmatches.org, who claim to analyse match information with a view to finding suspicious odds movements for making profitable predictions. Despite the name, based on their self-description they are evidently positioning themselves as a provider of reliable insider information rather than a source of matches for which the outcome or events of play have been fixed by third parties. At the time of my data collection, their betting history, dating back to 2011, contains nearly 9,419 picks (excluding postponed matches) with average odds of 1.963 and a yield of 39.8%. Such a record, of course, is entirely impossible in an open and transparent betting market, but for our purposes here I will forget about this little detail. I took the trouble to compare their published odds (FM) for the most recent 20 picks (at the time of writing) with the closing odds for both the market average (Avg) and market maximum (Max) closing price.

Betting pick	FM	Avg	Max	FM/Avg	FM/Max
Ankaragucu v Rizespor Under 2.25	1.98	1.86	1.92	1.06	1.03
TSC Backa Topola -0.75 to beat Backa	2	1.49	1.63	1.34	1.23
Tsarsko Selo v Botev Plovdiv Under 2.25	1.86	1.77	1.85	1.05	1.01
Goztepe +1 to beat Fenerbahce	2.03	1.86	1.98	1.09	1.03
CSKA Moscow -1.5 to beat SKA-Khabarovsk	1.86	1.71	1.83	1.09	1.02
Salzburg - 1.5 to beat Rapid Vienna	1.89	1.82	1.92	1.04	0.98
Trepca 89 + 1.25 t beat Drita	1.93	1.8	1.8	1.07	1.07
Altinordu v Adanaspor AS Under 2.25	2.07	2.16	2.32	0.96	0.89
Hearts -1.75 to beat Morton	1.84	1.83	1.9	1.01	0.97
Dordrecht +1.25 to beat Breda	1.96	2.25	2.38	0.87	0.82
Stabaek -1 to beat Raufoss	1.94	1.73	1.95	1.12	0.99
Brasiliense v Vila Nova FC Over 2.5	1.98	2.04	2.18	0.97	0.91

Betting pick	FM	Avg	Max	FM/Avg	FM/Max
Silkeborg -1.5 to beat Kolding IF	1.86	2.27	2.37	0.82	0.78
Al Nasr -1.25 to beat Ajman	1.83	2.15	2.21	0.85	0.83
Primeiro de Agosto -1 to beat Academica	1.8	1.83	1.86	0.98	0.97
RJ v Friburguense Over 2.5	1.97	1.96	2.1	1.01	0.94
Partizan -1.25 to beat Javor	2.03	1.76	1.82	1.15	1.12
Hap. Jerusalem v Hap. Umm al-Fahm Draw	3.36	3.4	3.58	0.99	0.94
Loures v Caldas Over 2.5	2	2.39	2.5	0.84	0.80
Police -0.75 to beat BUL	2.08	1.82	1.83	1.14	1.14

The last two columns show the strength and direction of the odds movement by calculating the ratio of their published pick price to the average and maximum closing price. A figure greater than 1 implies the odds shortened by closing; less than 1, it lengthened. Compared to the market average closing price, 12 of the 20 picks witnessed a shortening, with an average price ratio of 1.023, a shortening of 2.3% on average over the 20 matches, just enough to cover a typical margin for a sharp bookmaker. Compared to the best available prices at market closing, only 8 shorted relative to the tipster's quoted pick price, and the average price ratio was 0.973, or average price lengthening of 2.7%. Is this evidence of a tipster capable of finding average expected value of 40% in a football betting market? Is the moon made of cheese?

What is the probability of a tipster capable of finding expected value of 40% moving a market by an average of 2.3% over 20 picks? Let's do some back-of-the-envelope calculations. If we assume the closing odds perfectly reflect the true odds, then the expected price movement will be 40% plus the bookmaker's margin. Let's make the margin 2.5%. The standard deviation in price movement for these 20 picks is 0.125. The standard error in the mean price movement for samples of 20 picks is then $0.125/\sqrt{20} = 0.028$. The difference between 2.3% and 42.5% is 40.2%, or 0.402, equivalent to 14.4 standard errors. Excel NORM.DIST function just returns an associated probability of 0%; the number of standard errors is too large for it to cope. Using an online error function (ERF) calculator to do the job, I found that, given all these assumptions, the probability that they would have an average odds movement of 2.3% when the expected is 42.5% is roughly 1 in 20 quattuordecillion (or 2 followed by 46 zeros). I suspect that's a little less probable than the moon being made of cheese.

Granted, you might have noted that one of the odds shortened very considerably, from 2.00 to 1.49 as a market average. However, there were several which lengthened considerably, too, for example 1.86 to 2.27 and 2.00 to 2.39. Are those the sorts of movements you'd expect if Fixedmatches.org genuinely possessed insider information about the games? I could go on checking more picks for their odds movements, but what is the point? 20 is quite sufficient. Even if by some miracle I'd found a really unlucky sample, or the reliability of the closing line value hypothesis is less robust than assumed, the number of standard errors is so enormous that any further effort to clarify the probabilities more precisely would be wasted. Regardless, we don't need to rely only on the price movements to expose Fixedmatches.org. They have exposed themselves in the way they've compiled their results. All we need to know is the statistical trick to reveal it.

We are rather poor judges of randomness. We suffer from a cognitive bias known as the clustering illusion, with a tendency to erroneously consider inevitable runs or clusters arising in random distributions to be meaningful. By way of example, consider the following series of wins (W) and losses (L). One series is a random pattern of results from the world of sport whilst I've artificially constructed the other one; which is which?

LWLLLLLLWLWLWLLLWWLLWLWWLLWWWWWW

WLLWWLLLWLWLWWLWLLWLLWWWLLWLWLWW

Did you believe that the long sequences of the same result in the first series look manufactured? Did you think the shorter sequences in the second one make it appear more random? If so, you're experiencing the clustering illusion. In fact, the first series represents the 1973 to 2004 results for Cambridge University in the Boat Race. I made the second series with a pattern designed to fool the average person who may believe shorter sequences look more random than longer ones. When asked to actually create random binary sequences, most of us will switch from W to L or vice versa if they feel that one of them is happening too often. Long sequences of the same outcome are perceived as being non-random. In fact, they happen far more often than we might imagine.

It is statistically possible to test how random a binary series is. Named after Abraham Wald – we met him a little earlier on the topic of survivorship bias – and Jacob Wolfowitz, a Polish-American mathematician, the Wald–Wolfowitz runs test determines whether a binary data sequence, for example wins and losses, arises from a random process. The test was used by Thomas Gilovich,

Robert Vallone and Amos Tversky when investigating the misperception of random sequences in basketball shooting, the so-called hot hand fallacy. Even if a bettor or tipster's history arises through skill, with real expected value, the distribution of wins and losses, which remain independent of each other, will still reflect the underlying aleatory uncertainty associated with all those hidden variables in the system, in the same way that a coin biased 70-30 in favour of heads would. All we have done is change the arithmetic mean of the distribution. Fixedmatches.org, with nearly three times as many winners as losers would seem to possess a forecasting ability akin to Nostradamus, but the sequence distribution would nonetheless exhibit randomness. Indeed, Fixedmatches.org admit as much, recognising that it's not possible to guarantee wins, and that sometimes their tips can lose.

The Wald–Wolfowitz runs test works by comparing the number of observed runs (or streaks) of binary outcomes, for example heads and tails or winning and losing bets, to the number we would expect from a random series of the same number of those binary outcomes. Take a look at the following sequence of wins and losses:

$$\text{WWWLLLWWWWLLWLWWWWLWWLLLLLWWLW}$$

There are 17 wins, 13 losses and 13 observed runs (R_o), where a run is defined as a series of consecutive wins or losses (including only one win or loss). Determining whether this sequence is random or otherwise requires us to calculate the expected number of runs from 17 wins and 13 losses and compare this to the number observed. The bigger the difference, the less likely it is that the sequence is random. Provided that each outcome in the sequence is independent, and that the win probability for all outcomes is the same (although not necessarily equal to the probability of loss), then under the (null) hypothesis that the sequence is purely random with no causal influence, the expected number of runs (R_e) is given by:

$$R_e = \frac{2WL}{W + L} + 1$$

where W and L here are the number of wins and losses, respectively. Since N, the total number of outcomes, is W + L, the equation can also be expressed as:

$$R_e = \frac{2W(N - W)}{N} + 1$$

For 17 wins and 13 losses, $R_e = 15.73$. The distribution of the possible number of runs is approximately normal, with a standard deviation, σ, given by:

$$\sigma = \sqrt{\frac{(R_e - 1)(R_e - 2)}{N - 1}}$$

Here, the standard deviation is 2.64. I ran a 10,000-iteration Monte Carlo simulation to test the normality assumption and the mathematics. The outputs are shown in the frequency distribution below. The mean number of runs was 15.75 and the standard deviation was 2.63.

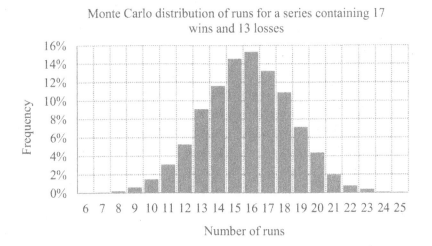

Monte Carlo distribution of runs for a series containing 17 wins and 13 losses

How many standard deviations does the observed figure of 13 runs differ from the expected figure of 15.73? We can pull out our friend the z-score, noting here that:

$$Z = \frac{R_o - R_e}{\sigma}$$

Since $R_o - R_e = -2.73$, $Z = -1.035$, implying the observed number of runs is a shade over 1 standard deviation below the expected number of runs. Its associated probability, or p-value, can be easily calculated with another Excel function, NORMSDIST, the standard normal cumulative distribution function, where the mean is 0 and the standard deviation 1. The syntax is simply NORMDIST(Z) and returns the proportional area under the standard normal curve to the left of the z-score. NORMDIST(-1.035) = 0.1504, implying the probability that 13 or fewer runs would be observed in a series containing 17 wins and 13 losses is 15.04%. You could also use the NORM.DIST function to make the same calculation, with the syntax NORM.DIST(R_o,R_e,σ,TRUE), which yields the same answer. Typically, such a probability would not be considered statistically small enough to abandon the null hypothesis of randomness, in favour of an alternative hypothesis that the sequence is not random. Arguably, a p-value below 1% or even 0.1% is required to consider switching the hypothesis which is favoured. Of course, in this example, I know the sequence was not made randomly; I constructed it to resemble a random sequence in order to present the mathematics to you. However, we can use the Wald–Wolfowitz runs test to investigate whether a sequence of wins and losses in betting has arisen randomly, as it should if it was genuine, or whether it might have been manipulated.

You might believe it would be easy to construct a sequence that looks random. Indeed, if you understand mathematically how often winning and losing streaks of a particular length should occur, you could make one that does. If, however, you just attempt to build one based on what you think it should look like, it's likely the clustering illusion will scupper your attempt. To find out just how easily one can be fooled by randomness, I attempted to construct 10 randomised binary sequences of 100 theoretical bets with win and lose probabilities of 50%, switching from win to loss in a way that I hoped was completely arbitrary, in much the same way as I might play rock–paper–scissors. Repeating this 10 times, I obtained the following p-values from the Wald–Wolfowitz test.: 1%, 5%, 1%, 1%, 1%, 3%, 16%, 16%, 5% and 3%. On four occasions I constructed sequences that one would normally expect to occur randomly only once in 100 times. Compare these to the p-values for 10 genuinely randomly generated sequences (using Excel's random number generator): 31%, 38%, 84%, 54%, 64%, 30%, 1%, 64%, 95% and 92%. Evidently, being statistically literate is not much of a defence against the clustering illusion, if you don't make any mathematical attempt to avoid it. It's rather like the Müller-Lyer illusion where, try as you might, you cannot convince yourself that the two horizontal lines are of equal length, unless you bother to measure them with a ruler.

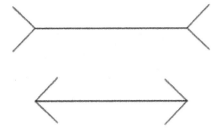

Let's subject Fixedmatches.org to the Wald–Wolfowitz runs test. I've already noted that a successful application rests on the assumption that the win probability of each independent bet should be the same. Although this is not the case, the variability of the tipping history's odds is small enough to assume that the violation of this assumption in this case will not prove to be unduly significant. (I will test this premise with a Monte Carlo simulation shortly.) In fact, 82% of the picks had odds-implied win probabilities of between 47.5% and 55%, with 95% between 45% and 57.5%. Furthermore, it was necessary to remove all the handicap-ties from the analysis since the sequence outcomes must be binary. There were 303 of these, leaving 9,116 picks in the record. However, since bets are independent, removing them will not influence the validity of the test, so long as the sequence of remaining bets is unaltered. Finally, half-wins and half-losses were treated as wins and losses. Again, this is a perfectly acceptable simplification; I could just as easily have defined the binary sequence elements as 'made a profit' and 'made a loss'; the mathematics are the same.

So, the results. The history of 9,116 picks had 6,798 winners and 2,348 losers. Plugging these numbers into the equation above gives R_e = 3,487.5, with a standard deviation of 36.5. The actual number of observed runs was 3,689, meaning $Z = 5.52$ and the p-value = 0.000000034 or about 1 in 29.5 million. This is stronger than the level of statistical significance that physicists demand when announcing the discovery of a new subatomic particle (z-score = 5), and far stronger than that demanded by the softer sciences analysing patterns, correlations and causal relationships in statistical data. The test tells us that the number of runs that were actually observed could have happened randomly just once in 29.5 million times. On that basis, we have just cause to rule out the (null) hypothesis of randomness in favour of a different one. What's the most likely explanation? The record was manipulated.

Let's take a look at the runs in more detail. The observed number is considerably largely than would be expected by chance. How could this happen? There must be fewer long streaks of wins (or losses) and more shorter ones. We can also use the mathematics to calculate the expected number of streaks of a specific length, k. Recall that for a history with a large number of bets, n, the expected number of times we will see a streak of length k (or longer) of the same outcome for a binary proposition, e_k, for odds, o, will be approximated by:

$$e_k \approx \frac{n}{o^k}$$

If we define p as the probability of that outcome, the $p = 1/o$. Hence,

$$e_k \approx np^k$$

Furthermore, the expected number of streaks of exactly length k is given by:

$$e_k - e_{k+1} \approx np^k - np^{k+1}$$

$$\approx np^k(1 - p)$$

$$\approx nqp^k$$

where $q = 1 - p$, the probability of the outcome not happening. Let's consider the winning streaks. The history of 9,116 picks analysed here had a win strike rate of 74.24%, so $p = 0.7424$ and $q = 0.2576$. Consequently, the expected number of winning streaks of exactly 5, for example, will be $9{,}116 \times 0.2576 \times 0.7424^5 = 529.6$. For streaks of exactly 10 wins, the expected number will be 119.5. I've reproduced them all for $k = 0$ up to $k = 29$.

k	Expected	Observed	k	Expected	Observed	k	Expected	Observed
0	2348.00	2348	10	119.47	51	20	6.08	1
1	1743.23	1845	11	88.70	24	21	4.51	1
2	1294.23	1419	12	65.85	14	22	3.35	0
3	960.87	1090	13	48.89	7	23	2.49	0
4	713.38	869	14	36.30	4	24	1.85	0
5	529.64	609	15	26.95	1	25	1.37	0
6	393.22	382	16	20.01	1	26	1.02	0
7	291.94	228	17	14.85	1	27	0.76	0
8	216.74	135	18	11.03	1	28	0.56	0
9	160.92	84	19	8.19	1	29	0.42	0

Take a look at the table; you will notice that the actual number of shorter streaks of length 1 through to 5 is considerably more than would be expected to occur by chance. By contrast, the number of streaks above 5 is fewer than expected, and for streak lengths above 12, the relative difference is huge. I've highlighted this in the two charts below. The first, a histogram, shows the excess of expected winning streaks relative to the actual number observed for k = 8 to 20.

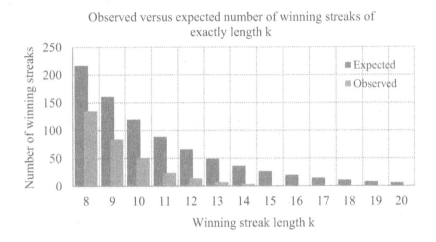

The second, shown as a scatter plot, compares the actual and expected number of winning streaks for k = 1 to 20, with the vertical axis redrawn logarithmically. Since k is roughly proportional to the logarithm of the expected number of winning streaks with length k, this will display as a straight line. Notice how the actual number of winning streaks departs from this linearity as k increases.

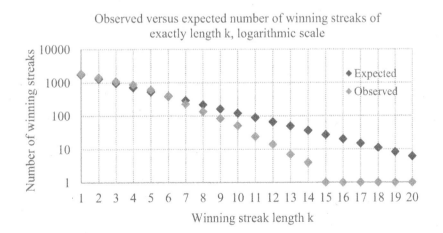

Fixedmatches.org has been fooled by randomness and the clustering illusion. A forecaster who could genuinely predict nearly three-quarters of bet outcomes successfully would have significantly more long winning streaks than has been reported here. The most rational explanation for this is that they have simply underestimated the probability of them occurring, or indeed not thought about it at all beyond a basic visual interpretation. Evidently, once a winning streak reaches around 12, it is believed that adding another win to it will start to draw suspicion. In fact, they've got it the wrong way round, but such is the power of the clustering illusion, neither they, nor anyone else would be aware that this had happened. By ending longer winning streaks artificially early, you introduce a new run. Consequently, if those long sequences are shortened more often than they should be, the overall history will contain more runs than would be expected by chance. And that, of course, is exactly what has happened. Naturally, if we have statistically proved that winning streaks have been artificially terminated with a loss, in a failed bid to make the record look more believable, it's not a stretch to conclude many of the winning bets are themselves just artificially created. Presumably, with a strike rate of nearly 75% and a yield of 40%, most of you had already concluded this anyway. However, it's useful to have a statistical tool to prove it. As a final way of demonstrating the power of the Wald–Wolfowitz test I randomised the history of 9,119 picks 10 times and calculated the z-score for each. The figures were, -1.55, 0.07, 0.92, -0.09, -0.01, 1.77, -0.18, -0.51, -0.12 and 1.71. None of the z-scores was statistically significant at even the 1% level. This just adds further weight to the evidence that the way this record of picks has been put together is entirely manufactured and with fraudulent intentions.

I've little doubt that Fixedmatches.org would wish to challenge my reasoning. Usually, it goes like this. 'You are a hater; our customers know the truth.' A little more sophistication in a rebuttal might attempt to challenge the validity of using the Wald–Wolfowitz test, and in particular the assumption that its use relies on all win probabilities being equal. Unsurprisingly, unless we are betting on coin flips or roulette spins, that's not going to be the case, and certainly not in sports, unless one knows the true probabilities for all bets and ensures they are all the same. To further rebut such a rebuttal, we need to test how reliable or robust the Wald–Wolfowitz test is when faced with variable outcome probabilities. For this, we can use the Monte Carlo simulation. To build one, there is an important consideration: for every iteration, the number of wins and losses should be the same; only the order in which they occur is randomised. Holding these figures constant whilst randomising which bets win and lose, based on their actual odds, presents a little bit of a computational challenge for a betting history this large. For each Monte Carlo iteration, I created a likelihood score for a bet to win by weighting a randomly generated number (using Excel's RAND function) with the win probability implied by the odds for each bet, thereby ensuring that shorter odds were more likely, on average, to win. I then used Excel's LARGE function to declare the 6,768 highest likelihood scores as winners. Thus, whilst the number of winners remains the same on each iteration, the order in which they occur is randomised, and hence the number of runs potentially different each time. Such a methodology, however, consumes a lot of memory. A simulation of just 100 iterations took over an hour. Nevertheless, that is sufficient to answer the question. The average number of observed runs in the Monte Carlo simulation was 3,487.7, almost identical to the expected number (3,487.5) calculated using the Wald–Wolfowitz test. It would seem that, for this set of odds at least, their variability makes no meaningful difference to the expected number of runs, and hence the use of the test as a means of exposing the manipulation entirely vindicated.

Just how variable would a set of odds have to be before the Wald–Wolfowitz test became less reliable? I've tested my Wisdom of the Crowd history, which, you will recall, has very sizeable odds variation. Of the 11,894 bets, 4,462 were winners, leading to 5,604 distinct runs of wins and losses. With R_e = 5,577.2, Z = 0.52, a statistically insignificant difference between the actual and expected number of runs, with R_o sitting at the 60th percentile within the distribution of possible runs given this number of bets and winners. That is as it should be, since the distribution of winners and losers will be random. But how reliable is the Wald–Wolfowitz figure for R_e? Another 100-iteration Monte Carlo simulation returned an average number of runs of 5,551.3. That's not nearly as close to R_e as for the FixedMatches.org history, but with a standard deviation of 47.9 in the simulation, it's still well within the limits of statistical error. Despite the large variation in my history's betting odds, the Wald–Wolfowitz test can still be used to provide a reliable estimate for the expected number of runs. Of course, if ever there is any doubt about the reliability and validity of a mathematical function, the Monte Carlo simulation will provide you with the information that you need.

It's likely that the reason the test still works fairly well for my history is because the order of betting odds is random, with no systematic evolution from shorter to longer odds, or vice versa. To test that premise I made a theoretical history of 999 bets, ordered from a win expectancy of 99.9% down to 0.1%, incrementally decreasing by 0.1% with each sequential bet. The reference sample had 499 wins with R_o = 326. By contrast, R_e = 500.5. It's fairly self-evident that the much smaller number of observed runs arises because of the ordering of the win probabilities. The earlier bets have short odds, with a high probability of winning. The first loss didn't occur until the 40th bet, and the next after that not until the 83rd. Similarly, at the other end of the history, almost all bets are losses. Consequently, the whole history has a few exceptionally large sequences of wins and losses, using up a large number of available bets, thereby reducing the total number of runs. Hence, the validity of the Wald–Wolfowitz test is completely compromised. The z-score for R_o is over 11, despite the fact that wins and losses were settled randomly; the sequence of odds, of course, was not random. By contrast, the average number of runs from a Monte Carlo simulation (100 iterations) was 323.4, a closer match for R_o. Clearly, when the numerical ordering of your odds (and implied win probabilities) is systematic and not random, the Monte Carlo simulation, and not the Wald–Wolfowitz function, will be the tool to use. However, I can't envisage any meaningful scenario in the real world where a bettor would have any reason to bet in such a manner. Certainly, I've never come across a betting history of such a kind in over 20 years of studying them, with the possible exception of tipsters who dramatically change a strategy following poor results. Such tipsters, however, should always be ignored anyway. If a tipster feels the need to introduce a dramatic change to their methodology, tipping is not something they should have been indulging in the first place.

My final method for uncovering attempts by a tipster to deceive paying customers with fake pick histories is another statistical one. It's relatively straightforward and utilises a statistic that I have already covered in detail: the standard error of the sample yield. Let me remind you of the formula:

$$SE = \frac{\sigma}{\sqrt{n}}$$

where σ is the standard deviation in a population of profits and losses and n is the number of your bets in your sample. If we have a large enough betting history (the population) we can break it up into a collection of equal-sized samples, calculate the yield for each sample and then their standard deviation. If the betting history has arisen randomly, that standard deviation in sample yields should be the same as the standard error calculated using the formula above. Let me give you an example to make things a little clearer.

Consider a theoretical history of 10,000 bets with fair odds of 2. The expectation is that 50% will win (for a unit profit of +1) and 50% will lose (for a unit loss of -1). Excel can tell you (with the STDEVP function) that the standard deviation, σ, in those expected profits and losses will be 1. Alternatively, you could have used the formula $\sqrt{r(o - r}$, where r (your expected return) = 1 and o (the odds) = 2. Using Excel's RAND function, I've simulated an example history of 10,000 bets. Each bet is settled with the following Excel formula: IF(RAND()<0.5,+1,-1), Next, I've broken this history into 100 separate samples of 100 bets each and calculated their yields. There's nothing special about the number 100. You just need a sufficient number of samples to make your analysis robust. Samples of 100 bets give me 100 samples, a decent size; samples of 1,000 bets, however, would only give me 10 samples, and any conclusions I draw could be less reliable. Finally, I've calculated the standard deviation in those 100 sample yields and compared that figure to the one obtained from the formula for the standard error. Since $\sigma = 1$ and the sample size, n = 100, the expected standard error = $1/\sqrt{100} = 0.1$. My standard deviation in the sample yields was 0.0986. Of course, this is just one possible history of 10,000 bets and one possible set of 100 sample yields. I can run a Monte Carlo simulation to see what the distribution of those 100-sample standard deviations looks like. Here it is below, for 100,000 iterations.

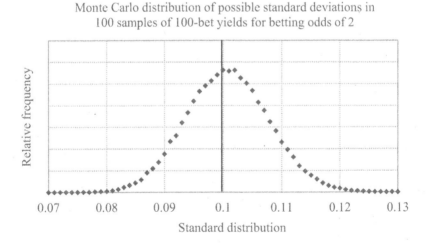

Monte Carlo distribution of possible standard deviations in 100 samples of 100-bet yields for betting odds of 2

The mean standard deviation, 0.998, is essentially equivalent to the expected value of 0.1, within typical margins of statistical error. This is hardly a surprising result, given that we know I created the history randomly. The distribution, however, gives us information about the possible variation of standard deviations in the 100-bet sample yields. The distribution looks a lot like a normal one and the spread of data conforms closely to the 68-95-99.7 empirical rule. However, there is an underlying positive skew which is hard to see visually, meaning the right-hand tail is slightly heavier than the left. The position of the mean standard deviation, marked with the vertical black line, perhaps helps illustrate the asymmetry a little better. In fact, a distribution of a sample standard deviations can be described by a gamma distribution, and the standard deviation of that distribution – in other words, the standard deviation of a sample of standard deviations – described by a gamma function. The size of the positive skew can be greater or smaller depending on the gamma distribution's characteristics, but under particular conditions, can be closely approximated by the normal distribution, which is likely to be the case here. I'm afraid my mathematical ability falls short of being able to interpret the gamma function, which is why I turned to the Monte Carlo simulation to estimate this figure for me. The standard deviation in my 100,000 standard deviations was 0.0071. With the Monte Carlo mean standard deviation in the yields for the 100 samples just 0.002 less than the expected figure of 0.1, a difference considerably smaller than the figure of 0.0071, this confirms that the observed 100-bet samples standard deviation and the expected standard error are not significantly different.

Let's run the same exercise for the pick history of FixedMatches.org. For each Monte Carlo iteration, I've again randomised the bet outcomes, using the history's actual average return to define the expected value, and therefore the expected win probability, for each bet. Of course, we can't be sure that different odds won't have different expected values; we already know that longer odds can typically have larger expected values. However, remember that the vast majority of the odds in this history lie within a very narrow range, so arguably my simplification should not invalidate my investigation. Similarly, we can't be sure that the actual returns were either luckier or unluckier than expected. I've had to assume neither, that is to say their actual returns are equivalent to their average expected value, since we have no other means of identifying what their expected value is. For example, then, with a yield of 39.8% ($r = 1.398$), their most recent bet of Ankaragucu v Rizespor Under 2.25 at odds of 1.98 would have an expected win probability of $1.398 / 1.98 = 0.706$ or 70.6%. Again, it's a simple matter of using Excel's RAND function to randomise the outcome, do the same for all 9,419 picks, and run a large number of Monte Carlo iterations. As for my theoretical history before, I've run 100,000 of them.

The distribution of 100,000 standard deviations of the 100-bet sample yields is shown below. The mean standard deviation was 0.0895, close to the figure predicted by $\sigma/\sqrt{n}$ (0.0866), and even closer to the figure predicted by $\sqrt{r(o-r)}$ (0.0889). The former is a little lower because a proportion of results were settled as handicap ties, half wins and half losses, the influence of which is to reduce σ, since the individual profits and losses are smaller. The proportion was quite small, however, at 15.7%, hence the relatively close match between the two methods. With a larger proportion of such results, the $\sqrt{r(o-r)}$ method obviously loses reliability.

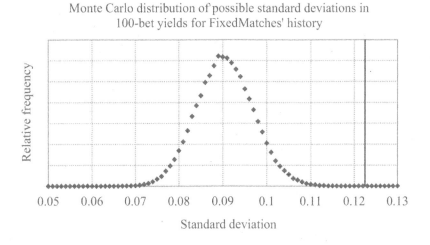

Monte Carlo distribution of possible standard deviations in 100-bet yields for FixedMatches' history

This time, the vertical black line marks the position of the history's actual standard deviation in the 100-bet sample yields. The figure is 0.1258. With a standard deviation in the standard deviations of 0.0065, it holds a z-score of 5.59 and lies on the 99.999998% percentile, assuming normality. In other words, you'd expect to observe a standard deviation in the 100-bet sample yields at least this large about once in 43 million occasions. It certainly didn't happen in the 100,000 Monte Carlo iterations. The largest was 0.1210, with only one other above 0.12.

Arguably, the true z-score could be even larger. In randomising the bet outcomes, I am only able to consider them as binary propositions: win or lose. In reality, some of the handicap bets could end as ties, half wins or half losses, the influence of which would be to lower both the mean standard deviation in the 100-bet sample yields and the standard deviation in the standard deviations. The observed figure of 0.1258 would then become an even less likely outlier. A z-score of 5.59, however, broadly similar to the z-score obtained by the Wald–Wolfowitz test, is already quite sufficient to make a conclusion, so let's do that: FixedMatches.org is cheating. There is simply too much variation in the actual 100-bet sample yields for that to have arisen randomly. If bet outcomes, which should be independent of each other, and therefore randomly distributed, have not arisen randomly, then one is forced to conclude that they have been manipulated. As the evidence from the Wald–Wolfowitz runs test has already revealed, FixedMatches.org has failed to adequately consider the natural way in which wins and losses, and samples of wins and losses, distribute. The word 'fixed' is clearly appropriate to describe this sports betting advisory service. It isn't the matches that are being fixed, however, but the picks themselves.

ODDS & SODS

We're coming towards the end of this journey; well done if you're still with me. I've covered all the topics I'd originally set out to address: modelling, winning, losing, staking and tipping. There are, of course, many other sorts of data analysis you can perform with a Monte Carlo simulation, so in this chapter, and the next one, I'd like to share a few of them. The list is by no means exhaustive but includes some ideas I've played around with over the years to improve my understanding of a betting market. I hope they might spark some more novel ideas in you, and perhaps improve your betting as well. Let's begin with scoring rules.

Scoring Rules

A scoring rule, or scoring function, measures the accuracy of probabilistic predictions, applicable where predictions assign probabilities to a set of mutually exclusive outcomes, typical to the vast majority of betting markets. Home-draw-away, or over-under are mutually exclusive results. Only one can happen, not two (or more) at the same time for a single event. The probabilities assigned to the full set of possible outcomes sums to 1, with each possible outcome holding a probability of between 0 and 1. That much you already know. Once an outcome is known, the forecast probability for that outcome is compared to the actual outcome. If something happens, for example a home win in football, an outcome score of 1 is assigned it. If it didn't happen, the outcome score is 0. These are the only possible outcome scores for binary propositions. The scoring rule then compares the difference between the probabilistic score to the outcome score, by means of some function or scoring rule. The smaller the deviation, the better the prediction.

Philosophically speaking, I don't like scoring rules since they appear to encourage a more deterministic view of events, in which it is assumed that one outcome or another was inevitable, but owing to a lack of information, we were unable to perfectly 'know' what that was in advance. This position chimes with Henri Poincaré's view of randomness, as just a measure of incomplete knowledge. Chaos theory and quantum physics, however, have revealed determinism to be an imperfect model of reality. Arguably, there are no such things as inevitable outcomes; they might offer a more coherent construct of cause and effect but rejecting them in favour of 'true' probabilities, where outcomes are not 1s and 0s but a fuzzy mess of values in between, helps to keep the bettor grounded in a more probabilistic interpretation of things. Nevertheless, scoring rules are a mainstay of statistical mathematics, so it probably wouldn't be wise of me to dismiss them out of hand.

There are scoring rules and then there are scoring rules, and some are more 'proper' than others. I'm not going to delve into the conceptual differences, largely because with my limited statistical background, I struggle to interpret them myself. Here, it is simply worth noting that a proper scoring rule is one that maximises its expected score by reporting the forecast probabilities truthfully. For example, a mean absolute difference (or error) between the observed outcomes and forecast probabilities is not a proper scoring rule, since we are actually incentivised to always report probabilities of 100% or 0%, depending on which is closer to our forecast probability. To eliminate this problem, and build a proper scoring rule, two possible solutions are to use the mean of the squared error (for example Brier score and rank probability score) or the logarithm of the forecast probability (for example the log-loss score).

The Brier score (BS) calculates the mean squared difference between the actual outcome of the event and the predicted probability for that specific outcome and sums the scores for all possible outcomes for that event. Mathematically, this is expressed as:

$$BS_{match} = \sum_{i=1}^{r} (p_i - o_i)^2$$

where, o_i and p_i are, respectively, the outcome and forecast probability for the ith possible event outcome with a total of r possible outcomes. Recall that the large Greek letter sigma implies 'the sum of'. For example, with home-draw-away football forecasts, $r = 3$. A worked example will illustrate the scoring rule calculation more clearly. Let's suppose Liverpool are playing Manchester United at home, and our forecast model has predicted a 45% win probability for Liverpool, a 25% win probability for Manchester United, and a 30% probability for a draw. Let's now also suppose the game ended in a draw. What would be the Brier score for our set of predictions? Given the draw outcome, $o_{draw} = 1$, whilst both o_{home} and $o_{away} = 0$. Thus, $p_{draw} - o_{draw} = 0.3 - 1 = -0.7$, whilst $p_{home} - o_{home} =$

0.45 and $p_{away} - o_{away} = 0.25$. Finally, the Brier score will be $0.45^2 + -0.7^2 + 0.25^2$ = 0.755. The smaller the Brier score, the better the original forecast probabilities. Suppose we had in fact forecast a draw probability of 100%, and 0% for the home and away wins. The forecast would have perfectly predicted the outcome, and the Brier score would be 0. At the other extreme, a perfectly inaccurate forecast will have a Brier score of 2, the maximum possible score for binary propositions.

If we'd just guessed randomly, assigning a one third probability each to home win, draw and away win, we'd have actually achieved a superior Brier score of 0.667. Of course, we should know enough about the randomness of sport to understand that judging the quality of a forecasting model on just one outcome would be more than a little foolish. To test the quality of the forecast model, we would like to know what the average Brier score is for a large sample of matches. To calculate it, simply sum the Brier scores for all match forecasts and divide the total by the number of matches. Thus:

$$BS_{sample} = \frac{1}{n}\sum_{i=1}^{n} BS_{match}$$

where n is the number of matches in the sample. I've done this for the 2019/20 English Premier League season (n = 380); the average Brier score for Pinnacle's closing odds (margin removed) was 0.575, better than random guesswork, but by how much? Quantitatively, 0.574 is smaller than 0.667, but qualitatively speaking, how can we measure how good the forecast probabilities, based on Pinnacle's closing odds, actually are? The 380 match outcomes represent one possible history. There are roughly two sexvigintillion googol of them (or 2 followed by 181 zeros). We can't calculate the average Premier League Brier score for all of those histories, but we can use a Monte Carlo simulation to estimate the possible frequency distribution, using Pinnacle's implied home-draw-away win probabilities as inputs for the model. I've reproduced it below, for a simulation with 100,000 iterations. The distribution is a good fit for a normal one, with the data conforming closely to the empirical rule. The distribution's mean and standard deviation are 0.561 and 0.017, respectively, meaning that the actual Brier score for the observed outcomes, marked by the vertical line in the chart, has a z-score of 0.81. That is to say, it lies 0.81 standard deviations above expectation, a figure well within typical statistical margins of error.

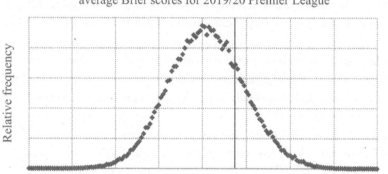

Monte Carlo distribution of possible Pinnacle closing odds
average Brier scores for 2019/20 Premier League

We might regard the mean Brier score as the expected Brier score, under the assumption that Pinnacle's closing odds capture the 'true' outcome probabilities perfectly. With the Brier score for the observed results higher than the expected score, we might also say that the Pinnacle model was a little unlucky given the specific outcome of games, but not so unlucky as to have us questioning the model's validity. The observant amongst you, however, may have noticed the underlying circularity in the methodological logic used to develop this analysis. Our aim is to test the quality of Pinnacle's forecast probabilities. To do so, I have randomised the outcomes to determine how unlikely the actual Brier score might be. However, to achieve this randomisation, I have assumed that Pinnacle's forecast probabilities perfectly capture reality and the likelihood of each possible outcome. What I have constructed here might be the statistical equivalent of the Escherian Stairway. One way out of this conundrum is to change the underlying outcome probabilities, but to what? Herein lies the problem, and actually the universal truth facing all bettors: we don't, and cannot, perfectly know the 'true' outcome probabilities, hence we have no direct way of calculating the real expected Brier score via a Monte Carlo simulation.

We can, however, test one set of model predictions against another to build a picture of their relative quality. Suppose, for example, the true outcome probabilities for all 380 games were one third for home win, draw and away win alike. If we re-run the Monte Carlo simulation, the average Brier score for Pinnacle's closing odds is now 0.773, with a standard deviation of 0.019. Since the Brier score for the actual results is over 10 standard deviations lower than the expected score for this simulation, with a vanishingly small probability that this could arise by chance if home win, draw, and away win were equally likely, we should conclude that all three outcomes being equally likely is probably not a good model to describe the 'true' outcome probabilities of these matches. Conversely, if we use such a model to describe the forecast probabilities instead, the average Brier score is 0.667 regardless of the true outcome probabilities. Again, since this is over 6 standard deviations higher than the Brier score for the Pinnacle model, this again suggests that Pinnacle's forecast model is far superior. Of course, it doesn't require a scoring rule to know that a bookmaker's odds are better than guesswork, but you could use this idea to test one bookmaker against another, or indeed your own forecast model against them.

A different way to interpret the accuracy for a probabilistic forecast model is by means of a likelihood estimation. Given some set of observed data, in this case the 2019/20 Premier League match outcomes, what forecast probabilities would be required such that the observed results were actually the ones most likely to occur? This statistical best-fit methodology is formally known as maximum likelihood estimation. It is an example of Bayesian inference; rather than test for the likelihood of the data given a particular model (or hypothesis), we reverse the process and test for the likelihood of the model or hypothesis given a particular set of data. There are advantages and disadvantages to Bayesian inference, which I will explore a little later in this chapter. For now, however, let's take a closer look at a commonly used method of likelihood estimation known as log-likelihood.

Return, for a moment, to my theoretical game between Liverpool and Manchester United. The game ended in a draw. If we assume that what happened was the most likely outcome to happen, then according to my forecast model, which had predicted a 30% probability, the likelihood of observing what we observed is 30%. My model, however, might not be the best model. The 'true' probability might not be 30%. The purpose of likelihood estimation, however, is to discover what the most likely 'true' probability would be, given the outcome. Under the assumption that football matches are independent, the likelihood of observing the 380 match outcomes that did occur can, following the multiplication rule, be calculated by the product of the observed outcome probabilities. When you multiply fractions, you end up with an even smaller fraction. If you do that 380 times, you will end up with an exceptionally small number indeed. I've done it for the Pinnacle model probabilities and the likelihood of precisely this set of outcomes was 2×10^{-161}, or about 1 in 5 novemdecillion googol (5 followed by 160 zeros). Such numbers can create brain fog. For match samples much bigger, Excel will get upset too. Instead, we can use the logarithm of the likelihood, and following the logarithm product rule, we can add their values rather than multiply them. For example, for two match outcomes where the forecast model had predicted win probabilities of 50% and 25%, the log-likelihood for these outcomes would be log(0.5) + log(0.25). If the base of the logarithm is 2, then the answer is (-1) + (-2) = -3. For a log-likelihood estimation, we can use any logarithm base we like. It is common to use the natural logarithm, Ln, with the number e as the base. Doing so for the 380 outcome probabilities yields a log-likelihood figure of -369.87. Sometimes, it's preferable to lose the minus sign and divide by the sample size, in this case 380. This is then known as a log-loss. Here, that would be 0.973 for Pinnacle's fair closing odds.

The ultimate goal of a likelihood estimation exercise is to find a set of forecast probabilities that maximises the likelihood of seeing the outcomes we have seen. In terms of log-loss, the smaller the number the better the forecast probabilities, in exactly the same way as for the Brier scoring rule. In fact, the log-loss is an example of another scoring rule and is just a reformulation of log-likelihood. The formal equation for the log-loss (LL) scoring rule is:

$$LL_{match} = -\sum_{i=1}^{r} o_i Ln(p_i)$$

where Ln is the natural logarithm. Thus, for a sample of matches, we also have:

$$LL_{sample} = \frac{1}{n}\sum_{i=1}^{n} LL_{match}$$

The log-loss score can be interpreted as a measure of how wrong or far away your forecast probabilities are from the outcome distribution. In one sense, we might regard 'loss' to mean a loss of certainty. Many mathematicians prefer the log-loss scoring rule to the Brier score because it exhibits what is known as locality, where only the forecast probability of the actual outcome is used to compute the score. For the Brier score, by contrast, and for another called rank probability score, the other possible outcomes contribute too. Intuitively, locality might be considered a desirable property of a scoring rule; if one particular outcome happens, why should we care about the probabilities for the other events? I'm sure Henri Poincaré wouldn't care since he might argue for the inevitability of the observed outcome. Werner Heisenberg or Edward Lorenz, the fathers of quantum mechanics and chaos theory respectively, might take a different view. The logarithmic scoring rule also has the property of penalising large forecast errors more severely. For Brier, the worst possible score is 2; for log-loss it is infinity.

Let's compare Pinnacle's log-loss score to those for some other possible forecast models. For a model that assumes the home win, draw, and away win are all equally likely, the log-loss score is 1.099. However, guessing is hardly much of a model; we can do better than that. What about one that assigns the average home win, draw and away win percentage to every game? These are roughly 45%, 27% and 28%, although the 2020/21 season witnessed a dramatic departure from these values, evidently on account of the absence of crowds and a weakening of the home advantage. The score is a little better at 1.067, but still a long way short of Pinnacle's forecast model. Next, let's try a proper match prediction mode; I built one using the Dixon-Coles methodology described earlier in the book. It achieved a log-loss score of 0.978, far superior to my two rudimentary models but still not quite as good as Pinnacle's closing prices. That's probably to be expected; I should hardly assume that my simple Dixon-Coles model could be superior to Pinnacle's forecasting algorithms, in addition to the models of the 'client-status' bettors who help to improve the accuracy of the forecast percentages.

How does the Pinnacle closing-price model fare against other bookmakers? Take a look below. I've compared Pinnacle's log-loss score for the 2019/20 Premier League season with 5 other bookmakers, in addition to the market average. I've also shown the Brier scores for additional comparison.

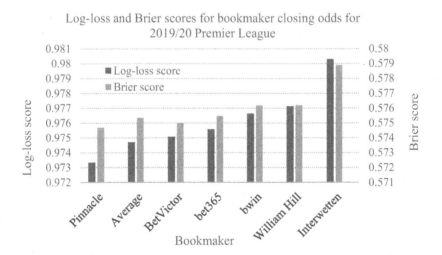

Firstly, you will notice that the two scoring rules correlate reasonably well. Whilst obviously they have different scales, bookmakers with superior (lower) log-loss scores also tend to have superior (inferior) Brier scores as well. Secondly, you can see that according to both scoring rules, Pinnacle has the most accurate forecast probabilities. We already knew this to be true from the evidence of the Wisdom of the (Pinnacle) Crowd methodology, but it's helpful to have it confirmed. You will also notice that Pinnacle appears to be superior to the average market. Whilst the average betting odds do contain Pinnacle's prices, they are just one bookmaker of around 35 in total that contribute to the average. Nearly all of the rest are recreational bookmakers, which as explained earlier may be offering prices which intentionally deviate from the most efficient (accurate) ones. I have been asked by bettors whether the market average price offers a reliable consensus price that is more accurate than individual prices, according to the principles of the wisdom of the crowd. Whilst such a process may go some way to help cancel out random errors in bookmakers' prices, my answer is always the same: ignore the average; if you want a good measure of 'true' probabilities, use Pinnacle's odds instead, their crowd is always the wisest. The average, here, is better than all contributing recreational bookmakers, but not better than Pinnacle.

Even Pinnacle's scores, however, are not perfect. A perfect score would be 0, where the forecast probabilities exactly match the outcomes. Such a forecast model, however, would need to understand all of Henri Poincaré's hidden variables perfectly, to be able to predict with certainty how the potentially infinite number of causal mechanisms combine to produce an outcome. As argued, this is both practically impossible from the perspective of chaos theory and theoretically questionable from the perspective of quantum mechanics. Whilst outcomes might seem inevitable in hindsight, these modern sciences have taught us that there is no such thing as inevitable, not because we lack all the information but because that is the fundamental nature of reality. Indeed, it is for precisely this reason that I dislike the whole concept of scoring rules since, philosophically speaking at least, they appear to be more deterministic than probabilistic in their design. Arguably, a better scoring system would be one that could compare a prediction model's forecast probabilities to the 'true' probabilities. Of course, if we could do that, we would have no need for the model in the first place, and the whole business of bookmaking and sports betting would not exist.

In principle, we could use a scoring rule to investigate which betting markets are more efficient, and which less so. A more inefficient betting market, with less accurate prices, presents more real expected value opportunities for bettors.

Traditionally, it has been assumed that the more popular the market, the more efficient it will be, on account of there being more interest, more available player and team information, therefore better initial bookmaker prediction models, and more bettors betting more money. According to that reasoning we should expect the English Premier League, for example, to be more efficient than the French second division. Let's investigate whether that is so. For the 280 matches played during the 2019/20 French second division season, Pinnacle's fair closing odds log-loss score was 1.103. Eureka, hypothesis proved. Or has it been? Different sets of 'true' probabilities will give you different scoring rule scores, even if your forecast model for both correlates perfectly with those 'true' probabilities.

Consider the following scenario: a forecast model for a fair coin flip predicts 50% heads; 6 out of 12 coin tosses land heads; the log-loss score is 0.693. Now consider a second scenario: a forecast model for a fair 6-sided die predicts one-sixth 6s; 2 out of 12 die rolls land 6; the log-loss score is 0.435. The second forecast model looks superior by virtue of its lower log-loss score, but in fact the two models are both perfect. Although this is a theoretical example where we know the underlying probability distribution for both coin tosses and die rolls, the point I wish to make still stands: you should not compare scoring rules scores for two different sets of data with potentially different underlying probability distributions. In this example, there is a greater asymmetry (and variance) in the binary outcome probabilities for a die role (1/6 versus 5/6) compared to a coin toss (both 1/2). To put it another way, there is lower aleatory uncertainty. The greater the asymmetry in the 'true' binary probabilities, the lower the scoring rule score for a perfect forecast model. The standard deviation in Pinnacle's implied Premier League probabilities is 0.209. By contrast, for the French second division it is just 0.117. The Premier League has a far greater asymmetry of team quality between the best and worst teams than the French second division. As a consequence, the best/worst teams will have proportionally higher/lower 'true' win probabilities.

From these figures it is essentially impossible to determine whether the Premier League is genuinely more efficient than the French second division. Indeed, it could be the case that Pinnacle's closing odds for the latter are more accurate, but that truth remains hidden. If you'd foolishly predicted a fair die to land 6 one third of the time, your log-loss score accompanying two observed 6s in 12 rolls – 0.521 – would still be less than for the probabilistically perfect coin toss prediction model. A scoring rule is unable to distinguish between aleatory (random) and epistemic (model error) uncertainties. In this case, you've artificially increased epistemic uncertainty above 0, by using a die roll prediction model that doesn't conform to the known true probability distribution. However, the aleatory uncertainty for rolling versus not rolling a 6 is less than that for tossing versus not tossing heads on a coin. Thus, despite an increase in epistemic uncertainty, your flawed die roll prediction model exhibits less overall uncertainty as measured by the log-loss scoring rule.

Similarly, it is impossible, from a scoring rule, to determine whether your own prediction model for one division will be better or worse than another model for a different division. Furthermore, you will face the same problem attempting to reveal whether betting markets have increased in efficiency over time, as one might expect given the increasing numbers of people betting in them. Different seasons have a different make-up of teams and players, and no two seasons will have identical underlying 'true' probability distributions. All things considered, I don't find scoring rules to be a particularly useful metric for use in sports betting analysis, but now at least you have a better idea about how they work and what they do.

Bayesian Inference

I've mentioned the phrase 'Bayesian inference' three times so far. What exactly am I talking about? Cast your mind back to the chapter on winning. The probability distribution of possible betting performances (yields), given a prior hypothesis about the expected value we hold is true, allowed us to calculate the probability of the actual outcome we had of occurring. With such an approach, the starting point is always the hypothesis, which is assumed to be true. This might be that we have no expected value at all and can expect to lose a percentage over turnover defined by the bookmaker's margin. Alternatively, it might be a belief that we do hold expected value, for example an average of 5%. The number doesn't actually matter; what is important is that it is assumed to be true. Then, given that our hypothesis is true, what is the probability of seeing the data that we have seen? If the probability is small enough, we may be motivated to throw out the prior hypothesis in favour of a new one that might better explain the observation. This method of hypothesis testing is something called the frequentist methodology; it involves looking at the frequency of data.

Bayesian inference turns this approach on its head. Instead of 'given the hypothesis, what is the frequency, probability or likelihood of the data?', the Bayesian method asks the question in reverse: 'given the data, what is the probability that the hypothesis is true?' As you've just seen, scoring rules are a form of Bayesian inference. The probability of the forecast model being true is inferred from the data that has been observed, which is assumed to be the most likely. The statistical process begins with the specification of some prior probability of a hypothesis being true. For example, this might be that I am a skilled bettor holding expected value of 5%. This probability is then updated in the light of new evidence, for example with the winning and losing of bets. With Bayesian inference, there is no such thing as absolute truth or certainty, just probabilities. The truth of the hypothesis, for example that I am a skilled bettor, is merely provisional, open to reappraisal and correction as I acquire more information, but never to be absolutely determined.

Bayesian inference takes its name from the reverend Thomas Bayes, an 18th century statistician, philosopher and church minister who formulated a famous law of conditional probability which bears his name: Bayes' Theorem. It describes the probability of an event conditional on some prior knowledge that might be related to the event, and its formula, or rule, provides the precise method by which prior probabilities can be updated given the new information. The formula is easily derived from the more generalised multiplication rule for dependent events. At the beginning of the book, I showed you the specific multiplication rule for independent events. As a reminder, here it is again.

Multiplication Rule for independent events:

$$p(A \text{ and } B) = p(A) \times p(B)$$

The multiplication rule for non-independent events, that is to say, where the probability of B depends upon what happens with A, involves a little tweak.

Multiplication Rule for dependent events:

$$p(A \text{ and } B) = p(A) \times p(B|A)$$

The notation $p(B|A)$ means 'the probability of B , given that A has happened.'

Let's briefly look at an example. Suppose you remove two cards from a standard pack of cards, one after another, without replacing the first card. What is the probability that the first card is the ace of spades, and the second card is a heart? The two events are dependent events because the first card is not replaced. There is only one ace of spades in a deck of 52 cards, so the probability that it is removed as the first card is 1/52. There are then 51 cards left in the deck, of which 13 are hearts. Thus, the probability of removing one on the second card draw is 13/51. So, by the multiplication rule for dependent events, we calculate the probability of removing the ace of spades on the first draw AND removing a hearts on the second draw, conditional on having removed the ace of spades on the first draw, as 1/52 x 13/51 = 13 / (52 x 51).

What happens if the dependence is reversed? This time, we would like to calculate the probability of removing a heart on the first draw AND removing the ace of spades on the second draw, conditional on removing a hearts on the first. The calculation is now 13/52 x 1/51 = 13 / (52 x 51). Notice that the solutions are exactly the same. Thus, we have demonstrated that p (A and B) = p(B and A). From this, we can show that p(A) x p(B|A) = p(B) x p(A|B). Finally, we can derive the following formula:

$$p(A|B) = \frac{p(B|A) \cdot p(A)}{p(B)}$$

This is Bayes' formula. I've replaced the multiplication character 'x' with a more mathematically formal decimal point. Bayes' formula states that the probability of some event A, conditional on B occurring, is equal to the unconditional probability of A divided by the unconditional probability of B multiplied by the probability of B, conditional on A occurring. In the context of Bayesian inference, p(A) is the prior probability of some event occurring, or indeed some belief or hypothesis being true. Given that B, another event or some new information which influences A, arises, p(A|B) is what is called the posterior probability. The application of Bayes' formula can have most people tied up in mental knots. To untie them, it helps to break it down by means of an example.

What is the probability that Liverpool lose a game when conceding 3 goals? Let's suppose that p(A), the prior (unconditional) probability that Liverpool lose = 20%. Let's also suppose that p(B), the unconditional probability that Liverpool concede 3 goals = 10%. Finally, let's suppose that p(B|A), the conditional probability that Liverpool concede 3 goals when they lose = 25%. Using Bayes' formula, p(A|B), the conditional probability that Liverpool lose given they've conceded 3 goals can be calculated by 20% x 25% / 10% = 50%. I've no idea if these are true figures, so please don't go emailing to tell me they're wrong. Rather, the point is to demonstrate the application of Bayes' formula.

Amongst practitioners, there is much debate about the relative merits of frequentist versus Bayesian statistics. Arguably, they are two sides of the same coin. The frequentist believes that the parameters of a model (or hypothesis) are fixed, and the data is random; the Bayesian believes the data is fixed, and the model parameters are random. The answer to the question, which is better, is that it depends. The drawback with frequentist hypothesis testing and the use of p-values is that it offers little in the way of a judgement about the likelihood of a hypothesis being true. As I've previously argued, even when the likelihood of some data occurring is small, given the hypothesis that it should have arisen randomly, the leap from one hypothesis to another is subjective. Fundamentally, a p-value of 1 in a million still implies that there is a 1-in-a-million probability that what you have seen could happen by chance, assuming the null hypothesis to be true, for example a betting profit arising through luck and not via the skill of the bettor. A Bayesian method, by contrast, explicitly aims to say something about the probability of a model being valid or a hypothesis being true. Arguably, this works better when we have a clearer idea about the probability of the initial prior. Nevertheless, the underlying assumption is still that the data being observed is the most likely, and that may not be the case at all. Of course, the Bayesian would counter with 'that doesn't matter; we just collect more data and keep updating our prior to a new posterior again and again'. Anyway, enough of the philosophical musings; let's look at how a Bayesian approach might be useful for a bettor.

Perhaps the most important question a bettor wants to ask of themselves is whether they are skilled. Skilled could mean any number of things. More generally it could mean making a consistent profit. More specifically it could mean holding a specific expected value. It could also mean beating the closing line, regardless of whether the size by which it is beaten is enough to hold profitable expected value. What is clear is what not being skilled represents in this context. An unskilled bettor is one whose betting is effectively replicating a random walk through a prediction market, with an expectation defined by the bookmaker's margin; to put it more crudely, a coin tosser. Of course, that's not to say coin tossers believe themselves to be coin tossers. Overconfidence bias ensures that what people think they are and what they actually are do not correlate very well at all. That much was clear from the distribution of Pyckio's tipsters I showed earlier.

Let's design a Bayesian inference model. The hypothesis under scrutiny is that there is a probability that I am a skilled bettor. This is my prior probability. For the sake of argument, I'm not particularly confident in my abilities so I will assume the prior probability is 1%. I'm going to bet on fair 50-50 propositions with no margin. If I were completely unskilled, I could expect to show a yield of 0% after a large number of bets. What about if I was fully skilled? For my model I will define this as holding expected value of 5% but, as argued, I could define it any which way. Such expected value implies, if I were wholly skilled, I would be winning 52.5% of my bets. Let's suppose, then, that being 1% skilled means I might win 50.025% of my bets, since 0.025% is 1% of the difference between 50% and 52.5%. Similarly, being 50% skilled might mean I could expect to win 51.25% of my bets. Of course, this is just an arbitrary model assumption with no basis in reality, but I need some assumptions to run the model.

According to Bayesian inference, if I win my first bet, that should increase my belief (and the probability) that I am a skilled bettor; if I lose it, the reverse. Bayes' formula can crunch the numbers. The prior probability that I am a skilled bettor capable of holding 5% expected value, p(A), is 1%, and the unconditional probability of winning a bet, p(B), 50.025%. The conditional (and posterior) probability of winning a bet, given that I am completely skilled, p(B|A) is 52.5%, and 47.5% for losing it. Thus, following Bayes' formula, the conditional probability that I am fully skilled if I win my first bet, p(A|B), will be 52.5% x 1% / 50.025% = 1.0495%. It has indeed increased a little. Should I lose it, p(A|B) = 0.9505%, a slight decrease in my belief that I am skilled. We can re-run the model for the second bet. Now, the posterior probability p(A|B) which was determined from the outcome of the first bet becomes the new prior probability, p(A), that I am fully skilled. Similarly, the unconditional probability of winning a bet, p(B), is updated to reflect whatever skill probability my Bayesian inference model implies I currently hold. If I had won my first bet, p(B) is now 50.0262%. If I had lost it, p(B) would be 50.0238%. Using a true win probability of 52.5% I ran such a model over 5,000 iterations (bets) and plotted the evolution of the probability that I was a wholly skilled bettor, for three different initial prior probabilities that I am wholly skilled: 1%, 10% and 50%.

You can see that the evolution of my belief in the probability I am skilled is quite sensitive to the initial prior probability; indeed, it's one of the weaknesses of Bayesian inference. I will much more quickly conclude that I am wholly skilled if my initial starting point was a larger probability that I am.

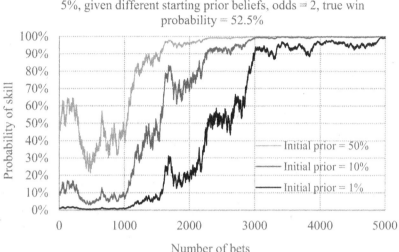

Evolution of the probability that a bettor is skilled with EV = 5%, given different starting prior beliefs, odds = 2, true win probability = 52.5%

Given that the model assumed a true win percentage equivalent to the final skill belief destination, it was simply a matter of letting the law of large numbers run its course. By contrast, if the underlying model win probability is set to 50%, the law of large numbers takes my belief that I am skilled in the opposite direction.

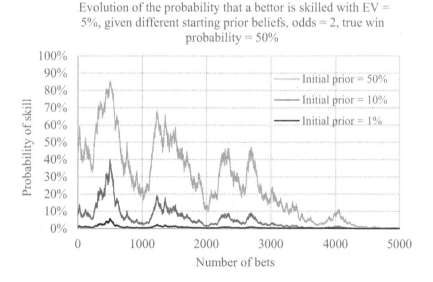

Evolution of the probability that a bettor is skilled with EV = 5%, given different starting prior beliefs, odds = 2, true win probability = 50%

You can see in the trends a lot of inherent randomness associated with the aleatory uncertainty of betting outcomes. These trends just represent one possible history. Below, I've shown 6 more mini plots for the original model to give you a flavour of the variability.

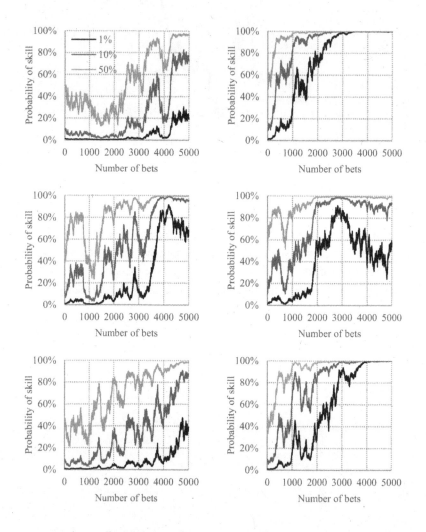

You won't be at all surprised to hear me say that we can remove the variability to see the underlying expected trend by means of a Monte Carlo simulation. I ran one with 10,000 iterations and plotted the average skill belief percentage for through the 5,000-bet history.

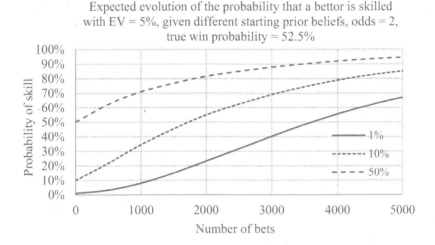

In addition to the model's sensitivity to the choice of the initial prior, p(A), it will also be sensitive to the way in which the unconditional probability of winning a bet, p(B), is updated as the model is iterated. In a sense, I fudged its calculation to help make the model work. Sensitivity to assumptions, however, is an underlying weakness with Bayesian inference modelling. There is, however, a compromise solution. Rather than test for the absolute probability of a hypothesis or model being true, one can instead compare two competing hypotheses to determine which one is more likely. Let me introduce you to the Bayes factor.

The Bayes Factor

At first glance, the Bayes factor, K, looks, to all intents and purposes, like a frequentist statistical function.

$$K = \frac{p(D|H1)}{p(D|H2)}$$

This is effectively a likelihood ratio of the probability of the data, D, arising given one hypothesis (or model), H1 is true, versus the probability of the data arising given another hypothesis, H2, is true. Suppose we have a coin. We think it might be biased, but we don't know. We previously tossed it 100 times and saw 60 heads, so we hypothesise (H1) that the coin is biased towards heads by a factor of 60% to 40%. After all, the binomial distribution tells us that seeing this many heads or more with a fair coin has a chance of only 1.76%. Of course, most coins are not biased, unless they belong to a magician. A competing hypothesis (H2) would be the coin is unbiased, and what we've observed really is just down to luck. With an unbiased coin, the relative weights of heads and tails are 50% and 50%. We now toss it 1,000 times and see 550 heads. Which hypothesis is correct? Let's calculate the Bayes factor, K. Here, the data is that we've seen 550 heads in 1,000 coin tosses. The probability of that happening exactly, assuming the coin is biased 60:40, p(D|H1), can be calculated via the binomial distribution. In Excel, recall, the discrete binomial probability of an observation is given by BINOM.DIST(heads,tosses,probability,false), where 'heads' is the number of heads, 'tosses' is the number of tosses, 'probability' is the probability of heads defined by the hypothesis, and 'false' specifies a discrete rather than cumulative calculation. Thus, p(D|H1) = BINOM.DIST(550,1000,0.6,FALSE). 0.6 is the probability of seeing heads, assuming our initial hypothesis about the bias of the coin is true. The answer is 0.0148%. How about the probability of seeing 550 heads with an unbiased coin? p(D|H2) = BINOM.DIST(550,1000,0.5,FALSE), the solution to which is 0.0169%. Finally, we can calculate the Bayes factor, K, as the ratio of the two probabilities. K = p(D|H1) / p(D|H2) = 0.0148% / 0.0169% = 0.871.

The 'Bayesian' in the Bayes factor can be revealed if we express it in its full form. Since, following the Bayes' formula,

$$p(D|H1) = \frac{p(H1|D) \cdot p(D)}{p(H1)}$$

and

$$p(D|H2) = \frac{p(H2|D) \cdot p(D)}{p(H2)}$$

we have,

$$K = \frac{p(D|H1)}{p(D|H2)} = \frac{p(H1|D)}{p(H2|D)} \cdot \frac{p(H2)}{p(H1)}$$

When the two prior hypotheses, p(H1) and p(H2), are considered equally probable, p(H2)/p(H1) = 1, and hence the Bayes factor becomes the ratio of the (posterior) probabilities of the two competing hypotheses, given the data.

$$K = \frac{p(H1|D)}{p(H2|D)}$$

The Bayes factor compares the relative merits of each hypothesis without saying anything about their merits relative to the true heads expectation. A ratio of 1 would imply that both hypotheses have equal merit relative to each other. With K a little smaller, that would imply we might favour H2, the unbiased coin, slightly more than H1, the 60-40 bias. Of course, given the tiny probability of seeing either 550 or fewer heads with a coin biased 60-40 (0.0741%), or 550 or more heads with an unbiased coin (0.0696%), a frequentist would likely argue against both H1 and H2. The Bayesian, however, is only interested in their relative likelihood, not the absolute probability of seeing the data, given either hypothesis is true. In fact, the equation above represents a maximum likelihood ratio. The true Bayes factor is the ratio of the integrals of the probabilities over the full distribution of possible heads. These are much harder to calculate, certainly in a software package like Excel. The likelihood ratio is also conceptually easier to understand for those not familiar with integral calculus and is quite sufficient for our needs.

More generally, how are we to interpret different Bayes factor ratios? Harold Jeffreys, the 20th century polymath, proposed an interpretation scale for the Bayes factor. A value between 1 and 3 implies anecdotal evidence favouring H1 over H2 or (1 to 1/3 for H2 over H1). One between 3 to 10 implies moderate evidence for H1 over H2 (or 1/3 to 1/10 for H2 over H1). 10 to 30 (or 1/10 to 1/30) implies strong evidence, 30 to 100 (or 1/30 to 1/100) very strong evidence and over 100 (under 1/100) decisive evidence. Suppose, instead, our hypothesis (H1) is that the coin is biased 55 to 45 in favour of heads, whilst H2 remains the unbiased coin. Our Bayes factor for H1 favoured over H2 would now be 150, decisive evidence that we had a biased coin.

We can calculate Bayes factors for betting histories too. With respect to my Wisdom of the Crowd record, let's consider two possible hypotheses. The first (H1) is that my average expected value, 4.12%, should be equivalent to my expected yield from unit-loss staking. The second hypothesis (H2) might be that the methodology doesn't work, and the best I should expect is to break even with a yield of 0%, given that I'm typically backing prices that are best-in-market, on average giving the bettor roughly fair odds. In fact, my yield from 11,894 bets was 4.35%. What is the probability of this yield given either hypothesis? As for the coin toss, let's use Excel to calculate those probabilities, replacing the binomial with the normal distribution since, as we know, it offers a useful and more easily calculated approximation, given binomial cannot be used when the outcome probabilities (the odds) are different. NORM.DIST(x,μ,σ,false) is the Excel function we need, where x is the observed yield, μ the expected yield defined by the hypothesis, and σ the yield standard error for that hypothesis. Thus, using $SE_{yield} = \sqrt{r(o-r)/n}$ to approximate the yield standard error, D|H1 = NORM.DIST(4.35%,4.12%,1.579%,false) = 24.99. Similarly, D|H2 = NORM.DIST(4.35%,0%,1.573%,false) = 0.55. Hence, K for H1 favoured over H2 = 24.99 / 0.55 = 48. This gives us strong, although not decisive, evidence that my Wisdom of the Crowd betting model does actually work.

Probabilities lie between 0 and 1, so you might be puzzled by a probability of 24.99. In fact, with the 'false' identifier, Excel's NORMDIST does not output a probability, but rather a probability density. Whilst conceptionally hard to visualise, a probability density can be thought of as equivalent to a probability per unit something; in this example, that something would be yield, so we have a probability per unit yield. A probability density is calculated using differential calculus; specifically, it represents the probability per unit yield at an infinitesimally small yield interval range (the derivative). In some circumstances, this can lead to probability densities greater than 1. Fortunately, because we are dividing one probability density by another, the 'per units' cancel out, leaving just a probability ratio, which is what the Bayes factor is.

With the Bayes factor, we could choose to compare any hypotheses we liked. One idea is to use it as a quasi-goodness-of-fit test. In such a test, when actual outcomes closely match those which were expected (predicted) *a priori*, this is an indication that our prediction model, and the hypothesis which is formulated from it, are valid. Let's change H2 to 'expected yield = observed yield'. That is to say, what actually happens was what was most likely to happen. In this case, that means a yield of 4.35%. Should the expected yield for H2 exactly equal the expected yield for H1 (4.12%), the Bayes factor will be 1. For anything else, the Bayes factor for H1 over H2 will be less than 1. Now, p(D|H2) = 25.25, predictably larger than p(D|H1) since we have stipulated that the hypothesis should match the outcome. Thus, K = 0.99. H2 provides the better model, but its favourability over H1 is barely worth considering. On this basis, we would have no reason to abandon the model of the Wisdom of the Crowd. Below, I've plotted a time evolution of the Bayes factor for my betting history. After each bet, H2 is changed to a new hypothesis where the expected yield matches the observed one. K is then recalculated each time. The maximum possible K is 1. The further it deviates below 1 towards 0, the less confidence we should have in the Wisdom of the Crowd betting model. The vertical Bayes factor axis is logarithmic. Remember, anything below 0.01 would imply a decisive rejection of the model.

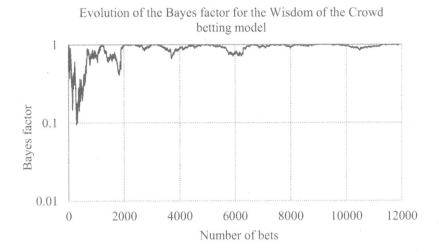

Evolution of the Bayes factor for the Wisdom of the Crowd betting model

You can see that at no point in the evolution was there ever any serious doubt about the validity of the Wisdom of the Crowd hypothesis. The largest deviations of K beneath 1 occurred in the early part of the history and are simply an illustration of the law of small numbers, and the law of large numbers that followed thereafter. Around the 300th bet there was a momentary suggestion there was strong evidence against the validity of the model, but it passed as quickly as it had arrived.

Obviously, even for a valid and robust betting model, results and histories are subject to the mercy of aleatory uncertainty. The actual Bayes factor of 0.99 is just one possible value. Assuming the hypothesis H1 to be true, that is to say, the expected yield for this history of bets is 4.12%, what would a distribution of possible Bayes factors look like? Using a 100,000-iteration Monte Carlo simulation, I randomised the 11,894 results in the same way as I have done for previous Monte Carlo simulations, defining the expected probability for a bet by the model forecast (bookmaker's odds divided by Pinnacle's 'true' odds), and the outcome by Excel's random number function (RAND). For each iteration I calculated the Bayes factor. Their distribution is shown below. The horizontal Bayes factor axis is logarithmic.

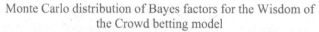

Monte Carlo distribution of Bayes factors for the Wisdom of the Crowd betting model

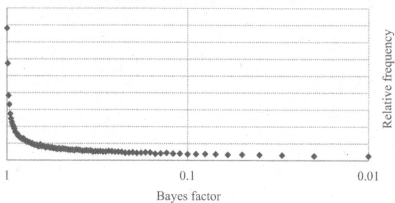

Just a small proportion of iterations (3.2%) returned a Bayes factor less than 0.1 and an even smaller proportion (0.24%) were less than 0.01. Consider the figures here: roughly 1-in-400 histories would see a decisive rejection of the Wisdom of the Crowd hypothesis, despite it being true, just because of randomness. We might compare the Bayes factor to the frequentist p-value. Here, for the Bayes factor of 0.01, the p-value is 0.0024. Philosophically, however, whilst related, they are not equivalent. Remember, Bayesian inference attempts to measure the probability of the hypothesis or model, given the data. Frequentist hypothesis testing, by contrast, measures the probability of the data given the hypothesis is true. Of course, the Bayes factor doesn't really make any claim to accept or reject the absolute truth of a hypothesis; rather, it simply measures the likelihood of one against another. Whether you adopt a frequentist or Bayesian statistical approach to testing the validity of your betting forecast model, it is important to maintain a sense of perspective. Validity and truth are not absolute but probabilistic, always updatable with new information. The more data we acquire, the closer we get to the truth, but there always remains the possibility that we are wrong.

A GAME OF LUCK OR SKILL?

Roger Federer has been paid well, not because he's good at tennis – plenty of people are good at tennis – but because he's better at it than almost everyone else in a professionally competitive capacity. Tennis is a game of skill, but professional tennis is a relative-skills contest. You are not paid to be skilful; you are paid to be more skilful than someone else. So it is with betting on tennis, indeed betting on anything for that matter. Forecasting is a skill, but you don't get paid to forecast the future; you get paid to forecast it more accurately than someone else. When I say 'accurately', I don't necessarily mean the outcome; that is influenced by aleatory uncertainty. Rather, I mean the underlying hidden 'true' probability of the outcome. Betting does not happen in a vacuum, by yourself. It takes place between consenting and competing agents. How much you will get paid will depend on how much the person you are competing against is willing to pay you if you win. Conversely, how much your opposition will get paid will depend on how much you are prepared to pay them if you lose. If either you or they deem the amount that has to be paid to the opponent in the event of a loss is too large, the contest will not take place. Only when parties reach a subconscious agreement about what is considered fair will a bet take place. Losing hurts, so most bettors take steps to ensure that doesn't happen. In this context, that means gathering information, constructing coherent narratives, and finally building models, to make a prediction of the likelihood of an outcome. If all participants are engaged in this process, a kind of Bayesian dance ensues whereby the amount that it is agreed will be paid on the settlement of an outcome becomes closer and closer to the fairest possible amount as defined by the 'true' outcome probability, assuming all participants are acting in rational self-interest. Economists call this price discovery. In the extreme, if all participants' prediction models were epistemically perfect, only aleatory uncertainty would remain, and betting would be reduced, like roulette, to a game of chance.

'This is all very well,' I hear you say, but there's plenty of error available in a betting market that can be exploited for real expected value. I would concur. Where I would disagree is how easily and systematically it can be revealed, and whether it is truly epistemic (model error) or aleatory (random error) in nature. 'Surely the error is systematic, right; if it wasn't, then how come so many people are making money from betting?' I've already explored the fallacy of studying a process by its outcomes. If all you see are the winners, you will arrive at an erroneous conclusion about how easy it is to win. Show me **ALL** the people who are playing, and then let's count how many of them are winning. Furthermore, why are they winning? Because of something they did, or just blind luck? Lots of bettors win, but have you bothered to find out if anything actually made it happen, or are you just judging it by the profits? It is my belief that, because of the process of price discovery and the Bayesian dance towards an ever more efficient (truthful) betting market, there is far less systematic error than you might think, and what error does exist is mostly aleatory in nature. Let's see if I can flesh out that belief with some data.

Is Betting Random?

What is the expected performance of a football team whose win probability is 50%, draw probability 30% and lose probability 20%? To make this calculation we need some way of scoring the three possible outcomes. In football, a team is awarded 3 points for winning, 1 for drawing and 0 for losing. This team here would have an expected points total of $(0.5 \times 3) + (0.3 \times 1) + (0.2 \times 0) = 1.8$. In betting, the scoring is a little different. Fewer points (or pounds) are awarded for outcomes that are more likely. For an outcome with a 50% probability, 1 point (or £1) would be awarded for a win and -1 point (or -£1) for a loss. For a 20% probability, the trade-off would be +4 points (for a win) versus -1 point (for a loss). For a win probability, p, we can standardise this scoring system as follows.

- If a team wins, award a score of $1 - p$
- If a team fails to win, award a score of $-p$

Such a scoring rule is not a proper one like log-loss or Brier, but it will suffice here. Now, all scores (or standardised profits) will lie between -1 (a team losing that had been predicted to win with certainty) and +1 (a team winning that had been predicted to lose with certainty). For example, if the win probability is 20% (or 0.2), the score awarded for winning will be 0.8, and -0.2 for losing. The expected score for such a team will be calculated by $(0.2 \times 0.8) + (0.8 \times -0.2) = 0$. For all values of p, the expected score will be 0.

As we know, a bookmaker's odds, o, represent an opinion about the probability, p, of winning, with $o = 1/p$. If the opinion is correct, that is to say, p equals the 'true' outcome probability, the expected score should be 0, and the average score for a collection of opinions should be 0. Using the last 8 completed seasons (2012/13 to 2019/120) of professional English league soccer (the Premier League, Championship, League 1 and League 2), I used Pinnacle's closing match odds with their margin removed to calculate a team score for every match outcome. The full dataset comprised 16,024 games and 32,048 individual team scores. The average standardised score (or profit) was -0.0004. Such a score would seem to indicate that, on average, Pinnacle had priced the teams almost perfectly, meaning that what variation will occur for bettors' outcomes will be almost entirely random, leaving little opportunity to exert any influence of superior skill to gain expected value. The observed history of results, however, is just one possible history of a large number of histories. The observed one may not have been the most likely. Assuming Pinnacle's implied fair probabilities to be representative of the 'true' probabilities, we can run a Monte Carlo simulation to find the distribution of average scores, by randomising the outcomes (home, draw or away) based on Pinnacle's probabilities. If a random number generated by Excel's RAND function is less than the implied home win probability, we award a home win. If more than 1 minus the away win probability, we award an away win. If neither, we award a draw. My simulation had 10,000 iterations. The distribution of average standardised profits is shown below.

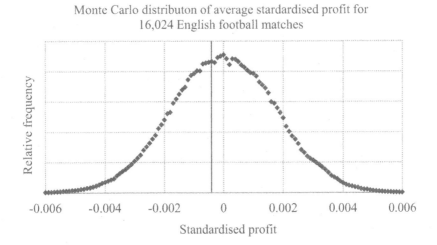

Monte Carlo distributon of average stardardised profit for 16,024 English football matches

The average standardised profit was -0.000007, or to all intents and purposes the same as the expected figure of 0. The vertical black line marks the position of the average score for the actual history of results, well within the typical bounds of statistical error.

There is no way to prove absolutely that a set of data is random, but one can make a statistical judgement as to whether it is likely to be. A common method in this respect is to see whether the dataset obeys the central limit theorem. I have already introduced you to this, but without naming it. The central limit theorem states that if you have a population with mean μ and standard deviation σ and take sufficiently large random samples from the population with replacement, then the distribution of the sample means will be approximately normally distributed, even if the original population of data is not normally distributed. As the sample size, n, increases, the degree of normality increases, and in the mathematical limit where n reaches infinity, the distribution will be perfectly normal. For most random data distributions, n > 30 is sufficient. Two important properties of the central limit theorem are that the mean of the sample means equals the population mean, and that the standard deviation of the sample means equals the standard deviation of the population divided by the square root of n.

Let's see if the population of 32,048 scores conforms to the central limit theorem. I randomly selected 10 scores from the population and used the Monte Carlo method to repeat this 1,000 times. The mean of the 1,000 sample means was 0.004 and standard deviation 0.150, implying its deviation from the population mean was well within the bounds of statistical error. The 32,048 scores within the population, which are themselves not normally distributed, have a standard deviation of 0.459. The standard error given by $\sigma/\sqrt{n}$ is thus $0.459/\sqrt{10} = 0.145$, close to the standard deviation in the sample means. Repeating for random samples of 100 scores, the mean of the sample means was -0.0008 and their standard deviation 0.0462, compared to the mathematically calculated standard error of 0.0459. The standard deviation in the Monte Carlo distribution above is about half the value predicted by $0.459/\sqrt{16,024}$. There is a simple explanation: this is a distribution of possible mean home **and** away team scores; they are not independent since the same result affects both teams in a match. If I run the simulation again treating the teams independently, the standard deviation in the sample means (0.00374) is a close match for the predicted standard error (0.00363).

I think these figures provide strong evidence that this population of standardised profit scores obeys the central limit theorem, and is thus likely to closely, if not perfectly, represent a random dataset. If any are still doubting this, let's consider the teams individually. The chart below shows the distribution of 10-match average scores for every team.

Distribution of 10-match average standardised profit by team

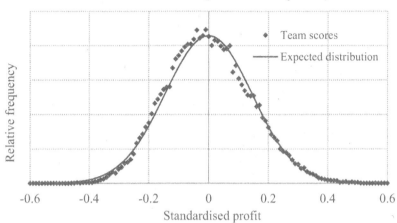

The mean 10-match team score is -0.0003. The standard error as predicted by $\sigma/\sqrt{n}$ is 0.145. The actual standard deviation in 10-match team scores is 0.142. Their distribution conforms closely to the empirical rule and is compared to an idealised normal curve. There is the slightest hint of positive skew, with slightly more data points in the right hand side tail. With a sample size of only 10 matches this is hardly surprising; the sample distribution hasn't fully converged on a normal distribution according to the central limit theorem. For a larger sample of matches, the convergence would be closer.

Regression to the Mean

There is one further test we can apply in the search for randomness: the degree to which these scores regress to the mean. A corollary of a normal distribution is that in a time sequence of independent random variables, more extreme ones will tend to move closer to the average on subsequent measurements. The phenomenon was first revealed by Sir Francis Galton, the Victorian polymath, as he experimented with the heredity of sweet peas. In cross breeding trials, Galton noted a tendency for the size of the offspring to show a smaller (but still normal) distribution than that of the parents. Crucially, whilst the offspring of larger parents tended to be smaller, the offspring of smaller parents tended to be larger. Galton described this tendency as reversion or regression to the mean. It is important to realise that there is no cause for this regression in a strictly deterministic sense; mean regression is merely a random process that sees extremes become less extreme. As if to demonstrate this point, paradoxically, regression to the mean is not time-dependent; if subsequent measurements are more extreme, the tendency will be for their earlier ones to be closer to the average. Regression to the mean, then, is entirely reversible.

Do my teams' 10-match scores regress to the mean? The scatter plot below shows the correlation between one 10-match score (horizontal axis) and the score for the next 10 matches (vertical axis). If a team's 10-match average score, as measured by Pinnacle's betting odds, was systematic, a positive/negative 10-match score would correlate with a positive/negative score for the next 10 matches. If the scores were random, we should expect no correlation at all.

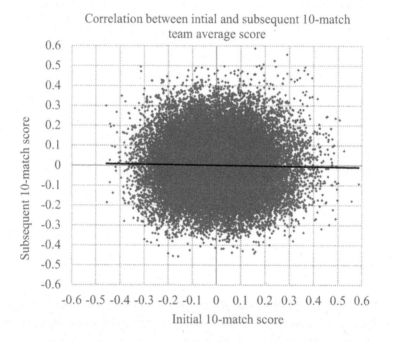

Correlation between intial and subsequent 10-match team average score

The correlation trendline is almost perfectly flat, implying almost no correlation at all. You can measure how closely one variable correlates with another by means of a regression statistic called r-squared (R^2). This varies between 0 (no correlation) and 1 (perfect correlation). Specifically, R^2 tells you how much the variance in a second variable is explained by the variance in the first. For example, people's heights and weights correlate to some degree, with taller people tending to be heavier. An R^2 of 0.2 would imply that 20% of the variance in people's weight is explained by the variance in people's height. How much of the variance in mean scores for the subsequent 10 matches is explained by the variance in the mean scores for the initial 10 matches? Just 0.03%. In practical terms, this represents almost complete regression to the mean. The average performance score of a team in one set of 10 matches, as interpreted by Pinnacle's betting odds, explains almost nothing of its performance in the next set of 10 matches. Effectively, there is almost no causal relationship between the two; instead, almost complete randomness. The 326 scores of less than -0.3 for the initial 10-matches regressed to an average of 0.006 for the subsequent 10 matches. Similarly, the 634 scores of more than 0.3 for the initial 10 matches regressed to an average of 0.0009 for the subsequent 10 matches.

Randomness in football matches is one thing, but no one is betting on all football matches. Surely bettors and tipsters are sufficiently skilled to find the subset of matches, no matter how small, that contain epistemic errors in the way they are priced. This, of course, is the rationale behind sports betting. Since 'true' probabilities, unlike for casino games, will always remain unknown, there exists the possibility to be better at estimating them than a bookmaker. I have no doubt that some bettors have such skills – I've met some – but there aren't many. Remember the Pyckio tipsters? I've already shown their z-scores distribute almost normally. For the 249 with records of more than 1,000 picks, I performed a regression to the mean test in the same way as for the football team performance above, dividing their records equally in half and calculating 1st half and 2nd half z-scores. Here is their correlation plot.

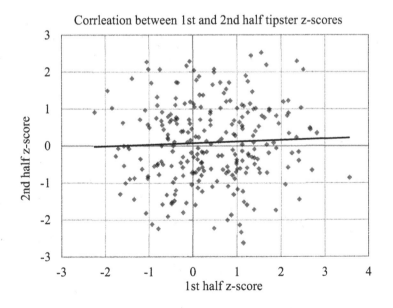

Corrleation between 1st and 2nd half tipster z-scores

The R^2 was just 0.2%. On average, these tipsters are almost fully regressing to the mean, implying almost all of what they are engaged in is just luck.

Correlation or Causation?

Regression to the mean, like the laws of large and small numbers, is not a concept that can be intuitively understood by a brain that prefers causal interpretations for the patterns that it sees. Even when you see a positive correlation between variables, can you really be sure that something caused it? If the answer is no, then the correlation is spurious, and the law of large numbers will eventually regress it to nothing. One of the biggest dangers facing bettors is being fooled by spurious correlations, or as Nassim Taleb puts it, being fooled by randomness. Incorrect interpretations of mean regression are part of a more general confusion of correlation with causation. Even where the distinction is understood, laziness on the part of the bettor looking to find explanatory relationships in data to support hypotheses – for example, that they are skilled at betting – can lead to invalid conclusions about what is really happening. Patterns in betting can look very meaningful without actually being so. Our brains our primed by evolution to see meaning in patterns even when there is none. Correlation without causation is essentially worthless. Consider the following time series of profitability from betting on all away teams in the English League 2 from August 2012 to May 2017, a total of 2,760 wagers.

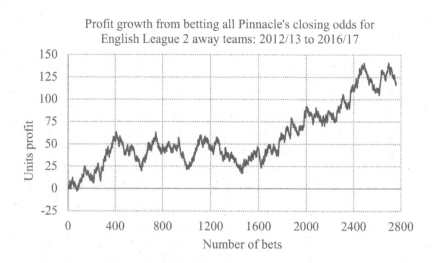

Profit growth from betting all Pinnacle's closing odds for English League 2 away teams: 2012/13 to 2016/17

So much for the theory that closing odds are efficient, right? The yield from unit-loss staking is 4.27%, at average odds of 3.49. With an average margin weight for these odds of about -3%, we would expect to see such a performance less than 1% of the time. Is that enough to declare statistical significance and something wrong with the hypothesis of closing line efficiency? If this was a standalone sample, it might be. However, there is no end to the number of ways we might choose to pick a sample of bets to back test for profitability. When a population of profits and losses is random, if we pick enough random samples from it, a few of them will always show profitability that appears to pass the usual tests of statistical significance. If multiple samples are tested, and hence multiple hypotheses retrofitted to explain the data, the chance of observing a rare event increases, and therefore, the likelihood of incorrectly rejecting randomness increases, even if there is nothing causal taking place. In 100 samples you'd expect one, on average, to have a p-value of 0.01; in 1,000 of them, one with 0.001; in one million, one with 0.000001, just by chance. As Taleb explains, on the fantasy of monkeys attempting to recreate the poetry of Homer on a typewriter, 'if there are five monkeys... I would be rather impressed with the Iliad writer, to the point of suspecting him to be a reincarnation of the ancient poet. If there are a billion to the power one billion monkeys, I would be less impressed...' Just because a pattern looks like it has a cause, does not imply that it has one.

The business of retrospectively looking for profitable samples is called data mining. Do so at your peril. There are several online betting services that offer 'strategies' or 'systems', simply based on some arbitrarily chosen criteria, for example a specific range of odds, or some specific recent performance in previous games, for no other reason than they seem to work when back testing them. The more arbitrary variables you include, the more likely that what pattern you will find will be, to coin a phrase of David Spiegelhalter, Winton Professor of the Public Understanding of Risk, 'complete bollocks'. Data mining effectively reverses the process of inference. Rather than test an *a priori* hypothesis that some variable, or set of variables, may cause a particular level of betting profitability, a pattern of profits is perceived to have a cause simply because it has happened. If you have no idea what is behind a pattern, you will have no idea why it disappears if it does. If we won't propose *a priori* hypotheses before mining our data for profitable patterns, then instead we should test a large number of samples to see how often we find something that looks statistically significant. By doing so we are effectively counting all of Taleb's monkeys. If the number of statistically significant patterns is what we would expect to see by chance, we cannot assume that any of them happened for a reason.

Using the same 8 seasons of English football league data I analysed earlier for evidence of randomness and mean regression, I used a Monte Carlo model to randomly select a large sample of different odds ranges (margin removed) and tested each for their profitability. Different samples had different numbers of bets, so I standardised their performances with the z-score. After discounting the model iterations that returned samples of fewer than 100 bets, I was left with 24,346 of them. Their frequency distribution is shown below.

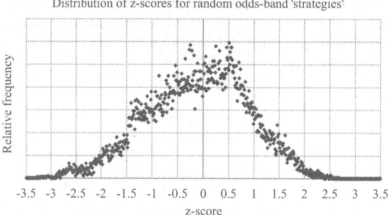

Distribution of z-scores for random odds-band 'strategies'

There's a significant departure from a perfect normal distribution, because there is likely to be a considerable degree of correlation between samples with overlapping odds ranges. The results of the population of 16,024 matches, after all, are the same. Nevertheless, we would be hard pushed to declare anything in this chart as systematic, with identifiable causes for why any particular sample showed the profitability (or loss) that it did. The average z-score for a sample was -0.05, close to the population score of -0.11. Below are the profit charts for two of the draw 'strategies'.

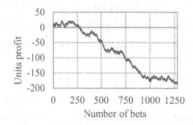

The first 'strategy' (left) included 1,279 bets where the fair odds (without Pinnacle's margin) were between 3.766 and 3.868. Betting the actual Pinnacle closing odds would have delivered a yield of -14.54%, with a z-score of -2.60 and a probability of performing worse of 0.5%. The second 'strategy' (right) included 964 bets where the fair odds were between 3.852 and 3.957. Betting the actual Pinnacle closing odds would have delivered a yield of +10.46%, with a z-score of 2.49 and a probability of performing better of 0.6%. What is most remarkable of all is that 186 of the bets are actually common to both 'strategies'. How would you go about attempting to retrofit a causal explanation for that?

Finally, let's compare the proportion of the 'strategies' which fall below a p-value threshold to the proportion that would be predicted by chance, where the p-value represents the probability of seeing more profit than was actually observed for that sample, assuming the data are random. Recall that we would expect to see 1 in 100 'strategies' to show a p-value of less than 0.01, 1 in 10 to show a p-value of less than 0.1, and so on. Here is the correlation.

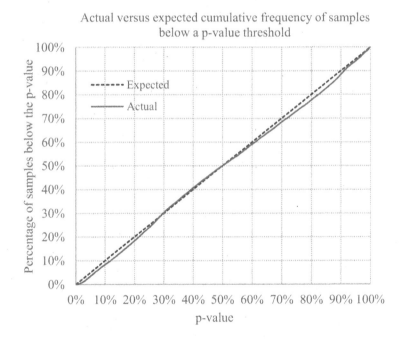

There are indeed a few samples with z-scores, either positive (profitable) or negative (unprofitable) beyond typically accepted thresholds of statistical significance which, in isolation, might have us questioning the basis of randomness. But their distribution does not deviate significantly from what we would expect to see simply by chance. Furthermore, we cannot treat these samples, and any inferred hypotheses to explain them, in isolation. This is the problem with data mining. When engaged in such multi-sample statistical testing, mathematicians typically apply something called the Bonferroni correction which reduces the required threshold of statistical significance for an individual sample. If your subjectively accepted significance level is 1% (p-value = 0.01), and you have 100 samples, the Bonferroni correction divides the desired overall significance level by the number of samples (and hypotheses) being tested. Each sample and hypothesis would then be tested against a significance level of 0.01%. With 24,346 samples here, we can categorically say that there is nothing meaningful to see beyond randomness. That's not to argue there isn't some non-randomness hidden somewhere in this English football league data; it's just that a crude retrofitting of odds bands will not reveal it. All you will find are lucky (and unlucky) patterns, which will simply regress to the mean if their underlying 'strategies' are played into the future.

I think we are done here. Data mining is a fool's game. By all means, develop a hypothesis that some aspect of a football match, or any other sporting contest, will predict what will happen, and then test it against the empirical data. However, if you're simply mining a dataset for patterns that you want to find, without having any *a priori* causal explanation for why you thought you would see them, future regression to the mean will be all but inevitable. Speaking of which, how did betting on all away teams in the English League 2 fare after the 2016/17 season? Here's the profit chart for seasons 2017/18 to 2019/20. The yield is -10.03%, and mean regression is almost complete.

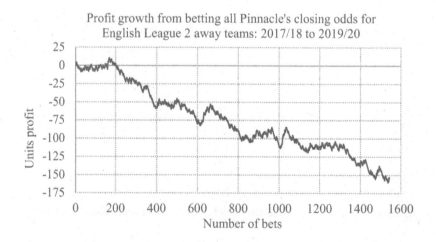

Profit growth from betting all Pinnacle's closing odds for English League 2 away teams: 2017/18 to 2019/20

Given that the original lucky sample size was 2,760, do you now see how easy it is to be fooled by the law of small numbers? 'Small' is relative. It can sometimes be a rather big number indeed. All the more reason to stop wasting time judging your forecasting skills by your outcomes; that can take too long and lead you up the garden path anyway. Far better to have a proxy method to make that judgement. That is the importance of beating the closing line; far quicker and far more valid as a means of linking cause and effect.

The Paradox of Skill

It is important for me to stress again that none of my discussion about luck and skill is to argue that all sporting outcomes are completely random. We know that better teams and players win more often; the number of points a football team collects in 10 matches, for example, will positively correlate with the number they will accumulate in the next 10 matches. Rather, it is that the prediction variables that have been used by Pinnacle to forecast the outcome probabilities have influenced the magnitude of the rewards and punishments for being correct and incorrect to the extent that the competition is reduced almost to a game of chance. It might seem paradoxical that as the quality of prediction improves, the impact of those skills diminishes, but with price discovery, that is exactly what is happening. It has a name: the paradox of skill.

In 1941, Ted Williams, a Major League Baseball player for the Boston Red Sox, had a batting average of 0.406. Considering that since the origins of the professional game in the 1870s, the average seasonal batting average has remained largely unchanged at around 0.25 to 0.28, this was a remarkable achievement, and something that has not been repeated since. Williams, however, would not score anything like that average in today's modern day league, given the improvements in training, fitness, diet and general professionalism. Why? The batting average is simply a measure of relative skill, between the pitcher on the one hand and the batter on the other. As Major League Baseball has become more professionalised, batters have individually become more skilled at hitting. At the same time, however, pitchers have become more skilled at pitching. Batters and pitchers are engaged in a kind of arms race: absolute skills improve across the board, but relative skills, on average, remain more or less the same. This, however, is only half the story. Whilst overall skill levels have improved, the difference, or variance, between the best and worst hitters (and pitchers) has shrunk. Imagine a 'wall' of human ability. In the early years of professional baseball, only relatively few players were already approaching the 'wall'; most were still quite some way away. Over time, progressively better hitters (and pitchers) were replacing the weaker ones, and as a consequence the difference between best and worst has narrowed. A similar shrinking of variance in abilities can be seen in other disciplines that face limits to conceivable athletic performance, including the marathon and the 100m sprint.

Whilst more conjecture than hypothesis, true score theory stipulates that an observed outcome is a combination of true ability (skill) plus random error (luck). More specifically, it states that the variance in outcomes is the sum of the variance in skill and the variance in luck. Recall that variance is the square of the standard deviation in a set of outcomes. With respect to baseball batting averages, whilst absolute skills have increased, the variance across them has narrowed. Consequently, according to true score theory, as the variance in skill diminishes, the variance in luck will assume an ever-increasing importance in the calculation of outcomes. Michael Mauboussin, the financial strategist and author of *The Success Equation: Untangling Skill and Luck in Business, Sports, and Investing*, calls this the paradox of skill. 'If everyone gets better at something, luck plays a more important role in determining who wins.' An example from Scottish league football will help illustrate the point.

The table below compares the final league points in the 2018/19 season for the Scottish Championship (left) and Scottish League 2nd division (right). The 'Points %' column illustrates the percentage of the maximum number of possible points (108 from 36 games) each team has achieved.

Team	Points	Points %	Team	Points	Points %
Ross County	71	0.657	Peterhead	79	0.731
Dundee Utd	65	0.602	Clyde	74	0.685
Inverness CT	56	0.519	Edinburgh C	67	0.620
Ayr	54	0.500	Annan	66	0.611
Morton	46	0.426	Stirling	47	0.435
Partick	43	0.398	Cowdenbeath	43	0.398
Dunfermline	41	0.380	Queen's Park	43	0.398
Alloa	39	0.361	Elgin City	43	0.398
Queen of Sth	38	0.352	Albion	27	0.250
Falkirk	38	0.352	Berwick	19	0.176

The standard deviation in these points percentage figures across each division are 0.110 and 0.185 for the Championship and League two, respectively. Squaring these gives us figures for the variance of 0.012 and 0.034. How much of this variance occurred because of luck? If all match outcomes were completely random, the expected likelihood of a home win, draw or away win would be one third. Of course, in reality, there's no such thing as a third of a win or a third of a draw, so let's randomly determine the result using Excel's RAND function and then simulate all 180 matches in each division 10,000 times. Doing so yielded a standard deviation of 0.073 in point percentage, and hence a variance of 0.0053. Finally, if, according to true score theory, the variance in outcome equals the variance in skill plus the variance in luck, the proportion of total variance contributed by luck will be given by the variance in luck divided by the total variance. For the Championship that proportion is 0.0053 / 0.012 = 43.8%. For League 2 it is 0.0053 / 0.034 = 15.4%. Despite the Championship having better and more skilful teams than League 2, far more luck contributed to the actual finishing league table. Why? Because within the Championship there was arguably a smaller difference in team ability between top and bottom than there was in League 2. When engaged in a contest, it is not your absolute skill that matters, but rather your relative abilities against your opponents.

Just like sports, sports betting is also a relative skills contest. Most bettors can predict winners, because most sporting contests have a favourite and an underdog, and you don't need to possess a huge amount of sporting knowledge to know that. The more important question is this: can you predict more winners than your opponent can? The betting odds act like a handicap system, ensuring you are rewarded less for more likely and easily predicable outcomes. Just as in many sports, which have seen a shrinking in the variance of skills between competitors, arguably there has been something similar taking place in the world of sports betting. A human can run only so quickly. None is ever likely to run 100m in under 8 seconds and probably not in under 9 as well. Similarly, there is a limit to how correct one can be about a forecast probability. The better prediction models become, the more epistemic error is reduced to aleatory noise, with successive reductions becoming harder and harder as forecasts converge towards what might be termed a wall of 'truth'. Whilst bettors may have become sharper in absolute terms, relatively speaking there may be less of a difference between them, and as a consequence, their performance will be progressively dictated more and more by luck. The fact that Pinnacle's odds are already so efficient, and the fact that bettors' performances are already distributing almost normally, suggests that the variance in absolute forecasting skills is already being squeezed by this wall of 'truth'. If this competition, and the price discovery it gives rise to, has pushed the odds for sporting outcomes ever closer towards the 'true' probabilities, whether one wins or loses is then largely a matter of chance.

I know this story is one that bettors dislike me telling. I'm frequently accused of reducing sports betting completely to chance. I don't. I reduce it **almost** to chance. There's a difference. The data on randomly distributing and mean-regressing performances cannot be denied. Nevertheless, to say a distribution looks random is not quite the same as saying it is perfectly random. If the percentage of bettors who do not regress to the mean is small, they will remain hidden within the more general distribution. Nishikori's data point is not visible in the mean regression scatter above, since he joined Pyckio after I had originally analysed the data, but it would almost certainly be positioned in the top right quadrant. Outside the usual business of short-term aleatory randomness, his longer-term profitability has been sustained over a period of 5 years. If his point were in the plot, however, how could you tell it wasn't just luck?

First, the good news. Betting, like a tennis match, is a relative-skills contest. It is also iterative, played again and again many times. The tiniest of advantages, for example in serving or forecasting a tennis match outcome probability, accumulate into much larger ones, if those advantages can be compounded. Thus, even if almost everything that happens to determine the outcome of a sporting event, and the bet that's placed on it, is chance, over many events, and many bets, the noise of good and bad luck should cancel, leaving only the signal. In betting, of course, this is what we call the expected value. You only need a tiny advantage for the influence of compounding to deliver the rewards in the long term, although as I hope the earlier chapters of this book have revealed, the harder tasks will be in dealing with the inevitable variance rollercoaster that accompanies the journey, and indeed knowing whether your advantage is real.

Now the bad news. A consequence of accumulated advantage is that those with marginally superior forecasting skills will slowly crowd out the competition. Any iterative, relative-skills competition which has finite rewards, as a betting market must surely do, will see a hugely asymmetric redistribution of assets, with the majority contributing a little and a minority acquiring the majority of the rewards. This is the 'winner-takes-all' effect, otherwise referred to as the Pareto Principle, named after the Italian economist Vilfredo Pareto, who, in 1896, noted that 80% of the land in Italy was owned by 20% of the population. In the Amazon rainforest, for example, where trees species are competing for nutrients, water and sunlight, just 1.4% of species account for 50% of all the trees there. Pareto asymmetry is recursive; the top 20% of the top 20%

will account for 80% of that slice of the pie, meaning 4% accounts for 64% and 0.8% accounts for 51.2%. Evidently, Amazonian trees follow the Pareto Principle closely. The precise numbers describing the asymmetry may vary; what is important to note is that betting, being the same kind of iterative, relative-skills contest, will be subject to the same power-law mathematics. There will be few winners and a lot of smaller losers. The small proportions of Betfair's customers paying their premium charge and Skybet's customers who have been restricted would support this supposition.

Let's build a simple Monte Carlo model to investigate the concepts of accumulated advantage, winner takes all, and the paradox of skill. Imagine a competition where you have to predict the number of points scored in a basketball match. In the NBA they typically have about 200 points. There are 20 competitors with forecasting skills that vary linearly from best to worst. We will assume that, with Henri Poincaré's infinitely powerful and infinitely well-informed mind, the outcome could be perfectly predicted to be exactly 200 points. Human beings are typically less skilled and make epistemic (model) errors in their predictions. Modelling epistemic uncertainty is more problematic than modelling the aleatory kind, since it's not at all obvious what kind of distribution such errors arising from it would look like. The Canadian actuary and gambler who goes by the Twitter handle @PlusEVAnalytics, and whose insights on betting are worth following if you have any aspirations to be as successful, has used a beta distribution to model it. However, he's a lot cleverer than I am, so I will resort to the laziness of the normal distribution. Furthermore, I will assume that this distribution of epistemic errors is centred about the true outcome probability, that is to say 200 points. Of course, if systematic biases were present in a forecaster's prediction model, that would not be true. Thus, the size of the prediction error will then simply be modelled by the size of the standard deviation in the distribution of epistemic uncertainty, where the mean of the distribution is 200 points. My best competitor has a standard deviation of 1 point, so that about 68% of their predictions will lie between 199 and 201 points, 95% between 198 and 202. In Excel, points predictions can be outputted using NORMINV(RAND(),200,1), where RAND() is a random probability between 0 and 1, 200 is the mean and 1 is standard deviation. The second best competitor has a standard deviation of 2 points, the 3rd best, 3 points, and so on down to the worst competitor with a standard deviation of 20 points. The competition is like a lottery: competitors pay 1 unit to compete, and the competitor with a prediction closest to the actual score of 200 points wins the pot of 20 units. 100 competitive rounds are played. What is the distribution of profits across the 20 competitors? I ran 100,000 Monte Carlo iterations to find out, and the results are shown below.

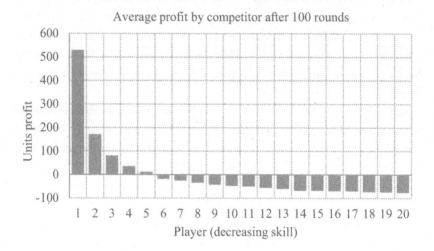

across the 20 competitors? I ran 100,000 Monte Carlo iterations to find out, and

Just a quarter of the competitors are profitable, with the most skilful competitor dwarfing the performances of all the others. The redistribution of assets follows a power law, with returns varying as a power of competitor skill. Below I've redrawn the chart as a scatter plot, changing profit to returns and with both axes logarithmic (base 2). The trend line is linear, as would be predicted for a power law relationship. The power law describing this distribution is not as strong as Pareto's 80-20 rule – about 60% of returns go to the best 20% of competitors, and 45% to the best 10% – but the underlying mathematics is the same.

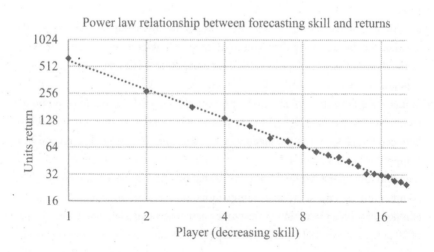

Throw in a bookmaker's commission for offering the competition, in the form of a margin weight of 50%, not uncommon for fair odds of around 20, and returns halve (since the bookmaker is taking the other half of total turnover). There are now only 2 profitable competitors. In a sense, the bookmaker acts as a super sharp, not because they are sharper, although that is also true in a real betting market, but because they are forcing competitors to accept playing at a disadvantage. To all intents and purposes, this has the same influence as being forced to use an inferior prediction model. Of course, in a real betting market, unlike in this thought experiment, bettors are not forced to compete unless they choose to. However, the point of this simulation is to illustrate how rewards for superior skill are distributed asymmetrically, with the most skilful taking the lion's share. In a real betting market, you may feel like you are competing against the bookmaker who has set the price but in reality, that price is, to a significant extent, a consequence of other bettors' opinions and money. You are not just competing against the bookmaker, but all other bettors in the market as well.

What happens if we reduce the variance across the competitors' forecasting skills? For a second Monte Carlo simulation, I took the square root of the original standard deviation in each competitor's epistemic error. Thus, whilst player 1 remains at the same skill level (the square root of 1 is still 1), all other competitors become considerably more skilled, with the difference between best and worst now much smaller, and the variance in skills across the competitors now over 33 times smaller. I've maintained the same vertical scale in the histogram below to allow comparison with the original model.

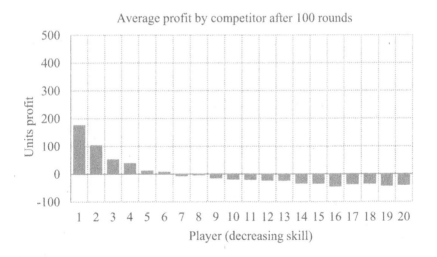

Average profit by competitor after 100 rounds

The most skilled competitors are now winning less, despite being absolutely more skilled than before. The shrinking variance across the competitors' forecasting abilities has created a paradox of skill: better absolute skills, but a relatively smaller difference, so outcomes are now more dictated by luck. You can see that some less skilled competitors actually lose less than those who are more skilled. This is just chance, but chance will play an increasing influence as the difference between players narrows. With the bookmaker's commission, only the best competitor still makes a profit. In the extreme where all players are equally skilled, regardless of their forecasting ability, returns will be completely random, and with a bookmaker's commission, all would face expected losses.

Arguably, prediction skills in a real betting market will not vary stepwise like I have assumed here. The majority of the market, made up of square money, is provided by bettors who engage in minimal forecasting beyond looking at a price and deciding whether they think the reward is large enough. What knowledge about teams and players they have is likely to be heavily influenced by cognitive biases: confirmation bias (what they already believe to be true); recency bias (with more recent events influencing decision-making more than older ones); and anchoring bias (where the bookmaker's price itself influences the bettor's belief about the outcome probability). Taken together, a square bettor's belief, in a market shaped by price discovery, is likely to be equivalent to guessing. I ran a third Monte Carlo simulation. In this one, 16 were squares (with an epistemic standard deviation of 20); the remaining 4 forecasters were what we might call (relatively) sharp, with standard deviations of 1, 2, 3 and 4 points. Here is their redistribution of assets for a model with no bookmaker commission.

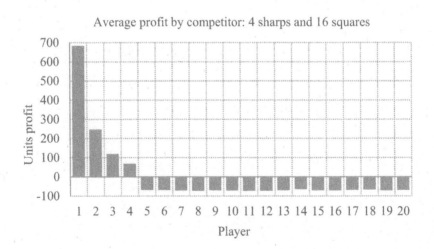

Average profit by competitor: 4 sharps and 16 squares

Unsurprisingly, only the sharp competitors are making any profit, and more than before since there are more square competitors to feed off. However, they are engaged in their own mini 'winner-takes-all' competition, which also displays a Pareto-type distribution. Now watch what happens when we increase their prediction skills but reduce the variance across this group, again by taking the square root of the standard deviation in epistemic error.

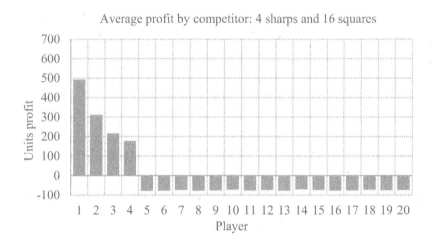

Average profit by competitor: 4 sharps and 16 squares

The best competitor is still the best competitor and has the same forecast skill as before, but the other three sharps have narrowed the gap to them. Consequently, they make less profit. This is the paradox of skill.

In my thought experiment, 20% of the bettors are sharp. If we plotted all 100,000 Monte Carlo iteration scores for the 20 competitors in a frequency distribution, we would see the sharps' performances as a long right hand tail, with the full distribution deviating significantly from normal. Yet Pyckio's tipster z-scores showed no such tail and no such asymmetry, just a symmetric normal distribution. There are two possible explanations. Firstly, the difference between sharps and squares is so small as to be practically undetectable. It would take a lot longer than 100 competitive rounds, as I have used in this thought experiment, for accumulated advantage to reveal itself against the background of luck. Alternatively, or indeed additionally, the proportion of sharps relative to squares is tiny. I ran one more Monte Carlo simulation, this time with just one sharp (relative to the rest) with a standard deviation in the epistemic model error of 1, and 19 relative squares with a standard deviation in the epistemic model error of 1.25. The frequency distribution of profits is shown below.

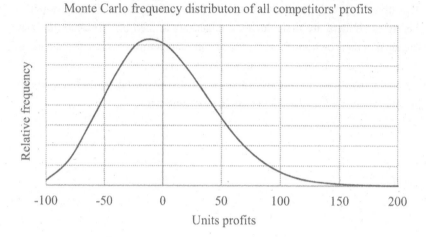

Monte Carlo frequency distributon of all competitors' profits

19 of the 20 competitors are effectively engaged in a game of coin tossing with each other. On their own, their profits would distribute normally. Despite the remaining competitor holding the most marginal of superior forecasting skills over the rest, it is still possible to see evidence of their existence in the distribution. The fact that I can't find such obvious asymmetry in a distribution of bettor or tipster performances tells me that the true number of sharp bettors is tiny. Fewer than 1 in 200 pay Betfair's premium charge. I would very much predict that the proportion of bettors capable of moving Pinnacle's lines and odds systematically, rather than randomly, or those of any other sharp bookmaker for that matter, will be similar.

For the few sharps who are winning the prediction arms race, the paradox of skill presents a further problem. They can choose to operate in less efficient markets, with less action and less liquidity, but as a consequence must accept lower stake limits, since the bookmaker will be guarding against greater liabilities. As a bigger fish in a smaller pond, their relative skill level may be greater compared to other competitors, and with that may come a greater expected value. However, because stake limits offered are smaller, absolute profits will be smaller too. To increase profits, the sharp may decide to go swimming in a bigger pond to find bigger stake limits. However, other sharps will be swimming there too, motivated by the same drive to increase absolute profits. The result? More sharps competing; a reduction in variance across skills; smaller absolute profits; and a greater influence of luck on performance outcomes. In terms of market action, this will all play out as a faster and more efficient price discovery process towards the 'true' odds. A sharp bettor will face such a decision every time they find some expected value in a market. Do I take what I have found now, but with smaller stakes, or do I wait a little longer for the larger stake limits, but run the risk of my competitors taking away some of the expected value from me?

The Environment of Skill

Betting is really just a machine for redistributing wealth. Financially, it is zero-sum, with the amount of money going in balanced by the amount coming out, with losers paying for winners. However, because it is an iterative competition played repetitively, marginal advantages for each iteration (bet) are compounded, and this redistribution follows an asymmetric power law function. Nevertheless, as the best forecasters find themselves pushed against a wall of 'truth' by those less skilled following on behind, relative skill differences narrow, and performance outcomes increasingly start to appear random, even if everyone playing is getting better at predicting the future. Machine learning, artificial intelligence and high-frequency trading are tools increasingly being used to find new advantages, but as more and more of these enter the competitive landscape, the same paradox of skill will continue to show its influence. The distinction between sharp and square, then, is relative, not absolute. A forecasting model that might once have delivered expected value may find itself overtaken in the evolution towards ever more accurate prediction.

Luck, then, will always be an ever-present feature in betting, both with regards to the aleatory uncertainty for a single outcome that makes predicting it with certainty impossible, and the wider distribution of performances where competitors are doing similar things. When everyone has the same prediction model, outcomes and performances are then just reduced to chance. The process of price discovery ensures that on a bet-by-bet basis, what advantages may exist for the handful of bettors skilled enough at finding them are marginal and hard to come by. Consequently, it takes time, or rather many iterations (bets), for that advantage to be accumulated into something that shows itself above the background noise of randomness. Perhaps, then, the question is not so much whether betting **is** a game of skill (as opposed to luck), but when it becomes one. My chapter on winning will have shown you how long it can take the law of large numbers to reveal this transition from luck to skill, although short cuts like the closing line value test are available for those in a hurry. Nate Silver, the ex-poker player and founder of FiveThirtyEight, suggested it might take as many as

100,000 hands, or 2 years of regular playing up to 40 hours per week, for skill to show its hand.

The means by which people acquire an expertise or skill is called 'naturalistic decision-making', where chunks or patterns of data are memorised and recalled periodically through prolonged practice and feedback. For this to be effective, the environment should be sufficiently regular and stable to be predictable, allowing cause and effect to be meaningfully connected. Clearly such an environment of skill exists for things like tennis. Can the same be said for tennis betting? When the game is competitive, and the likelihood of winning is determined not by absolute, but relative, skills, we are not necessarily rewarded for acquiring them if everyone else is acquiring them too. Skill in betting is not simply a matter of picking winners; rather, it's about whether we're better at finding more than everyone else.

Validity measures the strength of the link between cause and effect. The paradox of skill, and the price discovery that arises from it, ensures that in betting this link is weak. A betting market is complex and mostly random because the news that drives the movement of odds arrives to the market randomly. If news wasn't random, then it wouldn't be news. When the links between cause and effect are not strong, the scope for feedback is limited. Since feedback is the oil that drives the machinery of deliberate practice, it is much harder to develop expertise. In the extreme, where the link between cause (a prediction) and effect (an outcome) is nil, the opportunity for expertise is nil too. Imagine trying to practise a game of roulette. Can sports betting be practised? With 'true' probabilities remaining hidden, the possibility, unlike for roulette, must exist. The data, however, suggest that for most competitors, they are really just tossing coins. For them, betting is simply a zero-validity environment, influenced only by luck.

As I've said already, learning that betting is largely a game of luck is not something people want to accept. A large dose of overconfidence usually helps them circumnavigate this message. For most, however, their prospects of becoming a winner through real expected value rather than luck will not change. If you are one of those who wants to do more than just live in this illusion, let me offer you five points for consideration.

1) Betting is not roulette. The 'true' probabilities, and the precise probability distribution, will always remain unknown. This creates the opportunity, if not the guarantee, that the house edge, unlike in roulette, can be overcome. With possibility comes hope. I may tell the story that

betting is mostly random. 'Mostly' is NOT the same thing as 'Completely'.

2) Betting is a zero-sum, relative skills contest, with winners and losers Pareto-distributed until the paradox skill reduces all outcomes to luck. So long as there are competitors who exhibit systematic biases in their decision-making (the majority), the process of price discovery towards a perfectly efficient betting market will remain incomplete. In such a contest, to beat enough of your competitors to get paid takes hard work, and possibly a little talent too. Many people suggest betting is easy. They are either lying or stupid. The difficulty lies in knowing how to spot systematic (not random) errors in betting prices and knowing how to avoid making them yourself. The evidence suggests few are capable of it.

3) To increase your advantage, find markets with a higher variance of skill. Relative differences will be greater, the distribution of profits and losses more asymmetric, and the role of luck less pronounced. The downside may be having to accept smaller staking limits from the bookmaker.

4) Think relative, not absolute. You can make 95% of your decisions correctly and still lose your shirt if those you're competing against are making the right calls 99% of the time.

5) Finally, focus on your process, your model, your methodology, and not your results. Even for sharps, most of what happens in the short term is dominated by chance. Don't count your winners and assume your forecasts had something to do with them. Instead, find proxy measures to test the quality of your forecasting. The closing line is one good example. Where luck weakens the link between skills (causes) and profits (effects), a skilful player can lose money whilst an unskilled player (relatively speaking) can profit.

A CAUTIONARY TALE

We've arrived at the end. All the modelling and simulation is done. There will be no more random number generation, no more distributions and no more equations. (Reader breathes sigh of relief.). At the end, have I managed to demystify probability, uncertainty and luck and their roles in betting, as was the challenge I set myself? I hope so. However, teaching people to win at betting who don't have a mathematical background is arguably an impossible task. Perhaps that is as it should be, since to win in betting, like in any other walk of life, takes hard work. Those who work hardest, and in this case make the effort to understand the mathematics of probability, will be the ones most rewarded. For those of you who knew a little more, I hope you've found some of the concepts I've covered illuminating and helpful. Finally, for those of you who largely knew it all already, I hope it hasn't all been too tedious. This final chapter will tell a cautionary tale about the expectations of bettors aspiring to beat the bookmaker (or indeed their fellow competitors, as is really the case), and about the dangers that betting can present when overconfidence turns to greed, greed to loss chasing, and loss chasing to addiction. I do not use the word 'greed' here in any judgemental sense.

You have seen me distinguish between two types of bookmaker: the sharp one and the recreational one. The former is obsessed with 'true' probabilities. The latter with offering value and variety. The former considers betting as a means of facilitating a skill-based competition, rewarding those customers who are better at forecasting 'true' outcome probabilities than they and other customers are. The latter implicitly regards betting as a form of entertainment. Arguably, bettors can be divided in the same way as bookmakers. Bettors who aspire to be sharp, to beat the system and win with wits, versus bettors who simply like a bit of action to accompany the sport they are watching. The former are obsessed about expected value, the latter only with whether their bet will win. Sharp bettors are well catered for by sharp bookmakers. Recreational (or square) bettors are similarly welcome at recreational bookmakers. The problem occurs when bettors aspiring to play sharp wish to do so at recreational bookmakers. Whilst I have been told by traders of recreational bookmakers that they set odds with a view to challenging their customers to beat them, in reality there is no competition at all. If customers are skilled enough to beat their traders, they will be asked to take their custom elsewhere, or to their casino games which are impossible to beat. It has happened to me on numerous occasions. Bookmakers have figured out that recreational bettors far outnumber sharp ones, so it's much easier to build a bookmaking model that caters for them. It's also easier to make money that way, particularly in jurisdictions with tougher tax regimes and stronger gambling regulation. The fact that a small proportion of bettors becomes disgruntled about an inability to utilise their skillset is collateral damage small enough that recreational bookmakers are willing to accept it. Most of the large brands have shareholders to answer to, who want profit maximisation rather than principled bookmaking. It is for this reason that, just as for bettors, recreational bookmakers vastly outnumber their sharper counterparts. Great for squares, not so great for sharps.

If there is one thing more than any other to get bettors engaged in heated debate, it is the issue of bookmaker restrictions. Over the past number of years, attention has increasingly focused on the refusal by many recreational bookmakers to accept the custom of a small proportion of sharper customers whom they claim to be unprofitable for their business. The reason they are unprofitable stems from the business model recreational bookmakers are using. All bookmakers in the UK and Europe are using the recreational model. This is becoming increasingly true in America, once famed as a nation that honoured the action of anyone who asked for it, as it finds those ideals increasingly pressurised by a model that is more efficient at making profit. Let's review again the difference between the recreation model of bookmaking and the sharp one, why they exist, and what they mean for the bettor.

The quintessential sharp bookmaker is Pinnacle.com. It's been plying its trade as one for more than 20 years. Their unique selling point, for which they are famous and have built their reputation, is that they welcome winners, that is to say players who hold positive expected value. Leaving aside a few smaller exceptions and some Asian bookmakers where winners are also accepted, but arguably for slightly different reasons, there can only be one truly sharp bookmaker. The brief explanation for that is the mathematics of 'winner takes all' and the Pareto Principle, and to replace them at the top would now take very deep pockets to buy the kind of reputation and turnover that Pinnacle have acquired. Matthew Trenhaile – I referred to him earlier in my discussion about the tipster Nishikori – offers a more thorough and nuanced account in his medium.com resource *Haunted by Ignorance*, which is easily found via Google.

Pinnacle's model is what we might describe as the traditional bookmaker, and one that requires high volume. The greater the turnover of money coming through your markets, the more profit you should expect to take via your margin. However, to attract that volume you have to have low margins to offer the most competitive prices. Some of Pinnacle's margins are as low as 2% for their most popular markets; other bookmakers' margins may be three times larger for the same markets. As a consequence, you have to be right a lot of the time. If your errors are systematically bigger than your margins, your sharp customers are going to pick you off and erode your profits. Pinnacle make it their business to be right, with highly efficient odds keeping epistemic uncertainty in their models to a minimum. Pinnacle's trading director, Marco Blume, has explained that when it comes to managing his markets, it's 100% data science, 0% money engaged. The idea of trying to balance action on a bet-by-bet basis is more of an aspiration than a necessity. The law of large numbers, over many betting markets, takes care of liabilities a sharp bookmaker will face due to the betting habits of systematically biased customers anyway. Pinnacle CEO Paris Smith, furthermore, has explained that her company takes positions, doesn't lay off positions elsewhere, puts skin in the game and has confidence in their numbers.

Having the best models is expensive. Pinnacle's investment strategy is almost entirely devoted to data modelling, with little left over for advertising and marketing. Furthermore, refusing the business of the sharpest and potentially highest staking customers is going to be counterproductive to operating a high-turnover model. By willingly accepting sharp customers, however, Pinnacle kill two birds with one stone. Firstly, the 'winners welcome' policy is a cheap form of self-promotion, spreading the unique selling point of the product by word of mouth. Secondly, allowing the sharpest bettors to play helps Pinnacle improve the efficiency of their prices, ensuring that the proportion of positive expected value players is kept to a minimum. Bettors, Marco explains, are used as an information resource; Pinnacle are effectively incorporating customers' models into their own via the process of price discovery. He is always ready to upgrade his 'consultants' with superior versions. Yes, this involves risk, but they are good at it. However, Pinnacle's tight margins mean that it's not cost-effective to operate such a business model in jurisdictions with more costly tax regimes. The UK, for example, introduced its point of consumption tax of 15% in 2014 targeting offshore bookmakers registered in low-tax jurisdictions who were making profits off UK customers. It can hardly be a coincidence that Pinnacle left the UK market in the same year, and further withdrew their licence application to the UK Gambling Commission to rejoin four years later, just at the time that an increase of the tax rate to 21% was announced by Government.

Whilst a sharp bookmaker seeks volume, the recreational model caters for a much larger number of smaller-staking customers. From my own data on player turnover, average stakes per customer can be an order of magnitude smaller for these brands. They are smaller for two reasons. Firstly, their book limits (maximum stakes for a specific match) are smaller. They don't need to be as large as for the sharp bookmaker because their margins are greater, and they often have more available markets to bet on with a greater number of customers betting in them. Secondly, recreational bookmakers will readily limit or refuse stakes from their sharpest customers who hold positive expected value. Let's be clear, this does not include those who simply win through luck. Recreational bookmakers can quickly tell the difference. They only have to follow their price movements to identify which is which. Recall that identifying sharp play via the closing line value hypothesis is far faster than using one's results.

The term 'recreational' implies that bookmakers using this model see their product as a form of entertainment only, rather than as a means for their customers to make money professionally. This appears to be sufficient to satisfy the appetite of the majority of them, and in the UK at least, is compatible with a regulatory regime requiring advertisers to avoid portraying betting and gambling as a means to make money. In comparison to Pinnacle, less investment proportionally is directed towards data science and modelling efficient lines, more towards marketing and advertising of variety, bonuses and best-in-market prices. Consequently, because of their inferior market efficiency, it's actually easier to find expected value at a recreational bookmaker, despite their bigger margins. In contrast, Pinnacle's greater price efficiency means it's much harder to find it, even though, on average, they have the best prices because of their lower margins. 'Best-in-market' is not equivalent to 'most accurate'.

Indeed, some recreational bookmakers might be offering expected value intentionally as a loss leader to attract new customers and to promote the image of being a best-price bookmaker. The problem is that if they find you systematically exploiting it, they will take steps to prevent you from doing so. Recreational bookmakers consider that customers who are price sensitive are engaging in arithmetic value betting and arbitrage. Given that Pinnacle's price efficiency means recreational bookmakers are systematically on the unprofitable side of an arb – I have data to prove this – it is understandable why they would wish to stop this activity, and conversely why Pinnacle actively welcome it. It's how they acquire a lot of their turnover. Increasingly, however, sharper customers of recreational bookmakers are grumbling about the unfairness of these restrictions. Do they actually have a fair grievance?

A bet has always been regarded as an informal and consensual agreement between two parties to honour a redistribution of assets according to prior terms based on the outcome of some event. In the UK, this honouring of debts was more legally formalised in the 2005 Gambling Act. It was achieved by bringing gambling under the umbrella of contract law. This legislates that once a contract is made, the terms are legally enforceable, and all debts are liable. One crucial aspect of contract law is that parties are free to determine, without reservation or explanation, with whom they make a contract, and whether they may void one, provided they do not 'override any other rule of law that prevents enforcement on the grounds of unlawfulness.' One obvious example of unlawfulness that is routinely cited by restricted bettors is discrimination.

The 2010 Equalities Act in the UK identifies a number of protected characteristics which have been identified as illegal to discriminate against. Gender, race and faith are obvious ones. These are attributes that one cannot control. Sadly, intelligence, or to be more specific, the skill of finding expected value, is not one of them. Intelligence, like wealth for example, is something that arguably is more easily influenced by the individual, and hence discriminating on these terms is usually permitted under UK law. Furthermore, under contract law, as the outspoken gambling entrepreneur @ALuckyADay points out, a business has the right to discriminate for business reasons and has the right to refuse custom if it is in their business interests to do so. Unethical it may seem to be, but it's perfectly legal; to change this would require a change in the law, or a legal challenge creating a precedent that reinterpreted the existing law. Rather ironically, those of a more puritanical persuasion would paradoxically argue that the application of skill to acquire wealth from those less skilled amounts to cheating or fraud. I explored these gambling ethics in my previous book.

Attempts have been made to change the law with varying degrees of success. In the UK little headway has been made since 2018 when interested parties met with the Gambling Commission, the UK's official gambling regulator, and MPs to discuss the issue of customer restriction. Similarly, the action group Justice4Punters that investigated the opportunities for launching a legal suit have been advised against it on the grounds that they would probably fail. By contrast, in 2019 the bookmaker bet365 was ordered to unrestrict a group of Spanish customers following a two-year legal battle. Ruling in the plaintiffs' favour, the court decreed that, given the customers were not professional and had no right of reply, the account restrictions were a form of discrimination detrimental to consumer rights, and further that the contract terms they had been forced to accept were abusive. In Australia, minimum bet guarantees removing the right of bookmakers to refuse any bettor with a winning record were introduced in some states for racing, greyhounds and trotting, beginning first in New South Wales in 2014, that allowed bettors to win up to $2,000 (AUD) per bet. Surprisingly, the minimum bet guarantee has proved popular not only with bettors but with bookmakers too, who have found it easier to trade in a marketplace where turnover is strong, and a price must be honoured and available to all. Nevertheless, we should remember that it was introduced for only three betting markets. The remainder of sports, and presumably the majority of betting turnover, have been unaffected.

It should also be recognised that different nations have subtly different legal systems allowing for different interpretations and different opinions about what might be considered discriminatory or abusive. Perhaps more importantly different nations will have different cultural landscapes from which notions of fairness and discrimination are formed. Australians, whether because of the way the national identity has been forged or for some other reason, may have a more binary sense of fairness hardwired, believing that everyone should get a fair crack. In the US, with a gambling heritage rooted in the mafia, I have wondered whether bookmakers might be more inclined to 'honour' gambling contracts rather than 'boot' players for beating the line. PokerJoe, author of *Sharper: A Guide to Modern Sports Betting*, has said he's never heard, from the 'mobsters' he knew back in the day, any idea, ever, of banning someone for winning. 'I think they would have been humiliated.'

One crucial aspect of contract law is what is termed the invitation to treat. An invitation to treat (or invitation to bargain in the US) can be defined as an expression of willingness to negotiate. A person making an invitation to treat does not intend to be bound as soon as it is accepted by the person to whom the statement is addressed. Cassini, author of the sports trading blog Green All Over, explains this is not an acceptance of a contract but an indication of a person's willingness to negotiate one. It is a pre-offer communication. As such, this is precisely what publication of the odds represents. It is a form of marketing or window dressing designed to attract the bettor but placing no obligation on the bookmaker to accept their money, should there be any offered. If bettors choose not to make an offer, or the bookmaker chooses not to accept the bet, there is no contract. Provided the published price was not meant to deceive and is available to the majority of customers, the bookmaker is perfectly entitled to refuse money from bettors deemed bad for business. In the UK at least, the law still permits this. Unsurprisingly, it is the invitation to treat that causes the most consternation amongst restricted bettors. Bookmakers, they argue, should not be window dressers, or dressmakers as Spanky disparagingly likes to call them; they should be risk takers. If you put up a line or a price, then you should be prepared to stand by it, not discriminate according to which of your customers you believe think you've mispriced it. That, after all, is what Pinnacle is, a traditional bookmaker with skin in the game, not merely a facilitator of entertainment.

In an information market, knowledge is power. Sharp bettors use it to gain expected value and make a long-term profit. Sharp bookmakers use the knowledge they gain from their trading model and from the models of their 'consultants' to make more efficient numbers, with which to attract higher volumes from arbitrage players and others on the wrong side of value. In a sense, the two parties are engaged in a reciprocal and mutually-benefitting, if informal, contract: you scratch my back and I'll scratch yours. However, as @ALuckyADay reminds us, knowledge is only worth something if someone is willing to pay for it. If your knowledge has value, a fair price in an efficient market will be paid. The model the recreational bookmakers are operating, however, no longer requires bettors' knowledge. They have traders who already know roughly what an efficient number is, and what they lack, they can simply get from sharp bookmakers or exchanges effectively free of charge. Why bother paying customers who beat soft recreational numbers, like I can do with my Wisdom of the Crowd methodology, when you don't need them to tell you what the 'true' numbers are. Such knowledge, to a recreational bookmaker at least, is effectively worthless. Many recreational numbers, after all, are, in my view, intentionally inefficient and designed to attract more customers. They don't need to pay for something they already know. Given that it's only a small proportion of their customers who possess this knowledge, restricting them results in a bigger net profit than spending their budget on data, forecasting and 'consultants' to find 'true' numbers. Since there can only be one Pinnacle, let Pinnacle be Pinnacle, and the dressmakers can make money making dresses. Well, that at least is the theory.

The dichotomy between these two models of bookmaking may seem stark, and in some ways overly so. Certainly, recreational bookmakers do care about efficient numbers to an extent. If they simply posted anything and restricted everyone who beat it, they wouldn't have many customers and much reputation left. Furthermore, like Pinnacle, they will also be taking risk positions and facing liabilities. Even recreational bookmaking is not simply a matter of making your front window look nice. Nevertheless, the distinction between the two models has important consequences for the future of sports bookmaking. With the relaxation of betting laws in the US, the fear amongst bettors there is that the UK and European way of doing things is going to spread there too. Would that be such a bad thing? Well, that depends on your point of view. If you care about a sense of fairness and what a bookmaker should traditionally be supposed to be doing, or are one of the few sharps to hold expected value, then you will presumably be appalled. In contrast, if you belong to the much larger group who either don't know how to or don't care about beating a line, then the recreational model is nothing much to be feared. After all, it offers far more forms of entertainment.

Indeed, it might be argued that curtailing the current freedoms that recreational bookmakers hold through contract and consumer law would be detrimental to the interests of the majority who DO just see betting as a form of entertainment. Forcing them to accept winners could either see increases in margins or a move towards more efficient markets more generally. Both could be seen as being detrimental to the majority of bettors in terms of their losses, including those who currently hold a profitable edge via hitting soft numbers. Many of those currently complaining the loudest about being restricted might find themselves complaining about something worse: losing. Always beware the unintended consequences of what you wish for. It's much easier to look sharp at a recreational bookmaker. Take your betting strategy to Pinnacle, if you're allowed to bet with them, or to the Betfair exchange, and see if it still works. I can categorically tell you that my Wisdom of the Crowd methodology will fail. Since you know how it works, it should be obvious to you why.

There's probably a place for both the traditional (sharp) bookmaker and the recreational bookmaker to coexist together. They probably need each other. Pinnacle's turnover model is supported by the recreational money that floods in on the wrong side of arbitrage bets. Conversely, they signal to the rest of the market, better than anything else, what the 'true' prices of things are. Perhaps there can be only one Pinnacle, but a market with none just seems to jar against a bettor's sense of fairness. Even if they will never be sharp enough to win, perhaps it's having a realistic hope and means of trying that matters. Uncertainty and anticipation, after all, are lubricants that grease the wheels of betting. Bookmakers and exchanges who choose not to restrict winners help to facilitate those pleasures. So long as they remain pleasures, and don't stray into something more sinister, that, surely, is a good thing. Ultimately bettors vote with their money. To date it would seem the majority of customers who bet with recreational bookmakers are quite happy with the product they are being offered. If they weren't, they would leave, right?

If you're someone aspiring to gain a little bit more than entertainment from betting, where does the policy of restriction leave you? At one level, being restricted could be taken as a compliment and a proxy signal that you must be doing something right. If it happens, there are possibly a number of measures you could take. The obvious one is to move on to the next recreational bookmaker, but if your methods are the same, it's simply a matter of time before they will restrict you too. Reducing stake sizes to levels that will be less troubling for recreational bookmakers, typically small double figures, is an option but doing so will obviously impact your profits. This can be countered by having a large number of bets. My Wisdom of the Crowd method typically identifies around 2,500 bets per year. With an expected value of 4%, £10 stakes would give you an expected annual profit of £1,000 per year. That's not going to pay your bills, but it will contribute towards a holiday. There are automated services offered by TrademateSports.com and BettingIsCool.com that have taken my idea to the next level, scaling up to target a much larger number of markets and expected value opportunities than I do.

Small stakes, however, will only take you so far. If you're aiming to earn professionally from betting, your stakes will need to be considerably larger, unless you are able to find hundreds of expected-value bets every day. Ultimately, this will mean finding alternatives to the recreational bookmakers. Pinnacle and the Asian bookmakers will accept your custom, provided you live in a jurisdiction where they are licensed. Unfortunately, that is not the case for bettors in the UK. Brokers, who can give you access to a multitude of sharper bookmakers, are also an option, but again access to them will depend on the regulatory regime where you live. Unfortunately, there is no UK licensed betting broker. Asianconnect will accept UK bettors but only for deposit and withdraw via Bitcoin. The betting exchanges, which are available to UK bettors, should in theory offer you unrestricted liquidity. A few bettors have found their action refused, but it's hard to verify whether this is on account of departure from a specific country for regulatory reasons, or a breach of other terms and conditions. Exchanges and sharp bookmakers, however, are much harder to beat for the reasons identified. Taking your betting methodology there is no guarantee that it will continue to succeed. Intuition, and a little bit of theoretical modelling, suggests for every 10 bettors capable of systematically finding expected value at a recreational bookmaker, there is only one at a sharp bookmaker.

Miguel Figueres (who developed the maximum drawdown calculator) has offered an intriguing solution for those with restricted accounts, which makes use of new European Union General Data Protection Regulation (GDRP). Under the legislation you have the 'right to be forgotten'. The process would work as follows. 1) Seek clarification that your account has been restricted. 2) Request that your account be closed. 3) Request deletion of your personal data according to the terms of the GDPR legislation. 4) Open a new account. Whilst I am unaware of how effective such a strategy might prove to be – I tried it myself with BetVictor in 2018 but have not bothered opening a new account since – I fear that it may well be of limited use. By law, bookmakers are obliged to hold personal data about the individual for a period of 5 years (the Retention Period), for the purposes of combating money laundering and other fraudulent activities. Whilst in theory the information the bookmaker will keep is not to be used for any reason other than to comply with those legal procedures, it's unclear how bookmakers will draw the distinction. I suspect your 'right to be forgotten' will, in practice, be superseded by the bookmaker's obligation to counter money laundering, and it will be used, unfairly, to restrict you again. Perhaps customers will have to wait the full 5 years. Nevertheless, if all else fails, there is nothing to lose in trying.

Prevention, they say, is better than cure. What sort of things can you do to minimise the likelihood of being restricted? In the end, sharp bettors betting at recreational bookmakers are going to be restricted. It's as inevitable as night follows day. Every bettor leaves a trail. For the bookmaker it's just a matter of analysing it. Your job is to disguise your activity as much as is practically possible to look like a recreational bettor. That means making your betting look dumb. Bookmakers will initially use computerised algorithms to detect expected value bettors. If you mix your betting with wagers that throw these algorithms off your trail, you can stay under their radar for longer. TradremateSports.com has made a useful video (available on YouTube) with 10 tips on how to avoid being 'gubbed' by bookmakers. These include betting in bigger markets where liquidity is greater and sharper activity is more easily absorbed, rounding stakes so they look less like value betting and arbitrage, avoiding pushing the maximum limits and instead split stakes across several bookmakers, betting accumulators and other higher margin bets like correct score and first goal scorer, betting in their casinos, and limiting the frequency of withdrawals. Obviously, you still want the net impact of your betting to hold an edge but throwing in some negative expected value bets will hopefully confuse their detection methods for longer. Other things you can consider are not always betting the best odds – recreational bookmakers are able to see, just like you can, when they are best-in-market – and sometimes trying to lose, for example by backing a long price, but ensuring you hedge this position at a betting exchange. This list is obviously not exhaustive, but any measure I haven't included here will follow the same theme: look like a square.

A bookmaker restriction is arguably the best proxy method that you are a sharp bettor, or at least sharp enough at the bookmaker who's restricted you to be considered too unprofitable from the perspective of their business model. The corollary is that if you are not eventually restricted, you are not considered to be sharp. Many bettors do just bet for fun and entertainment, but there is a significant cohort who like the challenge of beating the system and winning with wits which, for many, is regarded as a form of self-actualisation. I must acknowledge it was the reason that drew me to betting more than 30 years ago. Humans are intrinsically wired to fear uncertainty. At the same time, they are attracted to trying to conquer it. Betting offers the opportunity to do just that, through predicting the future. Joseph Mazur, a Professor Emeritus of Mathematics, captures this idea in his book *What's Luck Got to Do with It.* '[G]ambling behaviour is primarily connected to an intrinsic desire to manipulate luck in order to validate life, to test the forces of uncertainty under a fantasy of knowing something unknowable or to experiment with the new.'

Winning with wits in betting, however, is no easy task, as I have tried to demonstrate in this book. Unfortunately, the correlation between those who can win and those who believe they can win is very weak indeed. The latter dramatically outnumber the former. 95% of bettors, if reported figures are to be believed, will not be restricted. For many, that is because they are only betting for entertainment, uninterested in finding the best price, expected value or a winning system. Nevertheless, even the majority of bettors who are trying to find an edge will be allowed to bet unrestricted. It's not that they are doing the wrong things; rather, they are not doing the right things well enough. In a competitive environment where small advantages can be compounded, and betting performances follow a Pareto distribution, it is easy to understand why. If they are failing, why do they keep trying?

Whilst uncertainty and anticipation may grease the wheels of betting, overconfidence is the spark plug. Overconfidence, or illusory superiority, is a cognitive bias whereby individuals overestimate their own qualities and abilities relative to others. Without it, almost all betting, for anything other than entertainment, would cease to exist. Daniel Kahneman asks the question: 'when you sell a stock, who buys it?' Both parties must believe they are right, otherwise we have to consign the theory of rational self-interest to the dustbin. The same is true for a bet. However, unless the odds or line are perfect, one side must be wrong, at least financially speaking. Given that both sides are happy to engage in a transaction, mutual overconfidence of their own abilities to assess a 'true' outcome probability accurately must account for why they are willing to do so. The fact that neither wants to be wrong is reason why odds typically converge towards the 'true' probabilities; it is the engine that drives the process of price discovery.

We might very well ask: what is it that breeds such overconfidence? The answer is the illusion of causality. Illusions of causality occur when people develop the belief that there is a causal connection between two events that are actually unrelated. In linear environments like hitting a tennis ball, the way I hold and swing a racket will have a significant influence on my quality of play. Such things can be acquired through learning, practice and feedback, the process of naturalistic decision-making. In complex, non-linear or largely random environments, like betting markets, where a forecasting arms race has reduced the variance of prediction skills, the links between cause and effect are far more tenuous. Remember, however, this is not to argue that Manchester City beating Sheffield United is a matter of luck - we know Manchester City's players possess more skill. Instead, in a betting market where the rewards for predicting the correct outcome are handicapped by its likelihood, whether I hold any expected value is then much more the subject of chance.

Randomness, however, is not something that human beings cope with easily. They would much rather prefer explanations and reasons for why things happen. Linear thinking, in terms of cause and effect, was an evolutionarily winning strategy, part of a general threat detection and avoidance mechanism that aided our survival. We extrapolate such linear patterns of cause and effect to more complex environments, even when it's unwarranted. Consequently, it's much easier to construct the narrative that when we win a bet, our knowledge and forecasting skill had something to do with it. 'I made money from my prediction $\Rightarrow$ I am skilled at prediction $\Rightarrow$ I caused my wealth to increase' is a far more coherent, appealing and psychologically rewarding story than 'I was merely guessing and got lucky', giving us a sense of control that is equally illusory. In a system dominated by the noise of chance, the appearance of any signal of skill can take time, and the law of small numbers is waiting at every opportunity to fool us. In the short term, indeed, even over quite long terms, many bettors will find themselves to be winning. It's much easier and psychologically comforting to believe that skill, and not luck, is the explanation. For almost all, this is an illusion.

Never has the dangers of illusory superiority been so starkly illustrated than with the collapse of Football Index, a UK-licensed and regulated gambling product that allowed customers to bet on the future success of football players. Customers purchased imaginary shares for the chance to win dividends based on players' performances, as well as to speculate on their future value, with Football Index earning a commission from the trading. The product was marketed as a stock market, when in truth it was nothing more than a hybrid of betting and fantasy football. Football Index entered administration in March 2021 and is currently suspended without a gambling licence, with customers facing collective losses in the region of £90 million. The events have cast a shadow over the way betting is regulated in the UK.

It was never clear where the money to pay dividends, £11 million in 2019/20, was coming from, but numerous observers, myself included, were sceptical. Almost nobody on the platform was losing. Indeed, even Football Index used this as a form of marketing, claiming that whilst 74% said they tended to lose money on traditional gambling, only 2% said they did so with Football Index. The product was not licensed by the Financial Conduct Authority. It would never have been granted a licence if it had applied. It was licensed by the UK and Jersey Gambling Commissions. It was a gambling game. A gambling game is financially zero-sum, a closed system where the money going in equals the money coming out, and all that happens is a redistribution. Unlike a real stock market, through which the engine of capitalism slowly converts natural capital into social and economic wealth, with the value of companies intrinsically linked to that process, the Football Index market of player values had nothing intrinsic at all. It was simply a game based on emotion and hubris, and amongst the Football Index community there was an awful lot of it about.

The owners of Football Index have attempted to defend themselves against this criticism, arguing that it fundamentally fails to understand how it is designed to operate. We might concede that they believed the fundamentals of the game could be scaled increasingly to more and more football markets. In the end, however, you run out of players to value. More importantly, they were confusing scalability with sustainability. Regardless of the potential for scaling, the product was, whether by accident or design, heavily invested in customer psychology. Such a market, by default, will be at a much greater risk of volatility if people's opinions change. That happened first when the company removed the opportunity for instant sell, allowing customers to 'cash out' their bets by selling shares back to Football Index at a small loss. and then more recently when it significantly reduced the size of the payable dividends. As some customers pointed out, it was akin to a bookmaker shortening the odds after your bet has been settled. Effectively, this was an admission that the source of those dividend payments was not sustainable. The crash in player valuations that it precipitated, as customers attempted to sell, ultimately led to the collapse of the platform. In doing so, it laid bare what many had long suspected. Rewards for success were not coming from any intrinsic player worth, but from new money chasing old, as more and more customers sought to join the bandwagon, and existing customers invested more and more of their personal wealth, often wealth that they could not afford to lose. Such an investment is known as a pyramid scheme or a Ponzi, named after Charles Ponzi, an Italian businessman and early 20th century con artist in North America, who paid early investors using the investments of later ones, rather than from the profit earned by the investment.

There is, to date, no evidence that Football Index was such a scheme; that must surely require intent to commit fraud. Nevertheless, as far back as January 2020 the UK Gambling Commission was warned of the possibility of the platform being a 'dangerous pyramid scheme' with 'users misled into believing they are investing rather than gambling.' A report, believed to have been handed to the Gambling Commission in person, and which I was sent anonymously three months later, was damning in its condemnation of Football Index's business model. The author estimated that in January 2020, Football Index's liabilities, on account of its dividend payments, exceeded £1 million per month, and that the only way the firm could continue to operate in this manner in the long term would be through a conveyor belt of new share issues to attract new money. Indeed, even after the value of dividend payments was slashed by 80%, Football continued to mint new shares for sale. Concluding the report, the author argued that 'should user growth stop or decline, the company would quickly find itself unable to pay these liabilities to users,' and that 'users would quickly see the value of their positions collapse.' Most damningly, 'Football Index users [were] unknowingly "betting" on continued user growth, [whilst] Football Index management [were] knowingly reliant on continued user growth to keep the system flowing and [avoid insolvency].' That is the very essence of a pyramid scheme.

If this hadn't all been so inevitable, we might have described these predictions as prophetic. It took the Gambling Commission four months to initiate a formal review, utilising specialist betting, financial and legal expertise to examine the business model, the finances of the company, and the complex legal questions over the appropriate regulatory framework. History may suggest it wasn't thorough enough, although the Commission has argued that an earlier licence suspension could have worsened the business' financial plight, and in turn put more customer funds at risk. We may also rightly ask why this examination did not take place before the licence was originally granted.

Ponzi or not, Football Index could reasonably be described as a 'castle in the air', a concept made popular in 1936 by the economist John Maynard Keynes, whereby investors attempt to build a castle floating in the air without foundations, with hubris rather than stock fundamentals driving future price rises. There is really only one way that 98% of players of a gambling product cannot tend to be losing: new money funding old, with price rises driven by customer sentiment that was firmly rooted in illusory superiority. It was not just the owners of Football Index suffering from it; its customer base, with a co-ordinated Twitter community, displayed an almost pathological overconfidence in the product. Arguably, customers were misled into believing the product was a stock market. There were, however, numerous observers trying to explain that it was just a game of fantasy football, and that the risks associated with this zero-sum game were unsustainable. Most of these warnings were met by a mix of denial and abuse, describing the product as revolutionary and hurling profanities and worse at those critical of it. I suppose this was inevitable since Football Index themselves claimed to have changed the game. Some of the old tweets made by those who will almost certainly have had their futures ruined now make for very depressing reading. Some sold ISAs and put the money into Football Index. One customer even sold their house. Unfortunately, Football Index didn't change the game. They just redistributed a large amount of money, costing many their futures in the process. That's not changing the game; it's just playing the same game very, very badly. By the time you read this, I would very much hope that at least some of the funds, currently being protected in a Trust Account, will have been redistributed back to investing customers.

I don't write this account to attribute blame; in my view, such judgement, as I will argue shortly, is not helpful, it doesn't provide sustainable solutions. On the contrary, this story should be seen by all parties, the owners of Football Index, its customers and the Gambling Commission alike, as something to learn from. Rather than look back with regret, look forward with more decision-making, learning from mistakes already made. As Joe Simpson, the mountain climber, whose near death experience was autobiographically told in *Touching the Void*, says: 'You gotta make decisions. You gotta keep making decisions, even if they're wrong decisions, you know. If you don't make decisions, you're stuffed'. Keep looking forward, not behind. That is a metaphor for life. Some Football Index customers may now be faced with wholly different life experiences than they might otherwise have had. No matter how bad things seem, there's little point in dwelling on what might have been. Time heals most things, and mistakes are life's great teachers. Instead, try to enjoy the new opportunities life's mistakes create. One can never know whether one path through life is better or worse than another; you only get to live one path within the Monte Carlo model of life, where there are potentially an infinite number of paths, and where the shape of the distribution is unknown. As I would say to all gamblers, focus on the process, not the outcomes, or as Buddha once said: 'Happiness is a journey, not a destination'.

Understanding the bias of overconfidence, and indeed the blind spot bias of failing to see its impact on one's own judgment, is arguably something that should be taught at an age as early as the individual is capable of understanding. I used the story of Football Index to illustrate it, but it just as equally applies to any other form of betting, or indeed investment for that matter. Overconfidence is triggered by a reliance on outcomes to form a view about the causality of success. The only thing customers of Football Index could see was profit but profit alone doesn't tell you what's causing it. Too easily, we build a narrative about why they happened that praises something we think we did, whether buying the 'right' players or making the 'right' bets, with our judgement about what is 'right' grounded in the perception of our skills. In a properly-managed gambling game, however, nearly everything that happens, particularly in the short term, will just be chance. There is almost nothing causal at all, and what is, takes many iterations to reveal itself above the background noise of randomness. The fact that almost every customer was winning should have been a huge red flag that Football Index was not being managed properly. Unfortunately, blindness to overconfidence meant that most ignored the warnings.

What can be learnt from a story like Football Index? When it comes to financial risk-taking, always understand what you are doing, and always question whether you really understand the product, market or system. Be self-critical and consider the range of possible histories that could unfurl, not just the one that presents itself in front of you. In effect, carry out a qualitative Monte Carlo simulation on yourself. That may not reveal all of the unknown unknowns, but at the very least it will give you a better insight into worst case scenarios and a rough idea of the shape of the distribution you are dealing with. In betting, and gambling, there is no such thing as a free lunch. If you think you have found one, the probability that you are suffering from illusory superiority is far greater than it being real. At the end of gambling games, where the opportunity exists to accumulate advantage, and where regression to the mean has followed its natural course, a large number of losers will have helped increase the wealth of a small number of winners. That is just the nature of the game. You might be astute, but given the small proportion of winners, do not assume that you will be one of them. The Pareto redistribution of wealth for such games is inevitable. If that hasn't happened yet, then it's simply a matter of time, and the longer the illusion that everyone is winning persists, the more probable it is that this redistribution will be catastrophic. Football Index, at its heart, did indeed facilitate the possibility to exercise skill. Its management failure was that this was dwarfed by the influence of player hubris. Sadly, for Football Index, the only skill that really mattered in the end was knowing when the castle would fall down.

If, for most bettors, the sense that making money from predicting the future is illusory, what has us trying and trying again? Even when the stories we tell ourselves, and the patterns we find, create an illusory sense of causality and control, this may not be entirely maladaptive, although in the case of Football Index, there was a heavy price to pay. Feeling in control reduces anxiety and a sense of helplessness, enhances motivation, even in low validity or random environments, and potentially leads to more effective performance and greater long term success. Evidently, evolution concluded that the payoff of winning big through luck outweighs the costs of failure or not trying at all. Rewards from betting may largely regress to the mean, but now we have an evolutionary explanation for why so many people choose to do it. Our brain acts as a kind of 'interpreter' or 'belief-engine' creating causal narratives about the world which, even when mistaken (for example conspiracy theories), help to reduce stress and imbue a sense of control. Natural selection may very well favour strategies that make many incorrect causal associations, including all those associated with gambling, in order to establish those that are essential for survival.

Betting is fundamentally about taking risks, specifically financial risks. When we are optimistic about the outcome of our risk-taking behaviour, paradoxically we actually perceive it as not being risky. This is the illusion of control. The engine for much of this risk-reward analysis is the limbic system, our reptilian and oldest part of the brain. The limbic system is responsible for endocrine (hormone) function and regulation, and is involved, amongst other things, in motivation and goal-directed behaviour. In large part it is the source of intuition and hence our predisposition to suffer cognitive biases, particularly in random environments. The hormone dopamine is implicated in directing you to get what you want. Contrary to popular belief, however, it is not about reward per se, but about the anticipation of reward, or the craving response. Paradoxically, dopamine levels for a bettor will be at their highest not when Sheffield United beat Manchester City, but when they are anticipating a successful outcome after backing them to do so.

The dopamine response, furthermore, is most elevated when outcomes are uncertain. Disappointment lies not so much in the failure to achieve a reward but in the habituation of a guaranteed one. When rewards are guaranteed, there is no longer any need for the brain to elicit a craving response, since reward expectation can be taken for granted. When rewards are uncertain, a craving response ensures that you keep trying, even after the reward has failed to materialise. This is the addictive power of 'maybe'. The largest dopamine surges correlate with the most uncertain of outcomes, the 50-50 propositions. Any wonder, then, why Asian handicap and point spread markets have proved to be so popular?

It's easy to see how the unpredictability of betting, and the disposition to building false narratives of causality through illusory superiority, can hijack the brain's reward centre. Games of chance prey on this dopamine system. Win a bet, or see a valuation rise in price, and the reward centre constructs a pattern of causality for the purposes of anticipating future rewards. Whilst the variance of betting is largely equivalent to tossing coins, illusory superiority ensures its denial. Now we have a neural explanation for the illusion of causality. Instead of switching off, of getting bored by the haphazard and random rewards, our dopamine neurons become obsessed, constructing a narrative of cause and effect which in reality are weak or non-existent. Being able to create such a story, with rewards predicted out of uncertainty, is more seductive than a more predictable or even guaranteed reward cycle, even if the story is illusory. Indeed, for many it is the uncertainty and anticipation in betting, rather than the financial rewards themselves, that provide the utility from playing. We might say that we are playing to play, rather than playing to win, and financial rewards are merely perceived as opportunities to extend the duration of play. Paradoxically, then, the disappointment of losing might be more attractive, neurologically speaking, than the thrill of winning, since it stimulates the reward centre into repeated action. Such a mechanism might conceivably provide an explanation for the prevalence of loss chasing, and the irrational attraction of systems like Martingale. The opportunity to predict, to explain and to control outcomes evidently matters more than the outcomes themselves. Those who become addicted to betting or gambling are, in fact, really becoming addicted to dopamine.

Pathological gambling is certainly a maladaptive behaviour, but the attractiveness of uncertain rewards is so widespread in the animal world that this tendency should surely have an adaptive origin. The evolutionary explanation for our inherent predisposition to gamble is known as the compensatory hypothesis. According to this hypothesis, reward uncertainty, rather than the reward itself, must necessarily be a source of motivation, otherwise it would have already been extinguished. Such an explanation would account for the neurological attractiveness of losses. Without the possibility of losing, taking risks to acquire rewards becomes dull. Assuming this interpretation is correct, gambling behaviour in humans exists because the motivation of reward uncertainty was an evolutionarily winning strategy. Far from being deviant, risk-taking, and more specifically in this context, gambling are adaptive behaviours honed by evolution. Perhaps the biggest paradox of all is that whilst we crave certainty, explanation and meaning, and the control those things reward us with, it is actually uncertainty and chance which ensures we keep demanding it.

My detour into the neurological, psychological and evolutionary explanations for betting and gambling has hopefully helped illustrate how and why such behaviours are normal, whilst at the same time striking a note of caution. The pleasure gained through the anticipation of uncertain rewards is as commonplace as the pleasure gained from eating and sleeping. It's hardwired. Thus, attempts to discredit the normalisation of gambling, and more specifically the normalisation of betting on sport, will routinely miss the mark. With the fallout of the collapse of Football Index still ongoing as I write – in April 2021, the Government announced a review into the firm's collapse – commentators, politicians and academics are decrying what they see as the 'gamblification' of sport, and the cultural embedding and normalisation of gambling within society, the end product of a 50-year timeline of gambling liberalisation whose chickens are now finally coming home to roost. At the same time, campaigns designed to stop gamblers making impulsive decisions squarely put the blame for such behaviour on the individual, ridiculing them for the decisions they make which might ultimately be regretted.

In its 12 Steps, Gamblers Anonymous emphasises the need to admit wrongdoing and the defectiveness of character, in a kind of theological self-flagellation. I fundamentally disagree with this approach. Ridiculing individuals like this, whose risk-taking **is** normalised and hardwired for evolutionary reasons, is not likely to bring about the behavioural change that is hoped for, and at a societal level moderate the behavioural excesses. Some research indicates success rates of only 8%. Furthermore, whilst we can argue about the reliability of the numbers, it is also highly questionable whether the liberalisation of gambling in the UK has had any significant impact on the rates of pathological gambling, which currently at 0.5%, have changed little over recent times beyond the bounds of usual statistical variance. Similarly, the view, expressed by some figures in authority, that we are on the brink of a gambling epidemic, surely has no credibility at all. This is not to deny the importance of a robust regulatory environment; the original Gambling Act, as @ALuckyADay has argued, did not go far enough to put safe gambling at the heart of the original regulation. The collapse of Football Index, and the failure by the Gambling Commission to prevent it, would seem to be a case in point. However, moral judgement against betting and gambling, in my view, is unlikely to have any impact on the small minority most at risk, and certainly not the vast majority who regard such proclamations as stupid and ill-informed, with proposed changes to the Gambling Act requiring bettors to prove their financial means to gamble an infringement on their rights to choose to spend their money how they please. With threats to ban gambling advertising and the use of credit cards already outlawed, these are sledgehammer reactionary measures that will probably do little to actually crack the nut that their proponents had hoped for. Would any of this have helped customers of Football Index understand better the risks they were taking? I very much doubt it. Rather than normalise the criticism and judgement of society for facilitating what is entirely a normalised behaviour, instead we should seek to understand how and why normal behaviour can occasionally lead to excess. We've already learnt, for example, how illusory superiority can lead to poor decision-making.

Most of the time, and for most people, gambling decisions are egosyntonic, in harmony with or acceptable to our needs and goals, that is to say, moderate, satisfying and rewarding, carried neurologically in the form of dopamine. It becomes egodystonic, for example through impulsivity and excess, only when our gambling habits come into conflict with our needs and goals, that is to say, self-defeating, maladaptive and pathological, and with an accompanying desensitisation of the dopamine system. The transition from harmony to dissonance inevitably involves a loss of control. Paradoxically, that arises because the craving for a sense of control becomes the problem rather than the solution. In the comfortable world many of us live in today, the motivation of reward uncertainty is no longer that essential, and the numerous opportunities available to gamble can hijack an evolutionarily designed adaptation to aid survival, in the small proportion disposed to such hijacking. Whether, as for most, our gambling remains egosyntonic and rewarding, or for a few becomes egodystonic and pathological, may in part be genetic, and influenced by our sensitivity to dopamine. Nevertheless, research has revealed that genes only explain a small proportion of the variance in gambling behaviours. Whilst the propensity to gamble is hereditary, our environment is just as likely to influence whether and to what extent we choose to do it. Our brain's neural connections are being constructed and reinforced by learning experiences all the time. A few of us might be born with predispositions to gamble excessively, but the events of life ultimately determine how much excess we indulge in. I would like to believe that increasing awareness about why so many of us choose to gamble, and what meaning it has for us, will ultimately be far more successful at reducing the likelihood of excess than moral condemnation, excessive regulation and prohibition.

Betting and gambling are often criticised for indulging a something-for-nothing ideology. However, whilst a market for speculating about uncertainty is, in a financial sense, zero-sum, with winners paid for by losers, there is evidently so much more to betting than money. The emotions of hope, anticipation, confirmation, success (and even failure) and control are all things that can be measured neurochemically (via dopamine). Through the consensual exchange of opinions about the likely outcome of a match, and how those opinions will be rewarded, bettors can engage in a positive-sum trade of beliefs about how they think the future will be. Ultimately, some will prove to be wrong and suffer financial penalties, but the emotional gains from this experience are potentially no less rewarding. Evidently, the vast majority of egosyntonic bettors who play solely for recreational purpose already understand this implicitly. If the purpose of gambling is to achieve authority over uncertainty, to feel in control of one's destiny, surely everyone who plays sensibly and reasonably is a winner, even if that control is illusory. Let's not criticise this behaviour, and let's not moralise about games that facilitate it. Instead, let's encourage greater understanding of the risk analysts that we are, why we take the risks that we do, how we may suffer from cognitive biases that lead to suboptimal risk-taking. and how an increased self-awareness of any dispositions to excess, whether it be gambling, or any other behaviour for that matter, will offer a far more reliable safety net than blaming a society for its wrongs. Betting, above all else, should be fun. If it is fun, praise yourself for being normal, but when the fun stops, stop.